Development, Globalization and Women

Development, Globalization and Women

Revisiting the Issues

Edited by
ASHA KAUSHIK

RAWAT PUBLICATIONS
Jaipur • New Delhi • Bangalore • Hyderabad • Guwahati

ISBN 978-81-316-0565-3

Published by
Prem Rawat for **Rawat Publications**
Satyam Apts, Sector 3, Jawahar Nagar, Jaipur 302 004 (India)
Phone: 0141 265 1748 / 7006 Fax: 0141 265 1748
E-mail: info@rawatbooks.com
Website: www.rawatbooks.com

New Delhi Office
4858/24, Ansari Road, Daryaganj, New Delhi 110 002
Phone: 011 2326 3290

Also at *Bangalore, Hyderabad* and *Guwahati*

Typeset by Rawat Computers, Jaipur
Printed at Chaman Enterprises, New Delhi

To

Prof. PAM RAJPUT

a mentor of generations engaged in

women's studies and advocacy in India

Contents

Preface xi

Contributors xiii

Introduction xv
Asha Kaushik

Part I
Conceptual Concerns

1 Women and Development 3
Susanne Hoeber Rudolph

2 Women and Globalization: Raising the Issues 8
Mary Grey

3 Gandhi and Nehru: Clash over Post-colonial Development 22
Lloyd I. Rudolph

4 Interrogating Development from a Gender Perspective 34
Asha Kaushik

Part II
Development–Discrimination Syndrome

5 Globalization and Economic Empowerment of Women: Some Issues for Policy Intervention 55
Kanta Ahuja

6 Economic Fallout of Globalization for Indian Women 65
D.D. Narula

7 Development, Deprivation and Gender Equality: The Context of Kumaon Hills 95
M.P. Dube

8 Development and Women's Political Participation: Challenges and Strategies 111
Leela Yadava

9 Women Empowerment: Political Dimension 126
Prem Krishna Sharma

10 Globalization and the Gender Imperatives in Environment 132
Kiran Soni Gupta

Part III
Questioning the Traditional Citadels

11 Gender Biases in Caste- and Kinship-based Organizations: A Study in Rural Haryana 147
P.S. Verma

12 Globalization-Islamization Interface: Implications for Muslim Women in the Indian Subcontinent 166
Surendra Nath Kaushik

13 Women's NGOs in the Context of Globalization 182
Deepa Mathur

14 Globalization, Media and Women 196
Urvashi Dev Rawal

Part IV
MDGs: Towards Bridging the Gaps

15 Millennium Development Goal 6 and Women: An Overview of the United Nations Agenda 211
Sandeep Gupta and Ashlesha Kaushik

16 Millennium Development Goal 3: Towards Gender Equality and Women Empowerment 222
Prerna Puri

17 MDGs, SAARC and Women 245
Shashi Upadhyay

18 Millennium Development Goals and Women's Health in Rajasthan 276
Meeta Singh

19 Globalization, MDGs and Women: Political Dimensions and Implications 293
Navneet Kumar Verma

20 Millennium Development Goals, Armed Conflicts and Women's Rights in North-East India 309
Manju Singh

Index 329

Preface

During my two tenures as Director, Centre for Women's Studies, University of Rajasthan, Jaipur, during 2000–2011, several seminars/conferences were held on different aspects of Gender, Development, Globalization, Culture and on interface of all these vis-à-vis women in India. The deliberations and discussions were academic stimulants *par excellence* for further interactions. The present book is one of the fruitions of such endeavours. The contributors deserve all the credit for making this collective wisdom concretize in this form possible. My grateful appreciation for each one for believing in me.

My students Hemant, Himanshu and Anuj deserve special appreciation for sharing burden of carrying out with cheerfulness umpteen chores in the process of bringing out the work.

On a personal note, words are poor substitutes for portrayal of unconditional love of dear ones without which no meaningful work is ever possible, love of my family – Prof. Surendra Nath Kaushik, Ashutosh, Ashlesha, Sandeep and darling Yasha.

Finally, thanks are due to Rawat Publications for being patient with me.

Asha Kaushik

Contributors

Ashlesha Kaushik, MD (Paediatrics, PGI, Chandigarh and Mount Sinai School of Medicine, NJ), Fellow, Paediatric Infectious Diseases, University of Texas, South-western, Dallas, Texas, USA.

D.D. Narula, Senior Fellow, Institute of Development Studies, Jaipur and former Member-Secretary, ICSSR, New Delhi.

Deepa Mathur, Assistant Professor, Department of Sociology, University of Rajasthan, Jaipur.

Kanta Ahuja, former Vice-Chancellor, MDS University, Ajmer and University of Rajasthan, Jaipur.

Kiran Soni Gupta, senior IAS officer, Government of Rajasthan, Jaipur.

Leela Yadava, former Professor and Head, Department of Political Science, Kurukshetra University, Kurukshetra.

Lloyd I. Rudolph, Professor Emeritus of Political Science, University of Chicago, Chicago, USA.

M.P. Dube, Professor, Department of Political Science, and Director, Institute of Gandhian Thought and Peace Studies, University of Allahabad, Allahabad.

Manju Singh, Assistant Professor, Department of Political Science, University of Rajasthan, Jaipur.

Mary Grey, Professorial Research Fellow, St. Mary's University College, Twickenham, and Professor Emeritus, University of Wales, Lampeter, UK.

Meeta Singh, MD, Chairperson, Dignity of Girl Foundation, Rajasthan.

Navneet Kumar Verma, Assistant Professor, Government College, Sirohi, Rajasthan.

P.S. Verma, Professor, Department of Political Science, Panjab University, Chandigarh.

Prem Krishna Sharma, President, PUCL, Rajasthan.

Prerna Puri, Assistant Professor, Department of Psychology, University of Rajasthan, Jaipur.

Sandeep Gupta, MD (Internal Medicine, Tufts University, Boston), Faculty, Pulmonary and Critical Care, and Medical Director, Intensive Care, Scott and White, Dallas, Texas, USA.

Shashi Upadhyay, Assistant Professor, South Asia Studies Centre, University of Rajasthan, Jaipur.

Surendra Nath Kaushik, Professor and former Director, South Asia Studies Centre, University of Rajasthan, Jaipur.

Susanne Hoeber Rudolph, Professor Emeritus of Political Science, University of Chicago, Chicago, USA.

Urvashi Dev Rawal, Bureau Chief, *Hindustan Times*, Jaipur.

Asha Kaushik, Professor of Political Science and former Dean, Faculty of Social Sciences, University of Rajasthan, Jaipur.

Introduction

ASHA KAUSHIK

Today, on the one hand, we see the paradoxical co-existence of unprecedented accomplishments in technological and economic spheres and, on the other hand, persisting discrimination, deprivation and marginalization of vast populace, particularly women. And, overcoming this is 'the central part of the exercise of development', as Nobel laureate Amartya Sen says. The key issues therefore pertain not only to the nature and dynamics of the dominant paradigm of development but also to how it has impacted various segments of society – men and women.

It is clear that development, hitherto conceived primarily as a West-centric project to modernize the post-colonial societies, has fallen far short of realizing the promised utopia of improved quality of life for all and greater equity. Instead, the dominant model of development has resulted in jobless growth and poverty, greater economic and gender inequalities and degradation of the environment. Globalization/liberalization-driven growth model has multiplied the socio-economic costs of development further.

Women have been the worst sufferers in this process. Why and how? Are the reasons just structural and institutional or matters of policy? Or, processual – resultant of the multi-layered interface between the state and the market on one hand and civil society and the state on the other? Or, there are deeper ideological undercurrents that need to be comprehended for a fuller understanding of the complex dynamics of hegemonizing the entire development process disfavouring women and others on the periphery. The issues need to be rethought, relocated and recontextualized.

The present volume is an endeavour in this direction. The essays, thematically arranged in four parts, look at development vis-à-vis women in the globalizing era with varied perspectives, focusing India. While the first part of the volume delineates conceptual concerns, the second part critically assesses the development-discrimination syndrome. The third part then raises the questions regarding traditional citadels. And, the last part, contextualizes the issues with an MDG perspective.

Susanne Hoeber Rudolph, in the opening chapter, raises several basic questions such as, whether development should be large-scale or human-scale whether it should be in the hands of the state or of non-state actors, and if non-state actors, who would they be – voluntary organizations or private capital acting through the market? Rethinking the scale of projects is part of a larger developing philosophical perspective on development as an encounter between humans and nature. She suggests, 'we can think about women and development in two ways: the effect women have on development and the effect development has on women'. In her view, civil society is the most significant arena for women's role in development. Thus, she urges to recognize the multiple faces of development – state, private capital, market and civil society.

Mary Grey presents a critique of the intrinsic tendency of globalization, in both its historical and current phases, particularly the tendency of domination, instrumental character and an all-consuming mandate for profit ignoring environmental, health and safety hazards. She further discusses how the patriarchal orientation of current unregulated economic system impacts women at large and poor women, in particular. Finally, she urges for a re-imagining of current economic structures reconnecting the economy to the normative foundations of society. This would result, in her view, in the recognition, visibility and valuing of women's contribution.

Lloyd I. Rudolph explores and revisits the Gandhi-Nehru debate on development or what he calls 'clash' over the nature and dimensions of pre-colonial development between state-led and large-scale industrialization-based urban model of development and the small-scale cottage-based rural model of development with minimum role for the state. The debate still continues in India in some form or the other, in the changed context of liberalization.

Asha Kaushik argues in favour of engendering development and draws attention to the inegalitarian fallout of the globalization-driven development model, particularly for women.

Kanta Ahuja advocates a holistic approach to address the women empowerment issue. She explains how women's autonomy, human dignity and economic rights are integrally related and how globalization has impacted the employment and social security scenario for women in India and in Rajasthan, in particular. Therefore, in her view, a re-prioritization of state policies is needed to facilitate both employment with growth and social protection mechanisms.

D.D. Narula, deliberating upon the nature and dynamics of globalization, highlights that globalization is a very uneven process with benefits and losses distributed unequally at both global and national levels. In the post-reform period in India, women's employment has suffered seriously despite a few bright spots. The cut back on public expenditure has added to the worsening situation. The economic fallout of globalization for Indian women has been dismal on the net. Therefore, he urges for a multi-pronged strategy to confront the multifarious challenges.

M.P. Dube, situating the deprivation syndrome of tribal women of Kumaon hills (Uttarakhand) in the gender-development discourse and development, comes up with a set of strategies to facilitate tribal women's participation in the developmental process.

Leela Yadava presents a strong case in favour of inducting a critical mass of women in the decision-making process. She argues that unless women become active participants in the political process at all levels, they will never attain empowerment, which has been recognized as a necessary condition for achieving the goal of human development. This is also central to the global development debate.

Prem Krishna Sharma contends that there is a clear political dimension to women's issues and that the issue of gender equality can best be addressed through united efforts of all progressive movements.

Kiran Soni Gupta, while analysing gender imperatives in environment vis-à-vis globalization, explores how women are victims of the economic process and also the potential for women as subjects of the process. She asserts that in order to ensure environmental sustainability and equitable human development, national policies need to be reformulated to accelerate democratization, gender sensitization and institutional development to keep pace with globalization.

P.S. Verma, exposing gender biases in caste and kinship organizations in the particular context of rural Haryana, stipulates that unless the framework of customary norms is interrogated and women given adequate space in caste/lineage-based organizations, gender equity and justice will remain unattainable in the countryside.

Surendra Nath Kaushik, covering the wider terrain of Indian subcontinent, analyses the manifold paradoxes in the globalization-Islamization interface and implications particularly for Muslim women. In his view, with focused attention to awareness raising, common action plan and joint strategies, it will be possible to guard against the negative fallout of globalization and religious fundamentalism.

Deepa Mathur argues that the role of women NGOs, particularly in the context of globalization, is crucial in ascertaining women's development and gender equality.

Urvashi Dev Rawal explores the multifaceted interface of globalization, media and women.

Sandeep Gupta and **Ashlesha Kaushik** argue in favour of a holistic and inclusive development strategy, particularly in relation to gender. They specifically focus on MDG-6 related to combatting HIV/AIDS, Malaria and other diseases within the larger ambit of the Millennium Development Goals and the pivotal role the United Nations has played globally.

Prerna Puri provides an overview of MDG-3 towards realizing gender equality and women empowerment, with details of global and national endeavours and constraints in adequate realization of the targets.

Shashi Upadhyay builds a comparative perspective on women's development issues in South Asia from the vantage point of both MDGs and SDGs and brings out the challenges that inhibit gender equality in the region.

Meeta Singh presents a comprehensive overview of women's health issues in Rajasthan with particular focus on MDG-5 related to improving maternal health. Situating the problem in the socio-cultural milieu and taking view of the present scenario, she highlights the gaps and strategies to address the problem.

Navneet Kumar Verma, situating women's vulnerable position in the globalizing economy, pins hope on 'mobilization against globalization' and the pro-active role of civil society organizations to ensure gender equality and also the realization of the MDGs.

Manju Singh brings out the challenges women face in armed conflict situations, with specific focus on North-East India. She upholds that the realization of MDGs and gender equality in the north-eastern region is largely contingent upon the united efforts of the women's organizations across ethnic lines to fight against both armed violence and gender discrimination.

It is hoped that the views expressed by the erudite contributors will stir more debate on the theme.

Part I

Conceptual Concerns

1

Women and Development

SUSANNE HOEBER RUDOLPH

Development does not just happen. There are agents that make it happen, and we need first to consider who those agents are. 'Development' too is not a self-evident concept. Who the proper agents are, and what the appropriate approaches are to development, has been vigorously debated over the last thirty years. The discourse on development is now much more contested than it was when I first came to India.

Let me tell you a story of my early engagement with this question. In 1962 Lloyd Rudolph and I were asked to speak at the National Academy of Administration in Mussoorie. An annual lecture on Gandhi was a required performance at the academy, a lecture not necessarily taken seriously, I might add, by all the probationers, many of whom saw this as a pious national formality. Lloyd had a paper on Gandhi as a critic of modernity, which he delivered with a good deal of conviction. In the question hour we had a hard time of it, as a lot of smart young men – there were not many women in the academy at that time – rose to their feet to protest that these young American academics were giving sympathetic treatments to a pious old 'dhoti wallah' and his outdated ideas praising village economies, decentralization, and critiquing large-scale industrialization. The need of the hour, they said, was centralization and state sponsorship of industrialization on a Fordist model, rationalized workplace, assembly line efficiency, and large-scale enterprises – the bigger the better. There was virtual unanimity in the room that large-scale, centralized, state sponsored development was best for India. This kind of unanimity has now disintegrated, and is being replaced by a heterogeneity of opinion.

The big issues these days are whether development should be large scale or human scale; whether it should be in the hands of the state or the non-state actors; and if non-state actors, who would they be? Two kinds of answers are: voluntary organizations or private capital acting through the market.

Most frequently, in India, we think of development as state generated. Development evokes the Nehruvian state's large development plans, its dams and steel factories and other basic capital goods which were too costly for the private sector to launch on its own and which built up India's industrial capacity; Indians used to be more enthusiastic about state directed development than they are now. The change of heart has come because most public sector industries have proved disappointing in the long run, uncompetitive and inefficient, incapable of generating even the revenues needed for their own internal investment. Also, the spectacular economic failure of the Eastern European state enterprise system was heard as a cautionary siren around the world. Indians are now more doubtful about the value of great capital projects, big dams and enormous irrigation facilities such as Bhakra Nangal, which has lost capacity due to silting, the Sardar Sarovar that is to be, and Rajasthan's own Indira Gandhi canal. Statesmen in the 1950s and 60s believed and preached the economies of scale that great size guaranteed greater productivity. When these verities are re-evaluated now, particularly the work on dams and large irrigation projects, critics stress the virtue of the small, of human size, of the locally controlled. Also, there is talk of water harvesting, of reviving old technologies of water conservation. Nowadays, people come to admire the extraordinary water harvesting system built at the site of Jaigarh (Jaipur), which I strongly recommend to any of our out of town visitors.

Rethinking the scale of projects, emphasis on the effectiveness of smaller projects, is part of a larger developing philosophical perspective on development as an encounter between humans and nature. There is a new recognition that science, with all its gains, has not generated an adequate understanding of the costs of human intervention in nature. Humans heedless and disrespectful of both the logic and the functioning of nature have ravaged her under the rubric of mastering her – and I use the gendered metaphor quite self-consciously. Ravaging takes many forms, such as the strip mining of coal in American Appalachian states and Pennsylvania, which destroyed lovely and ecologically supportive mountains and forests, leaving behind only slagheaps and unproductive stony wasteland; it takes the form of the enormous contributions to destruction of the ozone layer and to global warming made by the hydrocarbon emissions of industrialization in the Atlantic states; it takes the form of lime-stone quarrying of the Dehra Dun hills, which destroyed the forest cover and created massive erosion until Indira Gandhi personally intervened; or the stone cutting of the Jaipur and Udaipur hills which has stripped them, countering the ameliorating effect that forest cover had on the temperature and water supply of these two cities – to say nothing of destroying the beauty which is Jaipur's and Udaipur's greatest resource.

These are some of the reasons why the 1960s' enthusiasm for bold development in general has given way to more incremental approaches, to more thoughtful planning, to greater skepticism about the human costs and about the sacrifice of the earth. The enthusiasm about economies of scale which energized the commanding heights economy has waned as the negatives of such projects assert themselves – salination in the command areas of the Indira Gandhi Canal in Rajasthan; the possible disasters in Gujarat and Uttarakhand where dams are raised in earthquake-prone areas; the human cost of hundreds of thousands of tribals and cultivators displaced by great irrigation projects.

There is some progress in integrating long-term human and environmental considerations into development implementation. The Government of India now requires environmental impact statements in connection with large projects. So do international agencies and lenders, such as the World Bank, which pulled out of Sardar Sarovar. The Supreme Court polices its enforcement of environmental laws by scolding the Delhi administration for its lackadaisical attitude to the time limits fixed for repairing the poisonous consequences of thoughtless development schemes. It may in fact succeed in closing the polluting industries, which they say will move to Rajasthan, hopefully without the pollution. There are now fewer businessmen and bureaucrats who say that India being a poor nation cannot afford environment-friendly development.

Development can be imagined as the result of activities other than those of the state. They can be the, result of what the economist Paul Krugman calls 'unorganized activity'. He means that a number of major socio-economic developments coincide – let us say railroads are built by private or public enterprise and stimulate commerce, triggering a series of other economic developments, for example, making possible the shipment to markets of crops not previously shipped, thereby stimulating additional commerce and trade and social services – schools and clinics – in a farm area previously not very prosperous. Development here is unorganized in the sense that the railroad entrepreneur did not plan on developing this small agricultural area that the railroad passed, but he set off a chain of events that brought new economic activity, enhanced income, and generated social services.

Krugman has coined a term – unorganized development – as a way of talking about the development consequences of the market, of the economic activity of entrepreneurs. The idea of state initiative has become so firmly linked with the concept of development that we can scarcely imagine private enterprise as a vehicle of economic development, but it is well to remember that, after an initial and often fruitful statist phase under mercantilism, most European economies, including those with strong welfare policies, developed mostly via private rather than public sector. It is also well to keep in mind that in India today the role of public investment has shrunk and most investment, including that in infrastructure vital for development, is from household and corporate private savings.

But I want to stress another agent of economic development – the enormous role played by civil society, by voluntary groups, in India. By civil society I mean social action in a non-state autonomous sphere; empowerment of citizens; trust building associational life; and interaction with rather than acting as agent of the state. I want to stress the voluntary associations that constitute civil society because they are the most significant arena for women's role in development. We can think about women and development, in two ways. Pointing the causal arrow one way we can talk about the effect women have on development; and pointing the causal arrow the other way, we can talk about the effect development has on women. I want to talk mostly about women's role in development, and therefore about civil society and voluntary associations in development.

India has an enormous number of formal voluntary associations oriented toward social action. I have seen some counts by Smitu Kothari that place them in the 100,000 level, and since Kothari disqualifies associations with religious or religio/political character there must be many more. Such an account would include large and experienced organizations like Seva Mandir in Udaipur or Tilonia near Ajmer in Rajasthan as well as smaller less formal groupings. As a kind of development agent, such organizations are a better fit than is the state with recent attempts to redefine development as decentralized, close to the ground, stressing small or medium scale. They are also more hospitable sites for women to make a contribution to development. Women in town and country find it easier to make a contribution as social activists through organizations that are less formal, more flexible, and locally targeted.

Let me illustrate this point. The most frequently mentioned voluntary organizations in which women are active are the associations formed in connection with the Chipko movement in Garhwal for preserving forests, campaigning against forest contractors, and opposing the Tehri dam. In two villages studies by Niraja Jayal of JNU and her students, forest resources 'had been completely denuded as a result of overexploitation by the villagers themselves.' Community moblization among young people and women under the auspices of the Gandhian style Chipko movement took measures that, over a twenty-year period, restored the forest. The Mahila Mangal Dal mainly responsible for this action functioned without the supporting hand of state bureaucrats. As consumers and collectors of forest products, women had a unique interest in such preservation. The voluntary association approach to development provided an organizational form congenial to women, that was able to utilize their familiarity with local ecology, and that they could control. Jayal also tells us that with the passing of the Forest Conservation Act of 1980 by the UP government, the villagers' and women's interest in the forest diminished. Now, it was seen as government property, government responsibility. The state as development agent had no means for attaching local participants, let alone women, to its mandate to preserve the forest.

So let us recognize the multiple faces of development – state, private/capital market, and civil society. And let us deliberate on the forms by which women can make their best contributions.

2

Women and Globalization

Raising the Issues

MARY GREY

Even though the word *globalization* refers primarily to the financial and economic spheres within a world view of global capitalism, it is all too evident that its impact on the lives of women is all-pervading, with many serious and even life-threatening implications. Yet, the fact that *some* women can meet in international conferences and combine resources and experiences to write joint publications is one consequence of a globalized world – so globalization cannot be a totally negative phenomenon. The ambiguity of globalization, what aspects we want to encourage, and what must be rejected as disastrous for women and all poor communities – this is at the heart of our shared reflection. If you were to take a walk around the centre of London at night, looking for somewhere to have a meal, you are confronted by a bewildering choice of Indian, Chinese, Thai, Italian, Greek, French, Mexican restaurants. Not many Afro-Caribbean – even though there is a large community in London. You will equally be confronted with the ever-present McDonald's, Burger King, Kentucky Fried Chicken and so on. Right across the world's great cities such an array of choices will be offered – in American cities the possibilities probably multiplied by hundreds. But what are the issues – economic, social, moral – behind what looks like simply a delectable free choice? Let's pursue this global picture of cultural mix a little further:

> A traveller across the desert wastes of Sahara arrives at last at Timbuktu, where the first denizen he meets is wearing a Texan baseball cap. Pilgrims in the Himalayas in search of the ultimate wilderness in the furthest kingdom find Everest strewn with rubbish, in tins, plastic bags, Coca-Cola bottles and all the remnants of the modern global picnicker.

> Explorers of the Arctic complain that empty plastic bottles of washing up liquid are embedded in the ice. Tony Giddens opened his Reith lectures with the tale of an anthropologist trekking to a remote corner of Cambodia for a field study – only to find her first night's entertainment was not traditional local pastimes, but a viewing of *Basic Instinct* on video. The film, at this point, had not even reached the cinemas in London. (Polly Toynbee in Giddens and Hutton, 2000: 91)

There we have it – globalization in all its ambiguity. In this ambiguity, given that women's scholarship and specialisms span a diversity of disciplines like economics, social sciences, anthropology, history and religion, to name but a few, I am making the assumption that the shared focus is justice for women, especially poor women, a great concern that the structural systems in place around the world are causing yet more burdens and more suffering for women, their families and communities and a commitment to act to change this. The feminization of poverty is still a burning and unacceptable reality.

I will begin with a few definitions, and some historical background, before developing further what globalization means for women.

What is Globalization?

As I have already hinted, globalization has thousands of expressions: as Canadian writer Heather Eaton says:

> Ideologically, it appeals to a sense of adventure, entrepreneurship and superiority; with inviting expressions about global prospects for business, such as 'gateways to the world, go global, track global competition, spread global wings, crossing international borders, and becoming master of one's domain'. (*World Trade: For the Executive with Global Vision,* June 1998, passim. Cited in Eaton, 2000: 42–43)

Anthony Giddens, in his new book, *Living on the Edge: Living with Global Capitalism* (Giddens and Hutton, 2000: 1), asks this question of Will Hutton. He identifies many meanings – the world-wide communication revolution, for instance (this is not only air travel, but the opening up of the world wide web, e-mail, Internet). Secondly, he refers to what he terms the 'weightless economy.' By this he means the new 'knowledge economy' – with financial markets at its leading edge:

> Financial markets today are stunning in their scope, their instantaneous nature, and their enormous turnover.

It could be argued that it is this factor which is the crucial and all-encompassing one, with financial markets open 24 hours a day, with the growing trend in the north and west for 24-hour-a-day open supermarkets – a trend now also catching on in Indian and Chinese cities.

Thirdly, it refers to a post-1989 world, that is, a world after the fall of communism. Communism as a world view no longer exerts a force – even though Cuba, North Korea and China still have communist governments. And, fourthly, they refer to transformations happening on the level of everyday life. One of the characteristics of this, the authors consider to be the improved situation of women and the growing equality between women and men (this needs to be challenged in different contexts and a hermeneutic of suspicion raised over it: for example, does it scarcely applies to rural India, war-torn Africa and to the increasing poverty of women in some former communist countries?). The striking uniting fact for all these four points is that these changes are global and all-encompassing. Read these sentences:

> All borders are coming down; economic, political and social. There is a new conception of time, risk and opportunity. (Giddens and Hutton, 2000: 3)
>
> Globalisation is so powerful an idea because of the sense of there being no escape. Its coming down the tracks straight at you .... The food and chemical industries are coalescing; so are banking and insurance; so are information technology and television. (ibid.: 4)

and then, a sinister note:

> But don't forget globalisation also means the globalisation of crimes, drugs and the like. The Mafia now operates globally. Laundering drugs money is a global business. There are real fears that the laundering of Russian Mafia cash could pollute the entire Western banking system. And any police response has to be global too.

And now let us take another view, more critical and more historical.

Globalization – the Historical Process[1]

One could argue that globalization is nothing new. In any case the present scene has certainly been prepared for by five centuries of social, economic and political, imperial domination – as many Asian and African countries know only too well. For example, before the 16th century, there were of course great powers in the world: there were conquering powers (the Greek and Roman empires, the Mughal empire, the Chinese), but they were not global powers, in the way the United States has now become. The system whose consequences we now struggle with began with the expansion of western economic interests, and western political domination. Economically, this was the development of capitalism, which marked the rise of a new social class in the west – the bourgeoisie or the merchant class. By the end of the 17th century and the beginning of the 18th, it began to exercise political domination, through Britain, the

Netherlands, Spain and Portugal. Most of the great corporations that now rule the world began to mushroom from the middle to the end of the 19th century. This of course marked the transition from a more organic economy to an extractive economy of mining, according to Thomas Berry (Berry, 1999: 141). He refers to Standard Oil of Ohio 1970; Exxon 1882; Amoco 1889; Royal Dutch 1890; Texaco 1902; Mobil 1882.

Key features of this developing type of capitalism are, first, its dominating aim. It aims to subordinate every other interest in a domination that is deliberate, systemic, hierarchical and patriarchal.

Secondly it has an instrumental character. It controls the development of science and technology, aiming to manage nature (space) and history (time). One only needs to think of the impact of the GM food controversy. The results of this instrumentalism are an accumulation of things, artefacts, machines, gadgets – without which, so we are persuaded, it is impossible to live. And, tragically, *impossible for our children to live without.* In its male-dominated character, even though one of the myths it relies on is that of endless growth, progress, change, optimistic spin on culture, it is no different – despite the earlier rhetoric on gender equality – from pre-modern, pre-capitalist society in terms of patriarchal orientation.

Thus, ambiguity is built into its intrinsic rhetoric. Consider these paradoxical statements as Iulio de Santa Ana has written:

> It (global capitalism) aims at freedom, but imposes oppression. It aims at happiness, but creates pain and suffering. It says that it affirms life, but it brings death. ... It deals more with having than with being, but it is a having that influences the being.

Finally, even if globalization is a process where different projects co-exist, one project has always dominated, and still continues to dominate. This project has a fascinating, almost bewitching, effect on us. In fact, you could say capitalism is the new religion in the idolatry of money. It has hijacked our imaginations and desires. And it is global since there is no space where you can stand outside it. At least, that is what we are made to think!

The Current Scene

The particular characteristics of the current scene and the reason for the mounting concern is not only the accumulation of capital in the last five decades or so, but the decision taken under the presidency of Richard Nixon to end the stabilization of the market. Fixed, stable money exchange rates were abolished – so we now have the financial instability of the so-called 'free market' (think of the crash of the Asian economy, the so-called Tiger economies). During the Thatcher and Reagan governments came financial deregulation and the liberalization of domestic financial markets. Now, not the commodity but the money itself is the focus.

The actors in this changed scene are, first, the power of State institutions like the G8, the EU, the US and some geographical blocks in which India and China are now key players. Secondly, there are systemic pillars like the World Bank, IMF, WTO (which is the successor of GATT, set up at the Bretton Woods gathering in 1944), followed by research and development, the powerful corporations, banks, financial investors and certain key members of the public – Bill Gates of Microsoft comes to mind as well as Lakshmi Mittal. Remember that the motto of Microsoft is 'Make sure you make your product obsolete.' George Soros and his power to de-stabilize currencies would be another key figure.

The net result has become, as ecologist Vandana Shiva pointed out:

> With globalisation, life itself has emerged as the ultimate commodity. Planet Earth is being replaced by Life Inc. in the world of free trade and deregulated commerce. Through patents and genetic engineering, new colonies are being carved out. (Shiva in Giddens and Hutton, 2000: 118)

If the 20th century was the petroleum century, she argues, the 21st will be the century of biology:

> The 10 leading food companies – Nestle, Philip Morris, Unilever, Con Agra, Cargill, Pepsico, Pepsi Cola, Diageo Guinness, Mars and Anone – had revenues of $45.3 billion in 1992. These are setting up joint ventures with seed companies to control the crops grown and food eaten. (Shiva in ibid.: 119)

I will now pursue some of the consequences of these facts at a deeper level. First, there has been a loss of diversity as to what 'life' means. Its meaning has now shrunk to the business model of life:

> Implicit is that business is the greatest possible model of life; far superior to governments, nationalities, cultures, etc. There is no talk of differentiated and diverse cultures of people, of ethnicity or gender, of animals and land, of national or international regulations or indeed that there is any genuine limitation to this frontier of capital exchange. This 'globe' of which they speak is an utter abstraction with no accountability to anything but economics. (Eaton, 2000: 43)

Secondly, it is based on a drastically shrunken notion of what is economics. Women's contribution is certainly not factored in. There is a historical and philosophical development which made this possible, namely the separation of economics and politics, economics and value, economics and history. This is something that Mahatma Gandhi consistently refused to do.

This shrinking and splitting process itself has been made possible by the separation of money and commodities. Money – although paper money from the 18th century had been backed up by sold metal – became separated from it when the US came off the Gold Standard in 1971. Then money became a token of exchange with no intrinsic value (Gorringe, 1999: 86). With computerization and the linking of the world's stock markets, casino capitalism was born:

> The set of symbols developed to represent real assets has lost the link with any productive activity. Finance has progressively evolved into a sector all its own, only loosely connected to industry. (ibid.: 86)

David Korten points out that in the New York stock market crash of 1987,

> investors lost 1 trillion $ in 2 months, a sum that would feed the world for 2 years. In fact this one trillion dollars could not have fed the world for even 5 minutes for the simple reason that people can't eat money. They eat food and the collapse of the stock market values did not in itself increase or decrease the world's supply of food by so much as a single grain of rice. (David Korten in ibid.: 86)

How much harm does this do is the next question. The real threat – alongside the point that such growth is unsustainable – is the threat to democracy by the power being given to the corporations. Heather Eaton points out how corporations colonize everywhere – education programmes, television, art, energy, agriculture, colonizing even the cultural and religious symbols in which our values are enshrined, promising happiness and redemption in this car, gadget, bathroom, holiday, jewels or clothing. In fact, there is no aspect of personal or communal life which is not targeted. As Rowell *(Green Backlash*, 1996) put it:

> By stealth and by design big business has perverted the democratic process by buying politicians, by bribing them, by finding 'independent' think-tanks, by funding 'corporate front groups', by bullying citizens, by lobbying, by lying – all in the name of profit. (in ibid.: 89)

Because of the all-consuming mandate for profit, environmental, health and safety hazards are ignored. There are disastrous consequences for the lives of poor women. John Pilger (1998) cites the lives of factory women in Saigon, working for the equivalent of £12 per month, from 9–7 pm, never allowed to stop, given a hygiene card which they are allowed to use 3 times a day for personal hygiene, for no more than 5 minutes (Gorringe, 2000: 81). This reality can be multiplied all over the world – including the developed world. Listen to the story of women workers in contract clothing shops in modern, affluent San Francisco:

> Many of them are dark, cramped, windowless .... 12-hour days with no days off, and a break only for lunch .... And in this wealthy, cosmopolitan city, many shops enforce draconian rules reminiscent of the 19th

> century. 'The workers were not allowed to talk to each other, and they didn't allow us to go to the bathroom,' says one Asian garment worker. ... Aware of management zeal for bargain – basement prices, the nearly 600 sewing contractors in the Bay Area engage in cut-throat competition – often a kind of Darwinian drive to the bottom .... Manufacturers have another powerful chip to keep bids down. Katie Quan, a manager of the International Ladies Garment Workers Union in San Francisco, explains: "They say, 'If you don't take it, we'll just ship it overseas, and you won't get work, and your workers will go hungry'." (cited in Korten, 1995: 230)

This shows that wherever you are in the world, the forces of the unregulated market economy are impacting the lives of poor people. And this is without beginning to chart the effects on the health of children conscripted for factory life. The passage also introduces the lives of women specifically. Rather than developing this brief analysis of globalization, here I summarize 'the world of global dreamers' as one in which the world's money, technology, and markets are controlled and managed by gigantic global corporations, where a common consumer culture unifies all people in a shared quest for material gratification and where there is perfect global competition among workers and localities to offer their services to investors at the most advantageous terms. It is a world where corporations are free to act solely on the basis of profitability without regard to national or local consequences and where relationships, both individual and corporate, are defined entirely by the market: there are no loyalties to place or community (ibid.: 131). Such an analysis, of course, omits the violence and militarization inevitably accompanying such an economic system as well as its increasingly deleterious effects on the global climate crisis.

Now, in order to move us forward, both to define more clearly what this means for women, and to ask are there ways forward and movements for change, I offer here a poem written in Seattle, by one of the protesters against globalization:

> WHY WE ARE HERE – Seattle, 2000
>
> Because the world we imagined,
> the one we had always counted on
> is disappearing.
>
> Because the sun has become cancerous
> and the planet is getting hotter.
> Because children are starving in the shadows
> of yachts and economic summits.
> Because there are already
> too many planes in the sky.

This is the manufactured world
you have come here to codify and expedite.
We have come to tell you
there is something else we want to buy.

What we want, money no longer recognizes,
like the vitality of nature,
the integrity of work.
We don't want cheaper wood,
we want living trees.
We don't want engineered fruit,
we want to see and smell the food growing
in our own neighbourhoods.

We are here because a voice inside us,
a memory in our blood, tells us
you are not just a trade body,
you are the blind tip of a dark wave
that has forgotten its source.
We are here to defend and honour
what is real, natural, human and basic
against the rising tide of greed.

We are here by the insistence of spirit
and the authority of nature.
If you doubt for one minute the power
of truth, or the primacy of nature,
try not breathing for that length of time.

Now you know the pressure of our desire.
We are not here to tinker with your laws.
We are here to change you
from the inside out.
This is not a political protest.
It is an uprising of the soul. (Lewis, 2000)

Women and Globalization

First of all, echoing the last line of the poem, it is important to see that what we face is indeed an uprising of the soul: what we experience is a crisis of spirit. It is a crisis of spirit, dressed up as economics, and a system that progressively traps human desires, imaginations, and crushes what is noble about human beings through reducing us to be driven by crass greed, consumerism and caught by ruthless competition where, if you don't have the finance to play the market's games, you simply do not count as individuals and disappear into a faceless morass of poverty and famine on the one hand, or easy prey to depression, addiction, the drug culture, violence and possible suicide on the other.

Secondly, let us be clear that it is the systemic ruthlessness of an unregulated economy that is the focus. For there are many aspects of a global culture that do work to promote solidarity among women. Without the Declaration of Human Rights, and the oh-so-long-in-coming-to-birth consciousness that women, too, were human beings and deserving of rights, there would have been no UN Decade in Solidarity with Women, no Beijing Conference in 1995, when for the first time, violence against women became acknowledged as a global injustice. What needs to be striven *for* is to make such solidarity work, and to be effective in the transformations necessary for a just society.

Thirdly, what women struggle *against,* is the fact that when such an economic system rules the world, the invisibility of women from economics since the beginning of modern society seems far more ineradicable. Ester Boserup has documented how women's impoverishment increased during colonial rule:

> Those rulers who had spent a few centuries in subjugating and crippling their own women into de-skilled, de-intellectualised appendages, disfavoured the women of the colonies on matters of land, technology and employment. (Ester Boserup, cited in Shiva, 1988: 66)

While both men and women were impoverished, women suffered more grievously. The privatization of land for revenue displaced women more critically, ending their traditional land rights. Dalit women in India (and in other Asian countries) are particularly severely hit. In urban situations, where slum clearance has forcibly evicted Dalit families, the livelihood of vending goods in the informal sector on the streets is lost. It cannot be done from isolated suburbs. Vandana Shiva is sharply critical of the whole notion of development, since it emerges from western capitalized patriarchy, reproducing these structures within the family, in community and throughout the fabric of Third World societies. With Adam Smith and the development of western economics, Vandana Shiva believes, the wealth created by nature and women's work was made invisible. Thus labour and especially male labour became the fund which originally supplies humans with all the necessities and conveniences of life.

The UN Decade for Women had assumed that women's economic position would automatically improve from an expansion and diffusion of the development process. But there was a blindness as to the way the system excluded both women's work, values and links with caring for the processes which sustain life.

This widespread blindness and refusal to acknowledge that women are also right at the centre of economic life is at the heart of the problem: women are involved in all kinds of work, paid or unpaid, seen or unseen. In the west, there has been a long, bitter struggle to get housework to be recognized. Even now surveys show that while there is much rhetoric about equality and sharing the tasks of running a home, and whereas it is true that many men wish to share the upbringing of their children, research shows that what actually happens is that some men will sometimes participate in the more pleasant chores – cooking, sometimes, for example, but not cleaning bathroom/toilet. Women's involvement in the endless labour of sustaining life itself, from the search for water and kindling wood in many parts of the world, to the widespread responsibility for the long-term care for children and the elderly, is not a statistic ever factored into economic calculations. Yet economic life depends on this work. Thus the whole of the analysis of the Beijing report is flawed in the way it assumed that the purpose was to insert women into the androcentric model of economics which dominates public life.

What is needed is a re-imagining of economic structures, and the basic unit of exchange, from its narrow, monetary basis. If we began to honour the fact that the concept of exchange is many-layered, and that the most basic unit of exchange is actually a relational one, beginning with the primary relation, the exchange of relations between mother and child – could that be the beginning of redefining the economy towards an economy of care, based on relationships of mutual respect and responsibility? I would like to pursue this with reference to motherhood and how this is seen within a culture of globalization. I begin with the story of Vicky Diaz, a 34-year-old mother of five:

> A college-educated former schoolteacher and travel agent in the Philippines, she migrated to the United States to work as a house-keeper and nanny to the two-year-old son of a wealthy family in Beverly Hills, Los Angeles. (Arlie Russell Hochschild, 'Global Care Chains and Emotional Surplus Value', in Giddens and Hutton, 2000: 130)

This is a story of the globalization of mothering. Vicky is paid $400 a week, from which she pays her own family's domestic live-in worker in the Philippines (who is also paying for her own children to be cared for). Living in this global care chain is not easy. Vicky says:

> Even though it's paid well, you are sinking in the amount of your work. Even while you are ironing the clothes, they still call you to the kitchen to wash the plates. It was also very depressing. The only thing you can do is to give all your love to the child (the 2-year-old American child). In my absence from my children, the most I could do with my situation is to give all my love to that child.

The point is that global capitalism spawns global care chains like this, chains usually from a poor country to a rich one, or a poorer to a less poor, expressing an invisible ecology of care, one kind of care depending on another one. Increasingly the people migrating from one country to another will be women. (This is without quantifying the forced migration for the sake of prostitution, which is happening increasingly from the former communist countries as well as from Asia and Africa). Rachel Parrenas's research shows how women such as Vicky talk unceasingly about going home, their families, children and the birthdays and so on, *but it is their wages that go home.* We could compare with the situation of many black slave women in the United States, forced into caring for the white children of their owners, to the neglect of their own children, who had frequently been taken away from them anyway. And this was a situation which persisted even after slavery ended. The solutions to this global care chain are complex – including the political re-valuing of care and understanding that the low value given to care goes hand in hand with the declining value paid to basic food crops, relative to manufactured goods. The low market value of care keeps the status of women who do it, low. Production, not reproduction, is the focus of globalization.

A second example of the politics of mothering under globalization is even more chilling. The anthropologist Nancy Scheper-Hughes, in her book *Death Without Weeping*, researched the communities of the Alto de Cruzeiro in Northeast Brazil, where child deaths through chains of poverty was the norm (the context is the impoverished sugar plantations). Initially she was shocked and resistant to the way the mothers coped with the death of their 'angel babies':

> I resisted for a long time accepting at face value what impoverished Northeast Brazilian women told me about their lack of grief, regret or remorse accompanying the frequent deaths of their young infants – deaths they sometimes aided and abetted by reducing or withdrawing foods and liquids to babies seen as 'doomed' in any case. 'Infants are like birds,' women of Alto do Cruzeiro said. 'Here today, gone tomorrow. It is all the same to them'. 'They die,' other mothers explained, 'because they themselves wanted to die, because they had no "taste", no "knack" for life. We feel no remorse, only pity for the little creatures who die so young, before they have let us know what kind of person they are.'

Nancy Scheper-Hughes interprets this lack of grief and of maternal remorse for the over-production of these angel babies in terms of a political economy of emotions, within a culture of scarcity where there is constant anticipation of loss and premature death (Scheper-Hughes, 1992: 146). A cautious parallel might be made with the low value given to the girl child in situations of poverty in rural India, where female infanticide still occurs.[2]

If we set these two examples – out of possibly thousands – they manifest the consequences of globalization outlined above, where the market's lack of commitment to community and place even shapes how mothers interpret the (here inevitable) death of their babies, where money controls where maternal love should be directed.

The way forward must lie in making visible the labour which sustains life, and by re-connecting the economy to the foundations of society which promote a culture of peace, non-violence devoted to the flourishing of all interdependent life-forms. This means recognizing and valuing the contribution that women make and re-valuing the basis of the economy recognizing all the connections with nature – water, trees, seeds, air and its quality.

The economist Amartya Sen and philosopher Martha Nussbaum recognize this. They say that human rights are insufficient without ensuring proper quality of life. They suggest criteria to measure this. Here we are giving the necessary parameters for well-being and flourishing:

- Being able to live to the end of a human life of normal length.
- Being able to have good health, to be adequately nourished, adequate shelter, opportunities for sexual satisfaction, choice in reproduction.
- Being able to avoid unnecessary and non-beneficial pain.
- Being able to use the sense, imagine, think ... use imagination and thought in connection with experiencing and producing spirituality enriching material.
- Being able to have attachments to things and persons outside ourselves; to love those who love and care for us; to grieve at their absence.
- Being able to form a concept of the good and to engage in a critical reflection on the planning of one's own life.
- Being able to live for and to others, to recognize and show concern for other human beings, to engage in various forms of social action; to be able to imagine the situation of another and to have compassion for that situation; to have the capacity for both justice and friendship.
- Being able to live with concern for and in relation to animals, plants and the world of nature.
- Being able to laugh, play and enjoy relational activity.
- Being able to live one's life and no one else's.
- Being able to live one's own life in one's own surroundings and context (Nussbaum in Nussbaum and Glover, 1995: 83–85).

Nussbaum argues that a concept of 'the good,' or the good functioning of the human being, should underlie development policy and economics. Are people put in conditions of mere subsistence with respect to their functioning, or have they been enabled to live well? (ibid.: 87). She has continued developing this capability approach with economist Amartya Sen, and has specifically directed some of her ideas towards women's NGOs in Rajasthan (Nussbaum, 2000).

Without the re-valuing of economic life on the basis of a culture of peace where the poorest of communities not only survive but are enabled to flourish, where women's work is made visible and valued, without a re-valuing of the structures of care, and the sacredness of the earth's resources, the very future of our planet is endangered. And I end with the hopes and dreams of the women who came together in Beijing in 1995:

> Bread. A clean sky. Active peace. A woman's voice singing somewhere, melody drifting like smoke from the cook fires. The army disbanded, the harvest abundant. The wound healed, the child wanted, the prisoner freed, the body's integrity honoured, the lover returned. ... The labour equal, fair and valued. Delight in the challenge for consensus to solve problems. No hand raised in any gesture but greeting. Secure interiors – of heart, home, land – so firm as to make secure borders irrelevant at last. And everywhere, laughter, care, dancing, contentment. A humble, earthly paradise in the *now.*

Notes

1. For this section I am indebted to Julio de Santa Ana's analysis of globalization, presented at the *Kairos 2000* colloquium, Hofgeismar, June 2000.
2. I make the parallel with rural and not urban India, where the increasing incidence of female infanticide is related to the possibility of amniocentesis, and is becoming more of a middle-class phenomenon.

References

Berry, Thomas (1999) *The Great Work*, New York: Bell Tower.

Eaton, Heather (2000) 'Ecofeminism and Globalisation', *Feminist Theology*, 24: 21–43.

Giddens, Anthony and Will Hutton (eds.) (2000) *On the Edge: Living with Global Capitalism*, London: Jonathan Cape.

Gorringe, Timothy (1999) *Fair Shares: Ethics and the Global Economy*, London: Thames and Hudson.

Grey, Mary (2003) *Sacred Longings: Ecofeminist Theology and Globalisation*, London: SCM.

—— (2004) *The Unheard Scream: The Struggles of Dalit Women in India*, New Delhi: Centre for Dalit Theology.

Korten, David (1995) *When Corporations Rule the World*, London: Earthscan Publications.

Lewis, Robert Arthur (2000) 'Why we are here', Seattle.

Nussbaum, Martha (1995) 'Human Capabilities', in M. Nussbaum and J. Glover (eds.), *Women, Culture and Development*, Oxford: Clarendon Press, 83–85.

—— (2000) *Women and Human Development*, Oxford: Oxford University Press.

Pilger, John (1998) *Hidden Agendas*, London: Vintage.

Scheper-Hughes, Nancy (1992) *Death Without Weeping*, Berkeley/Los Angeles: University of California Press.

Shiva, V. (1988) *Staying Alive: Women, Ecology and Development*, London: Zed Books.

3

Gandhi and Nehru

Clash over Post-colonial Development

LLOYD I. RUDOLPH

In this paper I explore Gandhi's postmodernism by revisiting his October/November 1945 clash with Jawaharlal Nehru over the meaning and practice of 'development'. Nehru, like US New Deal President Franklin Delano Roosevelt, would have agreed that one should 'make no little plans' because little plans 'have no magic to stir men's blood'.[1] Nehru like Roosevelt preferred big plans and big dams. He admired America's multipurpose TVA (Tennessee Valley Authority) and tried to replicate it at the Bhakra Nangal complex and the Damodar Valley Authority.[2] Nehru expected big dams to become the temples of modern India.

Big dams, pre-eminent symbols of high modernist development thinking, are under fire these days – in India, at the Sardar Sarovar on the Narmada[3], at Tehri on the Bhagirathi and in the world beyond India at the Three Gorges on the Yangtse in China.[4]

Opposition to big dams symbolizes a crisis in the kind of modern development thinking that captured the imagination of Nehru's generation. Development has, in some circles, become a word for environmental destructiveness and human oppression.[5] The World Bank has tried to salvage modern development by continuously modifying economic, cost-benefit paradigms and criteria by factoring into the development equation such terms as equitable distribution of benefits, basic human needs, sustainability, environmental friendliness, protection of human rights and benefiting the poorest.[6]

The agent of development – the modern nation-state – has come under a cloud too. For Nehru and his inter-war years' generation the modern state was enlightened as a suitable instrument for the economic and social transformation. Today, as money, commodities, services, ideas, images, persons, disease, drugs and terrorism circle the globe with accelerating speed and deeper penetration, the modern state is increasingly seen as obsolescent, less and less able to cope. With decreasing effectiveness, its exclusive claims to sovereignty, and the use of force have lost credibility and legitimacy.[7] The modern state's apparent inability to reduce much less eliminate 'poverty,' the most widely agreed development objective,[8] has cast doubt on the developmental state, an idea and practice that Nehru wholeheartedly embraced and that Gandhi for the most part rejected.

The Gandhi-Nehru debate over development and the modern state began in 1928. Nehru had recently returned from a tour of Western-European countries and the Soviet Union. The trip left a deep impression on him, reviving and sharpening his modernist proclivities. The debate resumed briefly in 1940 and culminated on the eve of independence in October and November 1945 when the two men clashed over their visions of an independent India.

Six decades later, we can see more clearly than most of their contemporaries could how and why these nationalist comrades in arms differed. When they first met in December 1916 in Lucknow at the annual meeting of the Indian National Congress, Gandhi was 47 and Nehru 27. Gandhi had recently returned to India after 21 years from South Africa – a colony on the periphery of the British empire. His reputation as a Satyagrahi on behalf of Indians' civil rights and against racism preceded him. Nehru had returned to India in 1912 after seven years in the homeland of empire – England. He had been a public school boy at Harrow, done science tripos at Cambridge and studied law at the Inner Temple – an education common to the empire's governing class.[9] From 1920, when Jawaharlal began playing an important role in Indian politics, Gandhi was his mentor. It was through Nehru that Gandhi 'captured the imagination of the younger people ... .'[10] By 1926, when Jawaharlal left for an extended tour of Europe, it was clear that Gandhi had chosen him as his political heir.

Why did Gandhi choose Nehru 'despite the latter's known basic differences with him?'[11] In retrospect it seems clear that their world views were poles apart: Gandhi championed the village, civil society, craft production and simple living, whereas Nehru the city, the modern state, industrial production and material well-being.

The apogee of their positive relationship may have been in 1929 when Gandhi signalled that Nehru was to be his successor by proposing him for Presidency of the Congress because 'the nation is safe in his hands,' after which Nehru presided at the 'historic' Lahore Congress in December that year.

But Nehru soon reports himself as 'bored' with Gandhi's rather uneventful 'constructive programme' and not pleased with Gandhi's references to 'an idyllic Ram Raj'. In the mid-thirties Nehru recorded in his diary, 'I am getting more and more certain that there can be no cooperation between Bapu and me. We had better go our own different ways.' And Gandhi wrote to his English friend, admirer and collaborator, Agatha Harrison, that 'Jawaharlal's way is not mine. I do not accept his methods'.

But, in 1942, when Gandhi launched the 'Quit India' movement, the kind of political action Nehru liked, Gandhi could tell the Wardha session of the AICC that 'when I am gone he (Nehru) will speak my language.'

In an exchange of letters and one meeting in October and November 1945 Gandhi tried to determine if Nehru would in fact speak his language when he was gone. The exchanges focused on what kind of 'development' would be best for an independent India. This episode will be analysed in the text below.

Despite their profound differences in 1945 over development, including Nehru's outright rejection of Gandhi's plan for village swaraj , in June 1946 Gandhi persuaded Vallabhbhai Patel, who held a 6 to 1 lead over Nehru in Provincial Congress Committee nominations, to withdraw from the crucial Congress presidential contest. As a result of Patel's withdrawal, Nehru was unanimously elected Congress president – an event that paved the way for Nehru to head an interim government. Despite Patel's superior hold over the Congress Parliamentary Party after independence in 1947, the leadership of the party and government that Gandhi had arranged made it possible for Nehru to become independent India's first Prime Minister.

Nehru quickly rejected Gandhi's call, in his 'Last Will and Testament', to convert the Indian National Congress from a political party seeking power in the new state into a Lok Sevak Sangh, a People's Service Association. In the Constituent Assembly, Nehru avoided addressing Gandhi's request to provide for a 'predominately non-violent state' and saw to it that 'village swaraj' was watered down to non-justiciable Panchayati Raj clauses in the Directive Principles of State Policy.

Even though Gandhi was acutely aware of differences with Nehru, until his death on January 30, 1948 he supported Nehru over Vallabbhai Patel for leadership of the Congress party and of independent India.[12] Both men regretted their differences and tried to overcome them. Gandhi persisted until the end in asking Nehru to reconsider his commitments to 'modern civilization'.

Gandhi's assassination on January 30, 1948, put an end to their personal dialogue but not to the discourse it represented. When Gandhi died, two of his letters to Nehru about India's future remained unanswered. Nehru believed that the state directed and controlled industrialization would solve India's poverty problem and make it a power in the world. State patronage of science, higher education and research would promote and establish what Nehru sometimes referred to as a 'scientific temper,'[13] a modern secular culture that would do for India what the renaissance did for Europe.

The differences between Gandhi and Nehru came to the surface in October and November 1945 when Gandhi asked Nehru to discuss his goals for an independent India.[14] The story, based on extant correspondence, reveals Nehru's incomprehension of and indifference to *Hind Swaraj* – the primary text for understanding Gandhi's critique of 'modern civilization' and the kind of development and state it entailed. Gandhi started with the village and the villager, with local autonomy and employment, with work in small-scale industries, crafts and agriculture. Nehru started with the city and urban life, with centralized state planning and with work in large-scale, impersonal industry and offices.

Gandhi wrote to Nehru that the essence of what he said in *Hind Swaraj* 'is that the things required for human life must be individually controlled by every person ...' 'You will not understand me', he continued, 'if you think that I am talking about the villages of today'. 'My villages exist in my imagination.' As if to warn Nehru against privileging or naturalizing his vision of a modern industrial India, he continued with the remark that 'After, all, every person lives in the world of his own imagination'.

'The villager in this imagined village', Gandhi continued, 'will not be apathetic .... He will not lead his life like an animal in a squalid dark room. Men and women will live freely and be prepared to face the whole world .... No one will live indolently or luxuriously,'. The village of his imagination would be self-reliant, not self-sufficient. 'I can think of many things which will have to be produced on a large scale. Maybe there will be railways, so also post and telegraph. What it will have and what it will not, I do not know, Nor do I care. If I can maintain its essence, the rest will mean free facility to come and settle'. Gandhi's imagined village was to be voluntary, another of his experiments with truth. Gandhi ended his letter to Nehru by suggesting that they find time to sort out the issues between them.

Nehru agreed that they should meet, adding 'I don't know when to fit this in. I shall try.' Promising to reply at greater length, he sent off a short answer on October 9.

> Briefly put, my view is that the question before us is not one of truth versus untruth or non-violence versus violence ... I do not understand why a village should necessarily embody truth and non-violence. A village, normally speaking, is backward intellectually and culturally and no progress can be made from a backward environment. Narrow-minded people are much more likely to be untruthful and violent.

After arguing that 'we must find out specifically how to attain (a sufficiency of food, clothing, housing, sanitation, etc.) speedily', Nehru continued:

> It is many years since I read *Hind Swaraj* ... But even when I read it 20 years ago it seemed to me completely unreal .... It is 38 years since *Hind Swaraj* was written. The world has completely changed since then ... consideration of these questions must keep present facts, forces and the human material we have today in view, otherwise it will be divorced from reality.

Nehru then reminded Gandhi that '... the Congress has never considered that picture (portrayed in *Hind Swaraj*) much less adopted it. You yourself have never asked to adopt it except for minor aspects'. He then questioned whether it was desirable for 'Congress to consider these fundamental questions .... I should imagine,' Nehru continued, 'that a body like the Congress should not lose itself in arguments over such matters which can probably produce great confusion in people's minds resulting in an inability to act in the present'.

On November 12, 1945, Nehru found the time to discuss what 'development' should mean and be in independent India. The only account we have of this conversation is the memo Gandhi sent to Nehru summarizing what he took to be the gist of their discussion. 'I have realized', Gandhi wrote, 'after our talks of yesterday that there is no great difference between us with regard to our modes of thinking and understanding things'. He then recorded what he understood to be their areas of agreement:

1. In your view the real question is how to enhance the intellectual, economic, political and moral power of every human being. In mine too.
2. And every person therein have a similar right and opportunity to rise higher.
3. The condition of the country and the city should accordingly be similar in respect to food and water, habitation, clothing and recreation ....
4. ... To ensure that one person does not ride another, the basic unit must be an imaginary village or group that can remain self-sufficient[15] and within the group there needs to be mutual dependence. This way of thinking provides a picture of the relationship among human beings inhabiting the entire world.

Nehru did not respond but his silence speaks for itself; we can infer that he did not accept Gandhi's summary and wanted to exit silently. Gandhi, for his part, did not press for more meetings nor did he, as Nehru seemed to be daring him to do, attempt to have their differences over the nature of development in free, post-colonial India considered by a meeting of the Congress Working Committee. Perhaps he thought that this was not a time to weaken Nehru's leadership (we know that six months later, on

June 6, 1946, he backed Nehru against Patel for Congress president) and that he should wait for a more favourable moment. With the rush of events surrounding independence, the violence of partition, and Gandhi's assassination on January 30, 1948, that moment never came.

Gandhi died in 1948, Nehru in 1964, but the debate about development continues.[16] Starting in 1970s and with increasing force into the 21st century Gandhi's postmodern version of development gained in relevance and saliency.[17] Liberalization in 1991 changed the terms of debate by privileging the market over the centralized planning of the Nehruvian state.[18] The magic of Nehru's imagined India already had begun to fade in the 1970s, faltered in the 1980s and collapsed in the 1990s when what Nehru called 'the temples of modern India',[19] the 'big dams' and state enterprises, attracted more employees than devotees.

After 1991 property rights and market relations began to displace state agencies and policies as the driving forces of development. From a Gandhian perspective they have not changed, and may very well have intensified, development's destructive and oppressive consequences. For Gandhi the consumption-driven market, like the centralized modern state, was a central problematic of 'modern civilization'. Global warming and climate change threatened life on the bio-sphere and revealed the limits on growth that Gandhi's critique of modern civilization anticipated.

Notes

1. The aphorism, which has been attributed to the city planner Daniel Burnham, was said to be one of Franklin Roosevelt's. 'The quotation' a Bartlett footnote says, 'is now doubted'. See Henry M. Saylor, "Make No Little Plans': Daniel Burnham Thought It but Did He Say It?', *Journal of the American Institute of Architects*, 27(3), 1957. See *Bartlett's Familiar Quotations*, Sixteenth Edition, Jusun Kaplan, General Editor, Boston: Little Brown and Company, 1992, p. 555.
2. See Daniel Klingensmith's *One Valley and a Thousand: Dams, Nationalism and Development*, New Delhi: Oxford University Press, 2007 for how Nehru, and those of his generation who thought as he did, understood development, Klingensmith argues that what was established through the US-India exchange was '... a set of common metaphors, tropes, symbols and terms, a 'poetics' of development. But there is – no need', he continues, 'to assume that ... those ... who invoked the developmental model meant the same thing by it. TVA was ultimately not so much a blueprint as a signifier ... open to a variety of usages and ... meanings, in discourses about the state, civil society, the economy and the environment', pp. 2–3.

3. See K.K. Oza, 'Saga of Failed Dams', *Mainstream*, July 8, 1995, pp. 11–16 for an overview.

   Amita Baviskar's *In the Belly of the River: Tribal Conflicts over Development in the Narmada Valley*, Delhi: Oxford University Press, 1995, gives an account of the lives of Bhilala adivasis in the Narmada valley who are fighting displacement by the Sardar Sarovar dam.

   For a defense of big dams, see Dr Bharat Singh, Water Resources Development Training Centre, University of Roorkee, UP, 'Sardar Sarovar Project – More Beneficial than Baneful', *The Hindu*, 'Open Page', December 12, 1996. Dr Singh argues that the project 'is one of the most thoroughly investigated and meticulously planned projects in this country. It is unfortunate that is being opposed in India and abroad. The controversy over technical matters such as dam stability, water availability, water logging and siltation rate has no real validity as these aspects fall within the experts domain ... . No development since civilization began has taken place without changing environmental and social conditions. The only criterion is whether the gains are commensurate with the costs. The Sardar Sarovar Project is particularly advantageous in this respect ... . For every tribal displaced seven tribals in the command area will benefit'.

   The contest over the Sardar Sarovar dam on the Narmada river in Gujarat is reviewed critically, including an account of the World Bank's withdrawal from the project on March 30, 1993, by a leading opponent, Booker Prize winner, Arundhati Roy, in *The Greater Common Good*, Bombay: India Book Distributors, 1999. The essay first appeared in *Frontline* and *Outlook* edited by N. Ram and Vinod Mehta respectively.

   The Supreme Court lifted its four year old ban on construction of the Sardar Sarovar dam in February 1999.

   Arundhati Roy resumed her opposition to the dam in 'The Cost of Living', *Frontline*, February 18, 2000, pp. 64–75, where she covered much of the ground traversed in *The Greater Common Good* and updated her criticism. The essay 'The Cost of Living' was delivered at the Nehru Memorial Lecture at Cambridge University, November 8, 1999, at the invitation of Nobel Laureate in Economics, Amartya Sen, Master of Trinity College. N. Ram, editor of *Frontline*, published the lecture in full.

   Development high modernists such as Dr Bharat Singh are of course for the dam but the left is divided. Gail Omvedt, for example, on balance favours it because it will help cultivators who need the irrigation water but Roy, Sen and Ram are opposed.

4. The Three Gorges dam is likely to take upwards of twenty years to build and to cost upwards of $40 billion dollars. Upstream, it will inundate one of China's most revered landmarks and displace several million people;

downstream, it will eliminate vital, long established navigation and the livelihood of fishermen. Britain, the US, the World Bank and others, fearing a 'white elephant', have turned their backs on the project. For more on The Three Gorges dam project in China, see Patrick E. Tyler, 'Chinese Dam's Forbidding Future Dooms Rich Past', *The New York Times*, October 6, 1996, p. 1, 8 and Fred Pearce, 'A Dam Too Far?', *Guardian Weekly*, January 28, 1996.

5. See for example Claude Alvares, *Science, Development and Violence: The Revolt Against Modernity*, Delhi: Oxford University Press, 1994, where much of the anti-development literature and some development practices are reviewed and analysed from an evil versus good perspective.

6. For an evaluation of World Bank doctrine and performance over its first 50 years, see Devesh Kapur, John Lewis and Richard Webb, *The World Bank: Its First Half Century, Volume 1: History*, Washington, DC: Brookings Institution Press, 1997.

   For a critique of the World Bank's development thinking by an influential activist, see Bruce Rich, *Mortgaging the Earth: The World Bank, Environmental Impoverishment, and the Crisis of Development*, Boston: Beacon Press, 1993. Rich argues that economic development 'is now the organizing principle for almost every society and nation on the planet'. The World Bank's 'guiding principle', Rich argues, has been that central planners ... can devise universally applicable approaches to development. Because it ignores indigenous knowledge and local differences, the result has been rampant ecological destruction and the dislocation of millions of people'. Rich allows that the Bank has stopped some of its more egregious practices but holds that only a 're-invention' of the institution can cure its malaise.

7. Istvan Hont's essay, 'The Permanent Crisis of a Divided Mankind: 'Contemporary Crisis of the Nation State' in Historical Perspective', in John Dunn (ed.), *Contemporary Crisis of the Nation State?*, Oxford, UK and Cambridge, MA: Blackwell, 1995, argues in a section entitled, What 'Crisis'? (167–72) that 'Some of the problems facing contemporary 'nation-states' have been recognized as acute difficulties for a very long time; and only by recognizing their longevity can we be in a position to judge whether the various solutions proposed in the past might prove workable.

8. In 'Future of Poverty: Development and Destitution', Ashis Nandy distinguishes between poverty and destitution. Before development undertook to eradicate poverty large sections of the population were poor but not destitute. The commons, the community and their kin and neighbours kept most of the time above a subsistence line. Karl Polanyi

in *The Great Transformation* makes a similar argument. Nandy distinguishes pre-modern poverty from modem destitution in another way. In pre-modem societies, the poor and the rich lived differently; their lifestyles were distinguishable. In modern societies the destitute and the affluent share lifestyles but not income.

9. See Rupert Wilkinson, *Gentlemanly Power: British Leadership and the Public School Tradition*, New York: Oxford University Press, 1964 for the tight relationship between education and power before World War I when the empire seemed to be at its apogee.
10. Madhu Limaye, *Mahatma Gandhi and Jawaharlal Nehru: A Historic Partnership 1916–1948, Vol. 1, 1916–1931*, 4 vols, Delhi: B.R. Publishing Corporation, 1989, p. 80.
11. Limaye, *Mahatma Gandhi*, Vol. I, p. vii. These are the words of Madhu Limaye, whose four volume work is devoted to trying to answer this question.

    In his Preface he says that 'The freedom movement drew into its fold the finest elements from the various Provinces of India. Gandhi's magic touch made them into heroes. I often asked myself as to why did Gandhi pick up from among half a dozen eminent leaders – Rajaji, Vallabbhai, Rajendra Prasad, Abul Kalam Azad, Jawaharlal Nehru and Subhas Chandra Bose – Jawaharlal Nehru as his heir despite the latter's known basic differences with him? This question troubled me', Limaye continues, 'because it was difficult for me to conceive Jawaharlal rising to pre-eminence either without Gandhi's decisive intervention in India's politics or Gandhi's deliberately and persistently promoting his succession. This question has interested me and mystified me, in turns, these last fifty years'.
12. S.C. Gangal assessed the Gandhi-Nehru relationship in 'Gandhi and Nehru: A Love-Hate Relationship?', *The Hindu*, 'Open Page', November 28, 1995.
13. Huiyung Wang, *Discourses on Tradition and Modernization: Perspectives of Gandhi and Sun-yat-sen*, New Delhi: Madhyam Book Service, 2001 for Nehru on 'scientific temper'.
14. Gandhi's attempt in 1945 to engage Nehru in their respective visions of post independence India first came to my attention when I read Nehru's *A Bunch of Old Letters*, London: Asia Publishing House, 1960. It reproduces their exchange of letters in October and November, 1945.

    Later I found the late Raj Krishna's article, 'The Nehru-Gandhi Polarity and Economic Policy', in B.R. Nanda et al. (eds.), *Gandhi and Nehru*, New Delhi: Oxford University Press, 1979, particularly helpful. An early account of the October/November 1945 exchange of letters can be found in Bimla Prasad's *Gandhi, Nehru and JP*, Delhi: Chanakya Publications, 1985, pp. 274–78. I would not agree with his statement that 'the correspondence only shows difference in emphasis but agreement on fundamentals', p. 274. Also helpful for constructing the relationship is B.R. Nanda's chapter on 'Man versus Machine' in his *Gandhi and His Critics*, New Delhi: Oxford University Press, 1985. Martin Green's accounts in *Gandhi: Voice of a New Age Revolut*ion, New York: Continuum, 1993, particularly at pp. 196–98, of Gandhi-Nehru relations are telling.

In writing about the Gandhi/Nehru debate about development in 1945, I have also drawn on Sudhir Chandra's 'The Language of Modern Ideas: Reflections on an Ethnological Parable', *Thesis Eleven*, No. 39, 1994, pp. 39–51. Anthony Parel's edition *of Hind Swaraj and Other Writings*, Cambridge, UK: Cambridge University Press, 1997, pp. 149–56, provides the complete texts.

15. Gandhi here refers to village communities as 'self-reliant', a usage frequently followed by Gandhi and interpreters. I have remarked in the body of the text above that Gandhi viewed village communities as self-reliant, not self-sufficient. As quoted above, he wrote to Nehru that 'I can think of many things which will have to be produced on a large scale. Maybe there will be railways, so also post and telegraph'. I take these remarks as supporting self-reliance over self-sufficiency. They also suggest that Gandhi accepted some of the technologies and economies of scale of his time and that he anticipated similar conditions and their consequences in the future.

16. At the official level Morarji Desai's Janata government (1977–1979) and V.P. Singh's Janata Dal government (1989–91) gave more credence and weight to Gandhian ideas about development than did Indira Gandhi's (1966–1977; 1980–1984) and Rajiv Gandhi's (1984–1989) Congress governments. Nehruvian discourse and practice about development remained the official creed of the Congress until June 1991.

    Faced with the threat of national bankruptcy in the form of a balance of payments crisis, a newly elected Narasimha Rao Congress government with Manmohan Singh as Finance Minister responded by 'liberalizing' the economy internally, abandoning inter alia the 'permit-license raj', and externally by abandoning economic nationalism and autarchy, lowering tariffs and moving toward participation in world markets and the global economy.

17. See Sumit Roy, 'Development, Environment and Poverty: Some Issues for Discussion', *Economic and Political Weekly*, January 27, 1996, pp. PE-29–PE-41. Roy addresses environmental concerns that have modified ... 'traditional' development goals and led to the concept of

'sustainable development'. He also takes account of 'a shift in emphasis from state to market forces in shaping development policies', PE-29.

Roy's analysis encompasses the 1972 UN Conference on Human Environment held in Stockholm where Prime Minister Indira Gandhi played a prominent role in ushering in 'the environment' to the international agenda, the 1987 report of the World Commission on Environment and Development (*The Brundtland Report*) which coined the phrase 'no sustainability without development' and held that environmental problems could not be dealt with unless 'factors underlying world poverty and international inequality' were addressed and stated flatly that poverty 'intensifies pressure on the environment'; and the 1992 UN Conference on Environment and Development, better known as the 'Rio Summit', where five agreements on Climatic Change; the Convention on Biological Diversity; Agenda 21 – devoted to environmental degradation issues primarily in the context of domestic policy; The Rio Declaration; and the Forest Principles, the latter two barely masking disagreements between the richer developed and the poorer developing countries were signed.

Roy's voice is quasi-official with a third world, developing country accent. Seemingly innocent of Gandhian development discourse about less is more, and better, he quite unproblematically accepts the notion that 'increasing the stock of wealth through growth' remains the primary goal of development.

Donald J. writing in the *New Yorker* of August 14, 1995 on 'E Pluribus Unabomber' argues that the Unabomber, who since 1978 in sixteen incidents killed three and injured twenty-three in his campaign against industrialism, 'is not alone in his dissatisfaction with industrial society. There has long been a kind of Unabomber strain in the West's ambivalence about science and technology (a strain that Gandhi called 'the other West') that have given it so much of its power ... critics (such as Gandhi) indicted it for not only technological unemployment but also the impersonalization and regimentation of work, the despoliation of nature, and, finally, the indiscriminate slaughter of total war', pp. 2–3.

Kevles says that Ned Ludd, the legendary leader of the rebellion against early industrialism, would have understood the Unabomber. Ludd, remembered in the triumphalist industrial canon as the eponymous founder of 'Luddites', led masked bands of cottage hand weavers and combers to smash power looms and bum down textile mills. The Luddite rebellion shook the North of England in 1811 and 1812 until it was brutally repressed. Destruction of machinery was made a crime punishable by death. In 1813, 24 Luddites were hanged.

Up to a point Ned Ludd would have understood Gandhi too. An early sub-altern, Ludd resisted what a Gandhi guru, John Ruskin, in *Unto This*

Last, written two generations after Ludd, called the 'satanic mills' of early industrial capitalism. When Gandhi wrote *Hind Swaraj* in 1909 a century of industrialism separated him from Ludd. That century of knowledge and of experience with industrial economies made it possible for Gandhi to distinguish between machines that empowered and machines that enslaved and to accept some of the infra-structural benefits of industrial technology.

In 1909 Gandhi's opposition to industrialism could be civilizational and moral as well as, like Ned Ludd's employment-oriented. Gandhi can be counted as a 'neo-Luddite' only if his critique of industrialism is read in the context of *Hind Swaraj*, his liminally inclusive and necessarily non-violent critique of and alternative to 'modem civilization'. If, as Daniel Kevles puts it, today's 'Neo-Luddism's sympathizers ... include some of us all of the time and all of us some of the time' it is in part because a postmodern Gandhi has helped them 'to be selective about disliking technology and its byproducts'.

18. I do not want to deal with the why and what of liberalization here except to say that in June 1991 when the Narasimha Rao Congress government took office the country was on the verge of bankruptcy. An IMF bailout was accompanied by Dr Manmohan Singh's 'reform' measures that signalled an end to Nehruvian style state led development. The implosion of the Soviet imperial state, the bankruptcy of communist ideology and, perhaps most important, the discrediting of centrally planned economies in the Soviet Union and Eastern Europe set the stage for India's turn to liberalization.

19. I am grateful to Baren Ray, another participant in the January 22, 1996 seminar on 'Postmodern Gandhi', for reminding me of Nehru's invocation of the phrase, 'the temples of modern India'. See Ray's 'The Burden of Population', *The Hindu*, June 1, 1995, where he argues that the Swaraj path established by millions of Gandhian activists was abandoned for a Nehruvian pursuit of 'science and technology (that) led to a concentration and over-centralization of all the entrepreneurial effort – of all the eggs being put in the same basket – namely in what Jawaharlal Nehru called the temples of modern India'.

4

Interrogating Development from a Gender Perspective

ASHA KAUSHIK

A paradoxical situation is perceptible in coexistence of unprecedented accomplishments in technological and economic spheres and persisting discrimination, deprivation and marginalization of vast populace, particularly women. Overcoming this is 'the central part of the exercise of development', as Amartya Sen says. The key issues, therefore, pertain not only to the nature and dynamics of the dominant paradigm of development but also to how it has impacted various segments of the society.

I

Development is a highly-contested concept. Following the ideological moorings of the 19th century liberalism versus Marxism, ever since the close of the 1940s, there has been a continuous debate on market vis-à-vis state-led development strategy. However, the larger implications became clearer during the 1980s and 1990s. Classical and neo-classical economic theories stress the centrality of the free market for development. Modernization theories argue that development is primarily an economic process and an identical development path should be followed by all countries. The logic and direction of pre-established patterns is predictable as exemplified by Walt Rostow's four-stage transition: (i) traditions with backward beliefs and technology, (ii) introduction of modern technology, (iii) take off towards modernization, and (iv) stage of modernity with mass consumption. Modernization-development equation, in this view, entails not only the procedural requisites such as a pre-eminent role of science and technology, large-scale industrialization, urbanization, etc., but also persistence of the Enlightenment world view denigrating and dismissing non-Western world views as pre-modern, uncivilized and undeveloped/underdeveloped. The development discourse, in this form, is clearly a power discourse.

Countering the growth-modernization equation, Marxist-dependency theories argue that development and underdevelopment are caused by unequal global power relations. Alternative development theorists of various hues describe this catching up development path as a 'myth'.

It is notable that ideological juxtaposition notwithstanding, both liberal-growth modernization and Marxist-dependency approaches have conceived development as a linear (rather unilinear) process. In this process, a nation or people moved from underdevelopment – equated with traditional institutions and values – to development identified with industrialization, rationality and modernity. Rooted in Enlightenment thought, the development discourse has remained West-centric and male-centric, rationalizing the economic growth model and technocratic control of productivity in terms of progress. The universalistic claims of the West-centric development-modernity discourse have been widely challenged by critics ranging from dependency theorists to post-Marxists, post-modernists and feminists, environmentalists and alternative developmentalists. Enormous diversity in the development critiques notwithstanding, the shared core conceptual argument pertains to acknowledging and accepting multiplicity of identity, ideas, frameworks of understanding and addressing problems from the vantage point of the situated/contextual reality.

In practice, however, in the footsteps of the global North, Southern countries driven by various reasons have been following the development path taken by the North. Today, structural adjustment policies as a manifestation of neo-liberal convictions have reinforced more than ever before the primacy of the market in economic development, multilateral agencies often using economic measures such as GNP per capita to assess development. Also, more often than not, national-level measures hide important spatial and social inequalities. Despite widespread decolonization, it is still suggestive to consider the role of colonialism in understanding development today. It needs to be understood that it is the drive to catch up with the West/North that has led to large debts resulting in the compulsions of adoption of SAP by the Southern countries.

Voices of resistance have been equally expansive and persistent. In the early 1970s, the 'trickle down' theories were questioned by women development professionals arguing in favour of bringing women to the centre of development debate. From 1970s, growing attention has also been paid to bottom-up or grassroots development, accepting decentralization and devolution as more efficient than large-scale activities. Civil society organizations have become key actors in the grassroots approaches in the move towards greater democracy throughout the world. During the 1980s, environmental concerns emanating from the economic growth model were voiced on a large scale with 'sustainable development' proposed as an alternative. As mentioned earlier, modernization theories and Marxist theories viewed development as involving social evolution into complex forms of social organization. Ethno-development analysts brought 'culture' into the precincts of the development discourse and, thereby, questioning it. Post-modern and post-colonial approaches to development stress on heterogeneity and argue that constructions of development are not neutral and have differential impact on men and women in differing contexts. And, as globalization processes intensify, neo-liberal arguments further support economic globalization, emphasizing upon the role of increased free trade in development process, privileging the interests of the North over those of the South. Accordingly, globalization-driven development paradigm raises pertinent questions of equity and justice.

Thus, development theories differ on definitions of 'development', key actors and approaches. Over time, what is regarded as 'development' has become more and more complex, contested and diversified.

It is not only defining development which is contested, the way that development, regardless of its definition, is 'measured' is also problematic. It is assumed that 'development' is something which needs to be measured or assessed. For various actors in development, measuring development is important for various reasons. For example, policymakers may want to find out what is the social development position (as defined by the policymakers) of a population in order to inform policy formulation. Governments or international agencies may want to assess the impact of a particular development initiative and, therefore, want to have measurements both before and after the project. Finally, campaigning organizations, seeking to improve living conditions for marginalized groups, may want information about the nature of marginalization.

Therefore, by the closing decade of the last century, development was redefined specifically in terms of human development, widely represented in successive human development reports of the UNDP since 1990. In these reports, the UNDP has posited human development 'as a process of enlarging people's choices to live a long and healthy life... to be educated and to have an access to resources needed for a decent standard of living by creating conducive environment for people... to develop their full potentials and to have reasonable chance of leading productive and creative lives in accord with their needs and interests' (UNDP, 1990: 1–3). It is argued that if human development and human rights advance together then they reinforce one another, expanding people's capabilities and protecting their rights and fundamental freedoms. Following large-scale global concern, the Declaration on the Right to Development was adopted by the United Nations in 1986. And finally, with the adoption of the Millennium Development Goals (MDGs) by the UN in September 2000, human and gender development has attained the status of a consensually-derived policy directive for all member-nations.

II

Globalization has exacerbated the impasse within development theory and practice. Globalization, theoretically speaking, has been the key concept of the 1990s, instrumental in comprehending the changes that have encompassed socio-politico-economic life at local, national and global levels in the recent past. Once it acquired academic significance, along with other conceptual frameworks like post-industrialism, post-modernism, post-liberalism and post-Marxism by the mid-1980s, it has occupied centre stage in mainstream development analysis. The global impact of globalization – also in development practice – is evident in its overbearing omnipresence, overshadowing other drivers of change. It is perceived as an anathema in some quarters and as irresistible in others.

Globalization is hardly a new phenomenon. It is merely a new name, a sub-code for capitalism that subsumes diverse socio-political and economic processes. The imperial historical origins have remained embedded in a matrix in which new actors compete for privileged access to networks and state support. Today, the principal agencies and multinational corporations fulfil the roles played earlier by the trading companies (these integrate and appropriate resources and exploit cheap labour, while the imperial states extract domestic resources to finance overseas expansion and to secure the conditions for the reproduction of global capital accumulation).

It would not be contrafactual to state that globalization in its current phase, indicating the desire to integrate nation-states within the overall framework of the WTO, is nothing but a modern version of the 'Theory of Comparative Costs Advantage' propagated by the classical economists to provide theoretical foundations for unrestricted flow of goods from Britain to the erstwhile colonies, the process is supposed to benefit both the countries entering into trade relations. The same argument is being brought forth by the advocates of globalization in favour of an 'export-led pattern of growth' in place of the 'import substitution trade' policies followed earlier. As revealed by historical evidence, the imperialist nations drained out resources from the colonized nations and thrived at their expense. In the Indian context, a major part of the Indian Freedom Movement was engaged in combatting this economic exploitation, beginning with the 19th century liberal 'economic nationalism' through the militant strategies of 'swadeshi' and boycott during the first two decades of the 20th century and leading to Gandhi's crusade of Swaraj in the subsequent decades. The anti-imperialist struggle was, thus, also anti-globalization (in its earlier sense).

The primary intervention of the globalizing process was admittedly felt in the economic arena but soon it expanded into the political and the cultural terrains as a clear ideological move. In this context, it is often argued that of all classical theorists, the most explicitly committed to a globalizing theory of modernization was Karl Marx, who argued that the bourgeoisie was recreating the world in its own image. What is missed in this argument is the exploitative core of the current phenomenon of globalization based on the liberal-capitalist logic of inequalities, intrinsic to the very organization and development of capitalism. The argument is also mistaken in synonymizing globalism and globalization. In our view, the two are not synonymous. They are distinguishable in terms of a deliberate ideological agenda in case of the latter and interactive international cooperation in case of the former. Not only this, globalism is not incompatible with the sovereign independence of the nation-states, whereas globalization threatens the same. In this sense, both Marx and Gandhi would qualify as proponents of globalism and not of globalization, in contrast to the liberal capitalists who celebrate freedom of the market as freedom of the human race (Kaushik, 2001: 82–89).

In view of the past historical experience of colonial repression, doubts are being raised, and rightly so, about the professed 'radically different' and altogether beneficial impact of similar policies, compared to the devastation of the earlier period.

Globalization has resulted in one-third of the global trade being conducted by the MNCs. This has been instrumental in liquidating not only national economies but also the sovereignty of the nation-states. In the political sphere, the nation-states find themselves increasingly constrained, as new centres of power emerge to delimit political sovereignty in terms of foreign aid, IMF loans, deregulation, etc. Growing concentration of economic resources and political power has also aggravated social schisms and conflicts. Plural cultural identities and normative structures are under threat through what has been described as the globalized 'culture industry' promoting not only a hybrid culture of newfangled consumerism, commodity fetishism and one-dimensional consciousness, but also 'hyper simulated' conditions and transmission of the 'culture ideology of consumerism' from the centre to the periphery of the world system. The mirage of 'abundance' is picturized in rosy colours and credit economy as a sure passage. Gandhi in India had warned about similar consequences of what he called 'mammon worship' (Kaushik, 2002: 9).

Even the journals of World Bank and IMF have confirmed that economic reforms introduced as part of the package of globalization in about 100 countries all over the world have resulted in a decline in the rate of savings on the one hand and increase in the rate of unemployment, on the other. Lower public/social spending and fiscal compression have also been noted. The inescapable impact of policies favouring globalization on intra-system functioning of the nation-states is also evident in terms of receding welfarist agenda of the State and fragmentation of political commitments.

Thus, as L. Sklair points out, although the nation-state is the 'spatial reference point' in these practices, but more significant reference point is the global capitalist system, based on a variegated global capitalist class, which unquestionably dictates economic transnational practices and is the most important single force in the struggle to dominate political and cultural ideological practices (Sklair, 1991: 7). Evidently, globalization is a totalizing process in terms of both hegemonization and homogenization, an extended and subtler American version of European colonial/imperialist ambitions of dominating, expropriating and transforming the world in its own image. Ideologically also, it is a derivative of the earlier conceptualizations of 'progress' and 'modernization', premised on the West-centric view of civilization, materialism and economism, glorification of the 'invisible hand' of the market, growth-obsessed industrialism, objectification of nature and instrumental treatment of humanity.

Thus, the globalized development paradigm epitomizes the complexities of 'technicized' developmentalism, enormous acquisitive attainments, spiralling politico-economic ambitions and shrinking space of human and normative concerns. Impressive cumulative accomplishments in all major spheres of human life notwithstanding, it is being gradually realized that the erosion of a sense of a common valued past, ideas about the superiority of the Western civilization, the desirability of the goal of economic growth, faith in scientific reason and knowledge and belief in the intrinsic value of the secular 'this worldly' existence indicate towards the conclusion that the Enlightenment idea of progress on which the current phenomenon of globalization largely rests, is in peril and the claims of globalization thesis as manifestation of 'development of all' are untenable at both theoretical and practical levels. In India, the arrogant imperialist West-centric world view of civilization and progress was challenged by Gandhi, most vociferously, at both theoretical and practical levels, at the beginning of the past century.

Admittedly, the world moves forward with commendable advancement of science and technology and expansion of opportunities in the new global order of borderless economy, culture and even politics. But the basic question, raised by Gandhi in his times, and earlier by Marx, remains pertinent as ever – the question regarding the real beneficiaries of the stupendous infrastructure of growth, development and the rhetoric of advancement? Answers to this question, by proponents and defenders of globalization, remain unsettling. The above 'basic' question should form the criterion of assessing the impact of what is appreciated as impressive development on nations and the common people that are still at the periphery of the globalizing world.

To combat the growing hegemony of the North, one of the strategies being contemplated and experimented with by the Southern countries is South-South cooperation, a strategy also suggested by dependency theorists about four decades back. If the strategy is employed with politico-economic sagacity, ills of the lopsided global development scenario may be reduced to an extent.

Resistance to the dominant development model is already widespread as evident in a large variety of people's movements in action all over the globe, bringing issues of marginality, plurality, oppression and disempowerment to the centre stage in development debates. And, gender figures in a crucial sense in these endeavours.

III

Gender discourse within the field of development has come a long way from building a case of 'inclusive' growth that prevents the marginalization of women to questioning of the predominant notions of development itself. The body of feminist critique continues to traverse new terrains and posit new challenges. The neo-liberal vision of society with a strong undercurrent of economic determinism often celebrates the atomistic, unconnected, self-maximizing individual – a conception that largely inhibits the space of both culture and development. In India, since women are considered to be the 'repositories of traditional Indian culture' the onus of 'maintaining purity' has also fallen on women, increasingly more so since 1990s, with globalization producing images of integration with the global consumer market on the one hand and marking destabilizing effect by attempting to exert control over cultural identities, perceived to be under 'western' threat, on the other hand. With new questions being raised as to what is global and what is local, women are becoming, once again, the ground on which questions of modernity and tradition are being framed. When reproduction and exchange involves not only the material but also the ideological issues, the discourse on culture and development need to establish a dialogue with multiple discourses outside its traditional ambit to address gender issues.

Historically, the first theoretical approach to development, namely, growth modernization theory, talked very little about women. In general, modernization theory was a manifestation of western capitalist modernity. It was argued that if modernization theory was pursued, the developing societies would catch up with the West.

Modernization theory was critiqued in several quarters in the late 1960s. Gender equality issues also began to be voiced around the same time. Since the early 1960s, the UN marked each official 'decade of development' with a declaration summarizing the lessons learnt from the past experience along with priorities for the coming decade. The declaration that announced the First Development Decade (1961–70) was devoid of any specific reference to women (Kabeer, 1994: 1). During the 1960s and 1970s, the feminist movement gained momentum and the research done by women scholars pointed out that the so-called modernization theory of development promoted by the development agencies had not benefited women and, in some cases, had adverse effect on women in the South. Women had not been given access to new productive opportunities, technology had not liberated them from domestic drudgery, and, in spite of the forces of modernization, prejudice and preconceptions about women persisted in society (Kabeer, 1994).

In terms of the impact of modernization on women in the South, a growing realization of the failure of the development enterprise was perceptible. Discontent among the First World women was also visible and was influenced by the second wave of feminism. These factors culminated in the emergence of the WID perspective, which was primarily inspired by liberal feminism (Waylen, 1996: 37). Remaining largely within the paradigm of liberal feminism, WID was, in part, a response to the inadequacies of the modernization approach. It was argued that the process of economic modernization marginalized women economically and socially, and increased their dependence on men (Boserup, 1970). Development projects largely benefited men, often at the expense of women, displacing women from their traditional productive functions and diminishing the power, status and income they had previously enjoyed (Moser, 1993). Development planners ignored women's productive activities, partly because their national accounting systems ignored much of women's work within the household and subsistence economy, assuming women to be only housewives (Rogers, 1982).

In the development projects wherein women were included, it was so on sex-specific terms as housewives, mothers and 'at risk producers' (Kabeer, 1994). M. Buvinic (1983) characterized these development projects as manifest welfare approach, identifying women as a vulnerable group needing help, particularly in their reproductive role. These projects concentrated on improving women's domestic skills such as childcare and nutrition (Rogers, 1982). Women's development projects were often ghettoized, leaving the majority to cater for men (Waylen, 1996: 38).

Several policy proposals emerged from the WID approach. The solution to gender inequality was visualized in increasing women's access to education, technology and resources. Women needed to be integrated into development more effectively. Development processes could not be allowed to pass them by. It was argued that women had to be brought into the development process through access to employment and the market place, thus placing emphasis on questions of equity. The WID approach was influential in determining the priorities for the UN Decade for Women 1975–85. Certainly, the WID approach was instrumental in increasing women's income, improving access to health care and resources in the short term, but the sustainability faltered as the question of unequal relations between men and women was left unaddressed. The focus on women in development, thereby, tended to be blind to the roles and responsibilities of men regarding women's position in society. This conformed to the liberal feminist position and did not question the existing social structure or explore the nature and sources of women's oppression. Nor did it take into account the impact of colonialism, capitalism and imperialism on women's lives. WID saw women merely as a unit of analysis and failed to consider the implications of class, race and gender having significant bearings on women's oppression.

Notably, as C.O.N. Moser argues, in spite of its essentially liberal feminist and reformist bent, the equity approach aroused hostility among development agencies and the Third World governments (Moser, 1993). This was so probably because the Decade's rhetoric of equity was perceived as difficult to translate into policy, as it required a redistribution of resources throughout the development process. Focusing on all women, rather than poor women only, called for equity at all levels, both among programme beneficiaries and among programme implementers (Kabeer, 1994). Nevertheless, WID continues to be commonly used by international organizations, including the World Bank, the United Nations and others.

Dependency model critiqued modernization theory and voiced disillusionment with economic strategies of development, especially as they had been applied in Latin America. It arose as a reaction to classical Marxism as much as from deeply held objections to modernization theory. Dependency theorists like A.G. Frank (1967), A. Emmanuel (1972) and D. Harrison (1988) argue that development and underdevelopment are two aspects of the same system, namely, the world capitalist system. Both development and underdevelopment are regarded as part of the world process of accumulation, a process that commenced in the mercantile period, carried through into industrial capitalism and culminated in imperialism. The colonies, the semi-colonies and neo-colonies existed primarily for the benefit of the capitalist metropolis throughout this process and as a direct result, became underdeveloped. Only breaking these links would lead to development, they argued. The dependency theorists' advocacy of self-reliant development coincided with the radical feminists' argument that women could develop only outside the patriarchal power structure (Daly, 1978). This resulted in the emergence of what is sometimes known as Women and Development (WAD) approach (Parpart, 1989). WAD is primarily a neo-Marxist, feminist approach with a strong emphasis on the significance of social class and exploitation of the Third World. WAD also derived some of its theoretical bases from Dependency theory. The WAD approach assumed that women have always been active participants in development. Advocates of this approach argue that both paid and unpaid labour of woman is essential to development. In contrast to WID, the WAD approach believed that under global capitalism based on exploitation and inequitous distribution of wealth, women's oppression and exploitation would not be possible to eradicate.

However, the WAD approach failed to undertake a full-scale analysis of the relationship between patriarchy and women's subordination and assumed that women's participation would improve if institutional structures change. Accepting work which women do inside and outside home as central to development, WAD preoccupied itself with the productive aspects more than the reproductive ones.

Towards the end of 1970s, an 'anti-poverty' emphasis emerged as another way of looking at the issue. In part, it was a toning down of the equity approach, which had required agencies to intervene in the scenario of unequal relations between men and women. An important part of this reorientation was the 'basic needs strategy'. The changed focus could be accommodated within the development agencies by linking women to poverty alleviation and basic needs (Kabeer, 1994: 7). Low income women could be identified, as a part of this new emphasis, as an important group to be singled out for particular attention. The anti-poverty approach stressed income-generation projects for poor women, yet it ignored their reproductive roles in interconnection with productive roles and also women's autonomy, which was implied in the equity approach (Waylen, 1996).

During this period, several studies traced the changes in class and gender relations in the household in industrial and agricultural production (Benaria, 2003). The Green Revolution in India was cited as an example of the way in which the introduction of new techniques such as high yielding seeds and fertilizers altered the class position of different peasant households and the amount of productive labour of men and women within the household and paid labour outside of it (Agarwal, 1992). This had an adverse effect on women.

In the 1980s, some scholars and activists in both the North and South began calling for a new approach to women's development. Drawing on concerns about the growing poverty of women (and men) in the South, as well as radical feminist concern with global patriarchy, a socialist feminist position gradually emerged in various parts of the world. Feminists in the South contributed to this debate. The series of international conferences celebrating the UN Decade for Women (1976–85) highlighted the unique problems facing women in the South and encouraged the development organizations to foster research and writing by Southern scholars. The scholarship emerging from these organizations (Sen and Grown, 1987) provided the basis for feminist theorizing and action grounded in Southern realities, commonly designated as empowerment approach to women's development (Moser, 1993).

The resulting dialogue known as Gender and Development (GAD), focused on gender rather than women, particularly the social construction of gender roles and relations. Gender seen as the 'process by which individuals who are born into biological categories of male and female become the social categories of men and women through the acquisition of locally-defined attributes of masculinity and femininity' (Kabeer, 1994). The possibility of transforming gender roles was, thus, established for the gendered division of labour and power was revealed as a constructed rather than a natural given. While GAD proponents rarely challenged the goal of modernization/westernization, some scholars believe the GAD perspective provides the possible (discursive) space to do so (Marchand and Parpart, 1995: 14).

GAD partly emerged as a critique of WID, questioning the patriarchal structures that maintain gender inequalities. Women's status in society was seen as deeply affected by material conditions and their position in the economy. GAD recognized the impact of patriarchal power in the society at national, community and household levels. Both the material conditions of women and patriarchal authority were defined and maintained by the accepted norms and values of gendered relations in a specific society. It was believed that this 'social construction of gender' could be transformed.

The GAD approach signalled a holistic perspective, recognizing inter-connections of social-economic-political factors in women's lives. GAD was positive towards the potential contribution of men, sharing concerns of gender equity and social justice. GAD acknowledged women as agents of change rather than as passive recipients of development services. Women's oppression was seen as interlinked with other issues such as power, colonialism, class, religion, etc.

Eclipsing both modernization and underdevelopment theories and dominant development thinking, in the early 1980s, Milton Friedman and Friedrich Hayek emphasized the unfettered working of the free market to promote economic growth. This provided one of the theoretical bases for neo-liberalism. While appearing to be gender-neutral, neo-liberalism has carried with it the implicit assumption of hierarchical gender relations and particular roles for women. At about the same period, advocating the efficiency argument, Rogers (1982) stressed that neglect of women's productivity was a costly mistake that planners could ill afford to make. Gender-specific occupational segregation, with concentration of men in higher-level jobs and women in lower ones, was a rather stable and rigid phenomenon existing in traditional as well as modern societies. Various studies underline the persistence of gender-segregated labour market globally as being independent of level of industrial development or occupational diversification (Anker, 1998). Even within the same occupation, women are paid lower wages relative to men and male-female earnings are not well explained by gender differences in human capital endowments (Olsen and Coppin, 2001). Anker argues that human capital approach is losing edge in view of increased empirical evidence.

Another movement, more radical in spirit, emerged in the 1980s known as DAWN (Development Alternatives with Women for a New Era). DAWN came up with a comprehensive critique of the development model for the 1985 UN third World Conference on Women in Nairobi. DAWN focused on the ways that growth-oriented macro-economics, neo-colonial international relations and militarism promote the marginalization of women in the South.

DAWN suggested that the problems of development were not unique to the South, within the North also women and men were marginalized in the process of marked-led growth. Dissent went unheard in the mainstream development discourse. It was argued that the priorities for marginalized poor women were frequently food, jobs and services manifest in the struggle for survival rather than the feminist agenda of equality with men. DAWN contended that equality with men, who themselves suffered unemployment, poor work conditions, low wages and racism within the existing socio-economic structures, did not seem an adequate or worthy goal (Kabeer, 1994). DAWN Report (1991) suggested that the need is to go beyond the discussion of empowerment as *desirable* for women and emphasise upon empowerment as *critical* for building accountability into the functioning of the public realm, both state and civil society (emphasis added).

On a different note, the post-modern feminist critique of development theory and practice interrogated numerous basic tents of the entire discourse. Post-modern feminism rejected universal constructs of truth, objectivity and neutrality. It replaced the unitary notions of 'woman' and 'feminine' gender-identity with plural identities and constructed conceptions of social identity, treating gender as one of the relevant strands among others, such as class, race, ethnicity, age and sex (Fraser and Nicholson, 1989: 390–91). It was argued that while some women share common interests, such commonalties are by no means universal; they are interlaced with differences, even with conflict.

This strand of feminism was sensitive to the local and diverse voices of women questioning the universalistic western predilections. Whereas earlier variants of feminism focused on understanding and recording commonly experienced oppression of women, the post-modernist feminism privileged contextualization of colonial/neo-colonial development discourse addressing the very real problems that women on the margins face (Parpart, 1993; Waylen, 1996).

The recognition of limits to development by nature fuelled the search for sustainable solutions to the crisis. In women's attempt to conceptualize sustainable development, the recognition of the connections between domination of nature and of women provided important insights. In the South, this recognition stimulated the debate on women, environment and sustainable development (WED) within the development context, while in the North it gave rise to nature feminism/eco-feminism.

In the 1980s, the WED theme became a prominent theme in discussions, publications and international conferences of women on issues of environment and development. As environmental degradation in the South accelerated fuel, wood, animal fodder and water scarcity, it was realized that those most severely affected were women, who had the responsibility to collect the same for the subsistence of their families. Northern development agencies, conveniently blame the poor people for large scale deforestation and desertification in the South. High level of population growth in the South is also held responsible for the global environmental crisis (Mies and Shiva, 1993).

The WED debate has been shaped and developed by prominent academicians, women from movements, non-governmental development organizations (NGDOs), non-governmental organizations (NGOs) from the South and from the North. Together they created a space for a large variety of women, eventually even women from the grassroots who are most affected, to voice their concerns in international fora which discussed solutions to global environmental crisis (Braidotti et al., 1994: 2).

The evolution of WED has been marked by a shift in positions and political priorities. While earlier the emphasis was on women as victims of the environmental crisis, it shifted to their roles as efficient environmental managers within the development process in the South. The argument for the increased participation of women in environmental management has been derived from their privileged knowledge and experience of working closely with the environment. A somewhat different line of argument has been advanced by Vandana Shiva and Irene Dankelman, who stress the 'feminine principle' based on the assumption of women's special empathetic and nurturing capacities in relation to nature. As a result, women are now seen by many people involved in the WED debate as privileged environmental managers or the source for solutions to the environmental crisis (Braidotti et al., 1994: 2–3).

Thus, the growing recognition of the connections between the crisis in development, the deepening global environmental crisis, growth of poverty and gender inequalities has reinforced the need of acknowledging significance of women's voices in the debates on sustainable development, stressing the social aspects of the sustainability.

The World Development Report 2012 reaffirms that gender equality is a core development objective in its own right. It is also smart economics as it can enhance productivity, improve development outcomes for the next generation and make institutions more representative (World Bank, 2012: XX).

IV

Thus, feminist interventions have impacted policy approaches to development in significant forms such as WID, WAD, GAD, WED, DAWN, eco-feminism, new economics movement, green economics and green politics. Issues of gender equality, equity, sustainability of development, women's equal access to and control over resources and voice in decision-making now find place in development debates and development planning as a result of effective feminist interrogations.

However, neo-liberalism remains the broad theoretical framework within which development perspectives and policies continue to be framed. Admittedly, in recent development planning framework, issues of poverty alleviation and social and gender inequalities have been addressed quite explicitly but the surfacial change of focus does not reflect a shift in the underlying philosophy of the dominant development paradigm. Shift in the direction of increased grassroots initiatives and rights perspective is a positive indicator, yet the overall market-driven strategies tend to overshadow and curtail people-centred/gender-centred development initiatives.

Globalization-driven development paradigm, therefore, presents a political challenge. The new structures and protagonists of world power are relatively anonymous. They lack accountability and often operate without controls. The power of the macro-structures and mega-corporations is enormous. While nation-states buckle under these immense pressures, in our view it is the 'social movements with fundamentally transformative social agenda' that have the potential to shift the focus and direction of the ongoing process of political restructuring.

It needs to be underlined that no social transformation is conceivable in the absence of participative democracy. Democracy has no meaning without equality and equality, particularly, gender equality is conspicuous by absence in the development process dominated by the hegemonic patriarchal politico-economic structures.

The role of women's movements also needs to be ascertained in this context. It is important, in our view that women's movement now enter into and strengthen coalitions/alliances with the forces of peace, progress and development for more impactive transformative alternative strategies. Admittedly, some feminist theorists caution that, in the context of a patriarchal society, the pursuit of gender equality is often entrapped by exaggeration and denial (Rhode, 1992: 149).

At a deeper level, the development debate could also be seen as a manifestation of the debates on distributive justice. Feminists working within the framework of gender justice tend to critique liberal-egalitarian theories of distributive justice as gender-blind and androcentric. For example, many theories of egalitarian justice assume that the concept of justice applies only to the public sphere, taking distributions within the family as given. Feminist political theorists have argued that analyses of social justice that are sensitive to gender, need to include the private sphere and consider the gendered division of labour within it (Bubeck, 1995; Okin, 1989; Pateman, 1987; Phillips, 1999). They have also challenged the individualism inherent within much mainstream egalitarian theorizing, which marginalizes the impact of social structures, ignores the significance of social groups, and fails to identify structural inequalities (Young, 2001). From this perspective, the liberal theories of equality have no theory of inequality and so fail to analyse the origins of the forms of inequality that they want to eradicate. Ingrid Robeyns, for example, finds (Dworkin's) liberal egalitarianism 'structurally unable to account for the cultural aspects of gender, race, and other dimensions of human diversity that create unjust inequalities between people' (Robeyns, 2003: 541).

The unease with the oscillation between recommending equal treatment and positive action has led to the emergence of another gender equality strategy, namely, gender mainstreaming. Recognizing that the criteria of equivalence used to establish fairness might themselves be biased, mainstreaming aims to identify 'how existing systems and structures cause indirect discrimination and altering or redesigning them as appropriate' (Rees, 2002: 46–48). The aim of the mainstreaming strategy is, therefore, to focus on the structural reproduction of gender inequality and to transform the policy process in such a way that gender bias is eliminated.

Meanwhile, as Judith Squires states, with the political theory literature more generally, the response to the limitations of liberal egalitarianism is to broaden out the account of equality of opportunity such that it engages with cultural and political forces as well as economic ones, and considers structural and institutional barriers as well as individual ones. This refocuses attention back on civil and political rights, highlighting the extent to which these are still to be fully realized for many marginalized groups. It also replaces the liberal egalitarians' apparent dichotomy between the 'choices we make' and the 'circumstances we face' with a more complex account of the ways in which social institutions and the decisions others make within them, constitute and constrain the context in which we act (Squires, 2006: 477).

Diversity theorists, attempting to negotiate a way beyond the apparent tensions of equality as redistribution or as recognition, invoke the importance of political voice and democratic inclusion. Bhikhu Parekh, for instance, suggests that redistribution requires principles to decide who is entitled to make what claims, and these principles 'can only be arrived at by means of a democratic dialogue, which generates them, tests their validity, and gives them legitimacy' (Parekh, 2004: 207). This emphasis on democratic inclusion shifts attention from the perennial 'equality of what?' question to the wider issue of who partakes in this very debate. Centrally, it focuses attention on the legitimacy of the actual process by which the norms of equivalence are derived. In this way procedural norms also become central to the pursuit of equality. A concern for democratic participation, therefore, complements the debate on substantive equality (Squires, 2006: 477).

Monica Mookherjee rightly notes that rectification of unequal circumstances 'cannot be achieved by applying preconceived interpretations of the term equality itself. This is because a necessary, if not sufficient, condition of equality is the enabling of excluded groups to unsettle and destabilize meanings and interpretations which the institutional culture has hitherto taken as universal and complete' (Mookherjee, 2001: 80). Enabling excluded groups to unsettle institutionally accepted conceptions of equality will require parity of participation, which makes democratic inclusion central to both the meaning and the realization of equality.

The earlier equality/difference debate within gender theory, which led to the development of mainstreaming as an equality strategy, could usefully be drawn upon. However, procedural concerns cannot supplant substantive concerns, for substantial economic equality may well be necessary for us to be political equals. This demands that debates about equality be iterative processes, for whilst fair procedures are needed to define what substantial equality entails, some form of substantial equality may be required to secure fair procedures (Squires, 2006: 484).

Accordingly, at practical level, women activists have recently turned to a rights-based approach to the development process, focusing gender equality/equity, in particular. A Rights-based approach sets the achievement of human/gender rights and the creation of an enabling environment in which these rights can be enjoyed as the main objective of people-centred sustainable development. A rights-based approach is significant in terms of legal enforceability, state responsibility and moral authority pertaining to human/gender rights. In our view, it is time that development as a basic human right of women – as of men – is accepted as a policy imperative at national and international levels within the larger democratic development discourse that is simultaneously inclusive and egalitarian.

References

Agarwal, Bina (1992) 'The Gender and Environment Debate: Lessons from India', *Feminist Studies*, 18(1): 119–58.

Amin, Samir (1980) *Class and Nation*, New York: Monthly Review.

Anker, Richard (1998) *Gender and Jobs: Sex Segregation of Occupation in the World*, Geneva: ILO.

Beneria, L. (2003) *Gender, Development and Globalization*, New York: Routledge.

Boserup, E. (1970) *Women's Role in Economic Development*, New York: St. Martin's.

Braidotti, R., E. Charkiwicz, S. Häusler and S. Wieringa (1994) *Women, Environment and Sustainable Development*, London: Zed Books.

Bubeck, D. (1995) *Care, Gender and Justice*, Oxford: Clarendon Press.

Buvinic, M. (1986) 'Projects for Women in the Third World: Explaining their Misbehaviour', *World Development*, 14(5): 653–64.

Daly, M. (1978) *Gyn/Ecology: The Metaethics of Radical Feminism*, Boston: Beacon Press.

Dankelman, I. and J. Davidson (1988) *Women and Environment in the Third World: Alliance for the Future*, London: Earthscan.

DAWN (1991) *Alternatives*, vols I and II, Rio de Janeiro: Development Alternatives with Women for a New Era.

de Groot, J. (1991) 'Conceptions and Misconceptions: The Historical and Cultural Context of Discussion on Women and Development', in H. Afshar (ed.), *Women, Development and Survival in the Third World*, London: Longman.

Emmanuel, A. (1972) *Unequal Exchange*, London: New Left Books.

Escobar, A. (1984–85) 'Discourse and Power in Development: Michael Foucault and the Relevance of His Work to the Third World', *Alternatives*, 10(3): 377–400.

Frank, A.G. (1967) *Capitalism and Underdevelopment in Latin America: Historical Studies of Chile and Brazil*, New York: Monthly Review Press.

Fraser, N. (1989) *Unruly Practices: Power, Discourse and Gender in Contemporary Social Theory*, Oxford: Polity Press.

Fraser, N. and L. Nicholson (1989) 'Social Criticism without Philosophy', in L. Nicholson (ed.), *Feminism/Post Modernism*, New York: Routledge.

Friedman, M. (1962) *Capitalism and Freedom*, Chicago: University of Chicago Press.

Harrison, D. (1988) The *Sociology of Modernization and Development*, London: Unwin Hyman.

Johnston, D. (1991) 'Constructing the Periphery in Modern Global Politics', in C. Murphy and R. Tooze (eds.), *The New International Political Economy*, Boulder, CO: Lynne Rienner.

Kabeer, N. (1994) *Reversed Realities: Gender Hierarchies in Development Thought*, New Delhi: Kali for Women.

Kaushik, Asha (2001) *Politics, Symbols and Political Theory: Rethinking Gandhi*, Jaipur and Delhi: Rawat.

——.(2002) *Globalization, Democracy and Culture*, Jaipur: Pointer.

Marchand, M.H. and J. Parpart (1995) *Feminism/Post-Modernism/Development*, London: Routledge.

Mies, M. (1986) *Patriarchy and Accumulation on a World Scale: Women in the International Division of Labour*, London: Zed Books.

Mies, M. and V. Shiva (1993) *Ecofeminism*, London: Zed Books.

Molyneux, M. (1985) 'Mobilization without Emancipation? Women's Interests, the State and Revolution in Nicaragua', *Feminist Studies*, 11(2): 227–54.

Mookherjee, M. (2001) 'Justice as Provisionality: An Account of Contrastive Hard Cases', *Critical Review of International Social and Political Philosophy*, 4(3): 67–100.

Moser, C.O.N. (1989) 'Gender Planning in the Third World: Meeting Practical and Strategic Gender Needs', *World Development*, 17(11): 799–825.

Okin, S.M. (1989) *Justice, Gender and the Family*, New York: Basic Books.

Olsen, R.N. and A. Coppin (2001) 'The Determinants of Gender Differences in Income in Trinidad and Tobago', *Journal of Development Studies* 37 (5): 31–55.

Parekh, B. (2004) 'Redistribution or Recognition? A Misguided Debate', in S. May, T. Modood and J. Squires (eds.), *Ethnicity, Nationalism and Minority Rights*, Cambridge: Cambridge University Press.

Parpart, J. (1993) 'Who is the 'Other'? A Postmodern Feminist Critique of Women and Development Theory and Practice', *Development and Change*, 24(3): 439–64.

Pateman, C. (1987) 'Feminist Critiques of the Public/Private Dichotomy', in A. Phillips (ed.), *Feminism and Equality*, Oxford: Basil Blackwell.

Phillips, A. (1999) *Which Equalities Matter?* Cambridge: Polity Press.

Rees, T. (2002) 'The Politics of 'Mainstreaming' Gender Equality', in E. Breitenbach et al. (eds.), *The Changing Politics of Gender Equality in Britain*, London: Palgrave.

Rhode, D. (1992) 'The Politics of Paradigms: Gender Difference and Gender Disadvantage', in G. Bock and S. James (eds.), *Beyond Equality and Difference*, London: Routledge.

Robeyns, I. (2003) 'Is Nancy Fraser's Critique of Theories of Distributive Justice Justified?', *Constellations*, 10(4): 538–53.

Rogers, B. (1982) *The Domestication of Women*, London: Tavistock.

Sen, A. (1999) *Development as Freedom*, New Delhi: Oxford University Press.

Sen, G. and C. Grown (1987) *Development, Crisis and Alternative Visions: Third World Women's Perspectives*, New York: Monthly Review Press.

Shiva, V. (1988) *Staying Alive: Women, Ecology and Development*, London: Zed Books.

Sklair, L. (1991) *Sociology of Global System*, Hemel Hempstead: Harvester Wheatsheaf.

Squires, Judith (2006) 'Equality and Difference', in J.S. Dryzek, B. Honig and Anne Phillips (eds.), *Political Theory*, Oxford: Oxford University Press, 470–87.

UNDP (1990), (1991), (1992), (1993), (1994), (1995), (1996), (1997), (1998), (1999), (2000), (2001), (2002), (2003), (2004), (2005), (2006), (2007), (2008), (2009), (2010), (2011) *Human Development Report*, New Delhi: Oxford University Press.

Waylen, G. (1996) *Gender in Third World Polities*, Buckingham: Open University Press.

World Bank (1997), (1998), (1999), (2000), (2001), (2003), (2005), (2008), (2012) *World Development Report*, New Delhi: Oxford University Press.

Young, I. (2001) 'Equality of Whom? Social Groups and the Judgments of Injustice', *Journal of Political Philosophy*, 9(1): 1–18.

Part II

Development–Discrimination Syndrome

5

Globalization and Economic Empowerment of Women

Some Issues for Policy Intervention

KANTA AHUJA

Empowerment

The term 'empowerment' defies a simple uni-dimensional definition. In itself, the concept of 'power' from which the term 'empowerment' is derived can be interpreted in more than one way. The prepositions attached to power such as power *to,* power *over* or power *with* add further meanings to the term. Power operates in a number of different ways. Power *over* involves a relationship of subordination, power *to* relates to having creative and enabling decision-making authority, power *with* involves people organizing with a common purpose or common understanding of collective issues, and power *within* refers to self-confidence and self-awareness that results in self-assertiveness to influence and change power relationships that operate in the social environment. The feminist thinkers have developed and stressed the power within concept even though other dimensions have been discussed. For example, Agarwal (1994) emphasizes the ability to challenge power relations of economic, social and political subordination. Kabeer (2000) interprets empowerment as the ability to make choices; the disempowered lack this ability. The HDR (1995) stresses the processes of participation.

Deshmukh-Ranadive (2003) defines empowerment as 'a process whereby constraints that impede equal participation are reduced so that the inequality starts moving towards becoming equality. ... These constraints are most often structural and connected to both the macro environment and the domestic environment that the woman finds herself in.' Further women have to be reached in different 'spaces' that encompass their lives. The *physical space* constitutes a woman's access to the physical space of her body, of mobility within and outside the house. The lack of ownership, access and control of physical space is a fundamental constraint for women in most societies. The *economic space* allows a woman ownership, access and control of goods and services, which in turn enhances her economic independence. The socio-cultural space places a woman within the hierarchy of a household and in the hierarchy of society. The *political space* defines a woman's access to public office and participation in the political process. Each of these spaces is not independent of each other. A holistic approach is required for analysing each issue. However, even though the term has been defined in various ways, economic self-reliance and autonomy is an important ingredient for empowerment in most conceptualizations. It may not be a *sufficient* condition for empowerment, but it cannot be denied as a *necessary* condition.

The UN has asserted that women's autonomy should be considered as a basic human right and essential to human dignity (UNDP, 1995). The subservient status of women inside the family as well as outside originates from lack of economic independence and the denial of economic rights to women. This denial is with respect to

- ownership of property,
- recognition of women's work as economically productive,
- providing education and market skills to girls,
- social obligations and restrictions put on them with respect to what work they will be permitted to do outside the home boundaries,
- equality in the matter of wages, salaries and opportunities for advancement at the workplace, and
- providing a facilitating environment to enable women to work and become economically independent.

These aspects have been extensively discussed in various forums – academic as well as policy planning. In this note, I discuss the general issue concerning women's work and women's empowerment to highlight the point that even though women's work is important there are several other aspects of work and the social environment of work that need to be considered. I then discuss some of the impacts of globalization that influence women's work. The priorities for action are summarized in the concluding paragraph.

Women's Work and Women's Empowerment

Size of the Female Workforce

Women's participation in economic activities is captured in the census data on the number of workers and their occupational characteristics.[1]

According to Census 2001, there were 27 million women in a population of 56.5 million in Rajasthan. The total number of women workers was 9 million. This implies a participation rate of 33.5 per cent compared to 25.7 per cent at all-India level. The participation rate for rural women was 41 per cent and for urban women it was only 9 per cent. The rate for rural women was higher than the all-India average but was lower for urban women. Participation rates in rural as well as in urban areas have increased since 1981. The overall female participation rate was 21 per cent in 1981, which went up to 27 per cent in 1991 and to 33 per cent in 2001.

The second source of data is reports of the National Sample Survey Organization (NSSO). The conceptual framework of the NSSO differs from the census. As a result, the two sets of data are not strictly comparable. The NSSO estimates of participation rates for 1999–2000 are somewhat lower for rural women and higher for urban women. For rural women it was 39 per cent and for urban women 14 per cent, compared to the census rates of 41 per cent and 9 per cent, respectively. The NSSO provides data on other aspects of employment also and is commonly used to obtain workforce profile. According to NSSO results for 1999–2000 most of the women workers (83% of total) were working as cultivators or as agricultural labourers. The remaining were employed in household industry and in a diverse range of service occupations – from teachers, doctors and administrators to laundry women and cleaning (*safai karamcharis*) workers. Despite small changes in the participation rates, the data shows that the structure of employment remains broadly unchanged at the macro level.

Structure of Workforce and Empowerment

Women's workforce participation is a central component of the Gender Empowerment Measure of the UNDP Human Development Reports. The first question is: does the increase in the number of women workers indicate greater empowerment of women? The answer will depend upon whether the increase in number is the result of economic need (poverty) or of more women working in capacities that they were earlier not doing. This would be the case if more women workers had higher levels of education and skill. In that case we may be right to conclude an improvement in women's empowerment status. In 1991, 77 per cent of women workers in rural areas and 47 per cent in urban areas or a total of 61 per cent were illiterate. The situation in 2001 was likely to be somewhat better as the state has achieved significant improvements in female literacy. This is the result of higher enrolment of girls in primary and middle schools, especially in rural areas. However, even though an improvement in the literacy status of women workers would be a logical outcome, yet the extent of change is likely to be small as literacy improvement has affected the younger age group of girls who are not in the labour force. More women workers belong to the higher age groups and therefore are not likely to be affected by improvement in literacy rate. Furthermore, macro data as well as some micro-level observations indicate that participation rates go down as the level of education increases. This again means that illiterate women continue to be the predominant part of the women workforce. When a larger number of women with no or low education, low skills, low productivity and getting low wages are working, it is also associated with low prestige and status. In short, it does not enhance the autonomy, self-reliance or empowerment of women. To achieve the latter, work must be associated with higher education and skills and must be at remuneration levels that are respected in society. This is not happening, as the structure of the workforce is not changing. Women are employed either in agriculture or in household activities and in the service occupations both in rural and in urban areas without significant changes in the status of their autonomy. Besides cultivation and work as agricultural labourers, the occupational categories that dominate the distribution of the female workforce are the occupation divisions 5, 6, 7, 8 and 9. Division 5 is service workers; division 6 is farming and other primary sector occupations like fishing and logging and divisions 7 to 9 are miscellaneous activities in production, transport and trade. A little less than half the number of female workers (excluding cultivators and agricultural labourers) in rural areas and 40 per cent in urban areas were employed in divisions 7 to 9 in 1981 as well as in 1991. The results of the Economic Census regarding the non-formal sector economic enterprises reinforce the absence of significant changes in female workforce structure.

Type of Work and Working Status: Conditions of Work

Does women's participation in economic activities result in greater autonomy for them? Autonomy in this context may be understood as the 'capacity to influence and control one's personal environment', and/or 'the degree of access to and control over material and social resources within the family, in the community, and in society'. We need to focus attention not only on the aggregate number of women workers (or the aggregate amount of work that they do) but also on the types and conditions of work. The Economic Census 1998 shows that 46 per cent women were working in 'own account enterprises' in agriculture, livestock and related activities whereas 54 per cent in non-agricultural enterprises mostly in manufacturing and in retail trade, restaurants and hotels. These results show that 30 per cent of workers in agricultural enterprises are women. Their share is 18 per cent in household manufacturing. In simple language such workers are also called 'family workers' or 'helpers'. The characteristic is that they are unpaid and their entitlement to earnings from such enterprises is not related to work but to social customs. Needless to add that in general, they lack control over their earnings and in decision-making. Furthermore, family workers not only work outside the protection of labour laws but are also denied the social interactions that workers in organized industry or workplaces have. Such conditions lower women's awareness of their bargaining position and therefore lower their autonomy. The self-employed in small household-based enterprises suffer from similar disabilities. On the other hand, women employers who manage a larger number of employees have greater self-reliance, self-confidence and autonomy. We tend to think of women employers mostly as an urban phenomenon.

However, there may be many activities in rural areas where the status of women workers is different from that of the household workers. For example, *beedi* workers may be working on contract. In the handicraft sector, women take orders and may sub-contract work to others. In retail trade (e.g., vegetable and flower sellers) or in restaurants, many women are not only self-employed entrepreneurs but are also responsible for day-to-day business decisions. Such women have more mobility and greater social interaction than home-based craft workers and therefore display more confidence and self-reliance. This is only an example to show that when we talk of the status of a woman worker, it is not only urban women that we are talking about. The focus is equally on women workers in rural areas who are engaged in diverse activities but only as unpaid household workers. Even in employment works, women are generally employed as workers who work under a supervisor, generally a literate male, called a 'mate' and cannot be described as a group of empowered women. However, in some areas (e.g., Tilonia in Ajmer district of Rajasthan) women struggled to get their right to work in the capacity of 'mate' as this was seen essential to get equal and just treatment by the workers in the matter of remuneration for work. When they got this position, it meant not only self-confidence for the woman mate but also power for the entire group of female workers in the matter of control over work measurement, the time and duration of work and the wages or remuneration for it. It also motivated more women to participate in literacy programmes and to acquire literacy and numeracy skills.

Work can be differentiated by remuneration (cash, kind or unpaid) or by location or by status. As discussed above, in Rajasthan, most of the women workers classified as cultivators are unpaid family workers. For them autonomy and empowerment are not in more work but in more productive agriculture and more productive economic activities. However, even if works were differentiated according to type of work, the relationship between work and autonomy would be difficult to capture. Unfortunately, it is difficult to find well-defined indicators of autonomy. The attempt should, however, be made to differentiate between type of work and also define indicators of autonomy carefully. This would enable development workers to focus on factors that are likely to enhance women's autonomy. The National Commission for Women may consider sponsoring some studies on this aspect.

In urban areas, there appear to be more visible changes in that more women are now seen in workplaces such as offices, banks, retail sales, media, schools, colleges and health professions. This is especially so in bigger urban centres. However, these changes have, so far, not increased the participation rates of urban women. Finding work has become more difficult even though more and more women are seeking work. As a result, the recorded urban unemployment rates are going up even though many women belong to the 'discouraged worker' category. Such women do not even 'seek work', as their perceptions about finding work are entirely negative. The issues in the urban sector are concerned largely with the impact of the new economic policies (globalization) on employment.

Globalization

Without getting into a debate on the meaning of globalization, aspects that have to be focused are: liberalization of trade and industrial policies, replacing market-based pricing policies for subsidy supported production and supply of goods and services, policy changes necessitated by the need for fiscal balance and privatization or withdrawal of the state from activities traditionally supported by it. All of these are interrelated aspects. I shall discuss only a few in the paras below.

Liberalization of trade and other economic policies has so far not impacted the rural areas in Rajasthan in a big way. However, the fact that the new policies are not generating adequate employment opportunities is widely accepted. Nevertheless, it should be recognized that the structural changes that have become necessary in the state sector would result in lower employment. One of the problems of the public sector in India has been an inflated salary bill because of an unjustified increase in the number of workers. Therefore, one of the things that became necessary was downsizing, i.e., reduction in the numbers employed. This is being achieved through voluntary retirement schemes and through a drastic reduction in new recruitment. The increase in employment is expected through higher rates of investment in several sectors. Unfortunately, Rajasthan is suffering because the flow of investment has been inadequate. This has a negative impact on the growth of employment. At the same time, several sectors such as road building and construction have become more capital intensive and more mechanized. This has further restricted the growth of employment. At the same time, employment has also become more skill intensive. Road building sector used to employ a large number of women. This is no longer the case. This can be observed on construction sites on national and state highways in the state. A crew of semi-skilled or skilled workers is now employed to work on the equipment used for getting the work done speedily and efficiently. Almost all such workers are male. Work is also organized differently so that women are no longer employed to provide water or do miscellaneous earth-work and stone/grit carrying activities. Most of the workers who have lost such work opportunities are from the poverty and the socially disadvantaged groups.[2]

Rajasthan is not an industrially advanced state although it has some large industries that contribute a significant share of industrial output of India. Agriculture continues to be the predominant production and employment sector in the economy. The impact of the new policies on this sector has, so far, been marginal. The main large-scale industries in the state are cement, synthetic fibres/textiles, fertilizers and non-ferrous metals (zinc and copper). None of these industries employ women workers in large numbers. In fact, it would not be an exaggeration to say that industrial employment in the state is predominantly male employment. And it so happens that none of the industries mentioned above are negatively impacted by trade liberalization. Copper is probably the only exception.

Industrial policy liberalization has meant the withdrawal of concessions to small-scale industry. Even during the eighties of the last century the small-scale industrial sectors in the state were not healthy. A large number of units were closed. This trend has accelerated further. This has a negative impact on the growth of employment of the sector. At the same time, some sectors like tourism and export of handicrafts are positively affected by liberal trade policies. Both these sectors employ relatively large number of women. Growth in demand of several handicrafts from the state has certainly given a push to growth of the handicraft sector. Ready-made garments and printing of textiles has emerged as an important employment creating sector. All the export sectors employ women in fairly large numbers but each of them is undergoing technical upgrading. This leaves women workers at a disadvantage. Garment making – from cutting to sewing buttons to ironing and packing – is increasingly handled by new machines. Women often are left out or displaced in these activities as they lack the required skills or training. Trained men are easily available because of the general lack of employment opportunities. They are preferred to female workers as some social disabilities, such as more absenteeism or non-availability of work in evening and night shifts, are associated with women workers. As a result, even though more women are employed in specific categories of work such as garment checking, packing, designing, etc., their share in total employment may not have increased. Except for designing and fashion co-ordination, most other female-dominated work in the garment making sector is lower paid. Educated workers familiar with the use of cell phones and computers can handle marketing of crafts better. These are only examples of technical upgrading that is now required even in the traditional sectors.

The new sectors related to information technology – radio, TV, journalism, computers, software development and related activities – are relatively more women-friendly. The same can be said about the new service sectors that are growing, viz., financial services, education and health. In short, except for small industries, most other sectors are not negatively impacted from the point of view of employment of women workers. But there are some aspects that are of concern. The environment in which these activities are operating has become highly competitive and employers have become cost conscious. This has been accompanied by privatization. As a result, many of these sectors are now characterized by long hours of work without any union pressures and also without any state support for meeting minimum wage or social security protection to the workers. One of the major concerns of state policy now has to be with provision of social security systems for workers in the private sector, particularly workers in the non-formal activities sector.

For women in these sectors there is an additional concern. This is of physical security while going to work or returning from it and in the process of job search. In urban areas, commuting to work has become one of the main problems. Low paid women workers in the service sectors are being relocated in order to create better urban environment through clearing slums or removing illegal occupation on public land. Both these are laudable objectives but the needs of the workers have not been given importance. Private costly bus service is provided but regulation of the number of passengers in a bus is, at best, ineffective. In most cases it is non-existent. People, including women, are packed in the bus almost like sardines during the morning and evening hours. How women are physically abused can only be guessed. There is no organized resistance or regulation of these conditions. Special buses for women have been withdrawn even where they operated in the past for reasons of economy.

Recruitment practices are another area of concern. The media often carries reports of workers wanting overseas employment being cheated by recruitment agencies. In the case of women trafficking is one dimension that gets noticed. However, recruitment in the private sector is increasingly being done through private placement agencies. This method provides another opportunity for exploitation, particularly of women workers. There is thus need for a regulatory system to monitor these agencies.

Another feature of employment practices is the substitution of contract work for salaried employment. This is euphemistically called flexi-work or work as consultants. Flexi-workers combine a disparate group of non-regular workers who lack entitlement to statutory protection but they also escape the restrictions that salaried employment may entail.[3] Some are in the high remuneration categories but many are earning low remuneration. Contract employment has become a common mode of employment in many urban service occupations, including state services. In order to escape the obligations (pension, leave, medical benefits) of government employment, the state government itself is using private contract agencies to get its work done.

The replacement of the welfare state with a market-friendly state has created a crisis of social protection that seems to be intensifying along with the crisis from a scenario of jobless growth. From the policy perspective, one of the prime concerns of political-economic policy has to shift to creating *employment with growth.* Without employment the other objectives of equity, poverty eradication and empowerment of women would become unachievable.

My suggestions for state action would be to:

1. Adopt economic strategies to create more jobs/work for men and for women.
2. Create social protection mechanisms.
3. Consider the impact on women more carefully in sectors like education in which withdrawal of the state from quality education or reduction of state support for education will have a greater negative impact on women.
4. Put greater emphasis on skill enhancement of women workers to cater to the needs of more sophisticated markets both in rural and in urban areas.
5. Consider the impact on women due to privatization of the health sector as well.
6. Cost recovery in drinking water needs to be pursued more gradually because of the impact of higher cost on household budget. Use of special purpose cess for collecting revenue would probably be a better option than pricing water to achieve fall cost recovery.

Notes

1. Attempts to improve the conceptual framework for data collection have not satisfied the feminist critique according to which women's activities are not recognized as 'work' as these are performed outside the market. However, the conceptual framework is based upon the notion that the

workforce numbers must be consistent with the estimation of the gross domestic product (GDP) that includes imputed values for some non-marketed products/services. This means that all activities that do not generate marketed or marketable output are not regarded as economic activities irrespective of who performs them. The problem is of valuation of output. Household works, like other forms of voluntary services, performed for oneself or for family/friends or for society are excluded form the GDP estimate as value for such services - even a notional value - is difficult to obtain unambiguously. This means that census/survey data on workforce may underestimate the number of women workers.

2. Most rural areas have socially defined hierarchy of wage work even when the nature of work is similar. Thus working on irrigation or soil conservation or construction of buildings is done by women of all caste groups in need of income earning, but road building is considered only by the socially disadvantaged category of women. Famine relief works are an exception as all households in need of income or grain participate in order to earn or to get entitlement to grain that gets distributed as part of wage.
3. A new category of workers who have a salaried employment but also perform services either as freelance consultants or as advisors in institutions registered by them or their friends or family members have proliferated. Doctors, architects, lawyers, accountants, teachers, researchers and computer literate persons are not the only ones in this category. So, on the one hand, there are not enough jobs to go around and on the other hand, there are many who have multiple jobs and multiple incomes.

References

Agarwal, B. (1994) *A Field of One's Own: Gender and Land Rights in South Asia*, Cambridge: Cambridge University Press.

Deshmukh-Ranadive, Joy (1993) 'Negotiating Spaces for Women's Empowerment', in S. Visalakshi (ed.), *Economic Empowerment of Women*, New Delhi: National Institute of Science and Development Studies.

Kabeer, N. (2000) 'Resources Agency, Achievements: Reflections on the Measurement of Women's Empowerment', in Shahra Razavi (ed.), *Gendered Poverty and Well-Being*, Oxford: Blackwell.

6

Economic Fallout of Globalization for Indian Women

D.D. NARULA

This paper is divided into three broad sections – the first section dealing with the period closing with the end of 20th century and the second, covering broadly the first decade of the 21st century and section three summing up the argument. It looks at the structure of sectoral output and productivity differentials between the broad sectors to contextualize women's employment in rural and urban India. The analysis reveals that the unpaid labour dominates women's employment, both in rural and urban sectors. It finds that the growth rate of employment was less than the growth rate of labour force, indicating an increase in unemployment rate. The study shows that female as well as male workers are concentrated in agriculture in the rural areas. The other sectors in the rural areas where women have significant presence are manufacturing, services and trade. The urban women workers were concentrated in services, manufacturing, trade and agriculture. The study shows that the proportion of the self-employed women was over 57 per cent at the end of the first period in the rural areas. The study further reveals that women self-employed workers are not decision-makers or independent agents but only unpaid workers in the family farms and enterprises. The patriarchal system dominates the scenario. The study finds women workers steeped in poverty. It also finds that apart from agriculture and construction, every other major industry has seen a reduction in the number of paid workers – a grim situation for women. The study reaches the conclusion that a sustained fight would have to be launched against the patriarchal system to liberate Indian women from thraldom and inhuman conditions of work and living.

I

Globalization has become the buzzword of the present age. However, economic globalization is not a new process; its origins lie all the way back to the colonial era in the 16th century. The process gained momentum in the 1970s, with the development of international capital markets. But, during the debt crisis of 1980s, several developing countries were coaxed/pressurized to implement the stabilization and structural adjustment programmes of the International Monetary Fund (IMF) and the World Bank to create conditions for liberalization of their markets. The process of outward orientation has accelerated due to various factors, such as technological developments, but especially the policies of liberalization that have swept across the world. It gained further momentum in the 1990s with the setting up of the WTO in 1995. Early 1990s was also the time when most South Asian countries, including India, heavily burdened by debt and deficits, entered into these programmes and opened up their economies to the world trading system.

The development paradigm underpinning the current process is based on an ideal view of the world, where markets work efficiently, capital and technology flow freely and people have all the knowledge, information and ability to take part in the market on an equal footing. But, in the real world situation, in most developing countries this process has had mixed results. According to Khor (2001), "While economic globalization is a very uneven process, with increased trade and investment being focused in a few countries almost all countries are affected by this process. While the opportunities and benefits are being stressed by its proponents and supporters, there has been increasing disillusionment among many policy makers in the South, analysts and academics, as well as the community of non-governmental organizations (NGOs) in both the South and the North."

India opted for the globalization scheme of the IMF and the World Bank in 1991. All types of quantitative restrictions on imports were completely removed with effect from April 2001. India joined the World Trade Organization (WTO) in 1995. Foreign investment was being competitively wooed. Short of capital convertibility, international financial flows were almost free. Public expenditures, especially capital expenditure, were sharply curbed for reasons of fiscal prudence. Disinvestment in public enterprises, initially proposed for chronically loss-making units, and now extended to profit-making units as well, was being actively pursued. Resistance to privatization of profit-making public enterprises watered down substantially. Financial sector was opened to private sector – both domestic and foreign. Multinational corporations and the corporate sector operated almost without any let or hindrance. Thus, the package of economic reforms comprising liberalization, privatizations and globalization has been actively pursued for over two decades now. What has been the fallout of these reforms? What have been the gains for the economy and what have been the ill-effects and danger signals? Who have been the beneficiaries and who have been the losers? How have women fared?

In order to examine these questions, we need to have a close look at the nature of our economy. An examination of Tables 1 and 2 shows that the informal/unorganized sector contributed 58.9 per cent to the output (GDP) and 91.66 per cent to total employment on Current Daily Status (CDS) basis of 336.75 million in 1999–2000. While the organized sector's contribution to output was 41.1 per cent, it was only 8.34 per cent to employment. Employment – its volume, nature and quality – is the key variable, indicative of the health of an economy, especially in developing countries, where the informal sector is the main source of employment. Economic theory and policy, as it developed in the advanced capitalist countries of the West, held that the level and rate of growth of employment was a function of the rate of growth of output and production technology.

Our policy makers and planners, right from the First Five-Year Plan, had included the maximization of employment and reduction of underemployment and unemployment as an important plan objective. However, the economic policies followed before the economic reforms, and more especially since 1991, had held that employment could be increased and unemployment reduced through maximization of the rate of economic growth, through percolation/trickle down effect. A reflection of this philosophy is found in the policy recommendations of the report of the Task Force on Employment Opportunities (Government of India, 2001). It is recognized that productive employment is not only a means of ultimate ends of economic well-being and poverty eradication but also an important end in itself. It is also a basic source of human dignity and self-respect. It promises social justice, social stability and social cohesion. The real issue, in practice, is how to combine the two objectives of maximization of rates of growth of GNP and of employment. What are the trade-offs between the two?

The Planning Commission (2002), obviously dissatisfied with the strategy recommended by the Task Force, appointed a Special Group on Targeting Ten Million Employment Opportunities per year over the Tenth Plan period, in September 2001. While the Task Force report had questioned the wisdom of spending more on job creation *per se* through special employment programmes, the Special Group assigned a specific role for such programmes, notwithstanding complaints of leakage of resources and lack of efficiency. The two reports also differed in the relative emphasis given to growth and employment. We propose to examine different aspects of women's employment to assess the economic fallout for them.

Table 1

Sectoral Net Domestic Product (NDP) Scenario: Organized and Unorganized Sectors, 1993–94 and 1999–2000

(GDP in ₹ crores at 1993–94 prices)

Sectors	*NDP (at factor cost)*		*NDP (organized sector)*		*%age Sectoral GDP (organized)*		*%age GDP (organized to total)*	*%age employment (private organized to total)*	*% age employment (organized sector to total)*	*Employment elasticity (organized sector)*	*Employment elasticity (total economy)*
	1993–94	*1999–2000*	*1993–94*	*1999–2000*	*1993–94*	*1999–2000*	*1999–2000*	*1999–2000*	*1999–2000*	*1993–94 to 1999–2000*	*1993–94 to 1999–2000*
Agriculture	229829	274858	8046	8808	3.5	3.2	0.9	0.26	0.41	–0.61	0.01
Mining and Quarrying	14950	20648	13861	19156	92.7	92.8	1.9	0.03	0.30	–0.25	–0.41
Manufacturing	103739	148121	65774	90168	63.4	60.9	8.8	1.54	2.0	0.165	0.33
Electricity, Gas and Water Supply	8801	14609	8169	13766	92.8	94.9	1.4	0.01	0.30	0.056	–0.52
Construction	38749	55696	18929	24107	48.9	43.3	2.4	0.02	0.35	–0.136	0.82
Trade, Hotels and Restaurants	96627	164064	10865	32751	11.2	20.0	3.2	0.10	0.15	0.069	0.62
Transport, Storage and Communication	37721	66110	21000	30801	55.7	46.6	3.0	0.02	0.94	0.024	0.63

Cont'd...

...Cont'd

Financing, Insurance, Real Estate and Business Services	80541	131527	39706	78739	49.3	59.9	7.7	0.11	0.49	0.358	0.64
Community Social and Personal Services	87035	143712	70499	120033	81.0	83.5	11.8	0.50	3.4	0.081	–0.25
Total	697992	1019345	256849	418920	36.8	41.1*	41.1	2.58	8.34	0.066	0.165

*Organized private sector 15 per cent of GDP.

Table 2

Per cent Sectoral Employment Scenario, 1999–2000

(in millions)

Sectors	Total					Organized									
	Employment Elasticity	*Employ-ment Elasticity*	*Current Daily Status (CDS)*			*Public Sector*	*Private Sector*	*Total*	*% of Organized Sector to Total Sectoral Employment*	*% of Public Sector to Total Employment*	*% of Public Sector to Org.*	*% of Private Sector to Total Org.*	*Absolute Employment% Composition*	*Sectoral GDP Growth (%)*	*Sectoral GDP Growth (%)*
	1983 to 1993–94	*1993–94–2000*	*1983*	*1993–94*	*1999–2000*	*1999*	*1999*	*1999*						*1983 to 1993–94*	*1993–94 to 2000*
	1	*2*	*3*	*4*	*5*	*6*	*7*	*8*	*9*	*10*	*11*	*12*	*13*	*14*	*15*
Agriculture,	0.70	0.01	131.25	190.72	190.94	0.52	0.87	1.39	0.73	0.27	37.16	62.84	56.70	2.9	3.1
Mining and Quarrying	0.59	–0.41	1.74	2.54	2.26	0.93	0.09	1.01	44.69	41.15	91.41	8.59	0.67	6.2	4.7
Manufacturing	0.38	0.33	27.69	35.00	40.79	1.57	5.18	6.75	16.55	3.95	23.25	76.75	12.11	6.0	7.8
Electricity, Gas and Water Supply	0.63	-0.52	0.83	1.43	1.15	0.96	0.04	1.00	96.96	83.48	95.91	4.09	0.34	8.4	6.8
Construction	0.86	0.82	7.17	11.02	14.95	1.11	0.07	1.18	7.90	7.42	93.97	6.03	4.44	4.9	6.3

Cont'd...

...Cont'd

Trade, Hotels and Restaurants	0.68	0.62	18.17	26.88	37.54	0.16	0.32	0.49	1.31	0.43	33.54	66.46	11.15	5.6	9.2
Transport, Storage and Communication	0.52	0.63	6.99	9.88	13.65	3.08	0.07	3.15	23.08	22.56	97.81	2.19	4.05	6.1	8.7
Financing, Insurance, Real Estate and Business Services	0.45	0.64	2.10	3.37	4.62	1.30	0.36	1.65	35.71	29.14	78.34	21.66	1.38	10.1	8.4
Community Social and Personal Services	0.68	−0.25	23.52	34.98	30.84	9.79	1.70	11.49	37.26	31.74	85.21	14.79	9.16	5.7	8.4
All	0.52	0.16	239.57	315.84	336.75	19.42	8.70	28.11	8.34	5.77	69.06	30.94	100.0	5.2	6.7

Source: National Account, CSO, NSO: 55th round, Economic Survey.

The data further reveal that the total output grew at 6.52 per cent per annum and employment at 1.07 per cent in the immediate post-reform period (1993–94 to 1999–2000). The organized sector's output grew during this period at 8.50 per cent per annum, with private sector growing at 12.30 per cent and public sector at 6.68 per cent per annum. Employment in the organized sector, however, grew at a negligible rate of 0.56 per cent, with public sector creating hardly any additional jobs (growth rate of 0.10% per annum) and private sector employment growth at 1.64 per cent during the period. While output in the unorganized/informal sector increased at a rate of 5.27 per cent per annum, employment grew only at 1.12 per cent per annum. Employment elasticity of output, i.e., job creation capacity per unit of output for the economy, as a whole, was 0.16 in 1999–2000, with that of organized sector being only 0.07 per cent, and that of the informal sector, 0.21.

Since women are employed predominantly in the informal sector, one needs to have a closer look at the evolving sectoral output and employment picture of the Indian economy. Table 3 presents the sectoral employment, 1993–94/1999–2000 and Net Domestic Product (NDP) scenarios of organized and unorganized sectors. It also presents alternative estimates of employment and labour force growth on UPSS and CDS bases for 1993–94 and 1999–2000. It shows that total employment on UPSS basis was estimated at 397 million and, that on CDS basis, was 336.75 million in 1999–2000. Agriculture provided employment to 190.94 million, i.e., 56.70 per cent on CDS basis and 237.56 million, i.e., 59.82 per cent on UPSS basis, in 1999–2000. The other sectors important for women's employment were manufacturing with 12.11 per cent of the employment; trade, hotels and restaurants with 11.15 per cent; community, social and personal services with 9.16 per cent; construction with 4.44 per cent; and transport, storage and communications with 4.05 per cent of total employment.

Further, it is noteworthy that informal/unorganized sector dominated all these industrial sectors providing employment varying from about 63 per cent in community, social and personal services to over 99 per cent in agriculture, among the few relatively women-oriented sectors. Organized sector provided only 37.26 per cent to total employment in services and 0.73 per cent in agriculture.

Sectoral distribution of workers in India (UPSS) by sex and locale shows that female as well as male workers are concentrated in agriculture in the rural areas though the percentage declined slightly from 86.3 per cent to 85.3 in the immediate post-reform period. The other sectors in rural areas where women have significant presence are manufacturing, services and trade, etc. Urban women workers in 1999–2000 were concentrated in services (27.1%), manufacturing (24%), trade, etc. (16.9%) and agriculture, etc. (17.6%). It may also be noted that during the

Table 3

Output Employment and Productivity of Organized, Unorganized and Public Sector, 1993–94 and 1999–2000

(employment in million; GDP in ₹ crore at 1993–04 prices)

	Organized			*Unorganized*	*Grand Total*	*% composition*		*Public sector (a)*	*Private Organized (b)*
	Total	*Public (a)*	*Private (b)*			*Organized (a+b)*	*Unorganized*		
Value added (GDP) (NET)									
1993–94	256849	180843	76006	441143	697992	36.80	63.20	25.9	10.89
1999–2000	418920	266519	152401	600425	1019345	41.10	58.9	26.1	15.0
Growth per annum per cent	8.50	6.68	12.30	5.27	6.52				
Outstanding credit of scheduled commercial banks (₹ thousand crore)*									
1993–94	80.8	28.1	52.7	94.9	175.7	46.0	54.0	16.0	30.0
1999–2000	247.4	66.8	180.6	145.9	393.3	62.9	37.1	17.0	45.9
Growth (in %)	20.5	15.5	22.8	7.4	14.4				
Employment									
1993–94	27.18	19.3	7.88	288.66	315.84	8.61	91.39	6.1	2.51
1999–2000	28.11	19.42	8.69	308.64	336.75	8.34	91.66	5.8	2.54
Growth (in %)	0.56	0.10	1.64	1.12	1.074				

Cont'd...

...Cont'd

Employment elasticity	0.066	0.015	0.133	0.213	0.165
Labour productivity	7.88	6.67	8.38	4.10	5.38
Growth per annum (%)					
(1993–94 to 1999–2000					
Relative labour intensity organized/unorganized					
(1999–2000)	0.1305				

* *Economic and Political Weekly (EPW)* (2002) Table 10. # Person years.

Note: The classifications of the economy by value added and employment are not strictly comparable. But even with reasonable margin of error, the dimensional differences in the features of the two sectors – organized and unorganized – are so significantly large as to give enough confidence about the robustness of the findings of this table.

Sources: 1. For organized employment, classified by DGE&T, reported in he Economic Survey, Government of India.
2. Organized sector GDP is as classified by Central Statistical Organization (CSO).
3. For bank credit, private corporate sector including public sector is equated with organized sector (March 2000 and March 1994).
4. Unorganized sector is by residual.

post-reform (1993–94 to 1999–2000) period, the share of rural women registered an increase in 'manufacturing' from 7 per cent to 7.6 per cent, in 'construction' from 0.9 per cent to 1.1 per cent and in 'services', from 2.9 per cent to 3.4 per cent. More rural male workers shifted to 'construction', 'trade', 'transport' and manufacturing' sectors from 'agriculture' and 'services' sectors. Chadha and Sahu (2002) observe, "a substantial slowdown of the process of weaning away of rural male workers from agriculture, and its complete halt, if not a reversal, in the case of rural females". This phenomenon "clearly signals their relative incapability of gaining access" to jobs in non-agricultural sectors "perhaps because of the low level of their human capital index. These infirmities are more pronounced in the case of rural female workers, because they have not only to compete with their male counterparts in the rural areas but also with their 'more qualified' sisters in the urban areas."

Another significant feature of women's employment is that a high proportion of women are self-employed, especially in agriculture and allied activities such as animal husbandry, fisheries, etc., and in small-scale industries.

The data show that the proportion of self-employed (both male and female), though declining marginally, continued to remain high (55% for males and over 57% for females) in 1999–2000 in rural areas; similarly, the incidence of casual labour, both male and female, was rising, in rural and urban areas, the rise being higher for rural male workers. It appears that casual wage labour was rising at the cost of self-employment in rural areas, which is a cause for concern. This implies, according to Chadha and Sahu (2002) that marginal and sub-marginal self-cultivators were being pushed out to become casual wage labour or were temporarily shifting to non-agricultural wage labour or as a seasonal supplementation. The index of casualization for rural females is disturbingly high and reflects partly the ridiculously low share that rural females have as regular salaried employees. Surprisingly, casualization for urban females declined in post-reform period, in contrast to a marginal rise in the proportion of casualization among rural male workers.

The results of NSSO round 55 (2001) on trends in employment and unemployment of women have baffled both scholars and policy makers. These indicated a considerable decline in crude worker-population ratios (WPRs) for both males and females in rural as well as urban sectors during the post-reform period; the decline being much steeper in the case of women. This cannot be explained by changes in the age structure since the decline was experienced by all the age groups. Further, there had not been any significant rise in unemployment rates in the period.

Table 4

Rate of Growth of Population, Labour Force and Employment

(% per annum)

Period	*Rate of Growth of Population*	*Rate of Growth of Labour Force (UPSS)*	*Rate of Growth of Employment (UPSS)*
1972–73 to 1977–78	2.27	2.94	2.73
1977–78 to 1983	2.19	2.04	2.17
1983 to 1987–88	2.14	1.74	1.54
1987–88 to 1993–94	2.10	2.29	2.43
(1983 to 1993–94)	(2.12)	(2.05)	(2.04)
1993–94 to 1999–2000	1.93	1.03	0.98

This implies that there was a decline in the labour force-population ratio (LFPR), i.e., the percentage of women offering themselves for work successfully or otherwise, or were willing to take up work or extra work, declined in the 90s. The decline in the WPRs, especially in the age groups 15–19 and 20–24, particularly for women, can be only partly explained by the rising student-population ratios. The other explanation for the decline in the WPR in the age group 25 and above, by the decline in subsidiary status for rural women, does not hold water for urban women and for rural and urban men. A further explanation that the 1993–94 WPRs are outliers when seen against WPRs of earlier surveys is also found to be deficient. In this context, Hirway (2002) argued that part of the explanation lies in the limited ability of the NSS surveys to capture the work and workers, in the economy. It seems to us that the concepts and methods used by NSSO to net work and workers are not able to capture the work of the poor and particularly of women satisfactorily. The decline in the WPRs in the 90s could be due to rise in the non-reported (by NSSO) part of the workforce employed in 'difficult to measure' sectors (such as subsistence work, home-based work or informal work) of the economy. This hypothesis was confirmed by the first pilot Time Use Survey (TUS) carried out in six major states in India in 1998–99. The TUS found that the time spent on unpaid activities constituted 85.99 per cent of the total time spent by women on economic activities in Haryana. Tamil Nadu women spent the lowest time (32.45%) on unpaid activities. For the six states combined, the proportion of time spent on unpaid activities was 50.52 per cent for females and 33.15 per cent for males. Hirway adds that an increase in 'the difficult to measure' sector of the SNA work[1] as well as in extended SNA work[2] do indicate a deterioration in the quality of employment. The former indicates an increase in employment with low productivity and low wages, while the latter indicates an increased burden on women who are primarily responsible for carrying on unpaid domestic services. The TUS seems to bring out under-reporting by the NSS of women's participation in the labour workforce and of women's unpaid work.

Chadha and Sahu (2002) compared the growth of labour force and employment for pre-reform period (1983–1993/94) and post-reform period (1993–94 – 1999–00), by all the four measures of work status. The data showed that employment had grown faster than the labour force during the pre-reform period (except for rural areas in both periods for UPS) but during the post-war period not only had the growth rates for both labour force and employment declined, employment growth rate was also lower than that of labour force by all the four measures, thus adding to unemployment. An examination by sub-sectors, however, reveals a mixed picture, with some sub-sectors, exhibiting higher growth rates of employment in the post-reform period; however, employment growth rates, in most sub-sectors, showed varying degrees of decline. Since, however, sub-sectors which are major absorbers of rural labour force and their number being much larger than those with improved employment growth rates, post-reform setbacks are more widely spread and greater in magnitude and, therefore, a grave cause for concern.

While overall employment grew for male rural workers at 1.94 per cent per annum in the previous period, it declined to 0.94 per cent in the latter period. For rural females, the growth rate of employment declined steeply from 1.41 to a low of 0.15 per cent per annum over the two periods. The decline for urban females was from 3.44 to 0.94 per cent per annum with urban males suffering a decline to 2.61 from 3.22 per cent per annum. It needs to be noted that the growth rate for both sexes was higher for urban workers than for rural workers. This implies that contrary to the claims made by the pro-reform lobby, employment growth rates suffered varying degrees of setback for every section of the workforce, most visibly in the rural areas and for female workers. Female workers in the rural transport-storage communication sector suffered a steep decline from 8.30 per cent to 0.15 per cent per annum in contrast to a sizeable rise from 4.51 per cent to 7.45 per cent per annum during the pre-reform periods.

With employment growth rates slowing down, during the post-reform period, unemployment and underemployment rates were bound to increase. According to Chadha and Sahu (2002), unemployment rates for rural male and female workers as also for urban males had gone up; however, the rate for urban females declined from 10.5 per cent to 9.4 per cent between 1993–94 and 1999–2000, according to Current Daily Status, which is true for the three other measures also. It hardly needs to be mentioned that open unemployment is not that serious a problem in developing countries with large informal sectors. It is the problem of self-employed and casual labour which gets worse. Scholars have noted the trend towards feminization of the labour market in urban areas, due to the preference of employers for labour flexibility or due to the rise in short-duration employment. But, why is female unemployment much higher in rural area?

Besides the supply side constraints mentioned earlier, an important factor operating more intensely in the post-reform period was the change in production methods with the introduction of mechanization and technology in agriculture, small-scale industry and construction. Women have a long history of losing their hold on jobs whenever there are changes in production methods. This is because of the mistaken notion that women cannot perform well on fast-moving, power-driven and complicated machines, because of their poor physique and poor intellect. Introduction of mechanization in Punjab and Haryana agriculture had the effect of displacing women workers there. Whenever production technology was upgraded, women lost jobs. However, this did not happen when land productivity rose due to rise of high yielding variety of seeds or in more intensive crop cycle. Techniques which increase productivity per worker without raising productivity per acre do not contribute to the overall solution of the problem of employment.

In the non-agricultural sector, all productive units are under pressure to keep their edge against their global rivals. For this purpose, Indian firms would have to extract value productivity per unit of labour similar to international standards while continuing to pay relatively lower wages to the workers. In the process, they are shifting to technologies using more of both physical and human capital and in the process, they are slashing their unskilled and semi-skilled workers and inducting workers with technical training and skills. Since women, especially in rural areas, lack these skills and training, they are the sufferers.

Jhabvala and Sinha (2002) cited a number of studies which showed that technical change had eliminated many women's traditional jobs, without creating alternative job opportunities for them: for spraying of weedicide by men replacing weeding by women, rice mills replacing hand pounding by women, mechanization displacing women in the textile and garment industry, etc.

Liberalization and removal of restrictions on imports displaced a number of Indian products with imports, e.g., China-Korea silk yarn imports displaced thousands of spinners and twisters in Bihar. The entry of large fishing vessels into Indian sea waters destroyed jobs of fishermen and women fish sorters. Import of cheaper gum from Sudan had destroyed jobs of women gum collectors in Gujarat. Besides toy industry, a number of handicrafts also faced serious problems due to cheap imports of toys and substitute products, creating serious problems of unemployment and underemployment.

It is often argued that in countries following an open economic policy, the work force in export-oriented industries, especially in manufacturing, comes to be dominated by female labour. Some writers have even argued about the empowering aspect of this development for women, who now have a wage income and a window to the outside world. It is no doubt true that there is a trend towards feminization of the workforce in export industries, especially in Special Economic Zones (SEZs) and Export Zones. But it is also equally true that the conditions of work offered to these workers are often quite horrendous and in any case, the process does little to close the male/female gap. Preference for women workers in the export sector, is principally because they are prepared to accept lower wages, and unfavourable conditions of work, due to their weak bargaining position.

Arup Mitra (2010) argued that the structural programme initiated by Government of India in 1991 aimed at increasing the long-run growth rate of GDP through deregulation in both commodity and factor markets. He felt that such a programme initially lead to reduction in both income and employment growth rates and thereby increase unemployment rate and/or low productivity employment in the short run.

Mitra further argued that Article 39 of the Constitution of India provided three directives in regard to wage and employment policies for granting equal opportunity to men and women. These are: (i) that the citizens, men and women, equally have the right to adequate means of livelihood; (ii) that there is equal pay for equal work for both men and women; and (iii) that the health and strength of workers, men and women, and the tender age of children are not abused and the citizens are not forced by economic necessity to enter vocations unsuited to their age and strength. Further, job reservation for women shift from welfare approach to equality approach and finally anti-poverty approach.

In contrast, Swarn S. Vepa (2009) in her book review argues that it is important to recognize the limitations of the study based on secondary analysis of very large data sets collected for national statistical analysis by Census of India, National Sample Surveys (NSS), Department of Agriculture, Labour Force Participation Reports, etc. The review of documents of the ways in which the land base had declined, forcing more and more people into dependence on wage labour. She pointed out how women's lack of access to technology, land and water had forced more and more people into dependence on wage labour. According to her, women tend to be an active force in conserving natural resources. On the issue of access to livelihood, she mentions three major concerns: (i) increasing burden of unpaid and paid work, (ii) inequality in wages, and (iii) women's low educational status.

Vepa criticizes the notion that the gender gap was decreasing and challenges the notion that women's well-being was congruent with that of the family. She argues that the Gender Gap Index was increasing and not declining.

II

A study by Nira Mehta (2010) has attempted to decipher recent employment trends, as shown by National Sample Survey Organization (NSSO) for 2009–10. The survey noted a significant deceleration of the rate of growth of aggregate employment. It noted that those reporting themselves as occupied in the 15–24 age group were 16.7 million for males and 11.9 million for females in 2009–10 as against 5.6 and 5.2 million respectively in the previous 5-year period; they were obtaining higher education, thus, reducing the number entering the labour force.

The government has claimed that this decline was substantially due to a fall in female employment level. Rural female employment, which had risen by 18.3 million between 1999–2000 and 2004–05, had registered a decline of 19.2 million during 2004–05 to 2009–10. Even urban areas had registered a decline from a positive 6.4 million to a negative 1.7 million. The government has claimed that NSSO 2009–10 had significantly

Table 5

Employment Trends for Men and Women Workers – Rural and Urban

A. Change in Number of Workers (in millions)

	1999–2000/2004–05	*2004–05/2009–10*
Rural Male	20.2	13.4
Rural Female	18.3	(–) 19.2
Urban Male	15.0	9.8
Urban Female	6.4	(–) 1.7

B. Usual Principal Status

Period		*Male Workers*	
	15–24	25–59	Total
1999–2000	55.0	190.2	264.9
2004–05	51.5	216.4	299.6
2009–2010	55.3	245.2	325.8
Self-employed	115.2	119.2	91.4
Regular	44.0	50.5	39.9
Casual	57.2	75.4	56.9

Female Workers (25–59)

	1999–200 0	*2004–05*	*2009–11*
Self-employed	32.4	43.2	35.5
Regular	9.9	00.4	21.0
Casual	28.6	39.6	29.2

under-estimated female employment, especially in rural areas. They have cast doubt on the official explanation for the decline. They have noted that changes in the 25–59 age group were 28.8 million (positive) and 28.2 million (negative) during the quinquennium (2004–05 to 2009–10) for male workers for principal status employment. In the case of females, employment fell during this recent period by 5.1 million as against a rise of 17.1 million during the previous 5-year period. Further, a positive feature of aggregate principal status employment for males in the age group 25–59 was paid employment instead of self-employment, which quite considerably could be distress-driven. However, female employment fell by 5.1 million in this age group as against an increase of 13.1 million in the previous 5-year period. Another distinguishing feature of this paid employment was that about two-third was in the casual work category. Further, a considerable part of this work was in the construction sector, a more volatile employment category, characterized by lower wages, and a higher uncertainty of employment and often, limited earning potential. According to this parameter, India with a poverty index of 0.296, poverty ratio of 41.6 per cent (in terms of GDP $1.25 a day) and national poverty ratio of 28.6 per cent is not favourably placed when compared with countries like China and Sri Lanka (see Tables 6 and 7).

The Economic Survey (2010–11) claims that the Government of India has been striving for inclusive development:

> In terms of gender equality index (GEI), India with an Index Value of 0.748 ranks 122 out of a total of 168 countries in 2008. The GEI captures the loss in achievement due to gender disparities in the areas of reproductive health, empowerment and labour force participation, with values ranging from 0 (perfect equality) to 1 (total inequality). The GEI index value of 0.748 indicates a higher degree of gender discrimination in India compared to countries like China (0.405) and Sri Lanka (0.599).

Despite over six decades of planned economic development vast sections of landless agricultural labourers, marginal farmers, SCs, STs and OBCs continue to suffer social and financial exclusion. To remedy the situation, the government has implemented economic and social as well as financial policies for their upliftment.

The Eleventh Five-Year Plan had recognized the multi-faceted exclusion and discrimination faced by women and envisaged action to ensure that every woman in the country was able to develop her full potential and share the benefits of economic growth and prosperity. It further recognized that success will depend on our ability to adopt a participatory approach that empowers women and mother partners in their own development. It further stated that the approach to gender equality is based on the recognition that interventions in favour of women

Table 6

Multidimensional Poverty Index, 1980–2010

No.	Country	1980	1990	2000	2010	Avg. Annual HDI Growth Rate (per capita) 1980–2010	1990–1010	2000–2010	Global Position
1	Norway	0.788	0.838	0.906	0.938	0.58	0.56	0.34	0.938(11)
2	Australia	0.791	0.819	0.914	0.937	0.57	0.67	0.25	0.937(2)
57	Malaysia	0.541	0.616	0.961	0.744	1.06	0.94	0.73	0.744(57)
65	Russia	—	0.692	0.662	0.719	—	0.19	0.82	0.719(65)
73	Brazil	—	—	0.649	0.699	—	—	0.73	0.699(73)
89	China	0.368	0.460	0.567	0.663	1.96	1.83	1.57	0.663(89)
91	Sri Lanka	0.513	0.558	—	0.658	0.83	0.82	—	0.658(91)
92	Thailand	0.483	0.546	0.600	0.654	1.01.	0.90	0.86	0.654(92)
101	Egypt	0.393	0.484	0.566	0.620	1.52	0.23	0.90	0.620(101)
108	Indonesia	0.390	0.458	0.500	0.600	1.43	1.35	1.82	0.600(103)
110	South Africa	—	0.601	—	0.597	—	(-)0.03	—	0.597(110)
113	Vietnam	—	0.407	0.505	0.572	—	1.70	1.24	0.572(113)
119	India	0.320	0.389	0.440	0.519	1.61	1.44	1.66	0.519(119)
125	Pakistan	0.311	0.359	0.416	0.490	1.52	1.55	1.54	0.490(125)
129	Bangladesh	0.259	0.313	0.390	0.469	1.99	2.03	1.86	0.469(129)
	World	0.455	0.526	0.570	0.624	1.05	0.85	0.89	0.624

Note: Figures in parentheses give ranking among 169 countries.

Source: Economic Survey 2010–11, Tables 12.1 and 12.2, Last column from Table 12.2.

must be multi-pronged and must (i) provide women with basic entitlements, (ii) address the reality of globalization and its impact on women by prioritizing economic empowerment, (iii) ensure an environment free from all forms of violence against women (VAW) - physical, economic, social, psychological, etc., (iv) ensure the participation and adequate representation at the highest policy levels, particularly in parliament and state assemblies, and (v) strengthen existing institutional mechanisms and create new ones for gender mainstreaming and effective policy implementation.

The Eleventh Plan laid down six monitorable targets:

(i) Raise the sex ratio for age group 0–6 from 927 in 2001 to 935 by 2011–12 and 950 by 2016–17.

Table 7

India's Global Position in Human Development

Country	*HDI/1980*	*HDI/2010*	*GNI per capita (PPP 2008 US$)*	*Life Expectancy at birth (years)*	*Years of Schooling*
Norway	0.788	0.938 (1)	58,810	81.0	12.6
Australia	0.791	0.937 (2)	38,692	81.9	12.0
Malaysia	0.541	0.744 (57)	13,927	74.7	9.5
Russia	—	0.719 (65)	15,258	67.2	8.8
Brazil	—	0.699 (73)	10,607	—	7.2
China	0.368	0.663 (89)	7,258	73.5	7.5
Sri Lanka	0.513	0.658 (91)	4,486	74.4	8.2
Egypt	0.393	0.620 (101)	5,889	70.5	6.5
Vietnam	—	0.572 (113)	2,995	74.9	5.5
India	0.320	0.519 (119)	3,337	64.4	4.4
Pakistan	0.311	0.490 (125)	2,678	67.2	4.8
Bangladesh	0.259	0.469 (129)	1,587	68.9	4.8
World	0.455	0.624	10,631	69.3	7.4

Note: Figures in parentheses give ranking among 169 countries.

Source: HDR 2010 as in Economic Survey, 2010–11.

(ii) Ensure that at least 33 per cent of the direct and indirect beneficiaries of all government schemes are women and girl children.
(iii) Reduce IMR from 57 to 28 and MMR from 3.01 to one per 1,000 live births.
(iv) Reduce malnutrition among children of 0–3 age group to half its present level.
(v) Reduce anaemia among women and girls by 50 per cent by the end of the plan.
(vi) Reduce dropout rate for primary and secondary schooling by 10 per cent for both girls as well as boys.

The Eleventh Plan considered an educated labour force to be critical for achieving faster growth and education to be the period to ensuring greater inclusivity. It proposed to build on ongoing efforts to strengthen elementary education. It stated that the infrastructure for primary schools had been almost completed under the Sarva Shiksha Abhiyan and that it was now necessary to focus efforts on issues of quality and expansion of infrastructure for secondary education. It recognized that higher education would be a key driver in an increasingly globalized and knowledge driven world needs to increase from around 11 per cent to over 21 per cent, over a ten-year period, requiring a massive expansion in the university system, combined with efforts to create competitive world class institutions of higher education. Given the scarcity of resources, it sought to encourage private sector initiatives in higher education and various forms of public-private partnerships.

The key strategy for achieving inclusive growth in the Eleventh Plan has been the generation of productive and gainful employment, with decent working conditions on a sufficient scale to absorb the growing labour force and for this purpose the plan has provided for creating 58 million work opportunities in 21 high growth sectors, thus hopefully bringing down the unemployment rate by the end of the plan. Economic Survey claims creation of 4 million work opportunities from 1999–2000 to 2004–05, as against 24 million from 1993–94 to 1999–2000. However, due to a faster labour force growth of 2.84 per annum, as against 1.25 per cent per annum earlier, unemployment also rose.

The United Nations Development Programme (UNDP) has supplemented measuring development with its Human Development Report (HDR), which uses Human Development Index (HDI) for this purpose. It captures progress in terms of three basic capabilities: to live a long and healthy life, to be educated and knowledgeable and to enjoy a decent economic standard of life, as shown by India's global position in Human Development. India's HDI at 0.519 for 2010–11 puts it at 119 out of 169 countries – an improvement over 2007 when HDI was 134 out of 182 countries.

There has been a surfeit of poverty estimates with the National Commission for Enterprises in the Unorganized Sector, chaired by late Arjun Sengupta, claiming 836 million (i.e., 77% of the population), being below the poverty line (BPL), with per capita consumption of upto ₹ 20 a day in 2004–05. The Central Minister of State complained that no justification had been provided for using the cut-off limit of ₹ 20 and put the estimate at 60.5 per cent. Gender earning differentials have been noted as being due to labour-market discrimination and also because of demand side constraints of the participants in the labour market, as shown by a study of floriculture market in West Bengal. This study also mentioned about a Haryana Agro-Economic Research Unit (2007) study of floriculture. The Expert Group, chaired by Dr N.C. Saxena, suggested that the national level poverty ratio could be assumed at 50 per cent, again without providing any justification. The Tendulkar Panel estimated 41.8 per cent head count ratio, on the basis of per capita consumption expenditure of ₹ 446.68 and ₹ 578.80 a month for rural and urban areas respectively for 2004–05.

The Economic Survey (2010–11) has estimated poverty at 55.4 per cent. A World Bank calibrated poverty line of $1.25 a day in 2008 put India's poverty at 41.6 per cent in 2005. The plan panel's official estimate had pegged the poverty ratio at 27.5 per cent in 2004–05.

In terms of Gender Equality Index (GEI), India with an index value of 0.748 ranks 122 out of a total of 168 countries in 2008. The GEI captures the loss in achievement due to gender disparities in the areas of

Table 8

Unemployment Rates: Alternative Measures

	Usual Principal Status (UPS)	*Usual Principal and Subsidiary Status (UPSS)*	*Current Weekly Status (CWS)*	*Current Daily Status (CDS)*
Rural				
1977–78	3.26	1.54	3.74	7.70
1983	1.91	1.13	3.88	7.94
1987–88	3.07	1.98	4.19	5.25
1993–94	1.80	1.20	3.00	5.63
1999–00	1.96	1.43	3.91	7.21
Urban				
1977–78	8.77	7.01	7.86	10.34
1983	6.04	5.02	6.81	9.52
1987–88	6.56	5.32	7.12	9.36
1993–94	5.21	4.52	5.83	7.43
1999–00	5.23	4.63	5.89	7.65
All-India				
1977–78	4.23	2.47	4.48	8.18
1983	2.77	1.90	4.51	8.28
1987–88	3.77	2.62	4.80	6.09
1993–94	2.56	1.90	3.63	6.03
1999–00	2.81	2.23	4.41	7.32

Note: These estimates of employment are based on NSS data combined with census 2001 data. The NSS gives Labour Force Participation Rate (LFPR) and Work Force Participation Rate (WFPR) for four categories: rural male (RM), rural female (RF), urban male (UM) and urban female (UF) separately. We obtain estimates of the total labour force and total work force in each year by applying LFPR and WFPR to the total population of each category (RM, RF, UM and UF) obtained from the interpolation for inter-census years. However, for the year 2001, the four component (RM, FR, UM and UF) were not available in the key results of census released in April 2001. Hence, estimates of populations for these four categories made by the Technical Group (which was chaired by Registrar General) in 1996, had been used to combine the component-wise LFPR's and WFPR's to the level of rural, urban and all-India.

reproductive health, empowerment and labour force participation, with values ranging from 0 (perfect equality) to 1 (total inequality). The GEI index value of 0.748 indicates a higher degree of gender discrimination in India compared to countries like China (0.405) and Sri Lanka (0.599).

Another study on female employment in India reveals that the employment structure in India has led to polarization of skills such that women predominate in low-paid, low-skilled work, forming a high proportion of service sector. The study has also noted the high concentration of female workforce in low productivity industries, negating the premise that economic reforms would create more employment opportunities in modern sectors. The study has pleaded for spread of education and skill development for empowering women as well as women workers. It has also advocated for direct employment generation and fiscal incentives for expansion of activities that use female labour.

Table 9

Unemployment Rates: India and Selected Countries (Current Weekly Status Basis)

Country	*1996*
India*	4.4
Australia	8.6
Bangladesh	2.5
China	3.0
Indonesia	4.0
Korea, Republic of	2.0
Malaysia	2.6
Pakistan**	5.4
Philippines	7.4
Sri Lanka	11.3

*Pertains to the year 1999–2000 (55th round).

** Figures relate to 1995.

Source: World Employment Report.

The decline in the percentage of self-employed women from about 61 per cent in 2004–05 to 55.9 per cent in 2007–08 and a further decline to 53.3 per cent in 2009–10 confirms the hypothesis that 'volatility or uncertainty in a crisis inherent to self-employment-driven increase in FWPR'. The downturn in women's employment from 2004–05 to 2009–10 is in sharp contrast with the surge in GDP growth rates in the same period.

Figures 1 and 2 describe the characteristics of self-employed women (UPSS) in rural and urban areas respectively over the three quinquennial rounds from 1993–94 to 2004–05 and 2004–05 to 2007–08. Figure 1 brings out that three-fourth of self-employed women are unpaid workers and a quarter of rural self-employed women are own-account workers (again unpaid). And, this unpaid work in the NSS data does not include domestic work, such as cooking, cleaning and child care, but only the economic and non-market activities leading to production of primary goods for own consumption or relate to own-account production (such as construction of houses, roads or of any private or community facilities free of charge) (see Table 5).

Figure 1

Work Participation Rate of Women in Rural India

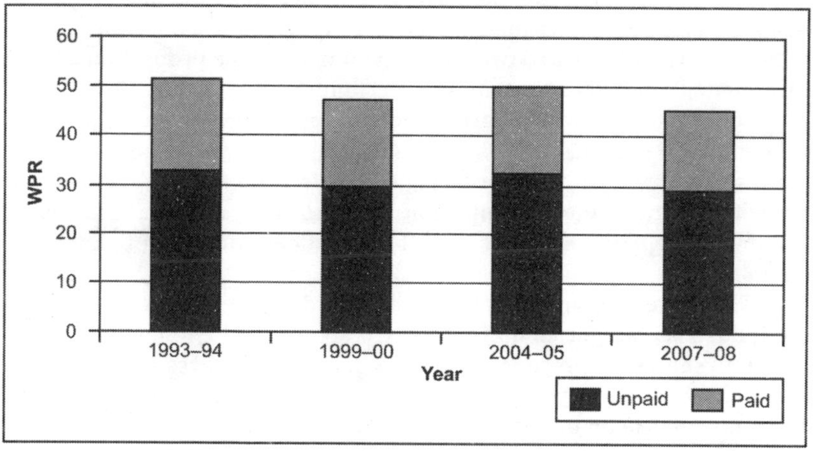

Figure 2

Work Participation Rate of Women in Urban India

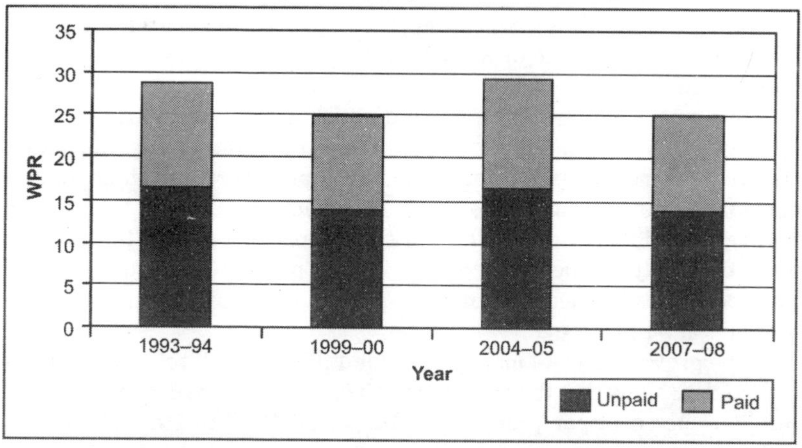

Among urban women (see Figure 2), own-account workers include piece rate workers in homes, on the streets the like, who are paid for their work. Unpaid labour forms a substantial proportion – 49 per cent in 2004–05 – among urban self-employed women. Casual labour accounts for 64 per cent of the women in the paid workforce in rural areas in 2004–05. It seems that a significant number of unpaid self-employed women tend to go for casual work when they are unable to find such work.

Men too are involved in unpaid productive work, but not on the same scale nor does it have the same social significance. Women's unpaid productive labour is deeply rooted in the patriarchal nature of their households or families and property rights. It articulates their condition of economic dependence and patriarchal domination. The proportion of paid rural female population shows a declining trend from 1993–94 to 2007–08. In contrast, the proportion of paid rural males increased between 1999–00 and 2007–08. This suggests that rural women are either more seriously constrained or facing more discrimination in the paid job market. Further, the urbanization process has affected increasing employment opportunities for men, the same does not appear to hold true for women.

The share of women workers in standard UPSS estimates for each of the industrial categories up to 2009–10 and in paid employment up to 2007–08 shows a high concentration of female workforce in agriculture as well as that of only paid workers. While the number of female workers as a whole has been increasing across each of the quinquennial surveys, the female workforce has seen a reduction of 21 million between 2004–05 and 2009–10, and more than 20 million of it in agriculture. The withdrawal of such large numbers of unpaid workers from the agricultural workforce without a simultaneous increase in the overall number in paid work is a negative development – an expression of greater domestication and dependence of women on construction industry, absorbing more than 3 million.

But, apart from agriculture and construction, every other major industry appears to have seen a reduction in the number of paid women workers – a grim situation for women's employment and their further marginalization in the economy. It is a shocking reality that if one removes unpaid labour from the work participation in 2007–08, it would mean that only 15 per cent of the female population in the country received wages or incomes for their labour, with corresponding figure for males at 51 per cent.

The growth rates of employment and the labour force derived from the NSS data show that the rate of growth of employment declined sharply from 2.04 per cent per year during the period 1983 to 1993–94 to only 0.98 per cent per year during the period 1993–94 to 1999–2000. This sharp deceleration in the growth of employment has naturally been the focus of much attention and comment, raising fears that economic growth in the 1990s has been of a 'jobless' variety. However, it is important to recognize that the absolute level of employment in 1999–2000 is estimated by applying the percentage of employed workers to the total number of workers in the labour force observed in the survey to an estimate of the labour force in that year. The estimate of labour force, in turn, is obtained by applying the labour force participation rates (LFPR) in the survey to the total population derived from Census 2001 data. An important feature of the 1999–2000 survey is that LFPR declined sharply compared with position in 1993–94 and this is reflected in sharp deceleration in the growth of labour force from 2.29 per cent during the period 1987–88 to 1993–94 to only 1.03 per cent during the period 1993–94 to 1999–2000. The observed deceleration in employment, therefore, cannot be dissociated from the sharp decline in the growth of labour force and indeed is derived from it.

This is not to deny that the employment growth has been inadequate. The data clearly show that the growth rate of employment is less than the growth rate of labour force, indicating an increase in the unemployment rate and this is a matter of concern. However, the sharp deceleration in the growth rate of employment should not be compared, as is sometimes done, with the continuing growth rate of population. It must be viewed in the context of the growth rate of the labour force which is shown to have decelerated in the survey.

It is relevant to ask whether the observed deceleration in the labour force growth in some sense reflects a structural change in economy which is likely to continue in future. Some deceleration in labour force growth was expected because of the decline in population growth from 2.10 per cent per year during the period 1987–88 to 1993–94 to 1.93 per cent during the period 1993–94 to 1999–2000 and this would normally be associated with a slower growth in the working age population, which in turn would also lead to slower growth in labour force. However, the observed deceleration in labour force growth from 2.29 per cent to 1.09 per cent is much sharper than the deceleration in population growth. This is because the participation rates in all age groups have declined sharply. This decline needs to be carefully evaluated.

The participation rates thrown up by various NSS surveys from 1983 to 1999–00 have the following feature, which is worth noting:

> The decline in the Labour Force Participation Rate (LFPR) in the younger age group during the period 1993–94 to 1999–2000 is a part of long term trend reflecting the expected shift in the activity status of this group towards education. This trend is likely to continue in the future.

III

We have noted the following features about women's employment in the preceding sections:

(i) Majority of the women work in agriculture in rural areas. Since they work on family farms and family enterprises, they are not paid for their work.

(ii) A very high proportion of women are either self-employed or casual workers.
(iii) They have to combine work with family duties like rearing children, and doing odd jobs like fetching water, collecting firewood, tending livestock, etc. They work longer hours than men.
(iv) Most of the women workers, especially in rural areas, lack not only education but also literacy and skills.
(v) They suffer from other supply-side constraints such as irregularity in work due to reproductive, family and social responsibilities.
(vi) There has been increasing casualization of work due to liberalization, and more so, for women.
(vii) Even in the sectors where economic reforms have increased employment and/or feminization of labour has taken place, women workers are paid less than men and generally much below the minimum wages prescribed by law. Large manufacturing companies are increasingly resorting to sub-contracting work to smaller enterprises or resorting to putting out system, i.e., giving work to home-based workers, who are most often women. Quite often, home-based workers are paid on piecerate basis.

Due to the lack of bargaining power unionization, and working mostly in the sectors where productivity is low, women's earnings are much lower, even below minimum wages. According to estimates of poverty provided by NSS 55th and other rounds, rural poverty ratio declined from 37.3 per cent in 1993–94 to 27.1 per cent in 1999–2000. Similarly, urban poverty fell from 33.4 per cent to 23.6 per cent, during the post-reform period. There are no estimates available of poverty for women-headed households. However, the foregoing account of women's employment clearly brings out that they have suffered grievously during the post-reform period despite a few bright spots.

The Task Force (2001) recommended stepping up the rate of growth of output, through modernization, technological upgradation, dereservation of small-scale industry and allowing corporate sector to enter agriculture so that workers could enjoy a reasonable wage and income. The Special Group (2002), recognized the need for raising the growth rate of the economy and also of employment of the 92 per cent of the labour force which worked in the informal sector and a simultaneous tackling of the problems of the unemployed educated youth, which had grown dangerously during the post-reform period. Keeping in view the importance of the informal sector in the 21st century, we have to increase the growth rate of employment on a priority basis. Thus, the economic fallout of globalization for Indian women has been dismal.

What should be our strategy to wrestle with this stupendous and urgent problem? The Special Group has not addressed the problem of women's employment specifically, though its recommendations apply equally to women. We have to attempt to tackle both the supply-side and the demand-side constraints.

In this strategy the highest priority should be accorded to education and training for upgradation of skills to meet the challenge of globalization. This training should not be confined to women's traditional jobs such as stitching and typing but also in new promising emerging areas like information and communication technology. For this purpose, the state should actively help in creating infrastructure for this training and its financing (Jhabwala and Sinha, 2002). Women's cooperatives *a la* SEWA and unionization, pressure on the state to implement Minimum Wages Acts and provide social security to women workers in agriculture, construction and small-scale industry, with the active cooperation of NGOs, would help in breaking the logjam. Technological change also needs to be modulated, so as to cause minimum unemployment. Simultaneously, a sustained campaign would have to be launched against the patriarchal system for its discrimination against women.

We noted in our introductory paras that globalization is a very uneven process with benefits and losses distributed unequally. In this process, investment resources, growth and modern technology get concentrated in a few countries (like North America, Europe, Japan and East Asian newly industrializing countries. A majority of developing countries are excluded from the process or participate in it in marginal ways that are often detrimental to their interests. Nationally, the globalization and liberalization have caused increasing inequality in employment opportunities, with the economic opportunities created being highly unequal. The better-endowed, with better access to skills, to markets, with more resources or with better international links, have been able to benefit. Women from upper income groups, with better education and skills have now better access to quality as well as opportunities for employment. With rising social services expenditure by governments after 2004–05, economic opportunities have been rising.

Employment opportunities increase with the opening of new markets or expansion of existing markets. For example, in the crafts sector, now directly linking the big traditional rural economy with the distant metropolitan and global markets, the number of workers increased sharply from 48.25 lakh in 1991–92 to 81.05 lakh in 1997–98. Further, with male participation in crafts slowly declining, female participation has been rising, particularly in rural home-based crafts sector. Women have also started entering into this sector traditionally considered male bastions such as stone carving, metal work and wood work. However, average daily earnings of women crafts workers are low, almost half of those paid to male workers.

Another area where opportunities have been expanding, especially for women, is the services sector. Personal services, health services, dairy sector, manufacture of garments and associated work are areas where employment opportunities for women have been expanding, especially with the extension of credit to women workers. However, in most of these sectors, women workers are paid less than men, and in many cases, much below the prescribed minimum wages. Besides gender discrimination in wage differentials there is also discrimination in access to higher positions and promotions.

Another sub-sector where women from urban areas are doing well is information technology. India's IT sector, at present, is doing remarkably well over the past two decades and has good potential for development in the future too.

Women, especially in white-collar jobs in the urban areas, have also benefited from the expansion of financial, banking and entertainment industries in the private sector. There is also marked presence of women in the highly paid professional and technical jobs in the private sector. In sharp contrast, poorly educated urban women's job opportunities are getting concentrated in domestic sector alone.

With the education facilities expanding in rural areas in late 80s and early 90s, rural women also got job opportunities within rural areas. However, with the cutback in public expenditure in the 90s, these opportunities dried up. As noted earlier, these have again risen only after 2004–05.

Women's handicaps on the supply side are too well known and also of long standing – a majority of them are without any educational qualifications, even literacy. During the six years ending 1993–94, unemployment rates among rural women with middle level and secondary education did fall and might have persuaded parents of girls to change their attitude to girls' education. A withdrawal of public support at this juncture may, however, put the clock back.

Other constraints on the supply side, in both rural and urban areas, which women workers suffer from, are:

(i) Women self-employed workers are not decision-makers or independent agents, but only unpaid workers in family enterprises.

(ii) The controls and bindings are put on them by their families under sanctions from the entire society and even the state. Child marriage is still being condoned by the administration. Families seldom give women a choice about where and when to work. The heads of the households have full authority to decide on how to use labour of their family women, with nowhere to appeal against such decisions.

(iii) The general assumption is that women are supplementary earners of their families, hence it is claimed that they do not need or deserve higher wages. Both the employers who are generally males and the male-dominated trade unions subscribe to the myth which implies that there is a marked bias against them.

(iv) Women, especially during their reproductive period, need frequent breaks due to child birth and care of newly born children and other family responsibilities.

(v) Family responsibilities and social constraints are a handicap on their mobility. Even salaried women employees, quite often, refuse promotion, if it involves moving away from family.

These constraints oblige women to choose specific jobs because these jobs are easy to combine with their family duties and/or allow interruptions in their careers. It is widely accepted that women suffer greater irregularity and intermittence of employment.

Notes

1. SNA activities are activities covered in the system of National Accounts and falling within the SNA Production Boundary.
2. Extended SNA activities are activities falling outside the SNA Production Boundary but in the General Production Boundary, consisting mainly of unpaid services.

References

Chadha, G.K. and P.P. Sahu (2002) 'Post-Reform Setbacks in Rural Employment: Issues that Need Further Scrutiny', *EPW*, 38 (21).

Chakravarty, Sanyukta and D. Sarkar (2011) 'Gender-earning Differentials in Flower-trading Market in West Bengal', *Indian Journal of Agricultural Economics*, 56(1).

Chandrasekhar, C.P. and Jayati Ghosh (2011) 'Deciphering Employment Trend', *The Hindu-Business Line*, July 21.

—— HDR (2011) 'Ranks India 129th Out of 146 Countries on the Gender Inequality Index', *The Hindu-Business Line*, November 3.

Economic Survey (2010–11). 'Human Development, Equity and Environment, HDR and HDI (2011)', Ch. 12, Government of India, Oxford University Press.

Government of India (2001) Task Force on Empioyment Opportunities – Report.

Hirway, Indira (2002) 'Employment and Unemployment Situation in 1990s: How Good are NSS Data?', *EPW*, 37(21).

Jhabvala, Renana and Shalini Sinha (2002) 'Liberalisation and the Women Worker', *EPW*, 37 (21).

Khor, Martin (2001) *Rethinking Globalisation*, Books for Change, Bangalore.

Mehta, Nira (2010) 'Female Employment in India: Trends and Underlying Processes in the Era of Reforms', Working Paper No. 3, Sardar Patel Insitute of Economic and Social Research, Ahmedabad.

Mitra, Arup (2010) 'Changing Labour Market and Women Employment', Survey Report, Asian Productivity Organisation (APO).

Planning Commission (2002), Special Group on Targeting Ten Million Employment Opportunities Per Year – Report.

Saxena, N.C., Chairman, Expert Group for Methodology for BPL Census in Rural Areas.

Tendulkar Panel on Methodology for Estimating Poverty.

UNDP (2010) Human Development Report, 2010.

Vepa, Swarna S. (2009) Book Review: *Bearing the Brunt, Impact of Rural Development on Women*, Sage Publications.

7

Development, Deprivation and Gender Equality

The Context of Kumaon Hills

M.P. DUBE

Development became the dominant global agenda in 1944 when representatives of 44 countries met at Bretton Woods and resolved to reconstruct Europe after World War II. It is very difficult to conceptualize development. The concept of development reflects a particular set of social and political values. 'Development' can be conceived only within an ideological framework. Different people use 'development' in different senses. It is highly ideologically loaded; it means different things to different people. Some see it in terms of a purposive and planned project; others prefer to talk of processes of social transformation. Some define it as the enhancement of individual choice; others see it as the equalizing of opportunities; still others see it as redistributive justice. Some emphasize ends, others means; and still others focus on the interrelationship between ends and means (Kabeer, 1994).

In a survey from the mid-1980s, 72 different meanings of the term were registered (Riggs). There is, therefore, no consensus on a particular definition of the term. At the most a working definition can be given of the term 'development'. It refers to a process in which resources are put to better use – in a country, a region, or a sector of society (like industry or agriculture). The resources in question include natural resources, technology and capital – and human labour, planning and co-operative capacity too. In other words, development is advances in economic and cultural progress, and in the quality of everyday life for most people; it is an increase in the availability and widening of the distribution of the basic life-sustaining goods; and, it relates to the expansion of the range of economic and social choices available to individuals and the nation. Thus, development aims to improve human well-being and to enable human beings to achieve their potential.

As early as 1943, Polish-born economist Paul Rosenstein-Rodan became a prominent spokesman for massive industrial development as the way to growth and progress for backward areas. In 1957, he expanded this argument further into a theory of the 'big push' as a pre-condition for growth. Big push is just like an aeroplane's take-off critical ground speed. He said backward areas were generally characterized by low income, low purchasing power, unemployment, and underdevelopment. It necessitates state involvement in education of workforce and in planning and organizing of large-scale investment programmes. Later on, Ragnar Nurkse took over and further developed many of Rodan's major points.

Since the Second World War, the core ideas and assumptions of the dominant view of development have been the possibility of unlimited economic growth. These believed that economies would reach a 'take-off' point and thereafter wealth would trickle down to those at the bottom; that 'western' model and knowledge was superior; that the process would ultimately benefit everyone; there was also belief in domination and exploitation of nature. Development was measured by economic growth, domestic product (GDP) per capita income, industrialization, including of agriculture, migration of labour to industrial areas, division of labour, etc.

During the 1970s, focus shifted to life expectancy, infant mortality reduction, and increase in literacy. It aimed to increase the productivity of the assets owned by the poor; and to provide for the old, sick, children outside the family, and others unable to earn. However, during the 1970s and 1980s, human rights became one of the main concerns of development. Later this was broadened to include enhancement of civil society, effective governance, and democracy.

An alternative view of development gradually put forward a serious challenge before mainstream development paradigm thinking during 1980s and onward. It is concerned mainly with entitlement and distribution. Those who advocate an alternative approach therefore place more emphasis on the pattern of distribution of gains within global society and within individual states. The alternative conception of development argued that the process of development should be (Baylis and Smith, 1997: 458)

need-oriented (material and non-material);
endogenous (coming from within a society);
self-restraint (in terms of human, natural and cultural resources);
ecologically sound; and
based on structural transformations (of economy, society, power relations)

Thus, development makes advances in economic and cultural progress, and in the quality of everyday life for most people; it is an increase in the availability and widening of the distribution of the basic life-sustaining goods; and it relates to the expansion of the range of economic and social choices available to individuals and the nation. The terminology of alternative conceptions of development has, however, been incorporated to a limited degree into the mainstream: 'sustainable development' or 'growth with greener face' are the buzz words (Baylis and Smith, 1997). Development is sustainable when economic and social development meets the needs of the present without compromizing the ability of future generations to meet their own needs. It relates to programmes which maintain an appropriate balance between economic development, social development and environmental protection.

A very striking feature of alternative model of development is that it ensures visibility of women. This is reflected in the shift from 'development' to 'women in development' to 'women, environment and development'. During 1970s, there was a shift from women being invisible or appearing only as housewives and mothers, relegated to a privatized notion of reproduction, to seeing them as producers and economic actors – as agents of development. Ester Boserup rightly says that development policies that failed to include women or to study their roles were doomed to failure.

The subordination that women experience at a daily level, regardless of the class they might belong to, takes various forms – discrimination, disregard, insult, control exploitation, oppression, violence – within the family, at the place of work, in society. We see that son preference, discrimination against girls in food distribution, burden of household work on women and young girls, lack of educational opportunities for girls, lack of freedom and mobility for girls, wife-battering, male control over women and girls, sexual harassment at work, lack of inheritance and property rights for women, male control over women's bodies and sexuality, and no control over fertility or reproductive rights are common in India, irrespective of class, caste and region.

There is worldwide gender-based division of household labour. The work assigned to a gender is arbitrary; that is any given task can be considered women's work in some cultures and men's work in others. But one thing usually in practice everywhere is that the tasks assigned to women are much more time consuming than those assigned to men. This has been called by some as a patriarchal economy, where household women provide many more of the goods and services needed by household men than vice versa. Men's time is freed up from household tasks to go out and earn income in the economy beyond the household, to formally or informally govern the public sphere of the larger community, to engage in leisure activities or to do all three. Because men have more authority in the larger community, and because most of the income available to the household comes to the men, who thus control the financial resources, the gender division of labour is an unequal one. It establishes and perpetuates the subordination of women to men in the society (p. 194).

Ester Boserup, in his classic work *Women's Role in Economic Development*, maintained that in some cases, development results in even 'greater disempowerment of women, expanding men's control over resources and shrinking even those spheres of domestic life where women's influence was traditionally more important. Men leave their subsistence work in the farm fields of the household economy to take up education and paid employment in the state or private sectors of the modernizing economy. They leave more of their former household work to women, and their new paid employment displaces traditional informal sector work that used to provide some income to women. This process is summed up by Maria Mies under the concept of 'housewifization'. However, sometimes development empowers women and increases gender equity.

Women's subordination is rooted in patriarchy. Patriarchy is both a state of affairs (i.e., men control social institutions) and an ideology (embedded in languages). Kate Millett's *Sexual Politics* (1970) was a landmark in the study of patriarchy. Questions of gender, the nature of the family and the process of socialization were highlighted in understanding the nature of male supremacy. For Millett, the political relationship between the sexes was central to patriarchy, and male power was expressed and contained in the sexual act itself.

Gerda Lerner (1986) makes a telling point:

> Men and women live on a stage, on which they act out their assigned roles, equal in importance. The play cannot go on without both kinds of performers. Neither of them 'contributes' more or less to the whole; neither is marginal or dispensable. But the stage set is conceived, painted, defined by men. Men have written the play, have directed the show, interpreted the meanings of action. They have assigned themselves the most interesting, most heroic parts, giving women the supporting roles.

Thus, development needs shifts in consciousness and shifts in strategy. It leads to empowerment of women only when its goal is gender equity. Empowerment of women is generally defined as a woman's increased voice in the everyday decisions that shape her life, especially decisions regarding family formation and family planning; a woman's right to participate equally in the economic, civil and political life of the community and the nation; and a woman's increased experience of the social-psychological dimensions of empowerment, increased economy, and self-esteem, along with decreased dependence, fatalism and passivity.

Kumaon is a region in Uttarakhand whose political economy has distinctive features. It is a land of snow-capped mountains, high hills, perennial rivers and nature-gifted forests. Its history, culture and social anthropology has marked dissimilarity with that of the plains of UP. Its more than 60 per cent of the area is either forests or mountains. The cultivable area forms only a small proportion of the total area of which nearly 11 per cent is arable. People of the region have immense fortitude and endurance. They are known for their bravery and courage in the battlefield, their integrity and honesty. Though several Chief Ministers and important leaders belonged to this region, G.B. Pant, followed by K.C. Pant and N.D. Tewari, yet the region could not come out of backwardness; the region is steeped in poverty and backwardness.

Women are overworked and underpaid throughout the world. Woman labour accounts for two-thirds of the world's work hours, yet it earns only 10 per cent of the property (UN, 1980); whereas in Kumaon hills woman labour accounts for three-fourths of the work hours. Here also their subordination is rooted in patriarchal set-up. Dominated by men and guided by traditions, women in hills live a very hard life. A woman has to do even some of those productive works that belong to male domain in planes. Her day is typical. She rises at 4 a.m. She cleans the house, washes clothes, prepares the meal for her husband and children, and after feeding cattle and milking, leaves for the fields at 8 a.m. She works there until 6 p.m., in the meantime nursing the small children she took with her. On her way back home, she collects fuelwood and, if necessary, drinking water. She cooks the evening meal, cares for the children and tends to the animals. At about 10 p.m. she goes to bed. She is the backbone of the family economy. The survival tasks, work in the household, and income generation are the three areas of her productive work.

Women grow the food crops, provide water, gather fuel and perform most of the other work which sustains the family. Most of the subsidiary agricultural work is done by women; they are responsible for sowing, weeding, crop maintenance and harvesting. At the same time activities in the home are almost exclusively the responsibility of women, yet women are often the last in the family who may eat, and they consume less than the other family members do. Women contribute substantially to the family budget through income generating activities – food processing, trading of agricultural product and the production of handicrafts.

Generally, steep footpaths connect villages to the roads; some villagers have to walk several days on foot to reach the nearest bus station. The terraced village fields yield hardly enough food to provide an average family's requirement for six months, so they migrate to the cities in search of jobs. Women bear the multiple burdens of tending the fields and domestic animals and carrying out their normal domestic chores. The drudgery of collecting fuel fodder and fibre takes its toll on Kumaoni women: their average life expectancy is 45 years, compared to 52 years of men. They labour sometimes more than 10 hours daily to collect the resources they need, primarily from the forest. As wood supplies become scarce, women walk substantially longer distances and spend more time and energy in fetching firewood. In a study on rural energy and the position of women, Irene Tinker concludes that 'the real energy crisis is a lack of women's time'. In the foothills of the Himalayas, just a generation ago the gathering of firewood and fodder took no more than 2 hours; now it takes a whole day and involves walking through difficult terrain. Today health hazards are also increasing. Wood and other biomass burning cause respiratory and eye diseases, which are so abundant among Kumaoni women and children. Exposure brings acute bronchitis, pneumonia and death where respiratory defences are impaired. Where emissions contain high concentration of carcinogens, nasopharyngeal cancer is common among young women who have been exposed since infancy. Development intervention in agriculture sector has made women over-burdened. A woman hardly gets time for herself.

Their life of drudgery, hardship and degradation cuts across caste and communities, and spans the entire region. Their living conditions can be improved only when they could be able to take decisions about themselves and actively participate in the decisions about the family, and get politically empowered. In a democratic system, empowerment is possible only by ensuring that women reach positions of decision-making. This can be achieved through their participation in the political process and ensuring that they get adequate representation from the grassroots upwards.

Women's empowerment demands a multi-pronged strategy: at a personal level its concern is women's self-confidence and sense of personal potency; at a higher political level, women's capacity to make public decisions and control resources. By enabling the women to analyse their own realities and thus influence development priorities, they would have a greater ability (more confidence and skills) to continue acting in their own interests. Empowerment is complex and carries an inherent contradiction, namely, the notion that 'some can act on others to give them power or enable them to realize their own potential'. If power is essentially about the 'transformative capacity of people or groups', then empowerment involves increasing people's capacity to transform their lives. It is more than inviting people to partake in needs assessment or a decision-making process. Empowerment is enabling to understand the reality of their situation, reflect on the factors shaping that situation and most critically, take steps to effect changes to improve it. As a result, it must include processes that lead the individual or group to perceive itself as able to occupy a decision-making space. It is enhancement of socio-political and economic potential and status of women. By implication, an empowerment focus involves the radical alteration of the structures which reproduce women's subordinate position as a gender. Along with sensitization of men, women's empowerment must focus on ability, willingness and opportunity to women for development. Two strategies can be adopted for empowering women: (a) of working with women in separate groups to improve their skills, increase their confidence and help them identify their own needs and priorities, and (b) working to sensitize men and change their attitudes

Development intervention can promote the well-being of the tribal societies when they are planned carefully keeping in view the cultural values, local beliefs, customs and traditions. There is, therefore, a need to take cognizance of the traditional values and practices of tribals while formulating schemes for their development. Effective development requires the full integration of tribal women in the development process as both agents and beneficiaries. Development agencies should take full cognizance of tribal women as a development resource. Changing tribal women's awareness about the political process will indeed require a virtual revolution. They need better access to human capital - education, skilled training, and extension advice; to factor markets - credit and landownership; to technology and raw materials; and to social organizations - membership to cooperatives, users' groups and village government.

The gender gap in command over property is a very important economic factor affecting women's situation. Arable land, a significant form of property, is a critical determinant of economic well-being, social status, and empowerment of rural women. But few women own land, fewer control it. It is fact of women's life that caught up in daily struggles for fuel, fodder, and wage, they have no time for anything else; women go about their daily chores in isolation, they are unable to share their experience of oppression with other women, and are, therefore, unable to tap their collective strength; they are alienated from decision-making, and even when they relate to government schemes, they do so as passive recipients.

In India, title to land is normally vested in men. Since the great majority of tribal people live in agrarian settings, this is a fundamental source of vulnerability for poor women. They often face more severe insecurities (for example, after the death of their husband). For preventing gender bias in land titling and promoting the rights of women, measures to be adopted are: making joint titling of land to couples mandatory; and fostering partnerships between government departments and NGOs that defend the rights of women - to increase women's awareness of their rights and support them in claiming title to land in the face of a possibly hostile bureaucracy or family.

Training is a dynamic and adaptable tool of interaction and a powerful means of bringing women into the process of development. Training can help to eliminate women's isolation and build confidence. Most of the existing training falls far short of these possibilities. Often the only training to which the women have access is in the so-called 'feminine' occupations of health, nutrition, sewing, handicrafts, childcare and home economics. These skills, necessary though they are, do not enable women to participate equally in development. They have to be helped to develop a capacity for income-earning, to be trained in leadership, decision-making and in new technologies.

Women play a very important role in integrating agriculture with animal husbandry. As a result of overwhelming reduction in grazing areas, women at some places have to walk 10–12 kms to fetch one headload of fodder. They leave for fodder collection in the early morning and return only in the late evening, all for a milk yield of 1–2 litres per day. Simply getting milk is not their sole concern, rather they are much more concerned about fertilizing their fields. Dung is composted and carried out to the fields by women. Under government schemes, loans are given for crossbred hybrid cattle but their adaptability to the local environment is very poor and due to inadequate feed quality, they are more vulnerable to diseases. In order to make such programmes successful, mechanisms should be evolved that address crucial related issues like fodder availability, management and care of livestock.

The development of women's dairy co-operatives is an appropriate mechanism to address women's needs as it is they who are engaged in a substantial part of dairying work. For organizing women's dairy co-operatives successfully, women should be paid twice daily, within 12 hours of the time. They should deliver milk to the society's collection centres, and the centres should be located in the villages where milk is produced. All the co-operative societies should be made up exclusively of villagers who supply milk and should be run entirely by villagers elected from among the society's members. The society should provide for hiring professional personnel to maintain accounts, ensure quality controls and efficiency in milk collection, manufacture and market milk products, and provide services for the co-operative's members for the growth of healthy and productive cattle. Care should be taken that co-operatives may not be converted into another means by which local elites solidify their power and control. The reluctance of bank officials to provide credit to poor women sometimes creates hurdles. Steps should be taken to provide easy loans to them. Generally, veterinary hospitals are located at Blocks. In addition to the cost of travelling, it means the loss of a day's wages.

Women, therefore, should be imparted training in livestock management and veterinary care. As para-vets, they should be trained in basic veterinary care, cattle physiology, animal care, feeding practices, etc.

Though women play a predominant role in agriculture and bear a disproportionately higher burden of farm production, they have been almost completely marginalized from extension service, training, technical information and access to productive resources. There is need to encourage the enrolment of women in agricultural universities. Extension services should focus on women. The aim should be to train and deploy female staff who would then act as a link in the dissemination of messages to other village women; the focus should be on giving them skill-oriented training in crop production, horticulture, post-harvest technologies, and depending on the requirements of the area, in daily management, poultry keeping and rearing other animals.

Provisions for easy access to credit facilities should be made for women. There are two main approaches to improving women's access to credit: fundamental change should be made in the banking system and a special women's credit fund should be established. The first approach would give banks more autonomy and responsibility and allow interest rates that would make it profitable to serve the rural poor. It would also necessarily enforce the repayment ethic by protecting the credit system from political pressures to write off loans to certain broad interest groups. Change would be needed in the concept and structure of the development programmes so that instead of a subsidized one-time dose of credit for those below the poverty line, there would be ongoing access to the formal financial system in return of repayment.

When agencies, government and non-government, make credit available to low-income tribal women, they can reduce the costs of delivery, greatly increase repayment rates, and substantially improve the well-being of poor families. Such credit would increase women's participation in decision-making, substantially improve household nutrition and raise aspirations for children's education. Therefore, focus should be on credit programmes which extend micro-capital to small-scale entrepreneurs.

Lending to the poor is an inherently risky business – high costs of operation and low repayment rates are common difficulties. There is, therefore, need to reduce transaction costs for both borrowers and the bank. The problem of filling out complicated forms, offering of collateral, investigating the credit-worthiness of each borrower can be handled by forming groups of borrowers which guarantee one another's loans; no one in the group may receive a second loan until all have repaid the first. Members of the group should be drawn from those in a similar socio-economic situation – social network or affinity groups. Sending a bank representative to meet with these groups, receiving their payments and disbursing new loans at one time and place may reduce costs. Or the borrowing group's representative may be sent to the bank to receive and to repay the loans. These groups should be given credit plus training, and assistance with marketing and supplies. However, a more sustainable, broadly replicable, and a long-term strategy of providing credit to the poor tribals does not lie only in trying to establish new banks, but also to recognize credit management groups as legitimate legal entities to whom full financial services could and should be extended. Mechanism should be evolved to make the poor more 'bank-friendly' and the banks more 'poor-friendly'. Tribals should be given organization skills needed to participate in the commercial banking sector.

Various legislations have curtailed access to forest areas, allowing only limited rights. Women's lack of awareness regarding what they can access and collect and the failure of the Forest Department to publicize people's rights have aggravated the situation and have resulted in the alienation of women. In Kumaon Hills, each household spends 6–10 hours every day on collecting fuel and fodder. This involves an uphill climb of nearly 5 kms with constant danger from wild animals. It also means harassment from forest officials who often demand bribes from the headloaders. Women should be organized in groups to deal with the issues, such as their alienation from the forest, harassment by the forest officials and other forest-related problems. A feeling should be generated that the forests belong to them and that they have rights in it. Forest Department should be made gender-sensitive. Women should be organized and trained in forest extension work, and awareness-generating training programmes should be conducted to make women the vanguard of forest protection. Tribal people on the fringes of forests should be encouraged to form village organizations to protect forests. The organizations might work with the state forest department, sharing the responsibilities and benefits of forest restoration, protection and management.

Horticultural development programmes and schemes should be implemented which are directly beneficial to women. Planting materials, plants and seeds, fertilizers and pesticides on subsidized rates should be supplied to small and marginal farmers of STs. As there is much scope for potato and vegetable cultivation in hills, subsidized seeds should be provided to vegetable and spice growers. At the same time, floriculture programmes should be popularized among women.

Generally, the cattle possessed by the hill people are of indigenous breeds, there is need for further improvement. Veterinary health services, breeding facilities in cattle and pig breeding farms should be expanded and improved. Sheep breeding farms and wool grading, marketing and health care, and Angora rabbit farms should be established in hills.

Intensive poultry development projects in hills can help in the economic uplift of women.

Hill women are more enterprising compared to their menfolk. While several men often waste their time in inconsequential pursuits like drinking and gambling, the women are more eager to make optimum utilization of their spare time in sericulture, mushroom cultivation, etc. Sericulture-related schemes would be very useful to them. Tropical tsar, oak tsar and silk mulberry production should be promoted for the benefit of women. The co-operative departments can revitalize the LAMPS for promoting credit and marketing facilities, including provision of consumer loans.

Wood, crop residues and dung are used as energy in hill areas. The burden of the decreasing availability of biomass fuels is borne disproportionately by women, particularly in rural areas where most of the fuel is gathered, either from forest, common lands, private farms or livestock, by them. Energy problem in hill areas can be tackled by popularizing the current interventions in the domestic energy sector that include introduction of non-conventional energy, improved cooking stoves, bio-gas plants and social forestry. The approach to social forestry should be directed towards not only achieving physical targets but also addressing sociological aspects and community participation. Targets should be to meet fuel, fodder and other bio-mass needs of the poor. The selection of the species to be planted should not be based on staff convenience, rather on the needs of the people. Non-browsable species that grow quickly and require little supervision should be discouraged.

In hills, water scarcity affects women much more harshly than it does men. As resources grow scarce, men invariably migrate to cities in search of work, leaving behind women who not only have to work harder to collect water, fuel and fodder, but also have to take on the additional responsibilities of the male members. Nearly 78 per cent of women spend four hours daily to fetch water, walking a minimum of 6 kms. Technology on rainwater harvesting from rooftops in the villages should be disseminated in hill areas. Water can be made available by using appropriate technology available on: (a) gravity flow streams for stream and spring water; (b) lift schemes for rivers, lakes, ponds, underground water channels, etc.; and (c) rain water collection schemes.

It is very common for women to suffer accidents or sustain injuries in the process of collecting minor forest products. Several women fall down from trees while plucking leaves or cutting twigs. Sometimes they become invalid, some even die a terrible death. Scarcity of water results in neglect of personal hygiene and causes disease and death. Sepsis, abortions, haemorrhage, toxaemia and anaemia account for the large majority of maternal deaths. A large number of maternal deaths are preventable, if attention is paid to three principal underlying conditions among women: poor nutrition and high and closely spaced fertility stretching from adolescence to menopause. It is suggested that teaching simple hygienic principles of clean hands, clean perineum and clean cord care can reduce the number of deaths from sepsis and neonatal tetanus. Moreover, adequate hospital facilities must be made available to villagers. There is need to develop female community-level health workers to reach women in the domestic setting. These workers need better training in the technical and the interpersonal aspects of their work. They also need more focused and clearly-defined job description, with a shift of emphasis from meeting targets and filling out registers to spending more time with clients during home visits. Concentrating on pregnant women and households where a child has just been born would reduce worker caseloads. Greater emphasis on reaching women in-groups would expand village coverage. Above all, health workers need to have the problem-solving skills, motivation and mandate to respond to women's specific health concerns, rather than to deliver Centrally-determined message and target-driven services. Under this approach, most health-care priorities would be determined locally by women users.

Little can rival female education as a means to weaken the inside-outside dichotomy and expand opportunities for women. School attendance familiarizes girls with non-family social settings and increases their skills and confidence to engage in public discourse. Literacy offers the possibility of almost unlimited exposure to new information and new ways of thinking. It leads to better hygiene, improved nutrition practices and greater effectiveness in caring for family health and seeking timely medical help. This results in better health status for women, improved maternal competence, and lower infant mortality. Female education can also mean delayed marriage, better knowledge of contraception and ways to obtain it, smaller desired family size and higher potential earnings which increase the opportunity costs of child-bearing. But the supposed beneficiaries rarely know about the various programmes and policies, including the relevant schemes and legislation for securing justice – social, economic and political. Efforts should be made to achieve 100 per cent literacy. There should be wider dissemination of information, which should be innovatively conceived and sensitively packaged and provided, through the help of the print and electronic media. At the same time, laws relating to rights and privileges of women should be included in a simplified form in the curriculum of higher and secondary-level classes.

More and more tailoring/sewing, knitting, carpet weaving, embroidery and handicraft training centres should be opened for the welfare of women. Mahila Mangal Dal can play a very important role in improving the quality of life. Village women should be assisted to form a

Mahila Mangal Dal in every village. At the same time, ICDS programmes, Anganwadi and, Balwadi programmes should be made much more extensive and intensive so as to benefit the larger section of society.

Rampant corruption and irresponsibility can be seen among the rank and file of employees. Sometimes project officials sanction and release grants to those beneficiaries only who agree to pay them a part of it as commission or bribe. In some cases this exceeds 50 per cent of the total grant. Access to information would enable people to hold their civil servants and politicians accountable. If information on budgets and on the use of funds is made available in newspapers and other information sources, people might hold their providers accountable for results. Legally-mandated dissemination of information would ensure public accountability and that in turn would help to reduce inefficiency and corruption.

For women to become partners in political leadership, they must move from the prevailing 'tokenism' to critical numbers at all decision-making levels of governance. The reservation for women should be extended to all representative bodies. Now, the 73rd amendment has made panchayats mandatory. It will lead to the realization of democracy at the grassroots level. There is provision for reservation for women in the local bodies. Though initially there may remain certain shortcomings in their implementation, there may also happen cases of proxy representation but surely and steadily it will lead to social revolution, towards women's empowerment. It is recommended that there should be enough devolution of powers in the matters that come in the purview of local bodies. The focus should be to refine the institution of Panchayati Raj, to strengthen it so that policy and budget blueprints arrive from down there to governments in state capitals, and not in the reverse order. Women should be imparted education, training and given access to information so that they could perform better in discharging the developmental functions of PRIs. Women should be helped to identify their more recurring problems. There is need to increase their self-esteem and make them understand the power that they can wield and the changes they can bring about in the lives of other women.

Poor hill people are exposed to a wide array of risks that make them vulnerable to income shocks and losses of well-being. And because shocks do not affect all members of tribal households equally, with women and children frequently the most at risk, inadequate risk management can cause long-term harm to girl children through malnourishment, child labour and loss of schooling. Integral to any poverty-reduction strategy should thus be measures to prevent and manage economic crises and natural disasters – and to establish safety nets, with ensured financing, to help women cope when these adverse shocks do occur.

Social norms and networks is a key form of capital that people can use to move out of poverty. Bonding and bridging social capital in local organizations is necessary for development. However, supplemented with linking social capital, these may lead to long-term development. External support from NGOs can help create social capital that increases the voice and economic opportunities of the poor people. This support is most effective when it is sustained over time, emphasizes capacity building, and is based on sensitive understanding of the local conditions and a relationship of trust and partnership. The focus, therefore, should be on social capital, bonding, bridging and linking.[1]

A promising strategy for new initiatives is the organization of women into groups. Group formation is particularly powerful in weakening the inside-outside dichotomy. It provides women a legitimate forum beyond the private domestic sphere and a more audible voice in demanding services and inputs. Membership in a group can initially substitute for the individual woman's lack of bureaucratic know-how and her unfamiliarity with public discourse. It permits a gradual building of her capacity to interact effectively with public, non-kin systems and with structures that increasingly attempt to redistribute economic opportunity in contemporary India. Most important groups can transform women from beneficiaries, who must be grateful for largesse, into clients with long-term reciprocal relationships with the institutions that serve them. Thus, greater women's freedom, higher levels of material advancement, improved health of women, stronger social organization, and an overall system of entitlement protection operate synergistically to increase tribal women's participation in the developmental process.

References

Altekar, A.S. (1956) *The Position of Women in Hindu Civilisation*, New Delhi: Motilal Banarsidass Publishers, 62–63.

Aryal, M. (1994a) 'Axing Chipko', *Himal*, 7(1): 8–23.

Atkinson, E.T. (1884) *The Himalayan Gazetteer: Kumaon Hills*, Vol. II, Dehradun: Trishul Publications, 624–27.

Bascom, W.R. (1981) *Four Functions of Folklore in Contributions to Folkloristics*, Meerut: Archana Publications, 40–44.

Baylis, J. and Steve Smith (1997) *Globalisation of World Politics*, Oxford: Oxford University Press, 451–52.

Beteille, Andre (1960) 'The Definition of Tribe', *Seminar*, October 14.

Census of India (1991).

Chakravarti, Uma (1993) 'Conceptualising Brahmanical Patriarchy in Early India: Gender, Caste, Class and State', *Economic and Political Weekly*, 28, April 3.

Desai, Neera (1986) 'Changing Status of Women: Policies and Problems', in A. Gupta (ed.), *Woman and Society*, New Delhi: Criterion Publishers, 72.

Dhar, T.N. and C.S. Shastri (1988) 'Industrial Development in Kumaon: Status and Possibilities', in K.S. Valdiya (ed.), *Kumaon: Land and People*, Nainital: Gyanodaya Prakashan, 312.

Dorchner, J.P. (1983) *Alcohol Consumption in a Village in North India*, Ann Arbor, MI: UMI Research Press, 96–98.

Elwin, Verrier (1994) *The Aboriginals*, London: Oxford University Press, 8.

Fernandes, Frank (1990) quoted by Surjit Sinha 'Rethinking about Tribes and Indian Civilization', in Buddhadeb Chaudhury (ed.), *Tribal Development in India*, New Delhi: Inter-India Publications.

Gupta, M.L. Chen and T.N. Krishnan (eds.) (1995) *Women's Health in India: Risk and Vulnerability*, Bombay: Oxford University Press, 60.

Hall, Stuart (1982) 'Popular Culture and the State', in Tonny Bennett et al. (eds.), *Popular Culture and Social Relations*, Part-I, London: Methuen, 7–9.

Hoon, Vineeta (1996) *Living on the Move*, New Delhi: Sage Publications, 66–67.

Huntington, S.P. (1968) *Political Order in Changing Societies*, New Haven: Yale University Press, 79–83.

Jetley, Surinder (1987) 'Impact of Male Migration on Rural Females', *Economic and Political Weekly*, 22(44).

Kabeer, Naila (1994) *Reversed Realities: Gender Hierarchies in Development Thought*, UK: Verso.

Kaira, Savitri (1989) 'Swatantra Andolan mein Kumaon ki Mahilaon ka Yogdan', Ph.D Dissertation, Kumaon University.

Khetwal, N. (1978) 'Impact of Community Development Programme on Agricultural Development in Kumaon Region', Ph.D Thesis, Kumaon University, 482–83.

Krishnamurthy, Sunanda (1988) 'Wage Differentials in Agriculture by Caste, Sex and Operation', *Economic and Political Weekly*, December 10, LXIII(50): 205–7.

Lerner, Gerda (1986) *The Creation of Patriarchy*, New York: Oxford University Press.

Mann, K. (1998) 'Status and Problems of Tribal Women in Uttar Pradesh', in H.S. Saksena et al. (eds.), *Perspectives in Tribal Development*, Lucknow: Ethnographic and Folk Culture Society, 110–12.

Manohar, Sujata (1975) 'Property Law and Women', *Bhavan's Journal*, June 8, 21(23): 61–66.

Martinussen, John (1997) *Society, State and Market*, London: Zed Books.

Melkania, N.P. and B.N. Johri (1988) 'State of Forests in Kumaon and Their Regeneration', in K.S. Valdiya (ed.), op. cit., 244.

Pande, B.D. (1937) *Kumaon Ka Itihas*, Almora: Shakti Press, 360–85.

Pande, G.C. (1988) 'Agrarian Scenario of Kumaon', in K.S. Valdiya (ed.), op. cit., 281.

—— (1988) 'Role and Status of Women in Kumaon', in K.S. Valdiya (ed.), op. cit., 167.

Pant, S.D. (1935) *The Social Economy of the Himalayas*, London: George Allen and Unwin, 216.

Pathak, Shekhar (ed.) (1985) 'Nasha ek Shadyantra', *Pahar Pustika*.

—— (1992) 'Uttarakhand Main Samajik Andolano ki Rooprekha', *Pahar Pustika*, 3.

Pye, Lucian (1966) *Aspects of Political Development*, Boston: Little Brown and Co., 31–67.

Roberts, G. (1984) *Questioning Development*, London: Returned Volunteer Action.

Sanwal, B.D. (1969) *The Report of Tarai Lands Committee*.

Shah, S.L. (1988) 'Agriculture, Horticulture and Animal Husbandry', in K.S. Valdiya (ed.), op. cit., 269.

Singh, J.S. et al. (1984) 'Man and Forests: A Central Himalayan Case Study', *Ambio*, 13(2): 80–87.

Singh, A.K., J.S. Sharma and D.K. Singh (1988) 'Participation of Rural Women in Agriculture in the Hills of Uttar Pradesh', *Journal of Rural Development*, 7(3): 289–97.

Tornquist, Olle (1999) *Politics and Development*, London: Sage Publications, 47–117.

UNDP (1996–2006) *Human Development Reports*, New York: Oxford University Press.

UNESCO (1980) *Division for Economic and Social Information Report*, 23.

Wallby, Sylvia (1990) *Theorizing Patriarchy*, Oxford: Basil Blackwell, 26.

Wedley, Susan (1977) 'Woman and the Hindu Tradition', *Signs*, Autumn 3(1): 113–25.

World Development Reports (1996–2006) Oxford University Press for the World Bank.

8

Development and Women's Political Participation

Challenges and Strategies

LEELA YADAVA

Human development has moved centre stage in the global development debate, where development is considered to be, more than an increased access to resources and improved welfare, a process by which these benefits are obtained and sustained. It entails members of the target group being involved as participants in the development process. They should not be passive beneficiaries of projected outcomes, but should improve their own capacity to recognize and overcome their own problems by being involved in the development process. This has brought into prominence the women issue, for, it is said that 'if you want to judge the level of development of a country, look at the position of women in that country'. Consequently, the roles played by women in society and their contribution as human resource are slowly becoming visible. The involvement of women in the development and political decision-making process has also been advocated by social and political thinkers, according to James Mill the condition of women in a society is an index of that society's place in civilization.[1] But an analysis of the condition of women in India shows that there is gender inequality, a few women have also been inducted into the political process but their impact has been negligible. The scales of gender equality are out of balance, the side marked women is weighed down with responsibility, while the side marked man rides high with power.[2] India ranks 115th among the 162 countries in terms of gender development. To overcome this discrimination, it is necessary to induct a critical mass of women in the decision-making process. The gender gap points to the need to investigate as to why women need to actively engage in politics? Why there is lack of political participation of women in India? Why so few women are a part of the decision-making process? and to device strategies to promote their participation.

Women form a major chunk of the society. Despite the rights granted to them by the Constitution and laws, the gender bias continues. This is because they encounter many obstacles in the system and decision-making process due to traditions, prejudices and social and economic conditions. Thus, they remain a disadvantaged and discriminated group limited to the private realm of their homes. Politics and governance is regarded as a man's affair and political activity as a masculine activity. The only way to overcome this is to develop gender sensitivity in the system of governance, which can only be achieved by increasing the participation of women. The lack of women participation is indicative of the malfunctioning of the system of governance which does not fully represent the interests of the society. Consequently, the policy-making process too is not gender sensitive, the subordination of women has also affected the developmental process negatively. This aspect has been highlighted by the Nairobi Forward Looking Strategies, adopted in the Third World Conference on Women in 1985. It stresses that 'women, by virtue of their gender, experience discrimination in terms of equal access to the power structure that controls society and determines development issues and peace initiatives.'[3] The UNDP Report of 1995 shows that in no society do women enjoy the same opportunities as men. It also demonstrated that successful initiatives for removing gender inequalities do not depend on the wealth of nations. It has been observed that even though some countries have set targets for women's representation in national governmental structures, these often do not have significant impact elsewhere in governance.[4] Due to the gender imbalances women find it difficult to break the glass ceiling; thus, the less-than-equal status of women to men prevails.

Political Participation

The political status of women in any society can be defined not only as equality and freedom with which they share power with men, but also the value that society places on the role of women in politics. The Constitution of India promised 'equality of status and opportunity'[5] on the premise that the health of a system requires active participation by all segments of society.

But, the problem is that the concept of equality is understood as 'sameness'. This approach does not take into consideration the social and economic disadvantages that produce a set of differences between men and women. The demand for women's participation in governance on an equal footing with men is not new; it dates back to the 4th century BC, when women wielded considerable political power. For instance, classical philosopher Plato was no democrat, but his experience led him to conclude that intelligence and ethics were not limited to one class, ethnicity or gender. He believed passionately that education could cultivate these qualities in individuals and those who benefit from education could and should govern others, his ideal polity was a benevolent meritocracy.[6] The Indian epics too point to the effective role of women in decision-making. Indian women also actively participated in the political field during the freedom struggle.[7] Raja Ram Mohan Roy exploded the myth of male superiority and propagated equal opportunities for women by stressing, through a comparative study of the qualities of both the sexes, that women in no way were inferior, rather they were superior to men.[8] J.L. Nehru, in 1928, had stated that 'if we are to judge India today, we shall have to judge her by her women. The future that we build will also be judged by the position of women in India.'[9] Therefore, it is necessary to promote political participation of women, this is the realm in which mainstream decisions are made and here there is a need for providing a women perspective to policies which can be done only by women. Although women were in the forefront of various agitations and movements in the post-Independence era too, yet they found it difficult to make the transition from agitation politics to electoral politics which is predominately male dominated. To meet the needs of women effectively, women must be directly represented as a group in the political process, as the male-dominated political system often reflects male biases, in terms of policy and practices and does not really serve the needs of men and women equally.[10] Women's participation in decision-making plays a crucial role in the process of enhancing women's participation in public life and their overall development, yet women are largely unrepresented/under represented at most levels of the government, especially in ministerial and other executive bodies. The Committee on Status of Women in India points out that 'although women participate in the political process, yet their impact on sharing of basic rights with men has been negligible because of inadequate attention paid to their political education and mobilization by political parties.[11] Thus their participation in terms of legislative or decision-making bodies is low.

History shows that the modern era saw a disenfranchisement of women and the dominance of men in the public and private realm. It was only in 1970s that the movement for gender equality took force after the 1975 World Conference on Women held at Mexico. With this women realized that through the socialization process over the years, they had been rendered second-class citizens. This resulted in the movement for women rights and demand for gender parity in governance. Women have simply not been getting the kind of governance they deserve. Delhi has a woman chief minister, yet it is the most unsafe place for women. All this is because India does not have enough women in decision-making and in the political process. A few women here and there cannot make much of a difference.[12] Women's equal access to, and full participation in, governance was emphasized in the Platform for Action. It was stressed that for effective good governance, harmony must be maintained in the society. The policies should ensure that the interests of the maximum number in the system are served.[13] To realize these interests it is necessary that there is participation of these sections in governance, but it has been observed that they largely remain inactive and indifferent towards politics. This situation exists despite the fact that statistics show that they form a large part of the electorate. Women, who constitute nearly half the population, continue to be grossly under-represented in the Parliament and State Assemblies. They also continue to be marginalized in most of the prominent political parties in terms of seat allotments in elections and also within the party structure and hierarchy. Women have not moved in significant numbers beyond the ballot box into legislatures; besides, their participation as legislative elites too is remarkably low.[14] In a democratic system the legislators constitute the key elite of the society which plays an important role in the political and socio-economic development of a country. In this context the role of women as agents of socio-economic and political change becomes all the more crucial.[15] Unless women become active participants in the political process at all levels, they will remain passive observers being 'acted upon' rather than 'acting on' and will never achieve empowerment, which has been recognized as a necessary condition for achieving the goal of Human Development, which is central to the 'Global Development Debate.'[16]

Empowerment is about power and politics – and politics is the field where power is negotiated; thus, achieving empowerment requires women to operate in the field of politics, especially in the decision-making arena. There is a growing awareness that since governments matter, women must be a part of them. This awareness was also reflected in the 'Platform for Action' developed at the 1995 World Conference on Women in Beijing, of which one of the goals was to increase women's participation in political institutions. Women's claims on the political arena is not only to share power, but to change the nature of power; not just to govern, but to change the nature of governance. Empowerment of women can be meaningful only by enhancing the political ideological context of development. To be effective players in the distribution of power and resources, women have to stake their claim not only in the state's munificence, but also on state power and as a result, there is a demand for positive discrimination. In a developing country like India, the role of the legislative elite is very significant; they act as a catalyst in development, as they perform a crucial role in the formulation of the policies and programmes of the nation. In this process, the role of women legislative elites as agents of socio-economic and political change is all the more crucial.

The demand for women representation is partly based on the 1970s research conducted in the US on women participation in business. It was shown that within a decision-making body, 30 per cent representation by minorities could significantly influence the majority verdict. Drude Dehlerup of University of Stockholm extended these findings to women reservation in politics. She observed that quotas are necessary to jump start the process of equality. Representation is, thus, necessary as women represent half the population and, therefore, have a right to half the seats and Parliament decisions that affect their lives; women have different social and biological experiences that ought to be represented; women and men have partly conflicting interests; women in power position can inspire other women.[17]

In 1988, the National Perspective Plan for Women also suggested that a 30 per cent quota for women be introduced at all levels of elected bodies.[18] The demand for greater representation of women in political institutions in India was taken up seriously after the Committee on the Status of Women, in its report, suggested that women's participation especially at the grassroots level be increased through a policy of reservation. This was actualized through the 73rd and 74th amendments to the Indian Constitution which was hailed as a positive step towards ensuring women's equal access and participation in political power structure at the grassroots level. These amendments provided for 33 per cent of elected seats for women at the level of local governance. The issue of women participation in local-level politics may be viewed from the general understanding that women are subjugated in many ways and such state of subordination has affected the development process negatively. The subsequent participation of women on these seats has dispelled doubts about their functioning; the success stories of women sarpanches are many. The participation of women indicates that they are ready to avail of the opportunities and to some extent have also changed the quality, content and nature of leadership for development.[19] They have shown their potential to wield power effectively at the village level and challenge feudal traditions.[20] However, the number of women representatives in the Parliament, though steadily increasing, continues to be very low, which is obvious from the following table:

Representation of Women in 1st to 15th Lok Sabha

Lok Sabha	*Total no. of seats (Elections Held)*	*No. of women Members who won*	*% of Total*
First (1952)	489	22	4.4
Second (1957)	494	27	5.4
Third (1962)	494	34	6.7
Fourth (1967)	523	31	5.9
Fifth (1971)	521	22	4.2
Sixth (1977)	544	19	3.4
Seventh (1980)	544	28	5.1
Eighth (1984)	544	44	8.1
Ninth (1989)	529	28	5.3
Tenth (1991)	505	36	7.0
Eleventh (1996)	541	40*	7.4
Twelfth (1998)	545	44*	8.0
Thirteenth(1999)	543	48*	8.8
Fourteenth (2004)	543	45*	8.1
Fifteenth (2009)	543	59*	10.9

* Including one nominated member.

Source: Election Commission of India, New Delhi.

Women's representation in the Lok Sabha since the first general elections reveals that they continue to be grossly excluded, despite the fact that their representation has more than doubled since then. Still they are far from the required critical mass to make a difference. There is a need for affirmative action to ensure that women's concerns gain political prominence and a fairly representative number of women are accepted in the political arena. This can be done by practising positive discrimination and reserving seats for them in the political parties and the Parliament. But it is sad to see that the Parliament is still a man's world. It has repeatedly witnessed ugly exchanges and male muscle and lung-power battles over the Women Representation Bill of 33 per cent reservation in the Parliament. In one instance, the Speaker had to adjourn the House; in another, opposing law-makers grabbed the Bill off his desk. Consequently, the Women Reservation Bill has been gathering dust in the absence of consensus among political parties. The Samajvadi Party, along with the BJP, claim that the Bill should include a sub-quota for Other Backward Classes (OBCs) and Muslim women otherwise, they argue, the quotas will only promote the interests of the elite.[21] The BJP ideologues Murli Manohar Joshi and Lalmani Chaubey are on record decrying women's organizations' demands for the said seats. They argue that reservation of seats for women would be a waste of seats. One government after another has held meeting on this issue, but never arrived at a consensus. Despite the opposition, women feminists have welcomed the introduction of the 'Bill.' They are of the view that the 'male plot' has actually done women a service by uniting women parliamentarians across party lines like never before.[22] In contrast, neighbouring countries like Nepal, Pakistan and Bangladesh have already implemented a bill granting 33 per cent, 22 per cent and 14 per cent, respectively.[23]

Women's equal participation in political life plays a pivotal role in the general process of advancement of women. Their equal partnership in decision-making is not only a demand for simple justice or democracy, but can also be seen as a necessary condition for women's interests to be taken into account. It is also generally believed that the induction of women in governance would improve the standards of governance as women are motivated by altruism and community-welfare concerns, whereas men are motivated by personal power and interest. Women are expected to bring about an empowering community-oriented, clean, honest and participatory governance in contrast to power over the present capital-oriented, corrupt and top down model of politics that was identified with the traditional masculine and transnational politics. Women prioritize issues differently as compared to men, as they are believed to be less corrupt and more socially-oriented than men. Even the public agenda of elected men and women as people's representatives are quite different – women representatives address issues of long-term benefits such as education, health, violence against women and basic amenities that affect community. On the other hand, men concentrate on issues that need immediate attention, such as roads, community and commercial centres. Thus, men's agenda of public work tends to neglect women's issues and is detrimental towards women's advancement and progress in the larger interests of society.

This view has many critics who point out that the practice in various states speaks otherwise. They are of the view that when women come into power they behave like their male counterparts.[24] Here it is necessary to keep in view the fact that this is due to the process of socialization. It is believed that the role of a decision-maker demands masculine stance. But this is not true if one looks at the corporate culture, which is successful. It is observed that it has adopted the feminine traits of mentoring, nurturing and building up of a participatory and committed culture. Thus, breaking the gender bias in governance would lead to empowerment and development of women in India, but this is easier said than done and has its own challenges.

Challenges

Traditions and values have deep roots in the social system which consequently affects the lives of people. India, being a male-dominated society, has not yet succeeded in breaking away from its age-old traditional shackles. The system seems to be modernizing, but the thinking is still traditional. Though a few women have come to the forefront in various fields, yet the ground reality is that the social values and psyche still restrict the participation of women in active politics. It has been observed that if women succeed in breaking the glass ceiling, by entering the decision-making arena, they still face many challenges.

Socio-psychological

The social set-up is still feudal and conservative and no effort has been made to tackle the issue at the base, which is obvious by the way in which women are treated in the public and private realms. Despite the claims of modernization and development, the socio-psychological environment is backward and the society continues to be male centric. She has been socialized to undervalue herself and is subject to the worst conditions, such as wife beating, family violence, etc., despite the existing laws against such acts. Domestic responsibilities, lack of financial clout, rising criminalization in politics and threat of character assassination makes it difficult for women to be a part of the political framework. At the grassroots level, the traditional institutions that provide no space for women also act as an obstacle by virtue of the fact that they have no formal status, they are difficult to change by law. Women have not been able to make their material and household needs, that they recognize better than men, known to the policy makers. The traditional patriarchal attitudes regard women as physically, intellectually and socially inferior to men. With these inequalities in mind, they are not considered as important components of the decision-making process and are socialized in accepting this view.[25]

Socio-economic

Women's overall socio-economic status too acts as a hurdle; it places her in an inferior position.[26] She is economically dependent on the men in the family, she toils throughout the day, but her contribution is taken for granted. Statistics show that women do two-third of the world's work, yet two-third of the world's women live in poverty. Their work is usually unpaid, underpaid and invisible. Perpetuation of women's fiscal dependency occurs despite all the domestic work plus work outside the home. To make both ends meet, women have also started sharing the family burden by going out to work, which has, in fact, increased her burden; for, it does not relieve her of her domestic burden. Rural reality is even more complex; experience has taught these women to proceed slowly and, thus, approach their goals indirectly; politics to her becomes secondary. She has to decide if attending a meeting is sometimes worth missing her daily chores/wages.

This choice is even more important to women than men. Despite the fact that she is earning, she is not truly empowered, as she continues to depend on the men in the family. The condition in the lower strata is worse for these women are not aware of their rights, especially in the unorganized sectors, they are exploited in terms of wages and sex. Liberalization has increased the development process, but this has pushed the clock back for women, as, it has led to an increase in high technology and mechanization, leading to a reduction in the work force. The state has adopted the policy of state minimalization, due to which there is a growing reduction of the public sector, this has enhanced the vulnerability of women, the hire and fire policy has affected women directly or indirectly. For women absence of power results in lack of access to and control over resources a coercive gender division of labour, devaluation of their work and lack of control over their own labour and mobility.

Socio-political

Women as a marginalized section of society have been kept out of the socio-political realm.

They have not succeeded in overcoming the gender biases and other barriers that obstruct their access to decision-making. Men and women differ in their access to power, privileges and prestige. Laws are enacted to give women a position of equality, but due to lack of political will on part of the rulers, a vast majority has not been able to benefit; also, the political play field is uneven and not conducive to women's participation. The basic problem here lies in the laws which have not been translated into practice, courtesy resistance by the elites. Besides, a large section of women are not even aware of their rights as the efforts towards educating them about these rights have been inadequate. Women generally remain in the periphery of power and influence; their representation in the Parliament, which is important on grounds of social justice and legitimacy of the political system, does not easily translate into improved representation of women's various interests. Representation of women in public offices does not always mean better deal for women in general. Nevertheless, there is a need to demand greater representation of women in political life as women remain part of a tiny minority when dealing with women issues or while advocating a women's perspective on mainstream issues. No matter how firmly they promote their views, most find little or no support to make a difference in their chosen fields. Often, they are forced to take up mainstream positions on issues and in addition, absence of a critical mass reduces their bargaining/negotiating capacities. Thus, elected women are hardly able to make any difference. In such a (hostile) environment, survival of only those women is possible, who, in the long term, push the party's agenda rather than the women who conform to the standards and views of the (masculine) mainstream. When political parties support women it is often done with the intention of accommodating sectional or caste interests. They are never treated as political entities in their own right, instead they have been treated by political parties and power groups as a means to further their own agendas and gains or they are merely seen as serving a decorative purpose. Political parties too are reluctant to support women candidates as they are considered to have lesser chances of winning due to the prevailing patriarchal attitudes in the system.[27] Also, party funding becomes equally supportive to men candidates; thus, campaigning, finances and party politics become added obstacles. Most women who come into power belong to the elite class and are accommodated because of their family background and are unable to promote the cause of the general mass of women, for they cannot identify with them.[28]

It is, thus, seen that the system is not gender friendly, though women literacy statistics have improved, proactive laws in women's interest have been implemented and women in large numbers are also exercising their electoral rights. Women needs have remained invisible as they are not adequately represented in the policy-making structure. Hence, while formulating policies, their impact on women in particular is not considered. Protective laws are misused and not implemented in the desired spirit; the media too is insensitive and rather, exploits women. Policies of globalization and liberalization have had an adverse effect on women's health and status (leading to feminization of poverty). Consequently, their voice is not heard – the traditions and cultures of society restrict their voices – resulting in self-imposed barriers and loss of self esteem.

Strategies

There is a need to make the system gender-friendly by awakening the consciousness on women issues and helping women in overcoming self-perceived barriers and promoting their political participation, while preserving their gender values. Besides, it is necessary to promote education of women and empower them through economic and political participation. This is necessary as women's economic independence is critical for exercise of influence on decisions that affect their lives and families. Thus, individually and collectively, women have to expand their advocacy efforts through networking. Politics and participation range from home through the locality to the national level. Thus, women need to participate at the micro level of the home, the macro level of the community organizations and local government and at the macro level of the state. Gender sensitization of the society and empowerment of women, followed by political awareness and induction of women into mainstream politics, would help in creating an aware and vocal body of women in all electorates, including those of male politicians. This, in turn, can enable the voices of even women in minority to be heard and respected in the Parliament by men colleagues. When women MPs express an opinion, the men MPs will be obliged to take note, if they realize that many women in their own electorates can be a powerful force facilitating women's role in transforming politics.[29] To promote gender equality, women be accorded rights equal to men by giving them equal opportunities and by promoting participation of women in decision-making. Women perspectives should be reflected in all policies because the underlying cause of gender inequality lies in the socio-economic structure which requires to be targeted. There is also a need to promote equal and just relations between men and women and to rethink concepts and strategies for promoting women's rights and dignity. According to former UN Kofi Annan, 'gender equality is more than a goal in itself; it is a precondition for meeting the challenges of reducing poverty and promoting development' and it also helps in changing prevailing norms. There is a need for political socialization of women to reduce the gender gap in political attitudes, women's political capabilities and patterns of political participation.[30] There is an increasing evidence of the link between making progress on gender equality and progress in meeting all other development objectives. Tackling gender inequality increases women's productivity and reduces poverty and hunger; it also leads to a change in attitude and perception. There is also a need for levelling the play field for them to ensure that they get equal opportunity in developing their capabilities.

Women NGOs and community groups can serve as a rallying point, identifying women issues, and identifying and training potential candidates. They must hold the elected women representatives accountable and responsive to women issues and provide a women's perspective to all other issues. Women in decision-making positions can help adopt gender positive policies by lobbying for women causes and persuading their male colleagues to support them. Thus, an active women force can bring about a positive transformation in policies and take it a step further by promoting development through good governance. It cannot be denied that women in power will actually stick to the transformed platforms. Here, the civil society can serve as an asset in identifying women issues and make the women in power responsive and accountable for their actions. The national machinery for women advancement, in close cooperation with administrative bodies, should promote a broad range of measures for women empowerment.

The extent to which the strategies can contribute to political participation and development will not depend only on women's innate qualities as politicians. Rather, it will depend on the success of the women's movements in developing a strong and aware women electorate to support women candidate, while, at the same time, holding them accountable for promoting women's issues and women's perspectives on all issues. The greater the number of women at the decision-making level, more would be the articulation of their interests, with sufficient visibility in the political system and threshold representation. This group would be able to influence policies.

Conclusion

There is a need to develop a critical mass of about 35–40 per cent and enforcement of critical acts, which will help in changing the position of minority status considerably and lead to further positive changes in the condition of women by introducing quotas and development programmes for women. If a critical mass of women succeed in breaking the glass ceiling and reach decision-making positions, they can help adopt gender-positive policies by lobbying for women's causes and persuading their men colleagues to support them. Thus, an active women force can bring about a positive transformation in governance and take it a step further by promoting good governance, as this conforms to the general nature of women. It cannot be denied that women in power will actually stick to the transformed platforms. There is also a need for attitudinal changes in the male-dominated society to canalize the political potentials towards the real development of the nation through the untapped resources of half the country's population. Thus, there is a need to adopt positive attitudes and strategies for inducting more women into the political process at the level of policy makers and to educate and empower them so as to promote a participative culture of both the sexes within the system. Awareness about rights and opportunities and participation in the political process will help in overcoming the barriers towards women political participation and development. Kofi Annan has rightly stated that 'the role of women in decision-making is central to the advancement of women around the world and to the progress of human kind as a whole'. For the development of any society at the ground level, men and women should get a free and proportionate chance to enjoy and exercise their political rights, as lack of representation directly translates into a de-sensitized political leadership, which is completely cut off from the issues facing half the population. The inclusion of women in the political structure and their proportionate participation will not only correct the existing gender gaps but also bring gender issues to the forefront leading to women's empowerment and subsequent development and advancement of the society.

Notes

1. James Mill, *History of British India,* as cited in Sanjay Kumar and Praveen Rai, 'Gendered Political Exclusion: Crucial Implications for Indian Democracy', *Social Change,* Vol. 37, No. 4, 2007, p. 184.
2. For status of women, see Dalip Kumar Saikon and Neelam Deshmukh, 'Women Empowerment, Good Governance and Decentralizaton', *wed.nic.in/research/women empowerment,* pp. 2–8; also see, Tara Ali Baig, *India's Women Power,* New Delhi: S. Chand, 1976.
3. *UN Chronicle,* Vol. XXXI, No. 3, 1995.
4. *Human Development Report,* UNDP, New York, 1995.
5. Article 326 guarantees political equality and right to vote. Article 14, 15, 16, 19, and the Representation of People Act 1951 provide for equal participation of women in the political process.
6. As cited in Lina Hamedeh Banerjee and Paul Oquist, *Women's Political Participation and Good Governance: 21st Century Challenges,* New York: UNDP Publications, 2000.
7. For further reference, see Samita Sen, *Towards a Feminist Politics? The Indian Women's Movement in Historical Perspective,* Policy Research Report on Gender and Development, Working Paper Series No. 9, www.worldbank.org/gender; also see, Floria Agnes, 'Women's Movement with a Secular Framework: Redefining the Agenda', *Economic and Political Weekly,* Vol. XXIV, No. 19.
8. *Selected Works of Raja Ram Mohan Roy,* New Delhi: Government of India Publication, 1997, p. 157.
9. *Selected Works of Jawaharlal Nehru,* Vol. 3, New Delhi: Government of India Publication, 1972, p. 361.
10. www.dfid.uk/gender-equality-plan-2007
11. For details, see *Towards Equality: Report of Committee on Status of Women in India,* Ministry of Education and Social Welfare, Department of Social Welfare, Government of India, New Delhi, 1974. This aspect was also emphasized at the First 'Asia-Pacific Congress on Women in Politics', organized by Centre for Asia-Pacific Women in Politics (CAPWIP) held at Philippines in 1992.
12. To pursue women issues and bring forth the women perspective, 100 women along with Suman Krishan Kant as the President formed the first

all-women's party in India. It has also focused on 50 per cent women representatives in Parliament. See 'Women in India Form Their Own Party', www.//womennsenews.org.

13. The Platform for Action is intended to strengthen the implementation of the instruments and programmes which were adopted concerning the status of women and to broaden and place them in a timelier context. Its purpose was to mainly stimulate national action to solve the problem of underdevelopment and the socio-economic structure which places women in an inferior position. *Platform for Action, Five Years After: An Assessment*, Department of Women and Child Welfare, Ministry of HRD, Government of India, New Delhi, 2000.
14. For trends in political participation of women – their turnout in general elections and representation in Parliament, see *Records on Election Commission of India*, New Delhi.
15. Gender equality is an important factor in the process of democratization and development, for it is linked to the process of social and cultural change. For further reference, see Ronald Inglehart and Pipa Norris, 'Gender Equality and Democratic Functioning', . *havard.edu.*
16. The debate started in 1990, putting people at the centre of the development process, stressing on people's long-term well-being. For details, see S.P. Srivastava (ed.), *The Development Debate: Critical Perspectives*, Jaipur and Delhi: Rawat, 1998; For women perspective, see AWID-Global-www.comminit.com/en/node
17. Vaijayanti Gupta, 'Parliament is Still a Man's World', *India Together*, August 15, 2009.
18. *Report of Committee on the Status of Women in India*, New Delhi, 1997.
19. The Government has proposed to reserve 50 per cent seats in panchayats for women, which will empower them further and allow them to contribute substantially in the decision-making process; for further reference, see *The Hindu*, August, 29 and 31, 2009.
20. The potential of women for management and governance can be gauged from a write-up on 30 tribal women of Kenya who have built up an entire village only for women and are managing it effectively. For details, see Mehru Jaffer, 'A Village for Women', *The Tribune*, September 6, 2009.
21. For further reference, see Mrinal Pande, 'India's Nurseries of Politics', http://www.unesco.org/courier/2000–06.
22. Devki Jain, *The Eighty First Amendment Bill 1996: A Report*, paper presented at IAWS School of Women Studies, Jadavpur University, Calcutta, 1997.
23. *The Times of India*, March 7, 2009.

24. For a critique of women in politics in India, see Siddharth Srivastava, 'Indian Politics: The Women on Top', www.indolink.com
25. For further reference, see Shirin Rai, 'Class, Caste and Gender: Women in Parliament in India', http://archiv.idea.int/women/parl/studies
26. *Global Gender Report 2007, India*, www.weforum.org
27. This is ironical for history of elections shows that the success rate of female contestants has invariably been higher in relation to males. This too is a misconception, for, an analysis 'most of the women who have come into power shows that they have piggy-banked on the names of their fathers, husbands or glamour'. For further reference, see D. Bandyopadhyay, 'Gender and Governance in India', *Economic and Political Weekly*, Vol. XXXV, No. 31; also see, Bhawaha Jharta, *Women and Politics in India*, New Delhi: Deep and Deep, 1996.
28. For an analysis of women in Parliament, see Shirin Rai, note 19. Also see, Alladi Kappuswami, 'Indian Women's Rights: Myths and Reality', *Social Change*, Vol. 23, No. 1, 1993; J.K. Chopra, *Women in Parliament in India*, New Delhi: Mittal Publications, 1993.
29. Lina Hamadeh Banerjee and Paul Oquist, 'Women's Political Participation and Good Governance: 21st Century Challenges', *UNDP 2000: Women in Politics and Good Governance*, Development Bulletin No. 51, pp. 36–3.
30. For further reference, see R. Letha Kumari, *Women in Politics*, New Delhi: Authors Press, 2006.

9

Women Empowerment

Political Dimension

PREM KRISHNA SHARMA

Politics is actually the process of managing the social system in a particular way. In the present time nobody can remain unaffected by this process. It does not make any difference whether a person remains passive or active. The character of concern may vary from person to person. However, the person who becomes active may derive satisfaction for being able to make some intervention in the system. As a matter of fact, the course of history has changed a number of times because of such interventions. It is also true that this change has been negative for a number of times. The course of history has never been straight.

Generally, politics has been considered to be the art of acquiring capability to control the system. The end-result is the same whether it is monarchy, oligarchy or the so-called democracy. The visible differential is only on the basis of number of persons taking part in the process and deriving benefits out of it.

If we consider the place of woman in this process, we see that in the whole of history her role has either been passive or at the most supportive as a secondary member of the society. Of course, there have been exceptions but they were invariably by accident or as a male projection.

However, this aspect of politics is very myopic. We must consider politics in its widest sense. Still being in control of the seat of power is ultimate because other aspects can only manifest themselves properly through it. But in any case our understanding of politics in this sense will serve no purpose, particularly for the women who will be always forced to lag far behind if politics is not understood in its widest sense. As a matter of fact, the other aspects of political understanding are the basis of empowerment to reach the ultimate. A woman must realize that when she complains about the non-supply of water, she enters the political arena. This understanding will motivate her not to suffer the situation silently but to collectivize the complaint and seek avenues to express it effectively. Whether these efforts are successful or not is not relevant but every step to consciously intervene in the system is a political activity. Similarly, when a woman academician ponders over social conditions, analyses them, finds out reasons thereof and tries to evolve their solutions, the activity must not be considered simply to be academic. And, when this thinking is further publicized, discussed in seminars, it results in substantial awareness and streamlining of the thinking process of concerned quarters. The problem is that all these activities are considered and kept devoid of political perspectives. The result is that they fail to have any effective intervention in the system. It is strange that there are a number of women social activists who are zealously pursuing their goal, interacting with the people and spreading awareness about their plight, but they themselves consider their activities as apolitical. It is pathetic that howsoever important and worthy the activity is but it does not result in any change in the system. Therefore, when we talk about political dimensions with regard to women in India, the first step must be to identify and acknowledge every small effort relevant to any segment of the society as political.

It must be clearly understood that the political dimension is the core of the women empowerment. Without this basic approach there can neither be empowerment of women nor can they come out of the shadow of male domination. The deliberate limited interpretation that political dimension with regard to women means only her taking part in party politics, contesting elections or involving herself in governance in any way will not be sufficient for the ultimate goal.

In fact, this limited understanding has created a very ridiculous image of women who are in that type of politics. Most of the women in politics today have not come in the field on their own. They got their position because of their relations or as replacement of deceased or fallen males. You may call them proxy politicians. Vipul Pandey in his article 'Women in Indian Politics' has summed up the image of Indian women politicians as under:

1. Pallu groups or dynastic groups (Sonia Gandhi (why not Indira Gandhi also ... Auth), Vasundhara Raje Scindhia, Amma, Rabri Devi, Sheila Dikshit) having family ties.
2. Hysterical groups, Mamta, Mayawati, Sushma Swaraj, Uma Bharti. This is a broad generalization; some like Krishna Tirath, etc., have been left.

Among the Pallu groups the name which is most revered or has become synonymous with Indian politics is Sonia Gandhi. Leaving her, most of other Pallu group members are not able to set their foothold. This is also clear by the example of Vasundhara Raje, who has been made scapegoat after the loss of BJP in the state assembly and Lok Sabha elections. Also, Amma and Rabri are craving for power.

Talking of hysterical group on one hand Mayawati stands out as a clear winner as a woman who relies on vote bank of Dalits, and is CM of the most populated state of the country. Conversely, some like Mamta Banerjee are never able to outgrow their rebel image and have become more or less a relic in the changed political situation. The most interesting thing is that the Pallu group is no pushover. Sushma Swaraj is like Rahul Dravid of Indian team who never got what they deserved but still she also showed her immaturity in politics when she 'threatened to shave off her head if Sonia had become the PM?'

I do not agree with such image description but the facts remain as to how the common man views that image. This perspective has to be broken.

First, we may deal with the argument of biological differences. Biological differences are there and that is why they are men and women. With them, there are bound to be some natural differences with regard to their behavioural pattern, relationship-related responsibilities and emotional orientation. But this does not mean to show that these differences reflect on a woman's capability or ambition to 'shatter the glass ceiling to get to the top' as she puts it. I even agree with the remark that 'women are biologically hardwired to nurture their young, to prefer working with people they respect, to want flexible schedules that allow them to weave a social purpose in their work lives and to treat the needs of the people they love as important ...'. But, the question arises as to why these qualities come in conflict with their 'jobs' or 'career'. Actually it is the other way round. The system of 'jobs' or career' is so handmade that it automatically comes in conflict with capability parameters of a woman. And, is this what is known as social conditioning which has been created through centuries and man has used it to his advantage.

The findings of recent studies in brain imaging and neuro-endocrinology do not tell us anything new but to use them as explanation of psychological distress of women while working is misleading, to say the least. Why can not the work be so arranged so as to harmonize it with her natural behaviour?

In fact, the society has never tried to synchronize the career option with gender behaviour. Earmarking some jobs related to childbirth, nursing or easygoing teaching is misplaced. Work need not be identified by gender. It needs to be adjusted according to gender behaviour. There is vast difference between the two. In this way any work is capable of being handled by women. If children and family had been constraints for women, every single or childless woman would have been able to shatter the 'glass ceiling' and would have proceeded on the way to the top. But we know that this is not so. There are numerous examples to the contrary and for this, one need not cite names of Indira Gandhi, Margaret Thatcher or Pearl Buck but we should go to the village fields or vegetable markets to see bubbling energy of mothers along with their babies working side by side with men with the same level of productivity. Work culture is not the domain of the elite class only. Now, the job remains to convert this work culture into political culture without which there can never be women emancipation, which is the pre-requisite for real women empowerment.

I am conscious that the terminology to be used in this article may not be palatable to many, but I cannot express my views in any other way. Women empowerment cannot be carried on in isolation. It is, in fact, a part of continuous class struggle to change the whole spectrum of social structure, having constant and effective intervention in the system and keeping it directed towards the ever extending goals of comprehensive development, knowledge and well-being with equality in every aspect of life.

Without a conscious understanding about being a part of class struggle their movement will not be able to take strides in the right direction. This understanding implies spreading of class consciousness, which means affinity and commonness with all other sections of the society, which also have been subject of oppression, exploitation and discrimination. I can very well imagine that it would not be easy for everyone to come to terms with this line of expression but I am confident that once it is imbibed in the thinking process, made subject of discussion and applied in the field activities, the outcome itself is sure prove its worth.

The structural history of every society shows that only a small fraction of the population has dominated the social system and this has been possible by keeping the remaining vast majority under oppression and exploitation by means of keeping them divided, rather instigating one against the other. Thus, lack of affinity among this oppressed and exploited vast majority has kept the system afloat on their shoulders. Therefore, the political dimension of women empowerment cannot be women-centric. It has to be system-centric. The struggle is not to be against individual males but against the whole mentality under which the system works.

Now, we may revert back to that aspect of politics, which we call power politics in the present Indian situation. We are living in a democracy and whatever its aberrations, it is still a democracy, though very fragile. We may take three basic ingredients of democracy, which are present in the Indian system also. They are: firstly, general elections, i.e., periodic opportunity the people to elect their government; secondly, the freedom of expression recognized under the Constitution and; thirdly, independent judicial system. But if we analyse these ingredients with the help of ground realities, a very dark picture emerges. If the people are given the opportunity to elect their government, it must mean that they are electing of their free will, without any pressure or misdirected guidance. However, what we see is that this opportunity is tampered with money power, muscle power, communal feelings, caste system, regional feelings and so on. Can it be said that when so many negative factors are active and are deeply ingrained in people's minds, the elections are genuine and based on free will? The answer will obviously be an emphatic 'NO'.

Similarly, if we take the right to expression, the situation is no different. Right to expression means that every person must be free to express his views and he should have an opportunity that his views are communicated effectively to those sections whom he wants to address. Right to expression is meaningless if it is not communicable. But do we have the opportunity to communicate our views when the means of communication such as newspapers, publications, TV channels, etc., are confined in the hands of a few only? The reality is that it is only available to them who can have access to these means. A large number of right thinking people, even academicians, are left helpless in reaching out to the people with their views. Then, there is one more problem. Right to the expression does not mean simply giving expressions in a vacuum. This right becomes meaningful only when it is potential to have effective intervention in the system and this is not possible without acquiring knowledge about the working of the system. We all know that in spite of the right to information law, we are not able to have access to the complete information about the system and whatever we do, we get it with great difficulty.

Then again, if we take what we call independent judicial system, the less said about it, the better. The judicial system, because of its prohibitive procedure, frustrating delays, expensiveness, corruption and lack of people oriented mentality, is neither genuine nor approachable.

Thus, we can very frankly say that though it is a democracy but only in frame but without content. Still, we cannot give up the system, however fragile it may be. The real danger is from within. If efforts are not made to correct these aberrations, the whole system may collapse anytime. People's faith has already eroded and re-building it will need herculean efforts.

Therefore, when we talk about the political dimension with regard to women, we must ask this question: Do the women want to become simply a part of these aberrations by entering the present political arena in the same way? If this is so, it may not make any actual difference, reservation or not, women will not be getting anything, their movement will not successful. It will be a system with the same mentality which will be the winner. Therefore, it is essential that the women movement should understand the meaning of politics in its widest sense, enter the arena with a clear vision enriched by class consciousness and then endeavour to control it effectively. That will be real and genuine political dimension of women empowerment, which also includes decision-making power in every sphere, access to information, right to make choices through assertive but positive and collective approach, democratic perception and development of ability to overcome all types of stigma.

We are confident that women can do it and will do it.

10

Globalization and the Gender Imperatives in Environment

KIRAN SONI GUPTA

The welfare of human beings is the final reference point in judging the impact of what we do or fail to do. Women have an essential role to play in the development of a sustainable and ecologically sound system of natural resource management. Globalization brings with it potentially large benefits, as well as risks. The challenge is to manage the process of globalization in such a way that it promotes environmental sustainability and equitable human development.

While all dimensions of globalization affect the natural environment and through it human development, there are two axes of analysis of globalization from the gender perspective – one is of women as victims of the economic process; the other is the potential for women as *subjects* of the process. When women are perceived as an agency in the globalization process, they become a social force capable of acting in their own interest. This, in turn, focuses our attention on the relationship between the politics and economics of globalization, or 'the political economy of globalization' and its impact on environment and women. Countries and people have the potential to derive significant benefits from the globalization process but there is still the problem of realizing this potential optimally. Too much attention has been paid to the economic benefits of globalization and not enough to the social and environmental implications. As a result, the promise and potential of globalization as a force of sustainable human development is not being realized.

Contrary to the common belief that natural resources have an unlimited capacity to meet humanity's needs, the denudation of forests and environmental destruction has adversely affected the women in rural areas more than any other class of people. Each day, in the life of a rural woman, begins with a long march in search of water, fuel and fodder. Irrespective of age or physical ability of a woman, the crucial needs of every household have to be met each day. Nearly 84 per cent of the rural women are affected by the scarcity of fuelwood. This is becoming more and more arduous with the depletion of natural resources. The direct and critical relationship between women and natural resources draws its strength not from biology but from gender, and the socially-created roles and responsibilities that fall on women in households, communities and ecosystems.

Women's work and lives all over the world have long been intertwined with food. In every country, it is women who assume primary responsibility for preparing and serving meals. Not only do they prepare and serve food, they also grow food and contribute 60–80 per cent of the labour required for food production, both for household consumption and for sale as well as in food marketing. Vandana Shiva calls women the 'world's original food producers'. But, women are hardly given recognition in the process of food going from fields to tables. Women's work in the global food chain is chronically undervalued and underpaid and labelled unproductive. But not all food production is unrecognized. Women have primary responsibility for rearing children and ensuring sufficient resources to meet children's needs for nutrition, health-care and schooling. They are also the main managers of essential household resources like clean water, fuel for cooking and heating and fodder for domestic animals. Thus, women are caught in the intricate web of poverty and environmental degradation. As poverty persists and, in many parts of the world deepens, women's income from such activities becomes critical to family survival – reinforcing the importance of the environment in women's lives (and increasing the dangers posed by degraded environments). In the growing number of female-headed households, this work is essential, particularly for children. Women already head almost a quarter of rural households in the world's poorest countries.

The daily survival needs of predominant rural households are dependent on biomass food, water, fodder, fuel, manure and fertilizers for agricultural purposes, building material like timber and thatch and herbs as remedies for various diseases. Availability of water, which is directly related to the biomass in the country where monsoons are not only uncertain but also brief, is the most crucial resource affecting the lives of rural women. Water is present at many levels in the life of rural women. They collect and manage its use in the household; they farm irrigated and rain-fed crops, they know where the water can be found, how to store it and when it is scarce and whether it is safe for the family's use. Safe, clean water has often been taken for granted, but without adequate protection, water soon becomes contaminated by nitrates, phosphates and organo chlorines used in fertilizers and pesticides. These chemicals are used to increase crop yield, but their production and use are detrimental to health. Wages are low and hours long and while in the fields, workers and their families are exposed to another danger: pesticides. Children work in these fields and those too young to work accompany their mothers. Women's first priority is to put food on the table. Unfortunately, only a tiny fraction of that food arrives on their own tables. Nutritional deficiencies have increased as food has become more packaged and refined. Toxins and chemicals in the air also contaminate water. Rain absorbs these toxins, deposits them into the rivers and streams, which fill the wells and reservoirs that are used to irrigate the land, where the crops are grown to feed the people. This cycle results in the continuing contamination and pollution. One of the major factors in improving life expectancy in India has been the provision of portable water. The struggle for safe, clean water has been, and is increasingly so, women's daily struggle. With the disappearance of biomass in the surroundings, sources of water like ponds and streams dry up soon after the monsoons. Serious problems of water like the salinization of water for human consumption and for agriculture exist. The destruction of flora and fauna is alarming. Any development alternative, which intends to provide a more permanent solution, will have to ascribe high priority both to environmental and socially sustainable factors.

There are a large number of complex problems which women face – work burden, lack of property, unequal distribution of food and other resources within the family, duality of roles, poor health delivery system coupled with inferior social status bestowed on them and their total lack of control over cash and productive resources. All these problems get accentuated and heightened by environmental degradation. As these are becoming increasingly difficult to obtain, women are forced to spend inordinately long hours in search for them in addition to the multifarious domestic duties. The natural topography in hills and deserts, dry, and arid semi-arid areas poses a greater problem to women living in these areas, As agricultural production in these areas is extremely limited and alternatives to fuelwood are minimum, it is the poor landless woman who faces the brunt as considerable amount of time is spent for foraging fuel and fodder. Even in areas where animal husbandry and agriculture have improved the availability of crop residues and dung, it is not necessary that the landless woman should benefit. This shortage of cooking energy affects the food intake of a woman and other members of her family. Thus, scarcity of cooking fuel forces many a rural woman to reduce her energy for cooking. This implies nutrient losses and greater risk of infection and illness from eating stale food.

The study of rural water supply scheme in Andhra Pradesh in India revealed that the irrigation schemes have adversely affected the drinking water supply and thus women too as primary carriers of water. Another major activity of rural women is care of cattle and collection of fodder. Women play a major role in the livestock economy and there is a crucial linkage between dairy production and forestry. Government has paid little attention to the protection of fodder. Various social forestry schemes have not resulted in benefits commensurate with investment. Promotion of fodder on farmlands helps only those who own land while all others are left to fend for fodder themselves. The existing social forestry projects have largely failed women. Besides being insensitive to women's household needs, there has been no serious attempt to expand her employment opportunities for forest employment. The tribal women also need clear rights to forest produce and establishment of systems to their advantage. Women have an essential role to play in plantations and social forestry programmes. The new strategies for alternatives to fuel and fodder must enlist women's needs as they are the most affected. Therefore, environmental conservation is fundamental to the development process. But the gap between intent and reality is very large indeed. The women of marginal cultures like tribals and nomads encounter the maximum threat of environmental degradation.

In the production areas, planning has to be capable of assuring the productivity at a commercial level, making proper use of the natural resources and considering the improvement of the quality of life of the local population as well as preservation of the environment. Women farmers tend to use and perfect traditional cropping methods developed over time to protect and preserve the natural resources. This makes them the key players in the conservation of soil fertility. Ganganagar district of Rajasthan – where I was the District Collector for two years – is the granary of Rajasthan where the increasing use of fertilizers and pesticides, intense and concentrated mechanization and the large export-crop exploitation caused such an impact on soil, forests, inland water, and biological balance of pests and diseases that they cannot but trigger people's awareness. As chief food producers, women have a stake in the preservation of the environment and sustainable development. Land and water resources form the basis of all farming systems and their preservation is crucial to sustained and improved food production. Soil erosion, water shortage and crop failures reduce harvest yields and soil exhausted from overuse reduces the productivity of households.

The heavy environmental stress over the last 20 years due to deforestation and depletion of natural resources has drastically altered the relationship between women and the living systems which support their lives. Women tend to respond to these acute scarcities by limited cooking, washing and cleaning. Consequently, the scarcity of fuel, water and fodder has serious implications for health for all. Toxic chemicals and pesticides in air, water and earth are responsible for a variety of women's health risks. Because of their roles as home managers and economic providers, as well as their role in reproduction, women are susceptible to health problems. Pregnant women are especially vulnerable to environmental contaminants. Toxic substances in the environment can alter every step in the reproductive process. These toxic substances may increase the risk of abortion, birth defects, fetal-growth retardation and prenatal death. Environmental risks in the home and workplace may have a disproportionate impact on women's health because of women's different susceptibilities to the toxic effects of various chemicals. These risks to women's health are particularly high in urban areas, as well as in low-income areas where there is a high concentration of polluting industrial facilities. Strenuous work of the nature/accidents while performing these tasks results in miscarriages and other reproductive health issues. The deterioration of natural resources displaces communities, especially women, from income-generating activities while greatly adding to unremunerated work. Environmental degradation results in negative effects on the health, well-being and quality of life of the population at large, especially girls and women. Deforestation has affected the domestic economy of the poor households with greater severity and its impact has fallen primarily on women. For many women, degradation and deforestation have meant loss of jobs. Land degradation reduces yields, leading to a vicious circle of lower yields. Farmers may seek new land, but often find it only in frontier or marginal areas, especially if they are women and cannot close a sale or negotiate a loan.

Unfortunately, the increasing industrialization, urbanization and deforestation have shattered the biomass base. In the tenant farmer system, the male head of household who also receives the family wages signs the family contract. Production and processing of biomass like agriculture forestry and village crafts based on biomass as raw material are still the main sources of rural employment. The female rural labourer does not use the new agricultural technologies, which represent savings of the labour force. Biotechnology has brought about a longer harvest period as well as an increase in production of some agricultural products such as oranges, kinnows, cotton, etc.

The modernization of agriculture has brought about significant changes in labour relations, with new dynamics in the labour market. In the State of Punjab, the economic policies adopted have resulted in a gradual increase in the size of property and in land concentration. The smallholder units continue to be swallowed up by the larger ones and acquire a more mercantile nature. Simultaneously, rural hands are either overworked or, alternatively, part of the family acquires the status of temporary wage-earner, and the migration of some members of the family is rendered almost compulsory. As an alternative for survival, smallholders either sell their land and attempt to purchase another property in the agricultural border areas.

Men and women tend to occupy, use and manage aspects of biophysical environment in a gender-differentiated manner. Women have often played leadership roles or taken the lead in promoting an environmental ethic, reducing resource use, and reusing and recycling resources to minimize waste and excessive consumption. Women can have a particularly powerful role in influencing sustainable consumption decisions. In addition, women's contribution to environmental management has often taken place at the local level, where decentralized action on environmental issues is most needed and decisive. The traditional knowledge of women of ecological linkages and fragile ecosystem management is crucial to the enhancement and the preservation of the environment. Ganganagar being a border district sharing 210 kms of international border with Pakistan, women are generally the most stable members of the community, as men often migrate in search of greater economic opportunities, leaving women to manage the fields and thus have a greater role to play.

Many women are hit hard by natural disasters and gender relations in society tend to put women at special risk, some more than others. But focusing on women primarily as victims and the neglect of their capacities and resources misrepresents the actual experiences of women and men and negatively affects the culture and practice of emergency management. Gender relations significantly affect our daily lives – before, during, and after a calamitous event like a nuclear accident, earthquake, breaches or war. On balance, men tend to have greater access to key survival and recovery resources and hence are less vulnerable than women to disaster. Women are likely to become progressively more vulnerable with deterioration in environment and are not impacted identically by disaster, but have differential access. Community-based mitigation integrating disaster-readiness and sustainable resource management, fair housing, land rights, are increasingly becoming the order of day and women's active participation is essential to success. Finally, women need to take up the challenge of disaster planning, information about local hazards and specific conditions creating vulnerability and learn about existing emergency plans, personnel and resources. Each new disaster is a wake-up call – a strong reminder that we must not continue the past into the future. In all societies, women's expertise and leadership need to be reckoned with as we shift from disaster aid to disaster mitigation through sustainable development.

Efforts aimed at rehabilitation of ecologically-sensitive areas should necessarily take into account the burden of work of rural women, especially the women in hilly areas where the ecological destruction is at its worst and the work burden is the highest. Efforts at the government level like promotion of new technology, like biogas plants, fuelwood plantations, and fuel conservation through use of smokeless *chullahs*, handpumps, etc., will lead considerably to reduce the rigours of rural living. However, what is most important is to envisage the role of women in the implementation of various schemes that impact them. At the same time, women have little power over the conditions of their lives. Decision-makers often overlook this reality, even though women's use and management of local environmental resources is fundamental to household and community well-being. Agricultural extension services are heavily biased towards men. Education and outreach efforts in support of sustainable farming and land management methods often pass them by.

What has been the environmental intensity of technological change? The economic dimensions of trade, investment and capital flows of globalization need to be recognized. Globalization affects both the nature and the rate of technological innovation and diffusion through more liberalized international trade, capital flows and a more favourable investment climate, improved institutional and communication links and increased protection of intellectual property rights. The link between technological change and environmental quality and resource use with particular emphasis on the gender perspective of environment assumes greater importance. Globalization, in principle, could improve the environmental characteristics of technology through increased exposure to foreign markets from where cleaner technologies and more effective pollution-abatement equipment can be imported; increased access to export markets that may be more environmentally demanding than local markets; foreign investment that brings with it the technologies and practices of the home country with more stringent environmental standards than the host country; and increased diffusion of the fast-growing export-oriented environmental goods and services.

The environmental consequences of globalization differ from the economic effects both in time and space: environmental impacts are more long-term, dynamic and cumulative and are beset with uncertainty because of meagre knowledge of long-term damages. Environmental impacts involve both physical and non-physical spillovers. Globalization generates international interest in what traditionally were considered purely domestic policies, since economic integration implies that trade and investment are now being affected by such policies. Globalization increasingly brings into conflict notions of national sovereignty over production processes with globally-oriented life-cycle perspectives, where consumers want to know the overall environmental impact of what they buy and consume. The ability of nation-states to manage risks, inequalities and change is severely restricted by constraints and the need to remain competitive. Hence, the traditional instruments of trade barriers and control regulations would not work because of high operating costs. To manage globalization in the interest of people, particularly women, and the environment, it would be necessary to implement more efficient and innovative policies domestically and more effective global governance internationally.

Economic globalization – the process of opening up regional markets for global consumption – has played a large role in the transformation of agriculture from family gardens to a huge industry characterized by agribusinesses. Globalization of production has been a key element in re-shaping of the world economy with visible impact on our daily lives. This represents new organization of production processes, backed up by new technologies. Emanating from these changes, labour relations are being altered, in particular, to world trends of the flexiblization and feminization of labour. Globalization has stressed production for export – and hence, free trade agreements. Commercialized agriculture relies just as heavily on the work of women as did the family farm. Women are cogs in the machine of a globalized agriculture, e.g., harvesting rice in India. But while women still play a role in agricultural production, women's control over the means of food production has been significantly weakened. The forced migrations, environmental contamination, food insecurity and hunger that have resulted from this transformation, have been devastating. With increased emphasis on export production and increase in foreign direct investment, the feminization of the labour force has now been firmly set in motion in many Asian countries. The feminization of labour in Asia is rather unique compared to other core countries as it is characterized as the proletarianisation of women's labour. Many women wage workers engaged in capitalist production are still a central part of a noncapitalist or non-proletarian household economy located in rural villages. This continued direct link between waged labour in the formal sector and the reproduction of village subsistence economies is a key feature of the political economy of globalization and women's labour in Asia. Globalization has greatly increased the flow of goods between countries. Many countries have reorganized their economies in favour of export production. In some countries, especially in Asia, Export Processing Zones have been created to house production facilities. Women make up much of the underpaid workforce in these areas where regulations and labour protection laws are relaxed or not enforced in order to attract foreign investors.

From losing good government jobs, to less access to unionized jobs, to being left to pick up the slack when social services are no longer available, women are having a tough time coping with the reality of economic globalization. Women's experiences of both paid and unpaid work have been affected by this growing trend. Unions have always worked hard to protect women in the workplace. Unionized women earn wages much closer to that of their male counterparts than do non-unionized women. Unions also help workers who face sexual harassment and other workplace hazards and can bargain benefits like childcare.

Micro-finance, micro-credit, social insurance and social protection – national and international financial institutions need to operate according to social criteria. Credit facilities, markets, skills development and capability building must be provided to these sectors, particularly the women. Social protection should be accorded to all workers both in the formal and informal sectors. Women in poor communities cannot diversify their income sources for lack of skills and training. Education, training and human resource development are essential for the poor to be able to participate in the market. Government funds for vocational and technical training, quality of such training and teachers for the benefit of women currently engaged in the informal sector, need to be augmented. Governments must implement more innovative training approaches to reach out to those who need them most, e.g., urban poor communities.

Women are very differently positioned in relation to markets in different parts of the world. Where women are socially excluded from leaving their homes and going to market, the challenge is to find ways for women to participate and to create markets which are more women-friendly by establishing local sales outlets under women's control; participation in international trade fairs; markets to be regulated in ways that are fair to women's small businesses; bargain collectively for better prices; and setting up women's desks in major regional intergovernmental bodies that deal with trade issues. Globalization changes the 'balance of power' between markets, national governments and international collective action. It enhances the influence of markets on economic, social, and environmental outcomes and reduces the degree of freedom and unilateral management capabilities of national governments. It creates the necessity for all to cooperate both in the management of the global commons and the coordination of domestic policies. Globalization creates market-driven political pressures to gain or maintain competitiveness and this forces premature and not necessarily appropriate convergence of environmental policy. In the presence of diversity of environmental endowments, assimilative capacities and preferences, efficient environmental management requires sensitivity to local ecological and social conditions. Diversity of conditions calls for a diversity of policies. Yet globalization leads to uniformity and inertia in environmental policy in the absence of collective action. The main channel through which globalization influences environmental policy is through the cost of production. To the extent that environmental policy raises or is perceived to raise the cost of production, globalization inspired concerns about gaining or maintaining competitiveness, militate against any change of policy.

Globalization improves the prospects for economic growth worldwide but may reduce the economic prospects in individual countries, sectors and communities. Many factors contribute to wide disparities both within nations and between nations: lack of access to more efficient technologies, capital, inadequate flexibility to respond to changes in market demand, inability to manage structural change, weak institutions and absence of effective safety nets. These result in poverty-induced resource depletion and environmental degradation, which lead to further human deprivation, disparity and dispowerment. Globalization is likely to place significant stress on the environment if perverse subsidies and other distortions are not removed and environmental costs fully internalized, or if 'social adjustment' policies are not in place to cushion economic dislocation and avert marginalization of the poor. Globalization, by driving a wedge between what is produced and what is consumed, alters the distribution of environmental impacts and the costs.

Impact on women workers is vividly illustrated by the garments industry of Philippines as women workers lost their jobs due to international competitiveness and major garments and textile firms were shut down. With declining orders due to intense global competition and the shift to computer-aided technologies such as in embroidery, many workers now suffer from job insecurity and very low wages. The government may have to rethink its macroeconomic and trade policies that promote dependence on the export markets and neglect production for domestic needs. It must start to develop its own industries, relying on local resources and employing better technology and skilled workers. Developing an industrial base with high growth potential will absorb the labour force from the urban and rural areas and will stem the outward migration of women. It will also diminish employment of women in low-skill, low value-added economic activities such as those found in the informal sector. Strengthening and prioritizing food security alongside rural development will not only make food accessible to the poor, but will also stimulate and promote growth of rural-based industries, increase rural-urban linkages, make development more equitable, sustainable, less import-dependent and gender-fair. The continuing lack of safety nets for those adversely affected by globalization is a cause for concern as the poor continue to reel from the effects of the crisis.

Economic globalization has meant that many companies are cutting costs. They are doing this by downsizing. This means laying off staff, reducing salaries and benefits, hiring part-time staff as opposed to full-time, using home-based workers, firing older staff about to receive pensions, and giving remaining staff increased workloads. Because women are more likely to be at the bottom of the rung, they are often the most affected. Downsizing affects women's home lives as well. Women experience increased stress when men lose employment, as they are forced to take on more of the financial responsibilities. In a world where men's self-worth is often tied up in their jobs, women with jobless husbands may well need to provide extra emotional support.

Globalization reducing public services also affects women's unpaid work as they are forced to pick up the slack that the public sector leaves out. Women take care of patients sent home too early from the hospital, they find ways to teach their children things they're not learning in school because classrooms are overcrowded and special education services are gone, and cook meals for older neighbours when funding for community food programmes is cut. Women also keep families and communities stable through times of economic uncertainty. They improvise to feed their families when money becomes even scarcer. Women also find jobs in an even tougher job market and are willing to work for lower pay when that's all they can find.

Women have been taking a variety of initiatives to promote different, more gender-sensitive approaches to economic policy and global governance. These include improving economic literacy of women's advocacy groups; greater participation by women in economic policy processes; training policy-makers to review economic issues from a gender perspective; finding ways to 'engender' economic analysis; and pressing for changes in global economic governance, especially changes in the WTO. Ways have been identified of analysing links between economic policy and unpaid work. Gender issues in the WTO agenda have been identified. Women's groups are particularly concerned about the way in which the WTO and its rules and enforcement mechanism have enlarged the scope of policies that can be considered 'barriers to trade' to include most of national economic and social policies. The initiatives identified need to be gathered together in a global campaign for economic justice with a woman's face. Government and international organizations concerned with economic policy must make complementary changes so that ways of organizing the global economy recognize people as providers of care for one another and not just as producers of commodities, and subject markets to socially-negotiated regulations, in which social values as well as prices are recognized. Only then will the conditions for the progress of all women be secure.

Women are still very much in a minority among internet users. The internet is being used by women for e-inclusion, to overcome the constraints of seclusion; e-campaigns, to mobilize online for women's human rights and other objectives; e-commerce, to reach new markets; and e-consultation, to get women's views made known. But women still face huge imbalances in the ownership, control and regulation of this new information.

Women remain largely absent at all levels of policy formulation and decision-making in natural resource and environmental management, conservation, protection and rehabilitation, and their experience and skills in advocacy for and monitoring of proper natural resource management. Women are rarely trained as professional natural resource managers with policy-making capacities, such as land-use planners, agriculturists, foresters, marine scientists and environmental lawyers. It is often not ignorance but literally the distrust of women's abilities to cope with new technology and mystification of globalization that leads to their neglect in official programmes. Environmental change imposes new stresses and choices on women and men's lives. Evolution in gender roles induced by environmental change can mean better communication and shared decision-making, but negotiating new roles and responsibilities can be a painful process. There is a need for information, education and empowerment and to humanize the whole process of globalization to enable women to bring their perspective on environmental protection to the fore. Women gain knowledge and experience both in their home and working environment, yet this double contribution to society often denies them the opportunity to influence the decision-making process. It is essential not only to build on traditional knowledge, but also to ensure that women have the opportunity to use it to influence decisions at all levels – whether local, regional or global.

Men and women need to be alerted to the threats that globalization poses. Gender sensitization and humanizing the process of liberalization and globalization would not only improve 'our' today but also protect and preserve the environment for 'others' tomorrow. This situation is now changing as women assume an increasingly more visible role in the environmental community. In this context, women and children can be very active participants in the defence of the environment and can stop, or even reverse, the degradation of our natural resources. At a global level, there is growing awareness of the need to get women to contribute to the identification of environmental problems, as well as to help plan activities geared to the sustainable development of their communities. Public opinion is one of the most important areas of work for promoting environmental concerns and interests. Women in local organizations have a firsthand knowledge of the impact of environmental degradation in their communities. Through their work with the media, they can help publicize regional examples of the abuse of the environment. Within this framework of planning, women must be acknowledged as political subjects, capable of contributing to the economy in such a way that sustainable development can be reached. Women are bearers of a powerful impulse for change and, therefore, they are capable of contributing to the creation of a style of development that favours social justice and respect for the environment. It is important to maximize social flexibility and the resources people can bring to negotiations with each other and with the natural world.

National policies need to be reformulated to accelerate democratization, gender sensitization and institutional development to keep in pace with globalization. They should focus on increased accountability and transparency throughout the economy, and especially in the formulation and implementation of public policy and channel more public investment to human capability formation, and preserving the autonomy of the state to exercise fiscal and monetary policies to achieve both macroeconomic stability and growth. There is a need to reform domestic policies that both distort trade and have negative environmental impacts (e.g., energy subsidies) and correct existing market failures through efficient incentive systems (economic instruments) that internalize environmental costs, to avert their magnification by trade liberalization and economic integration. Improve the effectiveness of environmental policy through the involvement of businesses, NGOs and local communities in monitoring and enforcement rather than relying on the state's limited budget and weak regulatory enforcement, capacity. Instruments of empowerment include information disclosure in environmental performance of firms, and provision of training and other capacity-building services to communities. The social adjustment policies to cushion economic dislocation and avert the marginalization of the women and poor needs to be institutionalized. It must be recognized, however, that the autonomy of the state to act deliberately to protect the environment or to cushion the impact on women or other changes brought about by globalization is limited by the need to compete in the global economy for capital, jobs and markets.

Part III

Questioning the Traditional Citadels

11

Gender Biases in Caste- and Kinship-based Organizations

A Study in Rural Haryana

P.S. VERMA

The caste- and kinship-based organizations in rural India are so tacitly and irrefutably accepted that their framework of customary norms has become integral to the social action and behaviour of the people in the countryside. Even those who denounce the role of parochial identities and their normative perspective, which bolster patriarchy and are considered to be anachronistic, have often joined the race to secure access to the levers of power and patronage through the caste and lineage groups. Since the structures of caste and sub-caste are widely used to realize the socio-economic and political aspirations, our electoral democracy has also given them a new lease of life, resulting in frequent caste-based assertions to widen their space in the realms of power politics. 'We now have a plethora of assertive caste identities each privileging an angular hierarchy.'[1] The long-held assumption that the process of development and democracy would end the 'curse of caste' and strengthen secular politics and gender equality has been belied. In many states, including Haryana, politics cannot be analysed without comprehending the interlocking of caste or sub-caste with power politics.

According to some sociologists, 'nowhere in north-western India is the discourse of caste as prevalent as it is in Haryana'.[2] Normally, the caste and sub-caste identities take precedence over other identities in the state. However, the framework of cultural codes and customary norms, which provide splendour to caste and lineage ties, has buttressed patriarchy and disparaged gender equality. According to Prem Chowdhry:

> In Haryana, the control of women's behaviour through certain customs has been central to the affirmation of the solidarity of the dominant Jat peasant group. Such customs, emerging from the growth and demands of a patriarchy and interacting with specific geo-economic needs, have been largely constrictive for women. Further, when such customs came to be buttressed with the force of law by the colonial government, who became conscious agents in their perpetuation, the customs naturally became more binding upon Jats and other social groups in Haryana, making it either difficult or impossible for a woman to break out of their confines. The tenacious persistence of historically crystallized customs and attitudes made a mockery of attempts by women to contest these and often involved them in prolonged legal battles and open confrontations.[3]

The cultural milieu of the state of Haryana has been considerably impacted by the caste and kinship factors. A.B. Mukerji in his study on 'Territorial Expression of the Dominant Caste in Early Twentieth Century Haryana' observed: 'Stability of the traditional caste regions as evidenced by historical documents and folk recognitions has placed them in the network of culture area. Each major dominant caste in the state has been associated with a caste region named after it.'[4] Presently, if the Jats dominate in districts like Jhajjar, Rohtak, Sonipat, Bhiwani. Jind, Kaithal, Hisar, etc., the Ahirs dominate in the Ahirwal region covering Mahendergarh, Rewari and Gurgaon districts and the Meos exclusively in Mewat, encompassing the revenue blocks of Nuh, Taoru, Nagina, Ferozpur Jhirka and Punhana. Similarly, the Gujjars command hold in certain Assembly segments like Chhachroli, Samalakha, Mewala Maharajpur and partly Narnaul and Naraingarh, and the Rajputs in Ballabhgarh, Mundhal Khurd, Gharaunda, etc. The people in the countryside behave more as members of a caste or clan and the western notion of individualism has hardly penetrated into their customary and social terrain. The perceptions of dominant castes have also influenced the socio-cultural ethos of other castes and lineage groups in the respective zones. The 'ubiquitous domination by a single caste (despite internal economic disparities) set the tune and shaped the customs and attitudes that became common in rural Haryana. The emergent customs followed by most Jats came to be accepted and projected for the entire region ... .'[5] In fact, the Jats who were numerically dominant and owned landed assets, had emerged as 'a crucial community' in the political set-up of the Central and South-East Punjab during the colonial period. 'The British, who regarded the Jats as the best cultivators and excellent soldiers, reinforced their superiority as a social group over other communities and encouraged their customs and norms for women.'[6] With regard to gender relations, the 'patriarchal identity has been dominant among the Jats'. The same holds true about the other castes in the region, particularly in rural areas. The rural women are an asset to the economy and work harder than men, contributing substantially to the family income. They share agricultural work and undertake the tedious household duties such as cooking, rearing children and performing multifarious tasks relating to animal husbandry. But they hardly find any space in activities other than the domestic chores. In fact, most of them are kept away from decisions pertaining to public life. Moreover, most of the women in the rural areas, irrespective of caste, creed and religion, observe *Ghunghat* (veil). In spite of wide-ranging changes in the socio-economic sphere, the reality as expressed through a widely quoted proverb from Jainarayan Verma's *Haryanavi Lokoktiyan: Shastriya Vishaleshan* (1972) – '*Beerbani ghar ki bani*' (a woman who remains at home adorns it) – is yet to be invalidated in rural Haryana.

Similarly, the old mindset that identifies women with qualities of passivity, submissiveness and sacrifice has yet to be changed in the agrarian set-up. Like a proverb says, *'Nuan bhali jo chup'* (For the daughter-in-law it is proper to be bashful).[7] Another age-old local saying in the region has emphasized:

> *Andar baithi lakh di*
> *Bahr gayi Kakh di.*[8]

All this shows that the deep-seated patriarchal dominance and its supportive social structures have never allowed the women to enter into the public sphere. The aforesaid antiquated constructs still influence the people in rural areas. In other words, the archaic sayings which used to rationalize the superiority of men over women have yet to lose ground. Moreover, the factor of male dominance is not peculiar to any particular caste or sub-caste but commonly observed by the various socio-religious identities in the north-western region. The son preference stands to be the most salient feature of this region. It has been further strengthened by the customary norms and agrarian economy. People prefer sons over daughters. They need a male child to inherit property. During the colonial phase, the death of an infant daughter was perceived to be a sign of luck for parents and death of a son as a terrible misfortune, as vividly explained by a proverb:

> *Chora mare nirbhag ka,*
> *Chori mare bhagwan ki.*

(The one whose son dies is unlucky and the one whose daughter dies is lucky.)[9] Similar mindset is reflected in another folklore as *'Dunia mein do garib batae, aek beti, aek bail'* (there are two unlucky creatures in the world: a daughter and a drought bull).[10] The obsession with sons is also illustrated from the blessings often showered by the elderly women upon the young married women:

Budd Suhagin, sat puttari ho

(May you enjoy married status till your old age and be blessed with seven sons).[11]

The aforesaid blessings are widely prevalent in the region and the old women continue to bless the younger ones (brides, *bahus,* etc.) almost in a similar manner in the northern belt. In fact, the elderly ladies always shower such blessings when the younger ones touch their feet in reverence. The number of such discriminatory proverbs or, for that matter, sayings, songs, stories, etc., may be multiplied. The gender biases are also reflected in naming the daughters as Dhapali, Manbhari, Bhateri, Maari, etc.

The Adverse Child Sex Ratio

The craving for a male child, which is rooted in the patriarchally steeped cultural context, has also resulted in the adverse child sex ratio in the state and its neighbourhood. Of late, it has acquired alarming proportion and become a pandemic mainly because of the practices of preconception and pre-natal diagnostic tests, selective abortions, etc. According to a United Nations Population Fund (UNFPA) report, as much as 62,000 sex-selective abortions were recorded in Haryana during 1996–98, which itself indicated a clear gender bias in preference of a male child. Indeed, the state has become alert on the issue but the policies and mechanism of incentives to boost girl child ratio have failed to make much difference in the situation. The facts are revealing that the girl child is still unwelcome in Haryana. According to the 2001 census, out of the total population of 211.45 lakhs, the number of males was 113.64 lakhs and females as low as 97.81 lakhs.[12] 'Out of India's 50 districts with child sex ratio lower than 850, 17 districts are in Haryana.'[13] The phenomenon of adverse child sex ratio has hardly ceased to exist as revealed by the recent press reports as:

> From 860 females per every 1,000 males in 2007, the sex ratio went down to 854 in 2008 and further slinked down to 852 this year (2009), reflecting that the government's policies and incentives to encourage the girl child stand no chance against rigid mindset.[14]

The falling sex ratio could also be attributed to factors like the customary norms, rigid mindset, political economy of the agrarian order, matters of inheritance, etc. If this trend is not checked in time, it may cause social disequilibrium, resulting in a large number of males remaining single. Incidentally, the adverse sex ratio has been persisting since long. According to Chowdhry, 'the absolute number of married females is more than that of the married males in Haryana.'[15] In some parts of the state, the practice of bringing brides from far-off states, especially for the semi-literate, unemployed youths and those owning little agricultural land, has already begun. According to some studies:

> In Haryana and in Western UP, the Jat caste which dominates the region is suffering especially from what demographers call a 'male marriage squeeze'. With sex ratio in the low 800s, there is an accumulated male marriage squeeze; as smaller female cohorts are born and there are more men left unmarried in preceding and new cohorts, the greater the marriage imbalance. In Haryana, currently, at least one in every four men stands to remain unmarried and may have to resort to bringing a bride from Assam, West Bengal, Kerala and a myriad other states.[16]

A recent survey conducted by the AIDWA unit of Haryana, while narrating the pathetic condition of the brides brought from different states, revealed that 'many of these women from extremely poor backgrounds come in contact through migratory labour, through contractors or through people involved in transport business, etc. As many of these "bought wives" have no proper marriage ceremonies or registration of their marriages, they have no legal status as wives. This renders them vulnerable to sexual exploitation ... '.[17] Incidentally, the fewer number of brides in the state 'has in no way led to any decrease in dowry demands or enhancement of the status of local women'.[18] Those who have jobs or belong to economically well-off families hardly marry without handsome dowry. It was thought that the growing pace of change and the process of modernity and development would ease the situation and accelerate the pace for gender equality, but it has not come true. The various state-sponsored programmes and schemes such as *Ladli,* gender sensitization, women's awareness, award for rural adolescent girls, construction of Anganwadi centres, statutory laws, monitoring bodies, instructions for oath-taking against foeticide in educational institutions, etc., have failed to make a mark, so far. Even the growing rate of literacy among women and their increasing participation in the governance at the grassroots level has not been able to change the all-pervasive patriarchal framework.

PRIs' Contributions

There is no exaggeration in saying that an increased number of women in the three-tier structure of Panchayati Raj has brought about a silent revolution in the spheres of public life in rural areas. The number of women representatives elected to the village panchayats as on December 1, 2006 was as high as 23,897 (i.e., 36.1% of the total representatives) in the state of Haryana. Interestingly, some of them won the seats which were not reserved for women candidates. The dream of the 'bottom-upwards pattern of power sharing' may still be far off, yet the 73rd Amendment Act has marked a turning point in the life of women and widened their space in the governance at local levels. Mention may also be made here that the performance of certain women sarpanches has been better than their male counterparts. For example, Nirmala Devi, sarpanch of Risalva village panchayat (in Karnal district), succeeded in getting 128 acres of common land freed from encroachers after fighting a legal battle for 16 months in the Punjab and Haryana High Court. She won the case on March 15, 2003. Having won the battle, she claimed that her panchayat was the richest panchayat in the area.[19]

However, the participation of women at the local level is yet to cross certain limitations, like their lack of interest in politics, passivity and recruitment from relatively better-off families representing elitist background. But there is no doubt that thousands of women members in Panchayati Raj Institutions have very humble origins and belong to economically backward families of weaker sections. This, among others, has also made it untenable to hold that 'oligarchic forces are yielding no benefits to weaker sections'. Nonetheless, in most cases the decisive role of their husbands or male relatives in performing their responsibilities and actions cannot be overlooked. Many of the elected women function as figureheads with someone else acting as *de facto* representative. The epithet of 'Sarpanchpati' is hardly a misnomer in many cases. Most of the women have made it due to reservation and the support extended by the male members of their families and other relatives. The empirical studies 'clearly indicate that given the continued patriarchal culture of our society, most of the women who contest the panchayat elections would not be able to do so in the absence of reservations'.[20] Moreover, a vast majority of women remain split on caste basis than thinking in terms of gender solidarity. There exists a nexus between caste and patriarchy and when women identify with caste or lineage over the gender, it strengthens patriarchal institutions than promoting any gender equality. The upper caste women assert for their own hierarchical status rather than working hand in hand with the lower class women in a feminist movement. In other words, women generally remain within the bounds of a *maryada* of devotion to their husbands and also to the customary norms of caste or lineage, which obviously maintain the social equilibrium than challenging the existing hierarchical system and gender biases. Matters like male dominance, domestic slavery, exploitation of women, fight against traditional norms or cultural codes, etc., have hardly engaged their attention. Nor have the issues like women's right to property and landed assets been ever attended to. It is rightly said, 'What one sees in these local bodies today is public patriarchy whereby the women are included but not allowed to participate and their work is consistently undervalued.'[21]

Caste Organizations

The patriarchal norms are further consolidated by the well-organized caste associations or federations. 'A *Jati* (caste) does not just hang together like the parts of a cart, it must be actively maintained. To do so, men assume certain roles and support certain agencies. Central to *Jati* maintenance are the leadership roles and the panchayat patterns that are used at every level from family and lineage to regional council. These roles and patterns are highly formalized in some *Jatis*',[22] whereas in others such *Jati* organizations may be quite informal. 'Organisations need not be ineffective because they are informal; both formal and informal organizations have their respective advantages for social maintenance.'[23]

In the villages of Haryana, the caste associations and Khap Panchayats have been very powerful means of caste maintenance. Almost every caste in the state has its panchayat, which defends the interests of its constituents and guards against any outside encroachment in their respective domain. Regarding issues of common interests, the caste panchayats also work in alliance with other caste associations. Among the caste organizations, one may include the Haryana Jat Mahasabha, Sarv-Jatiya Mahapanchayats, Brahmin Mahasabha, Aggarwal Mahasabha, Rajput Pratinidhi Sabha, Yadav Mahasabha, Saini Mahasabha, Chamar Biradari Mahasabha, Dhanak Mahasabha and so on. In addition to single-caste associations, multi-caste organizations have also come into existence. The 'All India Punjabi Sabha' can be cited as an example in this regard. These organizations jostle for greater space and articulate the socio-economic and political interests of their constituents. Among the varieties of tasks which have engaged their attention include contributions to community institutions like dharamshalas, chaupals, schools, colleges, hostels, etc. Besides this, such panchayats have provided support to economically poor families of their group for education, marriage, shelter, etc. Almost every major caste has its own association at the district and state level. In the wake of elections, these organizations acquire phenomenal significance. They assert for share of power and also attempt to influence the major political parties in the state to allocate adequate number of seats to their respective candidates. Even the various Dalit castes which had suffered the agony of caste hierarchy in the past have started asserting through the caste associations. Ironically, such associations, though they have acquired a paramount importance in the state's polity and public sphere and also provided a link between the democratic system and the people leading to their increased participation, hardly provide any adequate space to women in terms of membership and decision-making. As a matter of fact, women are ignored as they have little space to assert for their interests through these preponderantly male-dominated associations. It is only a token participation granted to women in times of agitational politics launched to strengthen the cause of the respective castes. There is no exaggeration in saying that the caste associations hardly encourage women to enter into the realms of public life. Moreover, regarding the matrimonial alliances, the caste associations have invariably upheld the norms of caste endogamy and village and gotra (clan, an exogamous category to regulate marriage matches)[24] exogamy. The self-choice marriages outside the caste have been rarely approved and appreciated by caste organizations.

Khap Panchayats

The institution of Khap Panchayat is unique with the landowning Jats in Haryana, western UP, Delhi (rural) and Rajasthan. Since the Jats are 'organized into exogamous patri-clans', the clan councils as 'corporate group structures' have played a vital role in their socio-economic and political life. In spite of challenges and threats of elimination from one period to another, the Khap Panchayats have shown a great resilience. During the colonial period, the new land revenue system, judiciary and law and order mechanism had deprived them of many of their traditional powers and privileges. Similarly, in the post-independence period, the statutory village panchayats have divested Khap Panchayats of most of their functions and capabilities. Apart from this, because of the expansion of the activities of the state in the day-to-day affairs of the people and frequent judicial rulings against the khap leaders, the sanctity of these panchayats has been considerably diluted. Nonetheless, they frequently hit the headlines, particularly in the wake of contentious marriages, social disputes and periodic elections. Their followers, in disregard to diverse intellectuals and political campaigns against Khap Panchayats, still regard them as harbingers of culture and widely-accepted norm of Bhaichara (fraternity).

While defining the concept of *khap,* M.C. Pradhan in his study in the Meerut Division (UP) observed that 'the Jat clan has a compact geographical area of its own. The villages in which a clan is settled are organized into a clan council, and the area under its jurisdiction is called the khap'.[25] These socio-cultural and political institutions hold control and protect the customary norms in areas comprising one or more gotra-dominated villages settled in contiguity. Each clan council or Khap Panchayat is headed by a Pradhan or Chaudhary who convenes and conducts its meeting, whenever required. Some Khap Panchayats have hereditary headmen, whereas others are headed by the elected Pradhans, who are elected by the khap members on the basis of consensus, not through ballot. But, in most cases, they are elected only from the ancestral village inhabited or settled by the ancestors or founders of the khap. Most of the Pradhans are elderly persons belonging to relatively better-off agriculturist families and command understanding about the traditions and customs which guide the social relations and interactions of the people within the area of the khap. While highlighting the importance of the khap system, most of the Pradhans during the course of field study made a reference to the concept of *Panch Parmeshwar* (five panchas as embodiments of God delivering divine justice) and emphasized that Khap Panchayats had settled disputes without any discrimination or bias. According to them, the families or persons in dispute would never lie before the Khap Panchayat because the villagers participating in the meeting have known each other for long and interacted frequently for interpersonal matters. Further, while venerating the caste norms, they claimed that the Khap Panchayats had imparted justice on the basis of the time-honoured traditions and customs.

In terms of composition, the Khap Panchayats have been 'an all-male affair'. Women have been hardly allowed to participate in the meetings of Khap Panchayats. It was only recently (2010) that women participants were mobilized by the khap leaders to participate in the meetings of *Sarv Jatiya Khap Mahapanchayats* at Kurukshetra on April 13, 2010; Pai grain market on May 2, 2010; Kaithal town on May 10, 2010; Jind on May 23, 2010, etc. Basically it was done to counter the media and women organizations calling Khap Panchayats as *Talibani*, *Tughlaqi* and *Kangaroo* courts that follow the anti-women and anti-youth agenda. The Mahapanchayat also formed the women wing of the *Sarv Jatiya Khap* in its meeting at the Pai grain market on May 2, 2010. The president of the Mahila Wing of the *Sarv Jatiya Khap Mahapanchayat,* while addressing the meeting, declared that the Mahila Wing would launch a campaign against foeticide and dowry system. However, the Mahapanchayat vowed to fight for amendments in the Hindu Marriage Act, 1955 (5) to ban marriages in the 'same gotra, mother's gotra, same village and adjoining village'. Incidentally, on the eve of the meeting of Mahapanchayat at Jind on May 23, 2010, the Kisan leader Mahender Singh Tikait, Pradhan of the Balian Khap Panchayat in UP, said, 'We cannot tolerate such marriages. If the Central government fails to bring a legislation to ban such marriages, there will be no option but to gherao Parliament.'[26]

However, in terms of typology, most of the Khap Panchayats being kinship-based are single-gotra khaps, while some are based on multi-gotra and multi-castes. This apart, the *Sarv Khap Panchayats,* conglomerates of various khaps, clans, castes and communities, have also been organized from time to time. 'Though the *Sarv Khap Panchayat* as an institution is not based upon kinship affinity, it is an extension of the principle which acts as a charter for the khap, clan and caste councils.'[27] The matters relating to inter-caste disputes or problems involving more than one khap or, for that matter, resentment against the interventions and policies of the state have also been taken up by the *Sarv Khap Panchayats,* a quintessence of the *Sarv Jatiya Khap Mahapanchayat.* The representatives or delegates from different Khap Panchayats participate in the meeting of *Sarv Khap Panchayats.* Sometimes, the meetings of the *Sarv Jatiya Khap Panchayats* have also taken up issues concerning excessive expenditure in marriages, menace of substance abuse, etc. Similarly, the *Sarv Khap Panchayats* have articulated on development projects like roads, schools, electricity, irrigation, etc. In the past, the *Sarv Khap Panchayats* of the region had also fought against the invaders, autocratic rulers and the colonial regime. The major khaps of the region had actively participated in the 1857 revolt against the alien rulers. Bahadur Shah Zafar in his speech on July 1, 1857 also acknowledged and appreciated the support extended by the *Sarv Khap Panchayat* of the Haryana region.[28] While earlier these panchayats had enjoyed administrative and judicial powers, now they are left with only a customary mode of existence without any legal sanctity. But the customary norms and constituents of these panchayats have made them so ubiquitous and strong that even the politicians maintain a cautious silence on their controversial decisions. Strangely enough, in August 2009, all the 12 sarpanchas of the *Kadian* gotra-dominated village panchayats in Jhajjar district submitted their resignation in support of the Khap Panchayat's stand on the gotra row over a forbidden marriage with a girl of the *Kadian* gotra.

In terms of origins, the '*Khap Panchayats* are believed to have been there since the Mauryan times. They also find mention in the records of Pratiharas and the succeeding dynasties of Chahamanas, Parmaras and Chalukyas'.[29] Likewise, some writers have viewed that Khap Panchayats were organized and united in the 7th century AD during the reign of king Harshvardhna.

Presently, it is the gotra-dominated Khap Panchayats which have acquired prominence in Haryana and elsewhere. They are multi-village panchayats wielding considerable economic and political clout to act as 'instruments of social control'. They hold their control and protect the customary norms in an area comprising a series of villages in contiguity. They are based on the principle of local contiguity and *Khap Bhaichara.* Some Khap Panchayats comprise as many as 84 villages settled in contiguity. Their activities are now centred around the social issues or the customary norms concerning matrimonial alliances, patrilineal inheritance and the status and identity of the lineage group. While upholding the traditional caste values and cultural norms, they have opposed the inter-caste, inter-faith, intra-clan and intra-village marriages and sex relations. Moreover, they do not appreciate love or court marriages. Likewise, while protecting khap exogamy, they have opposed marriages of boys with girls belonging to a dominant gotra which wields leading influence in the village. In fact, the girls of dominant gotra could be accepted only as sisters, not as wives, even if they come from far-off villages. The breach of the customary practice of caste endogamy and clan and village exogamy has been vociferously opposed. The decisions of Khap Panchayats are taken on the basis of general consensus and a 'spirit of compromise'. Once a decision is taken, it becomes morally binding upon the persons or groups concerned. The defiance is not taken kindly by the Khap Panchayats.

Sometimes khaps have taken very harsh and regressive decisions on the pretext of honouring the traditional customary *biradari* norms, resulting in honour killings, annulment of marriages, grooms' dispossession of ancestral property, boycott, ostracism, exile, etc. In spite of such cruel dispensations, the Khap Panchayats have sustained, not diminished. Their edicts are overwhelmingly supported by the people in the villages for caste, clan, family and village pride. Of late, they have become controversial and their decisions have frequently been turned down by the judiciary. Yet they continue to exercise deep influence on the caste and clan's men. The community claims in the Jat villages have priority over individual rights and the caste, clan or lineal affinities backed by customary norms and practices are adhered to. Some scholars, while commenting on the Jat farmers, have observed: 'For the traditional Jats in the villages of west UP, freedom means the liberty to follow their traditions, lifestyles and customs without hindrance from outside. Many of them still believe that they would be better-off if they could settle disputes at the village or at the *Khap Panchayat* level.'[30] Since they preach and practice customary norms of caste and gotras, their social behaviour is largely determined by group identity than the factor of self or individual being as an autonomous or soul entity. Thus, they oppose any infringement with the norms such as gotra and village *bhaichara*. The Jats are neither primitive nor less modern and industrious, yet their social framework and values in villages do not find the liberal or, for that matter, the Marxian narrative of modernity as valid and tenable.

They even justify resentment against interventions by the state and judiciary in their normative spheres. They do not want laws that go against their cultural codes which determine their behaviour and inter-personal relations. Recently, the executive committee of the *Meham Chaubisi Khap*, while opposing alliances within gotras and villages, resolved that courts and government authorities had been according legal sanction to weddings within the gotra, 'which is not acceptable to the Hindu society and the Haryanvi society as same-gotra weddings are against our social norms'.[31] A khap leader, who considered Khap Panchayats as custodian of social norms, tradition, clan, culture, etc., 'claimed that khaps are above judicial courts as they were ensuring rules and regulation to run societies smoothly well before courts came into existence'.[32] The paternalistic interventions by Khap Panchayats are accepted over the considerations of autonomy of individual. In the villages, the Khap Panchayats have even settled cases of murder, rape, inheritance of property, inter-clan and inter-caste disputes, etc. People in the Jat heartland come to them for resolving long-pending disputes. 'In several areas these groups have helped resolve disputes on land and water, worked for development by getting the people to pool funds for village infrastructure and even banned liquor and dowry.'[33] Most people in the villages otherwise also prefer resolution of conflicts at local levels than approaching the police and judiciary because of expenses, delay in court cases and other hassles such as exploitation by the professionals, police, etc. Even the critics of Khap Panchayats maintain that factors like lack of faith in the legal system and fear of being humiliated by the police have turned illegal caste panchayats into law-enforcing agencies.

Patrilineal Inheritance

Being paternalistic in profile, the khap leaders in contravention of the Hindu Succession Act, 1956, have supported the view that the right of inheritance of property should confine to male descendants, which, according to them, would save the agriculturist families from faction fights and fragmentation of holdings. Most of the farmers in the north-western region of the country, irrespective of caste and religion, hold similar views on matters such as patrilineal inheritance, caste endogamy and clan and village exogamy. Women have been victims of abuses and violence for maintaining tradition by observing caste endogamy and gotra and village exogamy, which ensure that property remains within the patriarchal domain. The enactment of laws regarding the right of inheritance to women has rarely made any difference in the region. According to some scholars:

> The only ideal and honourable pattern of inheritance is acknowledged to be by males from males. This means basically that daughters and sisters, who are potential introducers of fresh blood and new descent lines through their husbands, are to be kept away from exercising their inheritance rights. The introduction of a non-caste outsider, the daughter's husband, into the family who can and may claim the property on behalf of his wife needed to be effectively stopped. As an outsider, he remains outside the influence of the family and caste/community rules and ethics which ensure a patrilineal inheritance. Similarly, the location of a married daughter within the natal village also spells danger to patrilineal inheritance as it facilitates and could lead to assumption of land inherited by her.[34]

It may be mentioned here that the Hindu Succession Act, 1956, which treats a daughter on par with a son regarding parental property, has hardly received any support from the political leaders in Haryana. Conversely, the State Legislature passed a resolution in 1967 requesting the Central Government to change the Succession Act. 'However, the then Indira Government refused to oblige. A similar resolution was passed in 1979. The President of India withheld his assent to it.'[35] Thus, despite the succession Act, women, barring exceptions, have no control over the landed assets.

Limitations and Support Structure of Khap Panchayats

The ideology and functioning of Khap Panchayats have invited sharp reactions from a variety of people in the media, civil liberty groups, academics, judiciary, etc. They view that khaps, which act as a parallel system of justice and advance the cause of stagnant and retrogressive socio-cultural milieu, need to be banned and tackled with a heavy hand. According to critics, these institutions defy law, ignore women and sanction murder, honour killings, social boycott, exile, etc. They are often labelled as *Talibani* organizations. The issue of honour killings also rocked the Indian Parliament in August 2009. The Union Home Minister, while replying in the Upper House, said he recoiled with shame after reading about the brutal killing of a young man in Jind (Haryana) and two teenagers in Meerut (UP). However, the khap leaders have rejected the allegation that they have ever taken harsh decisions or supported honour killings. Contrary to this, they have accused the media of writing wrong things to defame the Khap Panchayats. However, the media continue to criticize them as perpetrators of violence by annulling marriages and asking couples to live like siblings. Some academicians have viewed that 'khap today is a pale replica of its past, undemocratic in its structure and functioning. Women, who constitute about half the population, have no place in it.'[36] Likewise, the State President of AIDWA, while maintaining that Khap Panchayats openly defy the law of the land by issuing illegal diktats, said, 'As couples are selectively targeted, it is clear the real motive is to control women's sexuality and to ensure that property remains within the patriarchal caste domain.'[37]

Interestingly, some of the brides, whose marriages were annulled by khaps, have also approached the police and judiciary for justice. Recently, one of the affected brides with a ten-month-old son submitted an application to the SSP, Rohtak, demanding immediate action against the 21-gotra khap members who had pronounced annulment of her three-year old marriage. Unfortunately, her father-in-law 'was paraded around the village with a shoe shoved into his mouth' by the panchayat members.[38] Similarly, some brides approached the judiciary and won cases against khap leaders. The recent verdict, first of its kind, by the Additional District and Sessions Judge at Karnal, awarding death sentence to five persons, life term to one and seven-year imprisonment to another one, was also given on the basis of efforts made by an elderly woman.

Anyway, the khap system continues to persist in spite of heavy odds against it. The factors such as allegiance of people to the customary norms of caste and lineage, agricultural economy, role of khaps in history, their participation in the farmers' agitation for remunerative prices, supply of electricity, waiving of loans and power dues, etc., have sustained them in the state. Their followers always accept the paternalistic interventions by the Khap Panchayats. A survey carried out by *Hindustan Times* revealed that as many as 77 per cent of the respondents favoured ideology of gotra exogamy. Likewise, 63 per cent of the respondents favoured amendment to the Hindu Marriage Act, 1955 to bar same-gotra marriages. Interestingly, 34 per cent of the respondents replied that Khap Panchayats have the right to order the social boycott of the couple if it violates same-gotra marriage rules. Surprisingly, in Chandigarh city too, '65 per cent of the respondents opposed the same-gotra marriages'.[39] The survey was carried out in Chandigarh, Rohtak, Jind, Bhiwani and Kurukshetra. The people generally believe that the members of patrilineal clan share descent from a common ancestor and are bound by a morality of brother-sister relations. Any infringement of clan exogamy, according to them, becomes a blot on the honour of the clan, caste, village and family. Since people are born in a specific milieu, they abide by the norms of the society they are a part of.

This apart, the Khap Panchayats represent the largest vote bank which determines the political fortunes of around half of the MLAs and Parliament members in the state. Some Khap Panchayats like the *Meham Chaubisi* have invariably sponsored or adopted candidates, who, barring exceptions, have been successful in winning elections. In fact, the support pledged by a major khap has often ensured a sure victory. Sometimes, even the lightweight politicians have won against the powerful leaders due to the support of their Khap Panchayat. Since the Khaps wield tremendous political clout, the major political parties have never intervened in their affairs. The Chief Minister of Haryana maintains that Khap Panchayats are social organizations and they do not have any say in matters like honour killings. More than that, a senior Congress MLA and a former Home and Finance Minister of Haryana, while advocating a ban on the same-gotra marriage, said 'the Khap Panchayats acted as guardian in preserving our rich cultural heritage and values ...'[40] The ruling Congress apart, the Indian National Lok Dal, the major Opposition party in Haryana, has strongly backed the Khap Panchayats on the issue of same-gotra marriages. The state president of the party also demanded a special session of the State Assembly and gave a notice for a non-official resolution regarding amendments to the Hindu Marriage Act, 1955 for prohibiting such unions.[41] Similarly, a Rajya Sabha member from the Congress party also gave the notice, seeking permission to introduce the Hindu Marriage Act (Amendment) Bill, 2010 to the Rajya Sabha secretariat on May 6, 2010. He said that customs and age-old traditions prohibited marriages in the same village and in the same gotra and sapinda of each other.[42] These leaders have done so in view of the *Sarv Khap Mahapanchayat's* recent demand for amendment to the Hindu Marriage Act, 1955 to ban the same-gotra and same-village marriages. Another Congress MP, a US-educated business tycoon, said that these panchayats had given new direction to society and protected the social customs and traditions. He also said that he would carry their message and sentiments to the party and Parliament and support their fight.[43]

The inference that one can draw from the above analysis is that the caste and gotra-based panchayats operate in a milieu which is highly impregnated with the customary practices and cultural codes deep-seated in the behaviour, psyche and actions of the people. The nexus between the customary norms and the patriarchal system, which is sustained and strengthened by the structures of caste and lineage that mould the actions and thinking of the people in the agrarian mode, has yet to be broken by the modern state to facilitate the pace of a secular and progressive discourse. However, the electoral democracy, which weighs the caste-based vote bank over other considerations, has instead provided a new impetus to the primordial ties of caste and lineage rooted in the age-old hierarchical set-up in which the gender biases galore. The structures of caste, patriarchy, and the related customs and cultural nuances are virtually supplementary and complementary to each other. They have in-built gender biases and resist discourse on empowerment of women. Whenever the women assert for inheritance rights and dishonour the customary norms of caste endogamy and gotra and village exogamy, they become victim of male-intolerance. In other words, when girls prefer marriage of their choice, they face the wrath of kin or the lineage groups. If the lineage organizations annul such marriages and ostracize or exile the couples, the kin or relatives hack them to death, lynch, strangle, behead, stone to death, beat, etc. The problem has become endemic in the north-western region.

Recently, a study commissioned by the National Commission of Women (NCW) and conducted by the Shakti Vahini (a civil society organization) revealed that 72 per cent of the 326 documented honour-related crimes in states like Punjab, Haryana and Uttar Pradesh over the past one year involved couples that entered into inter-caste marriages. Of the remaining cases, only 3 per cent youngsters were involved in same-gotra marriages, 15 per cent in marriages without the consent of families, 7 per cent in runaway marriages and 1 per cent in interreligious weddings. According to the study, 'honour crimes are happening primarily in situations where girls are walking out of families to exercise their own choice of marrying a boy from other caste or someone their parents didn't consent to'. Basically, the study attributed honour crimes to patriarchal society intolerance for girl's empowerment. The fear of property division also led to honour killings. 'When girls marry against parent's choices, there is always a possibility that she might claim her property share as per the Hindu Succession Act .... In arranged marriages, that's less likely.'[44] Another startling finding of the report is that 84 per cent of the honour killings were committed by the girl's kin, 14 per cent by the boy's families and 2 per cent by both sides in equal manner.[45] In brief, in honour killings, which are perpetrated in the name of family pride, women have been the worst sufferers. These crimes are committed in many countries including India, Bangladesh, Pakistan, Turkey, Jordan and the Palestine Territories. They are carried out for a wide range of offences like adultery, premarital sex, flirting, choice marriages, etc. 'While statistics are hard to came by due to non-reporting of such crimes, United Nations Population Fund approximates that as many as 5,000 women are murdered in this manner each year around the world.'[46]

Apart from honour killings, sometimes the couples involved in violation of the customary norms of endogamy and exogamy have committed suicide. Most of such couples have been on the run like criminals after their marriage. On June 27, 2010, two lovers of different castes ended their lives by jumping before a train in Panipat district. The father of the girl was reportedly not grieved and the villagers were heard saying that 'she saved the honour of the family'.[47] In most cases of contentious marriages, the girl's family has been comparatively more aggressive in saving the family honour than that of the boy's. Safeguarding the honour of a girl, which has been the responsibility of the family, relatives, lineage group, etc., is regarded as saving the honour of the family, clan and village. This view is commonly shared by the people in the villages irrespective of their diverse social affinities. Unless the tradition is interrogated and rationalized in line with the secular and democratic framework and women are granted adequate space in the informal caste and lineage-based organizations, the dream of equity or justice to women may remain elusive in the rural areas of the region. The emergence of women as a strong group in the statutory as well as the customary or conventional institutions would change the prevailing nuances of dominance in peasant societies in the countryside. If their gender does not bar them from being sarpanches of village panchayats and chairpersons of Panchayat Samitis and Zila Parishads, the conventional panchayats that value customs and traditions must also keep their doors open for women to acquire positions of leadership and decision-making. The growing pace of social transformation also makes it imperative to permit or grant authority to women in matters of marriage and inheritance of property.

Notes

1. Dipankar Gupta, 'The Certitudes of Caste: When Identity Triumphs Hierarchy', in Dipankar Gupta (ed.), *Caste in Question: Identity or Hierarchy?*, New Delhi: Sage Publications, 2004, p. X.
2. Surinder S. Jodhka, 'Haryana: Change of Government and Beyond', *Economic and Political Weekly*, Vol. XXIV, No. 32, August 7, 1999, p. 2218.
3. Prem Chowdhry, 'Customs in a Peasant Economy: Women in Colonial Haryana', in Sumit Sarkar and Tanika Sarkar (eds.), *Women and Social Reform in Modern India: A Reader*, Vol. 1, Ranikhet: Permanent Black, 2007, p. 215.
4. A.B. Mukerji, 'Territorial Expressions of the Dominant Castes in Early Twentieth Century Haryana', in A.G. Noble et al. (eds.), *Geographic and Planning Research Themes for the New Millennium*, New Delhi: Vikas Publishing House, 2000, p. 397.
5. Prem Chowdhry, op. cit., p. 217.
6. Kamlesh Mohan, 'Clamping Shutters and Valorizing Women: Tensions in Sculpting Gender Identity in the Colonial Punjab', in Pritam Singh and Shinder Singh Thandi (eds.), *Punjabi Identity in a Global Context*, New Delhi: Oxford University Press, 1999, p. 167.
7. Quoted from Kishan Singh Bedi's (trans), *Agricultural Proverbs of the Punjab* (1972), in Kamlesh Mohan, op. cit., p. 171.
8. Quoted from Multan District Gazetteer, 1901–02, in ibid., p. 173.
9. Quoted from Jainarayan Verma's *Haryanavi Lokoktiyan: Shastriya Vishaleshan* (1972), in Prem Chowdhry, op. cit., p. 218.
10. D.R. Chaudhry, *Haryana at Crossroads: Problems and Prospects*, New Delhi: National Book Trust, 2007, p. 117.
11. Kamlesh Mohan, in ibid., p. 170.
12. Government of Haryana, *Statistical Abstract Haryana: 2005–06*, p. 23.
13. D.R. Chaudhry, op. cit., p. 118.
14. Geetanjali Gayatri, 'Girl Child as Unwanted as Ever', *The Tribune*, November 22, 2009.
15. Prem Chowdhry, 'Enforcing Cultural Codes: Gender and Violence in Northern India', *Economic and Political Weekly*, Vol. XXXII, No. 19, May 10, 1997, p. 1024.

16. Ravinder Kaur, 'Khap Panchayats, Sex Ratio and Female Agency', *Economic and Political Weekly*, Vol. XLV, No. 23, June 5–11, 2010, p. 15.
17. Manjeet Rathi, 'Female Feticide: Haryana's Experience', *People's Democracy*, Vol. XXIX, No. 29, July 17, 2005. Quoted from http://pd.cpim.org/2005/0717/07172005_haryana.htm.
18. Ibid.
19. Institute of Social Sciences, *Panchayati Raj Update*, Vol. XI, No. 8, August 2004.
20. Nirmala Buch, 'Reservation for Women in Panchayats: A Sop in Disguise?', *Economic and Political Weekly*, Vol. XLIV, No. 40, October 3–9, 2009, pp. 9–10.
21. Ibid., p. 9.
22. David G. Mandelbaum, *Society in India*, Vol. 1, Bombay: Popular Prakashan, 1970, p. 269.
23. Ibid., p. 269.
24. Ibid., p. 145.
25. M.C. Pradhan, *The Political System of the Jats of Northern India*, Bombay: Oxford University Press, 1966, p. 1.
26. Ravi Kumar, 'Khaps: Meet Demand by June 19', *The Tribune*, May 24, 2010.
27. M.C. Pradhan, op. cit., p. 134.
28. Nihal Singh Arya, *Sarv Khap Ka Rashtriya Prakram*, Delhi: Saini Printers, 1991, pp. 315–19.
29. Suraj Bhan Dahiya, 'The Rise and Fall of Khap Panchayat', *The Tribune*, September 13, 2009. Also see, P.S. Verma, 'Social Transformation and Khaps in Haryana', in Chetan Singh (ed.), *Social Transformation in North-Western India during the 20th Century*, New Delhi: Manohar, 2010, pp. 429–47.
30. Dipankar Gupta, *Rivalry and Brotherhood: Politics in the Life of Farmer's in Northern India*, New Delhi: Oxford University Press, 1997, p. 8.
31. Deependra Deswal, 'Want Change in Hindu Marriage Act', *The Times of India*, April 8, 2010.
32. Vijay Sabharwal, 'Khaps above Judicial Courts', *The Times of India*, May 3, 2010.
33. Navneet Sharma, 'The Tyranny of Custom', *Hindustan Times*, May 12, 2010.
34. Prem Chowdhry, *Contentious Marriages, Eloping Couples: Gender, Caste and Patriarchy in Northern India*, New Delhi: Oxford University Press, 2007, p. 264.

35. D.R. Chaudhry, op. cit., p. 120.
36. D.R. Chaudhry, 'Bringing Khaps to Justice', *The Tribune*, April 11, 2010.
37. Jagmati Sangwan, 'Khap Panchayat: Signs of Desperation?', *The Hindu*, May 8, 2010.
38. *The Tribune*, February 4, 2010.
39. *Hindustan Times*, May 12, 2010.
40. Bhanu P. Lohumi, 'Sampat for Change in Marriage Laws', *The Tribune*, September 14, 2009.
41. *Hindustan Times*, June 10, 2010.
42. Yogendra Gupta, 'Congress Rajya Sabha Member Seeks Leave to Amend Act', *The Tribune*, May 8, 2010.
43. *The Times of India*, May 10, 2010.
44. The major findings of the study are reported in Aditi Tandon, 'Inter-caste Ties Behind Most Honour Crimes', *The Tribune*, July 6, 2010.
45. Ibid.
46. The report is quoted in *The Tribune*, July 12, 2010.
47. Bhanu P. Lohumi, 'Caught in Caste Tangle, Lovers and Life', *The Tribune*, June 28, 2010.

12

Globalization-Islamization Interface

Implications for Muslim Women in the Indian Subcontinent

SURENDRA NATH KAUSHIK

Muslim women form the second largest group in the entire women population in the Indian subcontinent. In India, they are the second largest segment, whereas in Pakistan and Bangladesh, they belong to the majority community. Like women of other religious communities, the Muslim women are on the move for recognition of their human rights. They are confronting manifold challenges from two contradictory and almost antagonistic processes: Islamization and globalization. The process of Islamization, is dragging women backward, confining their roles within the four walls of their homes. Globalization process, on the other hand, has exposed women to the wider global environment, raising the level of their expectations and role performance.

Islamization as an indigenous, country-specific religio-cultural process and globalization as a global, world-wide phenomenon often result in contradictory pulls and pressures for women. In several Muslim countries, Islamization process has been imposed by the state to guard against the onslaught of Westernization. It has restricted women's freedom in accordance with Islamic laws. Globalization has opened new avenues for women's interaction across the cultures and nations. Mahbub-ul-Haq, the chief architect of Human Development Programme in Pakistan, had rightly observed: 'Globalization is no longer an option, it is a fact. Developing countries have either to learn to manage it more skilfully or simply drown in the global cross currents.'[1] Globalization process is basically driven by knowledge and revolution in the field of Information Technology (IT). There is a growing need not only to provide good quality primary, secondary and technical education but equally to spend more on higher education, especially on professional education. In the 21st century, globalization has become an inescapable reality. Religio-cultural traditions can no longer be reasserted without confronting the process of globalization, which has shrunk the world and exposed even the remotest parts of the planet to its consequences.[2] The issue of women's development and gender justice is now widely accepted all over the world as an essential component of human development.

In spite of their distinct religio-cultural backgrounds, the women activists of the subcontinent are successfully articulating and projecting the women's rights issues on the global level. Global connectivity with improved communication channels has brought a tremendous change in the perceptions and attitudes of women the world over. The Muslim women are also a part of these changes. They are coming with their own fresh interpretations of *Quran* and *Hadith* and reminding the conservative *Mullahs* that Islam in its original form was a religion of women's liberation and gender justice. Owing to globalization, the Muslim women have succeeded in acquiring top positions in the government, administration and business. The so-called votaries of Islamization still want to keep women away from influential positions in society, polity and economy and go on denigrating the positive contributions of globalization. With their conservative mindsets, the Islamic fundamentalists want to maintain the status quo, which favours a male-dominated social system.

The global projection and articulation of women's rights has been facilitated significantly through the United Nations Organization (UNO) and several international women's fora, resulting in the member-countries of the UNO incorporating women's rights in their Human Development Programmes.

Women's human rights are clearly enshrined in international law. Starting from the United Nations Charter and the Universal Declaration of Human Rights, the principle found its way into the two main International Covenants: the International Covenant on Economic, Social and Cultural Rights and the International Covenant on Civil and Political Rights (1996). In addition to the principle of nondiscrimination, a number of other provisions of great importance to women are also contained in these instruments.

The Universal Declaration of Human Rights calls for equal rights as to marriage, which it stipulates shall be entered into only with the free and full consent of the intending spouses. It also calls for equal pay for equal work, and for the protection of motherhood. The Covenant on Economic

Social and Cultural Rights states that all workers must be provided with fair wages and equal remuneration for work of equal value without distinction of any kind; in particular, women being guaranteed conditions of work not inferior to those enjoyed by men, with equal pay for equal work. It also provides for the protection of motherhood, and calls for paid maternity leave or leave with adequate social security benefits. The Covenant on Civil and Political Rights prohibits the use of the death sentence on pregnant women, provides for equality between men and women during marriage and its dissolution, and for the right to participate in public life without discrimination while declaring, finally, that equality before the law and the principle of nondiscrimination are enforceable rights.[3]

One of the most effective tools for promoting women's equality has been the Convention on the Elimination of All Forms of Discrimination Against Women (The Women's Convention, or CEDAW 1979), laying in detail the duties that states have to promote women's equality in all areas of life, from family to workplace to government. This far-reaching legal instrument, however, has been saddled with reservations. Thus, from the point of view of international law, women's rights are human rights.

Reinterpretation of human rights law from a woman's perspective must lead to the recognition that violence against women, in the family and in the community, in peacetime and in war, is a violation of women's physical and moral integrity and their dignity as human beings. The artificial barriers between the 'private' and the 'public' spheres have to be removed, and the shield of silence that protects cultural, religious or other traditions and prejudices must be broken, so that acts such as the beating and raping of women (whether within or outside of the family), widow burning, and sexual mutilation, are clearly recognized as human rights violations.

But an important question that has been raised by human rights activists and that needs critical attention is: can we have an international discussion on human rights in a world of cultural difference? While the question of human rights has never been free from politics (in either its formulation or deployment), the cautionary call from 'culture and religion' has intensified in recent years. No social group has suffered greater violation of its human rights in the name of culture and religion than women. Regardless of the particular forms it takes in different societies, the concept of culture in the modern state circumscribes women's lives in several ways. However, while women are neither purely victims nor purely beneficiaries of religio-cultural politics, a recognition of their limited access to public defences of cultural practices can help us to contextualize the claims against rights on the basis of religion and culture.

For instance, the *Shariat* laws have drastically curtailed the freedom of Muslim women in the subcontinent. The ruling elite and the clergy manipulate the *Shariat* laws to serve their power objectives. The process of Islamization has further aggravated the situation.[4] In fact, the question of women's rights can be projected as a problem created and perpetuated by the fundamentalists. As these rights are in conflict with the interest of the theocratic elite, a furore is raised on the issue.

In fact, for a deeper understanding we must acknowledge change, complexity, and interpretive privilege in cultural formation. In the context of globalization, the tradition has to be reoriented to meet the requirements of human rights, democracy and development.

Without questioning the political uses of culture, without asking whose culture this is and who its primary beneficiaries are and without placing the very notion of culture in historical context, we cannot fully understand the case with which women become instrumentalized in larger battles of political, economic, military and discursive competition in the international arena. Progressive women organizations, human rights activists and the NGOs are engaged in the task of fighting for gender justice and human development. However, they find it extremely difficult to challenge the *Shariat* laws. There is a well-organized nexus between the ruling elite and the fundamentalists, which obstructs the work of the women organizations.

Muslim Women and their Rights in India

The Indian society is multi-cultural and plural in its nature which has been operating through a democratic and secular Constitution. All citizens of India are equal before law, irrespective of their religious and gender-based identities. Muslim women citizens despite being a major minority group in India enjoy equal rights like other women.[5] There is no state religion in India. Religion is treated as a personal matter of the citizens. Any citizen of India can seek justice from the judiciary. Educated Muslim women are gradually liberating themselves from the hold of the conservative and obscurantist religious leadership. There is strong realization among the educated Muslim women that without integrating themselves with the mainstream of Indian women's movements, they cannot fully realize their human rights. In the open society of India, there are vast opportunities for their development. However, uneducated Muslim women cannot dare challenge the patriarchal male-dominated social system. Muslim women, with lower economic background, find it extremely difficult to move the court of law. Without the support of either women's organizations or the NGOs, they are not in a position to challenge the *fatwas* (religions edicts) of the local panchayats and the *Mullahs,* even if they resent the same. Unfortunately, in the public sphere, political parties in both government and opposition, are concerned with their 'vote-bank' value rather than democratic or secular values. The judiciary has played a vital role in providing justice to women, including the Muslim women. Several civil society organizations have been demanding since long for a Uniform Civil Code (UCC) but the governments have shown reluctance towards this demand. The Muslim Personal Law has proved a hurdle in the implementation of many pro-gender decisions of the judiciary in India.

The issue of maintenance to a divorced Muslim woman, Shah Bano, was politicized in mid-1980s following a Supreme Court verdict that Section 125 of CrPC was a part of the criminal law of the country, hence was applicable to all Indians. It holds that a divorced Muslim woman has the right to maintenance under Section 125 of CrPC. Ironically, following strong pressure of the conservative Islamic lobby, Shah Bano in an open letter stated:

> Since the judgement of the Supreme Court is contrary to the *Quran* and the *Hadith* and is an open interference in Muslim Personal Law, I Shah Bano, being a Muslim, reject it and disassociate myself from every judgement that is contrary to the *Shariat*. The then Rajiv Gandhi government also gave in to the pressure exerted by the fundamentalists, passing the Muslim Woman (Protection of Rights Upon Divorce) Act 1986. The Bill removed divorced Muslim women from the ambit of Section 125 CrPC.[6]

There are a few instances when Muslim women in India have shown courage to challenge the retrogressive decisions (features) of the local clergy and the panchayats. In 2005, Imrana, a resident of Muzaffarnagar in UP was directed by the local clergy to accept her father-in-law as her husband and her husband as a son after she was raped by the father-in-law. In rape cases, the Islamic law punishes the woman victim and exonerates the real culprit. Imrana refused to accept the retrogressive decision of the clergy. The woman activists and the NGOs took up her case and fought for justice for Imrana. In 2004, the Arif-Gudiya case also evoked widespread criticism. Arif, an army jawan, had returned to his village after five years (following his release from a Pakistani jail) to find his wife Gudiya remarried. The local cleric directed Gudiya to go back to her first husband. Similarly, in September, 2008, Shabana, a resident of Lawar village in Meerut district, refused to accept the *fatwa* issued by *Dar-ul-Uloom* in Deoband that she should go back to her former husband Abid, who deserted her 14 years back. Shabana refused to accept the *fatwa* and decided to remain with her new husband Abrar, with whom she had two sons.[7]

Whenever there is a demand for reforming the obsolete laws regarding marriage, especially the child marriage, strong resistance comes from the orthodox *Ulama* who claim that India's Child Marriage Prevention Act of 1929 cannot be imposed on Muslims because their marriage laws are based on Islamic *Shariah*. The All India Muslim Personnel Law Board (AIMPLB) is the main authority to give directives in this regard.[8] However, the onus of change rests with aware and articute Muslim women ready to reform the obsolete Islamic laws. The secular-democratic environment of India can be used to their advantage. The women of all religious communities have to wage a united struggle for a Uniform Civil Code (UCC), to ensure freedom and security for the women victims of personal religious laws.

As human beings and bearer of human rights, all women deserve equal and fair treatment, including Muslim women. They should not bear the brunt of unequal field due to orthodox practices. The Indian judiciary has played a pivotal role in liberating the Muslim women whenever approached. The liberal Muslim males of India probably need to come forward to share responsibility for helping their women folk to achieve freedom and equality in a real sense. The combined efforts of the Muslim males and females will pave the way for internal reforms in personal law practices in favour of more gender justice and fair play.

Politics of Islamization and Women's Rights in Pakistan

Politics of Islamization initiated during General Zia's military dictatorship has adversely affected women's human rights in Pakistan. There was a systematic attempt by the ruling establishment to impose *Shariat*-based Islamic laws which perpetuated a 'culture against women'. The liberal ideals of the founder of Pakistan, Mohammad Ali Jinnah, were replaced by the fundamentalist ideology of *Jamaat-i-Islami*. Jinnah had an enlightened vision of women's rights and gender justice. In his address to the Aligarh Muslim University Union on March 10, 1944, Jinnah clearly stated:

'No nation can rise to the heights of glory unless your women are side by side with you. We are the victims of evil customs. It is a crime against humanity that our women are shut up within the four walls of the houses as prisoners. I do not mean that we should imitate the West. But let us try to raise the status of our Islamic ideals and beliefs. There is no sanction anywhere for the deplorable conditions which our women have been subject to. You should take your women along with you as comrades in every sphere of life.'[9]

Zulfikar Ali Bhutto, leader of Pakistan People's Party, assumed the leadership of disintegrated Pakistan in December 1971. Initially he took vital decisions in regard to women's rights. Under the Administrative Reforms Programme (1972), Bhutto's government for the first time permitted women's entry into Administrative Services – Foreign and Civil Services. Top-ranking political offices such as that of the President, Prime

Minister, Cabinet Ministers and Governors were opened to women. Begum Rana Liaquat Ali Khan was appointed as the first woman Governor of Sind. The new Constitution of the Islamic Republic of Pakistan (1973) contained specific provisions for gender equality and justice, such as the following:

Article 25 (2) states: All citizens are equal before law and there shall be no discrimination on the basis of sex alone.

Article 27 ensures safeguards against discrimination in respect of appointments to services of Pakistan.

Article 34 mentions steps shall be taken to ensure full participation of women in all spheres of national life.

Article 51 allocates 20 seats for women in the National Assembly for 20 years.

Besides his progressive reform measures, Bhutto took various steps for politicization of Islam. For his own political survival, he yielded to the pressures of the *Ulama* and the religious elite. A Ministry of Religious Affairs was constituted for the first time in Pakistan under Bhutto's regime. The 1973 Constitution for the first time declared Islam as the 'State Religion'. *Article* 2 states that 'Islam shall be the State Religion of Pakistan'.[10]

Bhutto's efforts for politicization of Islam proved counter-productive to the progressive sections. Religious parties always remained suspicious of Bhutto's Islamic credentials and joined hands with the military for destablization of his government. On July 5, 1977, Z.A. Bhutto was deposed from power by the army and within two years he was sent to the gallows (April 4, 1979). For several of his contradictory policies, Bhutto had to pay a heavy price.

The military dictator General Zia-ul-Haq introduced *Shariah*-based draconian Islamic laws. Following in the footsteps of the founder of *Jamaat-i-Islami*, Maulana Maudoodi, General Zia squarely rejected the western version of democracy and human rights. Maulana Maudoodi was a staunch critic of western feminism. General Zia identified women's rights in accordance with Maulana Maudoodi's fundamentalist thesis that 'women should be confined within the four walls of their homes'.[11]

In February 1979, Zia regime promulgated the Hudood Ordinance based on the Islamic *Shariah*. The Hudood Ordinance prescribed stringent punishment for the crime of *Zina* (adultery, rape and fornication). It prescribed stoning to death for married persons and 100 lashes for unmarried persons involved in the act of *Zina*. However, the proof required for the act of *Zina-al-Jabr* (rape) was quite complicated and anti-women. The eyewitness testimony of four adult Muslim males was essential to prosecute the rapist. Due to the lack of required evidence, the rapist often went scot-free and in most cases only women victims of rape were punished. Ironically, the Hudood Ordinance did not distinguish between adultery and rape.[12]

In December of 1980, the Council of Islamic Ideology, dominated by the clerics, suggested the imposition of *Qisas* and *Diyat* laws in Pakistan. Thereafter, General Zia-ul-Haq promulgated a Presidential ordinance for *Qisas* and *Diyat* laws. According to *Shariah, Qisas* (an eye for an eye) is defined as punishment by causing similar hurt at the same part of the body of the convict as he/she has caused to the victim or by causing offender's death in case of his/her committing murder. *Diyat* ('blood money') is the compensation payable to the legal heirs of the murdered victim. Ironically, *Diyat* for a man was fixed at 30.6 kg of silver and only half of this for a woman. The reason given for the reduced *Diyat* for woman by the propagators of this law was that it is man who is financially responsible towards his family and, therefore, with his death the family loses its provider.

The law on abortion formed Section 96 and 97 of the Law of *Qisas* and *Diyat*, which declared abortion illegal, carrying punishment of seven years for both the expectant mother and the person who performs it. The law reflected sheer insensitivity of the law-makers as it did not exclude the rape victims from it. So, there was not only the trauma of violence but a constant reminder of it in the shape of an unwanted child and also the extreme social stigma attached with it.

The Council of Islamic Ideology also prepared an Islamic Dress Code in 1980. Zia's government issued directives to all employees to observe the norms laid down in the Dress Code. It was mandatory for all women employees to cover their heads with *chadars* or *dupattas*. The female teachers were expected to set an ideal example for their students by wearing modest dresses with their heads covered. The government also issued notices to the advertising agencies that women's photographs be eliminated from all commercial advertising products. The women models were directed to wear modest dresses (full-sleeved dress and *dupatta*). In TV commercials, the women models were allotted specific time limit. Women were also debarred from national and international games. Obviously, Zia's military regime intended to reduce women's visibility from public arena.

In April 1982, the Zia government proposed a new Law of Evidence (*Qanoon-i-Shahadat*). Ironically, under the new Law of Evidence, witness of one male was treated equivalent to that of two females. The discriminatory provisions of this law were resented by women activists of Pakistan. *Qanoon-i-Shahadat* prescribed that in all cases other than those covered by the Hudood Ordinance and any other special law, either two male witnesses or witness of one male and two females would be required for a crime. Celebrating its first birth anniversary, the Women Action Forum (WAF, founded in 1981) criticized the Zia government for imposing a set of absolutely draconian laws against women. It alleged that the clerics, who were in majority in the Council of Islamic Ideology, had given irrational and inhuman suggestions for reformulating the legal structure through primitive methods. The WAF also demanded setting up of a National Commission for Women.[13]

Successive civilian and military regimes in post-Zia Pakistan found it quite difficult to reverse the Islamization policy of the Zia era. Although Benazir Bhutto during her two prime ministerial tenures (1988–1990 and 1993–1996) tried her best to introduce various schemes for women's welfare and upliftment, she found it quite difficult to reverse the Islamization policy of the Zia era. Benazir's political rival Mian Nawaz Sharif, also the Prime Minister twice (1990–1993 and 1997–1999), and a legatee of General Zia-ul-Haq, hobnobbed with the fundamentalist forces. Nawaz Sharif condemned Benazir's pro-women policy as 'anti-Islamic' and directed the state-controlled media to guard the women of Pakistan against the growing influence of western feminism. He legitimized all the Presidential ordinances of the Zia regime regarding Islamic laws through the Parliament. The controversial Bill regarding the supremacy of the *Islamic Shariah* was also approved by the Parliament in May 1991.

The military dictator General Pervez Musharraf, who usurped political power in October 1999 after dislodging the government of Nawaz Sharif, also relied heavily on the support of the religious parties. The right-wing religious parties formed an alliance: *Muttahida Majlis-e-Amal* (MMA) to contest the general elections held in October 2002. The MMA captured 50 seats in the National Assembly and gained majority in the provincial assemblies of the NWFP and Balochistan. The MMA exerted strong pressure on the Musharraf government to continue the *Shariah*-based *Hudood* laws. Owing to its majority in two tribal provinces (the NWFP and Balochistan), the MMA imposed draconian Islamic laws which adversely affected the interests of the women. The Islamic fundamentalists, also known as *Taliban,* terrorized women to abide by the Islamic laws in the tribal regimes of Pakistan. The women were asked to follow the Islamic Dress Code and keep themselves away from public life. Women in the rural areas meekly submitted to the dictates of the fundamentalists.[14]

Although the Pakistan People's Party was able to form the government after winning majority of seats in February 2008 General Elections, it had to sacrifice its great leader Benazir Bhutto. The Talibanized Pakistan was perhaps not ready to accept the reality that a woman leader of global stature should assume the office of Prime Minister for the third time. The surging popularity of Benazir Bhutto during the election campaign was probably not appreciated by the Islamic militants. Benazir Bhutto was assassinated on December 27, 2007 while she was returning after addressing an election rally.

Benazir Bhutto's assassination sent a shockwave throughout Pakistan and the world at large. This was a brutal instance of political violence against a woman leader.'

Pakistani society still remains feudal and tribal in character where women are denied their human rights in the name of religion or tribal norms. The inhuman tribal tradition of *Karo-Kari* (honour killing) is still in vogue in several parts of Pakistan despite the fact that the Musharraf government imposed a ban on it in April 2000. Rooted in patriarchal and cultural perceptions of women as male property, *Karo-Kari* ostensibly takes place to avenge (family honour) when a woman violates the cultural norms. In most of such cases, women are killed by male members of their family. The *Qisas* and *Diyat* laws have also encouraged the incidents of honour killing and violence against women in Pakistan. The practice of *Karo-Kari* (which was originally restricted to tribal areas) is now visible even in most advanced towns and cities of Pakistan. Although the Supreme Court of Pakistan announced a radical decision in 2003 permitting women to choose their life partners, women in Pakistan find it quite difficult to marry according to their own choices. The *Shariah*-based laws do not permit women to choose their life partners.

The incident of burying alive five women in Balochistan in August 2008 evoked controversy in Pakistan because it occurred during the present civilian regime of the Pakistan People's Party. Ironically, the Baloch senator Israr-ullah Zehri, while aggressively interrupting Senator Bibi Yasmin Shah, who condemned the brutal act of burying alive five women in Balochistan on charges of love marriage, said: 'it was part of their tradition and should not be negatively highlighted.' Senator Bibi Yasmin, however, continued and alleged that the government was not taking action against the culprits because of the involvement of a PPP provincial minister in the incident. She demanded that the government should take strict action against the culprits involved in the 'honour killing' which was a serious crime against humanity.[15]

Can 'honour killing' stop without debating the structure of Pakistan society and without wanting to change it? The religious clerics led by feudal or tribal leaders or the other way round will keep arguing that women have fewer rights than men. But their claims and counter-claims are all a farce till people begin to address the issue of restructuring the primordial culture, which is the basis of such crimes.

It is a fact that all governments in the post-Zia phase have shown sheer inability and lack of political will to shake the anti-women fundamentalist politics of Islamization. Instead of isolating the obscurantist forces, the rulers have forged alliances with them for their political survival.

Islamic Fundamentalism and Women's Rights in Bangladesh

The Constitution of Bangladesh guarantees equal rights and status for men and women. However, in practice, women are discriminated against in every field. The Islamic fundamentalists have taken undue advantage of the Islamic provisions of the Constitution. Under the pressure of religious parties, the military dictator General H.M. Ershad in 1988 declared Islam as the 'state religion'. Since 1988, the *Jamaat-i-Islami* has been assiduously insisting on Islamization of Bangladesh. Women activists, writers and journalists are warned by the fundamentalists to discard western feminism and secular ideology and abide by Islamic norms.

Taslima Nasreen's feminist writings aroused nationwide controversy. Her novel *Lajja* was proscribed by the government in 1993. The fundamentalist lobby issued a *fatwa* against Taslima Nasreen for death sentence as she 'hurt the religious sentiments of the entire Muslim community'. In view of the threats of the obscurantist forces, she had to leave Bangladesh. The district sessions court, Dhaka, declared her a 'fugitive from law'.[16]

To put the whole issue in historical perspective, it would be relevant to recall that the liberation (independence) movement of Bangladesh was indeed a struggle for human rights in which women contributed immensely. Following the call of the Father of the Nation, *Bangabandhu* Sheikh Mujibur Rahman, many women freedom fighters sacrificed their lives for the liberation of the nation. With his broad secular and democratic vision, Sheikh Mujibur Rahman defended women's rights and equality in every sphere of life. He constantly challenged the thesis of the fundamentalist *Jamaat-i-Islami* which intended to delimit the scope of women's freedom and equality through a parochialized version of Islam.

The *Jamaat-i-Islami* pressured the military regime of General Zia-ur-Rahman to Islamize Bangladesh. Gholam Azam, the chief of *Jamaat-i-Islami,* insisted on the imposition of *Shariah* laws and declaration of Islam as the 'State Religion' in Bangladesh. General Zia-ur-Rahman was also assassinated in a military coup in May 1981 as he failed to follow the dictates of the Islamic fundamentalists.

After the assassination of Zia-ur-Rahman, another military dictator General H.M. Ershad assumed leadership and remained in power for a decade. General Ershad went a step ahead of his predecessor in carrying out the Islamization plan. Through the Eighth Constitution Amendment (1988), General Ershad declared Islam as the 'State Religion' in Bangladesh, which provided a solid ground for the assertion of the fundamentalist lobby in Bangladesh politics. Progressive women organizations and the Awami League vehemently criticized the Eighth Amendment. The Awami League Leader Sheikh Hasina Wajid urged the progressive and secular forces to unite against the fundamentalists and the military dictator. The united ventures of the Opposition parties, progressive forces and human rights activists finally compelled the military dictator General H.M. Ershad to resign in December 1990.[17]

The General Elections of February 1991 were won by Bangladesh Nationalist Party (BNP) leader Begum Khaleda Zia, who assumed the office of Prime Minister on March 20, 1991 as the first woman Prime Minister of Bangladesh. Interestingly, the Leader of Opposition was also a woman, Sheikh Hasina Wazed. She urged the progressive and secular forces to unite against the fundamentalists and the military dictator.

The decade of 1990s heralded a new era of women's leadership in Bangladesh. Begum Khaleda Zia and Sheikh Hasina succeeded in assuming office of Prime Minister of Bangladesh. Alternatively, they also acted as Opposition leaders. The orthodox Islamic parties made concerted efforts to create hurdles in the way of women's empowerment. For her political survival, Begum Khaleda Zia forged alliances with the fundamentalist parties. On the contrary, the Awami League government under the leadership of Sheikh Hasina made conscious efforts to integrate various women's organizations and encouraged women's mass participation in politics and civil society. Sheikh Hasina upheld the secular, democratic and liberal cultural value premises of Bangladesh as laid down by the Father of the Nation, and her own father, Sheikh Mujib-ur-Rahman. The Awami League government gave priority to the institutionalization of human rights, especially the women's rights. Female education at secondary and higher secondary levels was made free. Separate police stations for women were set up on a priority basis. Prime Minister Sheikh Hasina was awarded a 'Medal of Distinction' for her services to the humanity by the International Association of Lion's Club in December 1998.[18] In April 1999, the Sheikh Hasina government took an 'epoch-making' step by making a provision for the election of women members of the Union Parishad by direct vote. Along with women's participation, she wanted to decentralize governance and strengthen the local governments administration.

Former Prime Minister and the Leader of Opposition, Begum Khaleda Zia, used every public platform for criticizing the Awami League government. The fundamentalist *Jamaat-i-Islami* also joined hands with Begum Khaleda Zia.

Begum Khaleda Zia assumed the Prime Minister's office for the second time following her victory in October 2001 General Elections.

The *Jamaat-i-Islami* being the major partner in the Khaleda Zia government zealously revived its Islamization programme. The *Jamaat-i-Islami* directed its students wing – the *Islami Chatra Shibir* (ICS) – to train the youth of Bangladesh according to Islamic 'code of conduct'. The *Islami Chatra Shibir* launched a massive campaign for the revival of Islamic culture and code of conduct on the university campuses. Women were specifically directed to wear what was called 'Islamic dresses' and discard *sarees*. It might be recalled that in the year 2000, the *Islami Chatra Shibir* also issued a *fatwa* (decree) imposing a ban on women's 'laughter' in public places as it was considered 'un-Islamic'. Thus, under the BNP-Jamaat government, the fundamentalists were given a free hand to dictate their terms to the people of Bangladesh. This was clearly an attempt to impose a 'Taliban type' social system in Bangladesh under the garb of Islamic ideology.[19]

It is an irony that in a country, pledged constitutionally to a democratic order, there are numerous villages where women are still not allowed to cast their vote. The *fatwa* issued by the religious leaders prevents them to exercise their entitlement of adult franchise. The fundamentalists maintain that 'vote of the male member is enough' and women are supposed to cast their vote at the dictates of the men in their family'. The Islamic *fatwa* issued in 1969 still persists in Kurigram's Berubari Union, while there are more than 4,000 women out of a total of 9,780 registered voters in the Union. The religious hardliners hold that women should not come out of their houses to cast their vote in public places.[20] The Pir of Charmani Maulana Syed Fazlul Karim, addressing a congregation of Islamic scholars on February 16, 2002, described 'women's leadership as an impediment to establishing Islam'.[21] Various fundamentalist parties of Bangladesh have also formed a movement, viz., *Islami Sashantantra Andohan* (ISA) assailing the Western concepts of secularism, democracy and human rights.

It is a positive sign that despite the state-sponsored Islamization programme, a majority of women in Bangladesh appreciate the democratic and secular ideology. They are deeply proud of their Bengali culture and heritage as they understand it and as exhibited by women's movements and human rights organizations in the country.

Conclusion

Diverse socio-cultural milieu notwithstanding, the women of the subcontinent share a common destiny. The crucial challenge before the governments and civil societies in India, Pakistan and Bangladesh is to recognize and understand women's cause and devise effective mechanisms to ensure a balanced perspective. The process of globalization has definitely raised the level of women's consciousness about their human rights. Irrespective of their religio-cultural distinctions, women by and large in the subcontinent are now asserting their distinctive identity and critically questioning impositions of various kinds. The Muslim women are gradually coming out openly against the fundamentalists and the conservative sections of their community, who wish to push them in the medieval era of Islam. A marked trend in conscious appreciation and other changes brought about by the process of globalization is visible. There is enough evidence to suggest that majority of Muslim women are against the *Talibanization* of society and culture. They are in favour of modern scientific education so that they could become well-equipped to meet the challenges of globalization. However, they are still placed very unevenly against fundamentalists of both religion and the market. The Islamic fundamentalists aim at exploiting them on various pretexts offered by growing avenues of the process of globalization. Thus, also being the beneficiaries of globalization, women are simultaneously facing its negative consequences. The global trends of liberalization and privatization have marginalized women in the economic sphere. In a highly competitive consumption-driven and market-oriented global environment, women are treated as mere products. The global culture of consumerism is spread by the powerful media, which gives priority to sustain and promote the interests of the market. Soft porn is easily available in the market, which is corrupting the youth and encouraging organized crime and violence against women. India, Pakistan and Bangladesh are often cited by the international agencies as source countries for global trafficking in women. There is an urgent need for creating awareness among women of the sub-continent against the forced labour and sexual exploitation. Hopefully, with common actions plan and joint strategies, it will be possible to guard against the negative consequences of both globalization and religious fundamentalism.

Notes

1. For details, see *Human Development in South Asia 2001: Globalization and Human Development*, Mahbub-ul-Huq, Human Development Centre, Karachi: Oxford University Press, 2002.
2. Malcolm Waters, *Globalization*, London: Routledge, p. 995; Carol C. Gould, *Globalizing Democracy and Human Rights*, Cambridge: Cambridge University Press, 2004.
3. *Human Development Report 2000*, New Delhi: Oxford University Press, 2000. *Human Development in South Asia 2000: The Gender Question*, Karachi: Oxford University Press, 2001.
4. See Surendra Nath Kaushik, *Politics of Islamization in Pakistan: A Study of the Zia Regime*, New Delhi: South Asian Publishers, 1993.
5. Generally, India's Muslim women are triply disadvantaged: as members of a minority, as women and most of all, as poor women. Gender discrimination coalesces with class inequalities and pervasive social hierarchies. Through secular agenda of development, the Muslim women of India can

get better opportunities. Merely reservations in jobs or legislatures will not help them much. According to Praful Bidwai, a path-breaking survey by Zoya Hasan and Ritu Menon demolishes many stereotypes and misconceptions about Muslim women in India. The Muslim women are not a monolithic category with their status virtually unvarying across regions or social groups. Nor is that status unchanging and immutable. Muslim women depending on their income group, location or work status, may have much more in common with Hindu women than other Muslim women.

6. For details, see Asghar Ali Engineer, *Islam, Women and Gender Justice*, New Delhi: Gyan Publishing House, 2001, pp. 73–75.
7. Shabana, daughter of Akbari Begum, resident of Lawar village in Meerut district, remarried after her first husband Abid disappeared in 1994 following a bitter quarrel between them. She has two sons by her second husband, Abrar. In September 2008, suddenly Abid surfaced insisting that while he may have left his wife (Shabana), he (Abid) had never divorced her and now wanted her back. Abid first approached the village headman Azhar Khan, who agreed that Shabana should go back to him. He summoned the local panchayat for a hearing, but the panchayat failed to reach any decision. There was much talk of approaching the renowned Islamic institutions closeby, *Darul-ul-Uloom* in Deoband, for an Islamic *fatwa* in the matter. Shabana, however, was never in any dilemma. She said: 'I am not going back to Abid, no matter what the *panchayat* says.' *Hindustan Times*, September 27, 2008.
8. In its meeting held on November 2, 2008 at Lucknow, the All India Muslim Personal Law Board unanimously resolved that the cases of Muslim women with regard to their divorce and property claims would only be decided in accordance with the *Shariat*. However, the judgment in such cases given by the Court of Law will not be binding on the Muslim community. *Hindustan Times*, November 3, 2008.

   Ironically, at an international Muslim women's conference held in Mumbai on November 7–8, 2008, the women belonging to various progressive Muslim organizations stated that the wall of religion should be demolished and several misconceptions regarding their marriage, employment and education should be removed. They vehemently criticized the negative role played by the conservation *Maulvis* and the clergy in interpreting the *Shariat* laws. *Hindustan Times*, November 9, 2008.
9. *Quaid-i-Azam and Muslim Women*, Islamabad, Ministry of Education, Government of Pakistan, 1976.
10. See *The Constitution of the Islamic Republic of Pakistan: 1973*, Islamabad, Government of Pakistan, 1973.

11. For details, see Surendra Nath Kaushik, 'Politics of Islamization and Women's Rights in Pakistan', *Pol-Sym*, A Socio-Political Journal of Symbiosis Society's Law College, Pune, Vol. 1, January 2004, pp. 37–51.
12. Surendra Nath Kaushik, *Politics of Islamization in Pakistan: A Study of Zia Regime*, New Delhi: South Asian Publishers, 1993, pp. 135–39.
13. Mumtaz Kanwar and Farida Shaheed, *Women of Pakistan: One Step Forward, Two Steps Backward*, London: Zed Books, 1987.
14. Surendra Nath Kaushik, note 11.
15. Pakistan's leading daily, *Dawn*, August 30, 2008 editorially commented under the title: 'Balochistan Taliban in Senate'. It stated that Senator Israrullah Zehri's defence of a barbaric incident involving the burying alive of five women in Balochistan smacks of a medieval mindset and one that is totally in tune with the Taliban's own obscurantist worldview. It takes one back nine years when similarly regressive-minded legislators refused to condemn the honour killing *(Karo-Kari)* of Samina Sarwar, who was shot dead at the behest of her own parents over a marriage-related issue in 1999. Clearly, then, this mindset that trivializes the sanctity of human life – especially if the life is that of a woman – and is dominated so easily by the interests of those who wield political, economic and social clout, is not confined to the representatives of the backward provinces alone. It has come to be a national set of mind.
16. Owing to her feminist writings, Taslima Nasreen has been criticized by the conservative *Mullahs* throughout the subcontinent. Even in a secular-democratic country like India, Taslima Nasreen had to face open threats to her life.

    See Iqbal A. Ansari, 'Free Speech-Hate Speech: The Taslima Nasreen Case', *Economic and Political Weekly*, February 23, 2008, pp. 15–19.
17. Surendra Nath Kaushik, 'Islamic Fundamentalism and Women's Rights in Bangladesh', *South Asian Studies*, Vol. 37, No. 1, January–July 2002, pp. 36–52.
18. Following landslide victory of her party Awami League in December 2008 General Elections, Sheikh Hasina Wazed also assumed Prime Minister's office for the second time.
19. *Bangladesh Observer*, May 24, 2000.
20. *Daily Star*, June 2, 2001.
21. *Bangladesh Observer*, February 17, 2002.

13

Women's NGOs in the Context of Globalization

DEEPA MATHUR

This paper consists of two parts. In the first section, an attempt has been made to define globalization and discuss its implications for women. The second section elaborates the development of women's NGOs and the challenges and prospects faced by them, in the changing milieu.

I

What is Globalization?

It is very difficult to define or point out what is globalization, because it means different things to different people. Globalization has effects on finance, industry, the environment and all of the many political and cultural ideas and institutions. It affects information flows, consumer trends and immigration flows between different parts of the world. Globalization has spread in an enormous way since the end of the Second World War and continues to do so as technology and communication improve between nations.

Globalization is a double-edged sword – it is widely perceived that the process of globalization produces both 'winners and losers'. For some, globalization is an inevitable, technologically-driven process that brings together people of different countries and areas in economic and political relations. They see globalization as an inevitable technologically-driven process which is natural and good for the world. To others, there is a much deeper concern about the related challenges and possible risks associated with the globalization process.

Globalization Defined

Globalization may be described as the most distinctive feature of the contemporary world. Broadly speaking, globalization refers to the expansion of global linkages – the organization of social life on global scale, and the growth of global consciousness. Hence, it implies a consolidation of world society. Definitions of globalization vary: 'time-space compression', 'action at distance', 'accelerating interdependence', 'networking', to mention a few. However, the meaning of the term is a topic of vociferous global discussion. It may refer to real processes, to ideas that justify them, or to a way of thinking about them. The term far from being neutral, expresses different assessments of global change.

The following definitions represent currently influential views:

- 'The inexorable integration of markets, nation-states, and technologies to a degree never witnessed before – in a way that is enabling individuals, corporations and nation-states to reach around the world farther, faster, deeper and cheaper than ever before ... the spread of free-market capitalism to virtually every country in the world.'[1]
- 'The compression of the world and the intensification of consciousness of the world as a whole ... concrete global interdependence and consciousness of the global whole in the twentieth century.'[2]
- 'A social process in which the constraints of geography on social and cultural arrangements recede and in which people become increasingly aware that they are receding.'[3]

Globalization involves all processes of integration. Globalization involves economics, cultures and political movements in different parts of the world. Actually the integration and working together of different countries is nothing new. What is new is the propensity at which this integration is now taking place. The speed of communication and exchange, the complexity and size of the networks involved, and the sheer volume of trade, interaction and risk give what we now label as 'globalization' a peculiar force.

Globalization involves the diffusion of ideas, practices and technologies. It is something more than internationalization and universalization. It isn't simply modernization or westernization. It is certainly not just the liberalization of markets. Anthony Giddens[4] has described globalization as the intensification of worldwide social relations which link distant localities in such a way that local happenings are shaped by events occurring many miles away and vice versa. This involves a change in the way we understand geography and experience localness. As well as offering opportunity, it brings with it considerable risks linked, for example, to technological change. Globalization thus has powerful economic, political, cultural and social dimensions.

Broadcasting technology and the internet have been major catalysts in this process. This is not to suggest that these twin forces are independent of other economic and cultural issues. They are neither ubiquitous nor omnipresent. This is one of the major problems with globalization; the world cannot be integrated effectively due to already existing power differentials between countries and cultures.

The reality of globalization is such that its implications are both impossible to ignore and equally impossible to comprehend. Governments are unable to forecast and deal with the realities of globalization because in reality and by definition, its force lies beyond the scope of any local government body.

Manuel Castells[5] has argued persuasively that in the last 20 years or so of the 20th century, a new economy emerged around the world. He characterizes it as a new brand of capitalism that has three fundamental features:

'Productivity and competitiveness are, by and large, a function of knowledge generation and information processing; firms and territories are organized in networks of production, management and distribution; the core economic activities are global – that is, they have the capacity to work as a unit in real time, or chosen time, on a planetary scale.'

De-localization and Supraterritoriality

Globalization has led to a significant measure of de-localization in social and economic exchanges. Gray[6] makes a spirited and well-argued polemic against the effort to create a global free market. One important aspect of this is the distancing of work from the home (and the move to the suburbs). But de-localization does not end here. Increasingly people have to deal with distant systems in smoothly running their day-to-day lives. Banking and retailing, for example, have adopted new technologies that restrict rather than inhibit face-to-face interaction. The only contact at the bank is in a call centre several kilometres away. Similarly, when goods are bought on the internet, the only personal contact is that with the delivery man. When we buy books from an internet supplier, our communications pass through a large number of computers and routers, travelling over thousands of miles on different continents; the books being located anywhere in the world.

Globalization is accompanied by the decline in power of national governments to directly influence their own economies. Changes in economic activity in say United States or Japan are reverberated all over the globe. The internationalization of financial markets, of technology and of some manufacturing and services impinge upon the autonomy of nation states. The emergence of institutions such as the World Bank and the European Union which is part of the globalization process remains 'pivotal institutions especially in terms of creating the conditions for effective international governance', as stated by Hirst and Thompson.[7]

Why is Globalization being Opposed by so Many People?

Globalization is a very controversial issue today. Opinions vary considerably over its pros and cons. T.L. Friedman[8] argues that the new era of globalization became the dominant international system at the end of the 20th century in an irrevocable process affecting everyone. The term globalization was once popular among business and corporate leaders. However, now, it has become the target of opposition by most people. The reasons given by its critics can be mainly listed as:

- It is used as an ideology by the powerful to deceive the people about illusory benefits.
- It perpetuates the inequalities and exploitation inherent in capitalism.
- It is not subject to democratic control and therefore cannot serve the interests of the people at large.
- Due to the scale of change, it intensifies long-standing problems such as environmental degradation.

The Negative Effects of Globalization

- Outsourcing of manufacturing and white-collar jobs to Third World countries (mostly India and China) is a common practice adopted by developed nations. The price of labour being comparatively low, costs are reduced considerably by this measure. Jobs in the customer service field are the ones that are mainly outsourced. The availability of a large English-speaking population – willing to accept five times lower wages than in the developed world – attracts this outsourcing. However, people of developed countries are unhappy with this loss of jobs. The resentment is further abetted on account of dissatisfaction with the lower standards of customer service provided. This has become a source of dissent and animosity between the peoples of the two 'worlds'.
- Globalization has been seen by several schools of thought to have become an engine for unethical and even illegal activities such as child labour and slavery. The reason for this is attributed to lack of accountability and corruption in these countries. Given the environment of fierce global competition, unethical practices are easily promoted.

- Another unfortunate by-product of globalization is seen to be the issue of environmental degradation. This has become a most vociferously debated issue at most international conventions. Indiscriminate use of natural resources to satisfy consumerist demands is depleting the earth of non-renewable resources. The pollutants emitted by industries and factories have had far-reaching effects on the quality of air, water and food resources – leading to spread of several ailments in an epidemic form. The presence of mobile towers and the radiation from them is an example of the dreaded effects on health.
- Fatal diseases like AIDS have now been known to have originated in Sub-Saharan Africa and reached developed countries like America. The interconnectedness brought about by globalization is the reason for the spread of this and other viruses to other parts of the world.
- Another problem seen as the negative effect of globalization, particularly by the developing nations, is the growth of urban slums and garbage-dumps in areas where most factories are concentrated. Several cities have become heavily polluted and the dumping ground for industrial wastes and unhygienic living conditions.
- Globalization has brought about an onslaught of fast-food or junk food culture to the developing world. McDonaldization is a seriously construed menace leading to obesity and several non-infectious diseases (usually termed as lifestyle diseases such as hypertension and diabetes). Sometimes cultural invasion has been perpetrated in the name of food chains. For example, legal notices have been issued to KFC and McDonald's for serving beef in their products.
- The free-flow of humans, food, materials has also created the menace of drug-trafficking and terrorism. Trafficking in women and children and terrorist activities are a serious threat to the civilized world.
- Globalization is often seen as a source of increasing the rich-poor divide. Globalization has led to creation of jobs and wealth but not of prosperity. The exploitative business practices have widened the chasm between the haves and have-nots.

These are some of the negative effects of globalization.

How does Globalization Affect Women?

In the words of Graham Greene, 'In the last 30 years women have come a long, long way. (Their) lives are nobler and richer than they were, but they are also fiendishly difficult ... the contradictions women face have never been more bruising than they are now .... On every side speechless women endure endless hardship, grief and pain in a world system that creates billions of losers for every handful of winners. It's time to get angry again'.[9]

Globalization has had such negative consequences for women and children that some commentators argue that 'globalisation is a man.'[10]

Although it is argued that some features of globalization may have liberating consequences for women, many critics fear that globalization in the sense of integration of a country into world society, will exacerbate gender inequality.

The traditional sexual division of labour may be further strengthened through the addition of new locations and forms of work (services industry, tourism, and work in free trade and export process zones). However, there is no change in the low economic value accorded to work performed primarily by women in conditions of exploitation, no job security and violations of human rights.

The shift to more knowledge-intensive production has not uniformly impacted women. New jobs have been created but women increasingly have to contend with vulnerable forms of employment. These range between technological redundancy, informalization of labour, as well as the health and safety hazards associated with new technology. This is especially severe in transition economies where women had the protection of the socialist state system; the opening up of the market to foreign capital has meant a loss of these rights.

Another unintended impact of globalization is the rapid increase in unemployment as hundreds of small and large firms across the region were forced to close their doors. Women were the first workers to be laid off – both because the industries in which they predominate (e.g., garment industry) were those most affected by the crisis and because women were less unionized and therefore, easier to sack. The unemployment situation was aggravated by increasing members of returning migrant labourers, many of whom were women, who were being expelled by countries which were experiencing their own unemployment problems. Moreover, cuts in public social sector expenditure that came in the aftermath of the crisis, brought even more hardships, especially for women who have primary responsibility for care of the family.

Thus, globalization may harm women, especially in developing countries, in more ways than one.

- Economically through discrimination in favour of male workers; there would be marginalization of women in the informal sector, and loss of traditional sources of income.
- Politically, through exclusion from the domestic political process and loss of control to global pressures, women will lose out.
- Culturally, through loss of identity and autonomy to a hegemonic world culture, women will be denuded of their roots.

According to V.M. Moghadam,[11] women play a distinct role in globalization, experience more harmful effects, and become a constituency for anti-systemic movements. Beneria and Bisnath[12] argue that gender influences both the causes and consequences of poverty; to compensate for women's weaker structural position and the bias in traditional development policy, their needs now demand special attention. Gita Sen and Sonia Correa[13] argue that the clash of free market globalization and patriarchal reactions poses new dilemmas for women committed to equality. Torry Dickinson[14] talks of the uneven effects of 'selective globalization' on women.

This is not to deny that in some ways globalization has made a positive impact on the lives of women. In many countries, the global pursuit of profit has enhanced employment opportunities for women, where previously they had not existed. Employment has brought economic independence for many women, which in turn has generated the self-esteem that comes from such independence.

The migration of women in search of better employment opportunities has helped to ease the problem of poverty in many cases and met the labour needs of a number of countries in the region. More remittances are generated for the home economy and there is also a greater possibility of technology transfer and enhanced skills formation.

II

But one of the most significant positive contributions of globalization has been the creation of new associations of women and the strengthening of their networks to offer mutual support and resources. The global social movement of human rights, in affirming women's equality, has empowered women's groups to rise against adverse national or local codes. Instantaneous communications have facilitated the formation of alliances and coalitions, lessened isolation of women in remote or secluded areas, allowed for rapid mobilization over issues and provided support on a global basis. In several countries, new information and communications technology (ICT) has improved the access of women to health, micro credit and employment opportunities. Access to ICT among rural women in recent years has been enabling them to participate in economic development through entrepreneurship and small-scale businesses.

Non-Governmental Organizations

Non-governmental organizations have mushroomed since the 1980s.[15] Today, NGOs remain as an important and large-scale presence on the landscape of international development; from the current international campaign to 'Make Poverty History' to the ongoing reconstruction efforts by outside and local NGOs still underway in Indonesia, India and Sri Lanka after the tsunami disaster of December 2004.[16] Alongside the more familiar roles of service delivery and campaigning, NGOs have also become active in a complex range of broader development activities that include democracy building, conflict resolution, human rights work, policy analysis, research and information provision.

Women's NGOs

Under the canopy of globalization, international agencies have emphasized the need to promote cooperation between the United Nations system and NGOs on economic and development issues (Non-Government Liaison Service 1999). The ESCAP (Economic and Social Commission for Asia and the Pacific) of the UNO has brought out seven booklets dealing with specific areas for government-NGO cooperation, including women-empowerment programmes. In this manner women's organizations shall be infused with life-blood. They will be strengthened and new vistas will be opened for them.

Women organizations sprang up in the 1970s and have mushroomed ever since. They have catalyzed action in the past few decades. This proliferation was so significant that the last decade of the 20th century may justly be described as the decade of the NGOs. The NGO has now become an integral part of the Indian social landscape. It has become part and parcel of the vocabulary of not only world languages, but of practically every Indian language too. The NGO sector in India is diverse and heterogeneous. NGOs differ from one another in size, in goals and membership.[17] Sociologists have not paid sufficient and systematic attention to the rise of this phenomenon. There is an urgent need to investigate and assess the nature, formation and working of NGOs. Women's organizations of different hues and shades of thought have emerged: liberal, socialist, Marxist, radical and cultural, to name a few.

The NGO acquires its significance mainly on two counts.[18] Firstly, being a non-governmental organization, it is distinct and separate from the state. Secondly, being a non-profit organization, it is detached from the market. Thus, the NGOs are part of the third sector in society, in which state and market are the first and second sectors. It is this distance from the state and separation from the market, which highlights the importance of voluntary associations. Voluntary action is the life-blood of a vibrant democratic society. Alex de Tocqueville[19] has very effectively brought to light this fact. In his account of democracy in America, he attributed its success to the natural inclination of Americans to form associations. As he stated: 'Wherever at the head of some new undertaking you see the government in France or a man of rank in England, in the US you will be sure to find an association.' He further states that 'the citizen of the United States is taught from infancy to rely upon his own exertions in order to resist the evils and the difficulties of life; he looks upon the social authority with an eye of mistrust and anxiety, and he claims its assistance only when he is unable to do without it.'

The Indian State was initially indifferent, if not averse, to the growth of NGOs in the field of development. Only relief organizations and charitable organizations were tolerated to a large extent. The situation underwent a change after the mid-1980s. First in the Seventh Five Year Plan and later in the Eighth Plan (1992–97), the government came out openly in support of NGOs and encouraged them to participate in the process of development. ₹ 150–200 crore was granted annually for NGO funding. This was by no measure an insubstantial amount.[20] Significance of NGOs and self-help organizations is particularly important in the case of women's movement. Women's organizations have pushed through radical change in two major directions.[21] The first is a fundamental change in the material conditions of women through income generation, asset formation and ownership of property. The second, which goes beyond economics into the realm of politico-social conditions, seeks to bring about fundamental changes in certain aspects of culture, in particular the system of patriarchal hierarchy. Much of the radical thinking comes from the feminist movement. The strategies used by most of these organizations have been skits, journals and social consciousness-raising movements.

Let us now examine the impact of globalization on this culture of voluntarism. Globalization has many components and ramifications. Some of the significant ones are: (1) the dilution of the state, which has already been preceded by disenchantment with the state, (2) upsurge of civil society, and (3) increasing intervention of global agencies. It is within this threefold scenario that the impact of globalization on NGOs becomes very significant.

Techniques and knowledge systems are not value-neutral. Those involved in changing the structures of society can ill-afford to ignore the normative and ideological dimensions of social existence. The onslaught of globalization has forced a rethinking and redefining of the structure of civil society vis-à-vis the state. The advent of international government organizations and multi and transnational NGOs has intercepted the two significant functions of the nation state – the nurturance of a liberal, democratic socio-political order and the nurturance of autonomous organizations that it must allow to emerge. With tremendous economic and managerial skills at their disposal, transnational and multinational NGOs are in a position to command and dictate to civil society organization/local NGOs. International agencies like the GATT (General Agreement on Tariffs and Trade) and WTO and even the World Bank are exerting pressure upon governments to share the burden of national development with local NGOs. In the context of globalization, the nation states are increasingly losing their freedom over their economic, and consequently, political agenda. In such a situation the local self-help organizations that are starved of resources and leadership could readily become targets of these transnational organizations. As Kothari[22] warns, the local state is to be side-stepped, the so-called voluntary agency, the NGO, is to be promoted, and the women's movement is to be adopted as an agenda of the new world order.

This has grave implications for the local NGOs. The local NGO, which is the bearer of the diverse range of protests responding to specific needs of the aggrieved, is being made an agent of the proposed integration, unity and interdependence which underlie the globalization ideology.

The NGO which may have secured autonomy, including financial autonomy, from the government, may not be able to enjoy autonomy from the international agencies to which it may have to turn to for funds in order to survive. This raises certain questions:

1. Can NGOs fill the entire space not occupied by either state or market?
2. Will the local NGOs crumble under the weight of transnational NGOs?
3. What strategies need to be worked out by the local NGOs to face the threats/challenges posed by globalization?

Let us address the first question. From the sociological point of view, it is preposterous to believe that NGOs can fill the entire space which is left vacant by state and market. NGOs may well form a key component of the third sector, but it cannot be the whole of it. There are other autonomous institutions which play a very vital role such as universities, and media. NGOs are based on mutual reinforcement and self-reliance. However, can NGOs be completely free of bureaucratic procedures, rational accounting and material incentives to its employees? Will NGO remain free from the social characteristics of caste and kinship? These are yet to be seen as NGOs are still in a nascent stage in India.

The second question is whether the local NGOs will withstand or totter under pressures of transnational NGOs. These organizations have to work on the agenda set for them by the funding agencies. There is a fear of derailment from pursuit of the cause of indigenous women's liberation and gender inequality. It seems that NGOs have come to stay. It may be possible that some of them may fade and disappear but as a social phenomenon, they shall endure and evolve mechanisms of survival and adjustment to the changing situation.

The most significant question is regarding the strategies which the local NGOs must evolve in order to combat the onslaught of globalization. Here comes the importance of committing mistakes which are not dissimilar to those made by the mainstream or which are imposed upon them by the transnational NGOs. Many of the grassroots experiments are wary of opening their doors to researchers for fear of criticism. Evaluation reports exist, but often lack the rigour of empirical research. The interface between social science research and grassroots activism must grow to enrich the frontiers of knowledge. They would strengthen voluntary action.

Moreover acquisition of knowledge and expertise will become the need of the hour. Activists must be trained. Training is not a one-shot affair. The stress should be on continuity. Without reflection, introspection and the sharing of experience, there is every chance of them rusting. Pressure must be maintained to ensure that the process remains vibrant. The NGOs must be made alive to the possible threats posed by globalization policies and become better prepared to face the challenge.

One of the issues that has been debated is whether self-help initiatives of women should remain autonomous or whether men and women should join hands in their organizational effort. Most successful ventures are wary of throwing open their doors to men. If given entry, men may undo whatever has been achieved against great odds. Women who need to gain confidence and exposure to the outside world may not find it conducive to negotiate and compete with men within the organization.[23]

When women organize or are helped to organize themselves, real social transformation begins. It has been amply demonstrated that organized voluntary efforts have provided the necessary protective environment in which women have gained confidence and self-reliance. The various examples of failure at self-help, on the other hand, prove the odds against them. The existing efforts, however, fall far short of the needs of innumerable labouring women. Large segments of the disprivileged women have neither access to an organization nor are there any attempts to organize them. E.R. Bhatt[24] observes, 'In every group we met, there were one or two bright, articulate, defiant young women ready to act as catalysts for a better future. These women are ready to absorb new ideas, more assistance, even to get organized to better their future. This is the most imminent challenge posed before us by these women today. If left to women's groups and to the poor women's own efforts, it is unlikely that such organizations will come up that soon, and in large numbers to make a significant dent on the situation of these women.' She further states that 'the course of their struggle is long-winded. While at one end there must be conscious effort to devise concrete strategies which can help to enhance the ownership of control over productive assets by these women. Perhaps it will be the most important intervention towards both their empowerment and economic well-being.'

Attitudes to NGOs have grown more complex, ambiguous and controversial. While NGOs were for some time favoured by development donors, they have in recent years been denounced for various reasons. There are many debates regarding the changing profile, extent, and role of the NGO sector.

Women Self-help and NGOs: A Case for Voluntarism

NGOs are no longer seen (by donors and others) as sources of 'alternative' development ideas at a time when mainstream neo-liberal approaches to development dominate. Many earlier ideas and approaches that were promoted by NGOs – such as empowerment and participation – have arguably been assimilated or co-opted into mainstream thinking.[25]

However, a strong argument for social change through voluntarism still exists, although activists feel that achieving social change through voluntary intervention is neither easy nor simple. The work of voluntary effort cannot always be tangibly measured. Often perceptible change is not visible even after tremendous effort. Social change is a gradual, long-winding process to alter the basic structures of society and end deep-rooted forms of exploitation entrenched in society. However the process of voluntarism is not less significant than the product. If collectivization and self-help activity can be achieved, it would not matter even if the gains trickle in slowly. In fact, collectivization itself may be the most dramatic achievement, and its momentum will help achieve concrete results as nothing else. Voluntarism coheres around the principles of freedom, self-help, self-reliance, importance of the group, mutual cooperation, accountability to the group and the consciousness that there is a common life situation. Freedom from external interference is also important. However, voluntarism must inevitably submit itself to critical judgement of its constituents. Voluntary action is not without responsibility. Critical questions as to whom should one be responsible and accountable, and what are the goals of voluntary effort inevitably come to the fore. In seeking to promote democracy and protect ideals of diversity and plurality, voluntarism emerges as a powerful body of ideas and values.

Prospects for the Future

Achieving social change through voluntarism is neither easy nor simple. Challenge and opposition are in-built into very concept of self-help. It is not easy to throw out presumptions on how NGOs should go about their business. Networking with each other and learning from each other's experiences can go a long way. The mechanics of keeping accounts, holding meetings, maintaining fields and running an office are increasingly important dimensions of running NGOs. This professionalization could be learnt from training programmes by engaging consultants. The right solutions may emanate from the abiding principles of voluntarism itself.

Notes

1. T.L. Friedman, *The Lexus and the Olive Tree*, New York: Farras, Strauss and Giroux, 2000.
2. R. Robertson, *Globalization: Social Theory and Global Culture*, London: Sage Publications, 1992.
3. M. Waters, *Globalization*, USA: Routledge, 1995.
4. A. Giddens, *The Consequences of Modernity*, Stanford: Stanford University Press, 1990.
5. M. Castells, *The Rise of the Networked Society*, Oxford: Blackwell, 1996.
6. J. Gray, *False Dawn: The Delusions of Global Capitalism*, London: Granta, 1999.
7. P. Hirst and G. Thompson, *Globalization in Question*, Oxford: Blackwell Publishing, 1999.
8. T.L. Friedman, op. cit.
9. G. Greene, 'Recantation', in *The Whole Woman*, London: Anchor, 2000.
10. R. Went, *Globalization*, London: Routledge, 2000.
11. V.M. Moghadam, *Globalization and Social Movements*, Lanham: Rowman & Littlefield, 2009.
12. L. Beneria and S. Bisnath, *Global Tension: Challenges and Opportunities in the World Economy*, New York: Routledge, 2004.
13. G. Sen and S. Correa, *Reinventing Social Contract: The Promise of Human Rights*, London: Zed Books, 2012.
14. T. Dickinson, *Community and the World: Participating in Social Change*, New York: Nova Publishers, 2003.
15. M. Edwards and D. Hulme (eds.), *Making a Difference: NGOs and Development in a Changing World*, London: Earthscan, 1992.
16. D. Lewis and P. Poku-Mensah, 'Moving Forward Research Agendas on International NGOs: Theory, Agency and Context', *Journal of International Development*, Vol. 18, 2006, pp. 665–75. Published online in Wiley Inter Science.
17. W.F. Fisher, 'Doing Good? The Politics and Anti-politics of NGO Practice', *Annual Review Anthropology*, Vol. 26, 1997, pp. 439–64.
18. R.B. Jai (ed.), *NGOs in Development Perspective*, Delhi: Vivek Prakashan, 1955.
19. A. Tocqueville, *Democracy in America* (2 vols), New York: Alfred Knopf, 1995.
20. M. Patel, 'Voluntary Organization in India: Motivations and Roles', in M.L. Dantwala et al. (eds.), *Social Change through Voluntary Action*, New Delhi: Sage Publications, 1998, pp. 40–56.

21. E.R. Bhatt, *Towards Equality, Report of the National Committee on the Status of Women in India*, New Delhi: Government of India, 1974.
22. S. Kothari, 'Social Movements and Redefinition of Democracy', in P. Oldenberg (ed.), *India Briefing*, Boulder: Westview Press, 1993, pp. 131–62.
23. *Shramshakti: Report of the National Commission on Self Employed Women and Women in the Informal Sector*, New Delhi: Government of India, 1988.
24. E.R. Bhatt, op. cit.
25. T. Wallace, L. Bornstein and J. Chapman, *Coercion and Commitment: Development NGOs and the Aid Chain*, Rugby: ITDG Publishing, 2006.

14

Globalization, Media and Women

URVASHI DEV RAWAL

In our daily lives we are constantly bombarded with images of scantily-clad, thin, beautifully made-up women in sexy poses staring at us from covers of magazines and newspapers or in the popular media, be it television, films or advertisements.

A UNESCO report described the images of women in the media thus: 'The glamorous sex kitten, the sainted mother, the devious witch, the hard-faced corporate and the political climber.'

The 2009 report stated that, at the current rate of progress on stereotyping women, it would take another 75 years to achieve gender equality in the media.

Several studies and reports have reiterated time and again the unfavourable impact of images of models splashed in the media on average women to look and act in a certain way. The pressure to be thin, to look good, to 'fit in' is leading to eating and psychological disorders in not only women but also young girls who are increasingly worried about their looks and bodies.

According to the Canadian Health Network, the average female model is not only much taller than the average woman, but weighs nearly 25 per cent less. Their bodies are pretty much unattainable for an average woman and leads to poor self-image and eating disorders among many women.

When an Australian magazine 'New Woman' published pictures of overweight and normal weight women, readers appreciated the realism. However, in view of negative reaction from advertisers, the magazine was discontinued. Other such initiatives have been few and far between.

Some fashion houses and magazines have experimented with 'plus size' models. There is now a smattering of 'larger' size models who are seen on ramps and magazines. And, while the overall reaction from people has been positive, this is still far from the norm.

Television, films and increasingly video games too are guilty of presenting overly sexualized and glamourized images of women. There is an obsession with the looks and physical attributes of celebrities. By and large, women in the popular media are still seen through the prism of male chauvinism. The depiction of women is all about looks, glamour and exposure. Women's bodies are continually used to sell cigarettes, liquor, cars, male perfume and other male-identified products, as well as magazines, newspapers and television programmes.

Writing in the online women's portal, WHRnet, Carolina Rodriguez Bello says that free market ideology and technological advancements in telecommunications have facilitated and compelled mergers among media corporations and have subsumed many small media companies. This has led to a concentration of media ownership under big corporations with strong market interests. Moreover, mergers and connections among global and national media corporations have made it possible for media to sway public opinions and attitudes more than ever before.

Globalized media spreads homogeneous images and sounds and, in turn, intensifies the alienation or 'othering' of peoples – immigrants, indigenous groups, people with disabilities, older women, etc.

Bello contends that through the homogenization of peoples and cultures, corporations have marketed their way to more societies and more into women's lives, both in developing and developed countries. Homogenization serves the market interest in women. The market and the media have intensified consumerism through advertisements that set the Aryan Barbie doll beauty as the ideal. Media has become an effective market instrument in creating needs to sell products that guarantee to mould women into the Aryan beauty.

More than ever, women are appraised on the basis of how they look and not on their abilities. The beautiful woman has fair and unblemished skin, is full breasted, slim, and a successful career woman. The ideal woman is not only beautiful but also a perfect mother and wife.

While feminists condemn the commodification and objectification of women's bodies in media, there are differing views on women's sexuality in the media. One view is that women in pornography and in prostitution are victims/survivors of sexual violence against women.

On the other hand, some feminists contend that censoring women's sexualized images would further deny women's reclaiming their own sexualities, and therefore, women's control over their own bodies. They say pornography and sex work are to be fought against only if they are done against a woman's will.

Bello points out that the rise of fundamentalism can be linked to globalization and western cultural homogenization. She says women are caught between market forces and conservative fundamentalist forces which oppose globalization and western economic, political and cultural imperialism.

With globalization and easy access to everyone through television, internet and social media, there has been a rise of fundamentalist tendencies in a number of states which are worried about 'inappropriate' content reaching the users. This has led to intensified control over media, regulation and filtering or even banning of some content.

Feminist approaches to fundamentalism have become more nuanced. The feminist analyses have focused on women's control over their own bodies. Both the free market and fundamentalist forces deny this control. The free market does this by exploiting women's sexualities by influencing attitudes and creating needs around women's bodies while religious fundamentalists do so by repressing women's sexual expressions and lifestyles.

Under the influence of globalization, India too is caught between contrasting images of women that are portrayed in the media. On the one hand, there are traditional, obedient, unthinking, unassertive women whose life revolves around their home and family while on other are bold, saucy, assertive women who are painted in shades of grey.

However, the matter is not confined only to the representation of women in the media. It is also linked to the larger issue of women's rights, not just legal or political but economic, social and even personal too. The 'commoditization' of women in the media and the denial of rights at the ground level are linked to the continuation of the patriarchal-feudal set-up in society.

In India, women are seen in primary roles of homemaker and childbearer. A woman is seen as a daughter, wife, mother, sister but rarely as an individual in her own right.

Continuation of the patriarchal system that sees women as less than equal and even subservient to men has run counter to women's rights. The position of women in society is not hidden from anyone. Though the founding fathers gave equal rights to women and men which are enshrined in the Constitution of India, in practice, it has been an uphill fight for women to find their place in the sun.

The situation in metros and larger cities has over the years improved somewhat with women breaking barriers and making strides in professional and personal life. Education has had an undeniable role to play in helping women break shackles of domesticity. It has emancipated women, helped them to find their potential, work in areas of their choice, become economically independent and thus have a say in deciding about their lives.

Paradoxically, however, it is not always true that women who are educated are also liberal. Literacy cannot be equated with being educated in the true sense of the term and modern in appearance is not always a synonym for a liberal mind. A majority of women, even those who are educated, continue to unquestioningly follow traditions that keep them bound.

These inconsistencies regarding women play out in different ways in society. Rajasthan too still clings to its feudal and patriarchal past where women are given a subordinate position and not allowed to participate in decision-making at home or outside. Men set the rules and women are expected to follow. Social customs like child marriage, *purdah* and restriction on widow remarriage still persist.

The statistics relating to the status of women in society reveal an unpalatable tale. According to the Census 2011, the sex ratio in the state of Rajasthan is 926 girls per 1,000 boys. The child sex ratio (0 to 6 years) is a worrying 883 girls per 1,000 boys. Female literacy is 52.66 per cent, the lowest in the country. Female literacy in urban areas is 71.53 per cent and in rural areas it is only 46.25 per cent.

The National Health and Family Survey-3 (NHFS) (2005–06) shows that Rajasthan's Maternal Mortality Rate is 677 per 100,000, Infant Mortality Rate is 80 per 1,000 live births, the mean age of girls at marriage is 15.3 years, and 53 per cent women and 80 per cent girls under three years are anaemic.

The NHFS-3 data also throws light on women in the social set-up. According to the data for Rajasthan, only 22.8 per cent of women participate in household decisions. The figure for urban areas is 37.9 per cent and for rural areas it is 17.3 per cent. The data further shows that 46.3 per cent of the married women have experienced spousal violence. The percentage in urban areas is 45.4 and in rural areas it is 46.6.

As per the data, the incidence of anaemia among children and adults is very high in the state. The data reveals that 79.1 per cent of children between 6–35 months are anaemic. There is not much difference in statistics for urban and rural areas. In urban areas, 78.5 per cent children are anaemic while in rural areas the corresponding figure is 80.2 per cent.

As for women, 53.8 per cent of the married women between 15 and 49 years are anaemic. In urban areas, the figure is 48.5 per cent while for rural areas it is 55.7 per cent. Equally disturbing are the figures for pregnant women in the age group of 15–49 years – 61.7 per cent of pregnant women are anaemic. Of this, the percentage of urban women and rural women is 64.5 and 60.8 respectively.

There is growing violence and harassment of women who are increasingly asserting themselves in the society. Police data reveals that Rajasthan and Jaipur have a worryingly high incidence of crimes against women.

According to the crime rate figures for 2009 released by National Crime Records Bureau (NCRB) in January 2011, the crime rate (number of crimes per 1,00,00 population) in Jaipur (722.4) was the third highest in the country and was next only to Indore (860.3) and Bhopal (836.5).

The NCRB figures showed a significant rise in crimes against women. Accordingly, Rajasthan stood fourth in the country in cases of outraging modesty (molestation) with 2,339 cases reported. In 2009, there were 189 cases of abduction of girls while 193 girls were abducted in 2010. The number of women kidnapped was 217 in 2009 while the figure in 2010 was 207.

In rural areas, the secondary position of women is manifested in a myriad ways. Girls and women are largely ignored when it comes to the question of their education, nutrition, health, marriage and employment. The discrimination really starts from the mother's womb. Traditionally, fewer girls are sent to school as compared to boys. As they grow up, they are pulled out of schools to be immersed in housework or to get married.

Girls are married young, often even below the legally prescribed age of marriage (18 years) and then they are pushed into a cycle of pregnancies, abortions and child births. Little care is taken of their nutrition during or after pregnancy and a large number of women still give birth to children at home itself with the help of local midwife.

With more and more women becoming educated and joining the workforce, they are challenging the traditional set-up and have to face resistance from their families and society. Sometimes they also have to face the wrath of their families or society for daring to tread their own path. Especially with regard to relationships and marriage, it is still quite difficult for women to make choices because the patriarchal notion of a woman representing a family's honour is still entrenched in society.

Media Portrayal of Women

The coverage of women and women's issues in the media remains by and large stereotypical. The print news media either tends to sensationalize or downplay issues related to women. The representation of women in the media and the status of women in society reflect and reinforce each other.

These are serious issues that need to be addressed not only at the government level but also at the level of the civil society. The media too has a role to play in highlighting the prejudice that prevails towards women.

A scan of newspapers and TV reportage on women shows that the coverage has been mixed. The media does highlight the unequal position of women in society. Both the English and Hindi newspapers regularly carry reports and stories on crimes against women, declining sex ratio, domestic violence, dowry deaths, female infanticide, malnutrition and health issues of women. Other news about women largely pertain to violence against them, dowry deaths, witch hunting, and honour killings. Of course, the more sensational stories make it to the front page of every newspaper but more often than not the news is relegated to inside pages.

Author and journalist Ammu Joseph, who has followed the industry trends for many years, writes that the Indian media like elsewhere focuses on events, especially dramatic, violent ones. This naturally implies that gender-related issues which fit into this narrow definition of news receive the most media attention. These include incidents of rape, dowry deaths, sexual harassment and the like.

A sensational case may bring a spurt in reporting about the event and there will usually be several reports exploring all angles related to the event. For instance, the media frenzy over the Arushi Talwar murder case or the Ruchika Girhotra suicide or the Bhanwari case in Rajasthan is well known. However, the attention span is brief and the news is soon overtaken by other more topical news.

Joseph makes a very valid point that the media's tendency to focus on events rather than processes often results in the neglect of many important issues concerning women. For instance, in Rajasthan, the issues of malnutrition, anaemia, maternal mortality, the continued practice of child marriage, witch hunting or the impact on governance and development patterns of the election of women sarpanchas call for in-depth reporting. When such issues do get covered, it is because of the efforts of women – both inside and outside the media.

The situation prevailing with regard to women as subjects in the media and women who work in or are associated with the media is monitored by the Global Media Monitoring Project (GMMP). The GMMP carries out research on gender discrimination in the news media.

The 2010 GMMP report titled 'Who Makes the News' threw up interesting highlights. In India, the GMMP process was coordinated by the Network of Women in Media, India (NWMI) – a professional association linking women journalists and other women working in or on the media across the country.

According to the GMMP report, in India, women constituted 22 per cent of the people heard or read about in the news. The corresponding global figure was 24 per cent. Across Asia the corresponding figure was 20 per cent.

Men remain the main subjects in news stories – 78 per cent or more than three quarters of the stories analysed revolved around men. An overwhelming proportion of experts/commentators (82%) and spokespersons (87%) featured in the news were male.

Only 22 per cent of the news subjects who were also sources of information (news sources) were women whereas 78 per cent of the news sources were men. Among news subjects, men outnumbered women in almost all occupational categories represented in the news. The only categories with a larger proportion of women than men were homemaker-parent, celebrity-artist-actor-writer-singer, and activist-civil society worker.

The largest proportion of women appearing as news subjects (82%) belonged to the homemaker or parent category; only 18 per cent of male news subjects were placed in this category. The next largest category of women news subjects (59%) was celebrities, artists, etc.

Nearly a third (30%) of the female news subjects in the Indian news media was identified by their family status while only 5 per cent of male news subjects were similarly identified.

Only 12 per cent of the news stories had women as the central focus (i.e., focused specifically on one or more women). That is marginally less than the global figure of 13 per cent.

Nearly two-thirds (63%) of the news stories from the Indian media that were analysed reinforced gender stereotypes while only 9 per cent challenged them. In contrast, globally, less than half (46%) of the news stories reinforced stereotypes.

Almost 51 per cent of activists or workers in civil society organizations in the news were women while 40 per cent of the academic experts, educational professionals and teachers and 35 per cent of bureaucrats, government officials and politicians in the news were women. Women sportspersons barely made it to the news, registering just 4 per cent in that category.

More female news subjects (27%) appeared in photographs accompanying articles than male news subjects (18%).

The GMMP report found that stereotypes about women and men abound in the media. While some stereotypes are fairly universal – for example, women are generally perceived to be non-ambitious, irrational, fragile and dependent while men are usually regarded as ambitious, rational, strong and independent – many others are culture-specific.

GMMP 2010 overwhelmingly found that gender stereotypes continued to prevail in a major way in all media. Nearly two-thirds (63%) of the news stories from the Indian media that were analysed were found to reinforce gender stereotypes while only 9 per cent challenged them.

The report showed that 73 per cent of the stories on crime and violence reinforced gender stereotypes, but so did 72 per cent of the stories on science and health, 62 per cent on economy, 60 per cent on celebrities, arts, media and sports, and 59 per cent on social and legal issues. Almost 87 per cent of the stories on religion, culture and tradition (which fell under the broad theme of social-legal) also reinforced stereotypes.

While 13 per cent of the news stories on politics and government challenged stereotypes, about 55 per cent of stories on that topic reinforced gender stereotypes.

The GMMP 2010 results also showed that 12 per cent of the stories by female reporters challenged gender stereotypes while only 7 per cent of the stories by male reporters did so. Further, 71 per cent of stories by male reporters reinforced gender stereotypes while only 49 per cent of the stories by female reporters did so.

Women in Media

Ammu Joseph, who has written extensively about women in the media, notes that over the years there has been a significant increase in the number of women journalists in the print, broadcast and online media. Women have moved out of the realm of only soft, feature or entertainment stories to cover the entire gamut of news, including crime, politics, business, international affairs, sports and even a few cartoonists.

Apart from women reporters and sub-editors, there are also a number of women editors, chief reporters, chiefs of bureaus, special and foreign correspondents and magazine editors. As Joseph writes, a number of women have managed to storm the citadel of hard news coverage. Many are recognized for their reportage from various areas of conflict in and around the country, having covered exclusive stories and secured rare interviews with leaders of militant organizations operating in these hot spots. Some of the most sensational scoops of recent years have been made possible only by the efforts of several women journalists.

However, this apparently encouraging state of affairs is far from universal. There are significant differences in the situation of women journalists across the country. In metropolitan cities, the situation is more conducive but in smaller cities, they face stronger biases and have fewer growth avenues. Resistance to the recruitment of women still persists in many places.

Joseph says women have contributed to broadening the scope of press coverage to include more and better reporting on issues that were usually sidelined like those related to women, development, human rights, social and economic justice. Women have been noted for their coverage of social trends. They are also credited with having introduced more humane feelings in the media, even while covering hard news.

Despite this, the capacity of women to influence the agenda, practice and output of the media is limited due to the fact that the number of women in key decision-making positions is still relatively small. This also influences women to adapt to the prevailing values and norms of the profession. Another factor is the preoccupation of the media with glamour and wealth. There is a fixation with the lives of the rich and the famous, the beautiful and the powerful. In the existing environment, there is less time and space for in-depth coverage of serious issues.

Call for Action

Internationally, various organizations, educational institutions, feminist and advocacy groups have called for fair and unbiased coverage in the media about issues relating to women.

Writing on WHRnet, Carolina Rodriguez Bello says that the 1995 Fourth World Conference on Women in Beijing, China focused international concern and action on the role of media in perpetuating women's subordination as well its importance in advancing women's rights. 'The Beijing Platform for Action (BPFA) gave an overview of problems and issues surrounding women and the media and spelled out specific strategies for governments, media organizations, non-government organizations and other civil society actors. It called for: (a) women's increased participation in and access to media and new information and communication technologies (ICTs); and (b) promotion of a balanced and non-stereotyped representation of women in the media.'

About five years after the conference, Women Watch, an initiative of the United Nations to assess progress and obstacles on BPFA held an online discussion. The discussion concluded that there have been few improvements in media portrayal of women both in advertising and news coverage. Women still scarcely occupy decision-making positions in the media organizations. Technological developments have made women's images in the media more complex and contributed to unattainable social expectations surrounding women's beauty and abilities.

However, it also noted that women and media monitoring groups have made some contributions in promoting positive images and role of women in media.

The 47the session of the UN Commission on the Status of Women (CSW) in March 2003 affirmed the importance of women's access to and participation in the media and ICTs to women's empowerment. The CSW called on governments, UN bodies, international financial institutions and civil society to continue mainstreaming gender perspectives and ensuring women's full participation in national policies, legislations, programmes, and regulatory and technical instruments in all areas of communications. The session also looked into the growing sexual exploitation of women through the traditional media and through new technologies and called for more research on the impact of media and ICTs on women and girls.

The CSW recommended the integration of gender perspectives in all aspects of the summit. It recognized the need to address inequalities that prevent women from gaining equal access to opportunities and benefits in the media and the emerging knowledge and information society. One way to do this is to ensure the participation of women, gender equality experts and women ICT experts in the World Summit on the Information Society (WSIS).

Human Rights Mechanisms

Article 19 of the Universal Declaration of Human Rights recognizes the media's role in facilitating the freedom of expression and opinion. It states: 'Everyone has the right to the freedom of opinion and expression; this right includes freedom to hold opinions without interference and to seek, receive and impart information and ideas through any media and regardless of frontiers.'

Article 19 (2) of the International Covenant on Civil and Political Rights (ICCPR) states: 'Everyone shall have the right to freedom of expression; this right shall include freedom to seek, receive and impart information and ideas of all kinds, regardless of frontiers, either orally, in writing or in print, in the form of art, or through any other media of his choice.' In paragraph 3, the ICCPR allowed temporary restrictions that may be placed by states upon media in 'respect of the rights or reputations of others' and 'for the protection of national security or of public order, or of public health or morals.'

In Resolution 2003/42, the United Nations High Commissioner for Human Rights defended the right to freedom of opinion and expression of media institutions and information professionals by warning against 'unjustified invocation of national security, including counter-terrorism'.

The Convention on Elimination of All Forms of Discrimination Against Women addressed all forms of discrimination that occurs in public and private spheres of women's lives. Specifically, it prohibits against any form of sex role stereotyping and prejudice, exploitation and prostitution of women, and discrimination in public and political life, education and employment.

The 1995 BPFA section on women and media provides the roadmap for women's advancement through women's access to and participation in expression and decision-making in and through the media and new technologies of communication. It also guides governments in promoting a balanced and non-stereotyped portrayal of women in the media.

The 1993 Vienna Declaration and Programme of Action affirmed the importance of the media in the promotion of human rights. Article 39 states: 'Underlining the importance of objective, responsible and impartial information about human rights and humanitarian issues, the World Conference on Human Rights encourages the increased involvement of the media, for whom freedom and protection should be guaranteed within the framework of national law.'

The Durban Declaration and Programme of Action that came out of the World Conference Against Racism in Durban, South Africa in

September 2001 recognized the role of the media in promoting human rights and in fighting against racism, racial discrimination, xenophobia and related forms of intolerance. Paragraph 93 affirmed that 'all states should recognize the importance of community media that give a voice to victims of racism, racial discrimination, xenophobia and related intolerance.' Paragraph 117 called on states 'to commit financial resources to anti-racism education and to media campaigns promoting the values of acceptance, tolerance, diversity and respect for the cultures of all indigenous peoples living within their national borders. In particular, states should promote an accurate understanding of the histories and cultures of indigenous peoples.' Paragraphs 140 to 147 focused on 'information, communication and the media, including new technologies'. This section called on states to come up with concrete measures to encourage marginalized communities' access to the mainstream and alternative media, promote the development of an ethical code of conduct and self-regulatory measures and policies, 'encourage the media to avoid stereotyping based on racism, racial discrimination, xenophobia and related intolerance ...' and encourage diversity among the workers of media organizations.

Conclusion

The situation is far from ideal. The coverage of women in the news media is far from adequate. Men remain the main subjects in news stories. Women are seen and heard less than men. And where they are seen, it is through a prism of a patriarchal society.

The media coverage remains biased as can be seen from the coverage of women politicians and sportspersons. Women professionals and athletes continue to be underrepresented in news coverage, and are often stereotypically portrayed when they are included.

For instance, in movies, on television, in magazines, the emphasis is on glamour and exposure. The unreal images of thin, fair, young, beautifully made-up models foisted on women and girls are leading to eating disorders and poor self-image. Women seem to be caught in a perpetual cycle of trying to shed weight, or get cosmetic surgery to improve their bodies and faces to look good. Their bodies are used to advertise and sell products. This commodification is a dangerous trend.

The media still relies on men as experts in fields of business, politics, economics, science and technology though there are increasing numbers of women professionals. Women in the news are more likely to be featured in stories about accidents, natural disasters, or domestic violence than in stories about their professional abilities or expertise.

Women media professionals too continue to face discrimination, especially at the higher echelons. There are still few women in top editorial and management positions.

The media fixation with hard news and short attention span does not allow for sustained coverage of an issue. Also, the undue importance given to celebrities and sensational news takes away from coverage of more important but less 'sexy' issues of development.

Academicians, advocacy groups, doctors and even the media have highlighted the of the prevailing situation. International agencies like the UN and human rights mechanisms have also called for elimination of discrimination and violence against women. They have urged for increased access and participation of women in the media. The need is to empower women by ensuring their participation in decision-making and framing of policies.

In recent years, there have been some encouraging examples of fashion magazines and some designers breaking away from the mould and using models who are closer to real women. More often than not, the editors of the magazines and fashion designers have been women.

Women in media too have brought a more humane touch to news. They tend to challenge stereotypes more and cover issues that are sidelined like those relating to women, development, human rights and social and economic justice. There is thus need to bring in participation of more women at higher levels in the government and media. This would lead to balanced coverage of women's issues and to a more real portrayal of women in the media. More awareness building and sensitization about issues pertaining to women is required in the media. And, while we expect the media to play the role of a vanguard in standing up for the right cause, there is need for sensitization of the media persons too so they may be true to their task.

References

Carolina Rodriguez Bello (WHRnet) (2003) 'Women and Media: Progress and Issues'.

Crime in India (2009) National Crime Records Bureau, Ministry of Home Affairs.

Global Media Monitoring Project (2010) *Who Makes the News*, National Report by Network of Women in Media, India.

Hindustan Times (2011) Jodhpur: 'No Child's Play: The Amorphous Knot of Child Marriages', Urvashi Dev Rawal, May 4.

Hindustan Times (2010) Govindgarh: 'Women Get a Shot at Panchayat Polls', Urvashi Dev Rawal, January 16.

National Health and Family Survey (NFHS-3) (2005–06).

Storming the Citadel of Hard News Coverage: Women Report alongside Men but their Impact can be Difficult to Discern, Ammu Joseph, Nieman Reports 2001.

World Savvy Monitor, Global Status of Women, Issue 9, May 2009.

Part IV

MDGs: Towards Bridging the Gaps

15

Millennium Development Goal 6 and Women

An Overview of the United Nations Agenda

SANDEEP GUPTA AND ASHLESHA KAUSHIK

Millennium Development Goals (MDGs) are eight goals to be achieved by 2015 that respond to the world's main challenges to development. They are derived from the Millennium Declaration – an ambitious document affirming the right of every human being to development. The Declaration was adopted by 189 nations and signed by 147 governments during the UN Millennium Summit in September 2000. MDGs synthesize the most important commitments made separately at the international summits of the 1990s; recognize interdependence between growth and sustainable development and acknowledge that development depends on democratic governance, rule of law, respect for human rights and are based on time-bound, measurable targets for monitoring progress. MDGs have become a prime focus of developmental work throughout the globe – a gold standard to which programme-planners aspire, and by which they measure their work. These goals are enumerated below:

Goal 1: Eradicate extreme poverty and hunger
Goal 2: Achieve universal primary education
Goal 3: Promote gender equality and empower women
Goal 4: Reduce child mortality
Goal 5: Improve maternal health
Goal 6: Combat HIV/AIDS, Malaria and other diseases
Goal 7: Ensure environmental sustainability
Goal 8: Develop a global partnership for development

All these goals are interrelated and mutually reinforcible. It is not possible to realize one goal in exclusion of or at the expense of other goals. The development strategy needs to be holistic and inclusive, more particularly, in terms of gender.

MDG 6 is the specific focus of discussion in the present paper.

MDG 6: Combat HIV/AIDS, Malaria and Other Diseases

MDG 6 specifically deals with HIV, Malaria and other leading infectious diseases afflicting the world like TB. MDG 6 has been further sub-classified as follows:

Target 6a: Halt and Begin to Reverse the Spread of HIV/AIDS

- 6.1 HIV prevalence among population aged 15–24 years
- 6.2 Condom use at the last high-risk sex
- 6.3 Proportion of population aged 15–24 years with comprehensive correct knowledge of HIV/AIDS
- 6.4 Ratio of school attendance of orphans to school attendance of non-orphans aged 10–14 years

Target 6b: Achieve, by 2010, Universal Access to Treatment for HIV/AIDS for All Those Who Need It

- 6.5 Proportion of population with advanced HIV infection with access to antiretroviral drugs

Target 6c: Halt and Begin to Reverse the Incidence of Malaria and Other Major Diseases

- 6.6 Incidence and death rates associated with Malaria
- 6.7 Proportion of children under 5 sleeping under insecticide-treated bednets
- 6.8 Proportion of children under 5 with fever who are treated with appropriate anti-malarial drugs
- 6.9 Incidence, prevalence and death rates associated with tuberculosis
- 6.10 Proportion of tuberculosis cases detected and cured under Directly Observed Treatment Short course (DOTS)

The Global Scenario

Every day, nearly 7,500 people are infected with HIV and 5,500 die from AIDS. Globally, an estimated 33 million people were living with HIV/AIDS in 2007. The number of people living with HIV rose from an estimated 29.5 million in 2001 to 33 million in 2007. The vast majority of those living with HIV are in sub-Saharan Africa, where about 60 per cent of adults living with HIV in 2007 were women.

Malaria kills over 1 million people annually, 80 per cent of whom are children under 5 in sub-Saharan Africa. There continue to be between 350 million and 500 million cases of Malaria worldwide each year.

Most countries struggled to meet the Goal 6 targets of achieving universal access to treatment for HIV/AIDS by 2010 and now, of halting and reversing the spread of HIV/AIDS by 2015. In countries for which information is available, no more than 40 per cent of men and 36 per cent of women aged 15 to 24 understand how HIV is transmitted and how to prevent infection, well below the 95 per cent MDG target.

The Situation in India

HIV/AIDS

In India, as per NACO statistics (July 2007), around 2.3 million people are living with HIV. Of these, an estimated 39 per cent are female and 3.5 per cent are children. The average HIV prevalence among women attending antenatal clinics in India is 0.48 per cent. Much higher rates are found among people attending STD clinics (3.6%), female sex workers (5.1%), injecting drug users (7.2%) and men who have sex with men (7.4%). The rates among different groups vary widely between states. By the end of 2005, the total number of reported AIDS cases in India was 116,905, of which 34,177 were women. Around a third of these were among people younger than 30 years.

Tuberculosis

Tuberculosis (TB) is a major public health problem in India. India accounts for one-fifth of the global TB incident cases. Each year nearly 2 million people in India develop TB, of which around 0.87 million are infectious cases. It is estimated that annually around 330,000 Indians die due to TB.

In terms of population coverage, India now has the second largest DOTS (Directly Observed Treatment, Short course) programme in the world. However, India's DOTS programme is the fastest expanding, and the largest in the world in terms of patients initiated on treatment, placing more than 100,000 patients on treatment every month.

Since 1993, the Government of India (GoI) has been implementing the WHO-recommended DOTS strategy via the *Revised National Tuberculosis Control Programme (RNTCP)*. The revised strategy was pilot-tested in 1993 and launched as a national programme in 1997. By March 2006, the programme was implemented nationwide in 633 districts, covering 1,114 million (100%) population. Phase II of the RNTCP started from October 2005, which is a step towards achieving the TB-related targets of the Millennium Development Goals. Since 2006, RNTCP is implementing the WHO-recommended 'Stop TB Strategy', which in addition to DOTS, addresses all the newer issues and challenges in TB control. TB is the single biggest killer of young women.

Malaria

Malaria has now staged a dramatic comeback in India after its near eradication in the early and mid-1960s.

India has spent up to 25 per cent of its health budget on Malaria control from 1977–1997, and starting in 1997, India planned to spend $40 million on Malaria control, a 60 per cent increase from the previous year.

Early setbacks in Malaria eradication coincided with DDT shortages. Later, in the 1960s and 1970s, Malaria resurgence was the result of technical, financial and operational problems. In the late 1960s, Malaria cases in urban areas started to multiply, and upsurge of Malaria was widespread. As a result, in 1976, 6.45 million cases were recorded by the National Malaria Eradication Programme, the highest since resurgence. The implementation of Urban Malaria Scheme (UMS) in 1971–72 and the Modified Plan of Operation (MPO) in 1977 improved the Malaria situation for 5–6 years. Malaria cases were reduced to about 2 million. The impact was mainly on vivax Malaria. Easy availability of drugs under the MPO prevented deaths due to Malaria and reduced morbidity, a peculiar feature of Malaria during the resurgence. The Plasmodium Falciparum Containment Programme launched in 1977 to contain the spread of falciparum Malaria reduced it in the areas where the containment programme was operated but its general spread could not be contained. *P. falciparum* showed a steady upward trend during the 1970s and thereafter. Rising trend of Malaria was facilitated by developments in various sectors to improve the national economy under successive Five Year Plans. Malaria, at one time a rural disease, diversified under the pressure of developments into various ecotypes. These ecotypes have been identified as forest Malaria, urban Malaria, rural Malaria, industrial Malaria, border Malaria and migration Malaria; the latter cutting across boundaries of various epidemiological types. Further, Malaria in the 1990s returned with new features not witnessed during the pre-eradication days. These were the vector resistance to insecticide(s); pronounced exophilic vector behaviour; extensive vector-breeding grounds created principally by urbanization and industrialization; change in parasite formula in favour of *P. falciparum*; resistance in *P. falciparum* to chloroquine and other anti-malarial drugs; and human resistance to chemical control of vectors. Malaria control has become a complex enterprise, and its management requires decentralization and approaches based on local transmission involving multi-sectoral action and community participation.

Gender Perspective

The Millennium Declaration explicitly recognizes that 'the equal rights and opportunities of women and men must be assured'. The MDGs therefore acknowledge that gender – what a given society believes about the appropriate roles and activities of men and women and the behaviours and status that result from these beliefs – can have a major impact on development, helping to promote it in some cases while seriously retarding it in others. MDG 3 (out of eight total) is, in fact, specifically about gender, calling for an end to disparities between boys and girls at all levels of education. There is general agreement that education is vital to development, and ensuring that girls as well as boys have full opportunities for schooling will help improve lives in countless ways. Nevertheless, it would be wrong to conclude – as a casual reader of the MDGs might – that the relevance of gender equality to development is confined to the educational sphere. Men and women, both, participate in nearly every aspect of life in communities throughout the world. Not surprisingly, then, the rules that regulate the behaviours and values of men and women in a given society and the status derived thereof have the potential to impact nearly every aspect of life. Therefore, while only one of the MDGs is specifically about gender, addressing gender is of critical importance to every MDG.

Recognizing this, the Department of Gender and Women's Health (GWH) of the World Health Organization has examined the health-related MDGs (numbers 1, 4, 5, 6, 7 and 8) with a view to identifying areas where gender considerations may have a bearing on work towards each goal. In each case where such an area has been identified, GWH has written a brief paragraph, specifying the relevant gender concern and pointing out factors which programme-planners and researchers should keep in mind to ensure that the concern is addressed. These paragraphs are meant for inclusion in the 'storylines' for the MDGs – accompanying texts meant to contextualize, explain the relevance of, and help operationalize the Goals. Health-related MDGs are expressed as national averages. They therefore do not reflect what happens to poorer groups, nor do they reflect how development processes impact differently the lives of men and women. As a minimum, relevant data collected for reporting on the MDG goals and targets should be disaggregated by sex, even where the indicators themselves do not call for disaggregation. The development of indicators that are able to capture gender dimensions is a next step. It is hoped that these 'storyline additions' will help 'en-gender' the health MDGs, ensuring that those who use the goals to guide their work will not fall short of maximum success through failure to address important, and relevant, gender realities.

HIV/AIDS and Women

HIV/AIDS is a leading cause of death for adults of reproductive age, and women are increasingly affected, constituting half of the number of people living with HIV/AIDS. Households affected by HIV/AIDS are more likely to be poor than those not affected by the disease, and women aged 15–24 are three times more likely to be infected by HIV than men of the same age. This reflects the uneven power relationship between men and women in both the private and public sphere of life. Women are not only physically more vulnerable to HIV infection than men, discrimination and/or violence limit their ability to access reproductive health-care facilities. Particularly intergenerational sex and transactional sex have inherent unequal power relations between partners, and makes it virtually impossible for women to insist on delaying sexual debut, abstinence, condom use, or to report abuse.

2002 was the first year when the number of adult women worldwide suffering from the disease approximately equalled the number of adult men, suggesting that the disease is spreading fastest among women. Indeed, in sub-Saharan Africa, the region most affected by HIV, prevalence rates among women are already distinctly higher than those among men. These figures reflect underlying realities of biological sex and social gender that programme-planners will have to grapple with if they expect to meet Target 7 of the Millennium Development Goals.

Creating opportunities for women's political and economic empowerment gives them the ability to seize control of their own lives. For most women, reproductive health-care services are the most accessible entry points for HIV prevention, treatment, care and support, explaining why investment in the areas of sexual and reproductive health are increasingly important.

Effective Prevention of Mother-To-Child Transmission (PMTCT) may require involving both mothers and fathers, even though planners of such programmes may be tempted to address only women. Although it is women who must take PMTCT drugs, yet they may not have enough autonomy or financial resources to do so on their own, without their partners' consent and participation.

Women and girls bear the brunt of the care-giving which this epidemic, by felling so many adults in the prime of life, renders necessary. The stigma of HIV may be felt most strongly by women, who are often physically, socially, and economically more vulnerable than men.

Violence is both a cause and consequence of HIV infection. Up to 30 per cent of women in some countries report that their first sexual experience was forced, which is one of the reasons that infection rates are so high among young women. Once infected, women often face violence from their partners and communities as a result of stigma and discrimination. Poverty, limited access to education and information, and ingrained gender inequalities fuel these problems. Progress towards the HIV goal is mixed. However, the aggregate story masks some deeply disturbing trends which, left unchecked, threaten to jeopardize progress on MDGs. In particular, women are increasingly at the centre of the AIDS pandemic and in Africa now account for 61 per cent of people living with the virus.

Among 16–24 years old in the region, 75 per cent of AIDS infections are among women. In the Caribbean, the percentage has risen from 37 per cent in 2001 to 43 per cent in 2007.

The Women Won't Wait Coalition, of which Action Aid is a part, is campaigning for action to address this often deadly intersection between violence against women and HIV. Despite the evidence that systematic violations of women's rights are drivers of the pandemic, the MDGs are silent on this issue. There is evidence that some progress is being made on halting the spread of HIV. However, this progress is under threat as the pandemic is increasingly feminized, driven by systematic violations of women's rights. Efforts to achieve women's rights and to tackle endemic violence against women must be a central part of government responses to HIV, if MDG 6 is to be reached.

The reasons for the feminization of HIV and AIDS are complex, but discrimination and the violence that often stems from structural inequalities between women and men are key drivers. It is therefore essential that national AIDS plans and strategies, as well as global initiatives such as the International Health Partnership, invest in consultation with organizations representing women and girls living with HIV and AIDS, and reflect their needs in interventions promoting prevention, treatment and care. Specific policies such as investing in female-controlled prevention methods, and training for health professionals to address violence against women, need to be accompanied by broader legal and political efforts to challenge and stop the discrimination that is helping to drive HIV and AIDS.

Malaria and Women

Pregnant women (and very young children) have unusually high incidence and mortality rates for Malaria, and warrant specific attention in Malaria-control programmes. It is also possible that gender norms may affect Malaria prevention and treatment via their influence on sleeping and work patterns, on use of bed-nets, and on which family members receive medicines and medical care. The direction of such effects probably varies from place to place – but their existence highlights the importance of recording and analysing all Malaria-related data by sex, in order to notice and respond to any patterns that do exist. More than 1 million people die of Malaria every year, mostly infants, children and pregnant women. International progress on tackling Malaria, like HIV, has been patchy. Every year, half a billion people – one in 12 of the world's population – become seriously ill with Malaria, and although the overwhelming majority survive, sickness diverts household time and money into care, interrupts education and carries particular dangers for pregnant women. For pregnant women without immunity, there is a 60 per cent risk of miscarriage and a 10 per cent risk of mortality, rising to 50 per cent mortality among those in severe cases. For pregnant women with some immunity, Malaria carries a high risk of anaemia and low growth in the foetus. There is also growing evidence that HIV-positive women are at a heightened risk. As with other diseases, tackling Malaria and reducing its impact demands an approach that addresses its effect on women in particular.

Tuberculosis and Women

According to the World Health Organiaztion, TB accounts for 9 per cent of deaths among women between the ages of 15 and 44. In comparison, war accounts for 4 per cent of deaths of women in that age group, HIV 3 per cent and heart disease 3 per cent. Worldwide, TB prevalence as well as latent TB infection rates among adult women are generally lower than those among adult men. Nevertheless, TB remains a leading cause of death among women of reproductive age. In India, deaths from TB are 27–41 per cent higher among young women and children compared to males.

Women of reproductive age who are infected with TB are more likely than similarly aged men to progress to disease. Furthermore, TB during pregnancy leads to significantly higher rates of poor pregnancy outcome, for both child and mother. Both of these gender-related aspects of the disease should be kept in mind by those designing programmes to combat it. Finally, studies suggest that genital tuberculosis, a relatively uncommon disease in men, may afflict up to 1/8 of women who have pulmonary tuberculosis and can lead to infertility and therefore, needs to be addressed. TB case detection is significantly lower in women compared with men. Women wait up to twice as long to seek treatment for TB – waiting until they are severely ill and more likely to die. Gender differentials in TB case detection and treatment outcomes may be due to a variety of factors such as differences in reporting of respiratory morbidity, delay in seeking care, gender-distinctive barriers to access, and stigma.

Implementation of MDGs: Global Partnerships

The Millennium Development Goals (MDGs) are the concrete targets agreed to by the international community which provide millions of individuals with the agency to improve their lives. Fulfilling the objectives around gender equality contained in mutually re-enforcing declarations such as the Programme of Action at the International Conference on Population and Development (ICPD) in Cairo 1994, and the Platform for Action at the Fourth World Conference on Women in Beijing in 1995, is essential to achieving the MDGs. Another underpinning to this effort is the Convention on the Elimination of all Forms of Discrimination Against Women (CEDAW), adopted in 1979, which mandates state parties to take all appropriate measures, including legislation, so that women can enjoy all their human rights and fundamental freedoms.

CEDAW is furthermore the only human rights treaty which enforces the reproductive rights of women and recognizes culture and tradition as particularly influential when shaping gender roles and family relations. In addition, the United Nations Population Fund (UNFPA) works with governments and non-governmental organizations worldwide to promote gender equality; equity and women's empowerment; address adolescent sexual and reproductive health needs; adopt a life-cycle approach to women's reproductive health; prevent HIV and reduce factors that make young women and adolescent girls vulnerable to HIV/AIDS; eliminate all forms of violence against women, including harmful cultural practices such as female genital mutilation/cutting; use culturally sensitive approaches to achieve sustainable gender equality and build ownership within communities.

By 2015, fulfilling the MDGs can save:

- More than 500 million people from extreme poverty
- More than 300 million people from hunger
- 30 million children from dying before the age of 5
- 2 million mothers from dying in childbirth
- 350 million people from unsafe drinking water
- 650 million people from living with unsafe sanitation

And plan to

- Halt HIV by 2015 and begun to reverse the spread of HIV/AIDS
- Halt and begin to reverse the incidence of Malaria and other major diseases.

Some Encouraging Results

As a result of the expansion of antiretroviral treatment services, made possible by increased international funding, the number of people who die from AIDS has started to decline, from 2.2 million in 2005 to 2 million in 2007. At 33 million people, the absolute numbers living with HIV are greater than ever before. Yet the global proportion of adults living with HIV and AIDS has remained stable since 2001. The number of deaths has fallen, from 2.1 million in 2001 to 1.7 million in 2007. This fall is mainly the result of the growing availability of antiretroviral drugs. These aggregate trends offer some encouragement. While the reduction in prevalence partly reflects natural trends in the cycle of the pandemic, it also demonstrates that progress can be made with the right mix of policy, funding and political commitment from national governments and donors. From 2005 to 2007, the percentage of HIV-positive pregnant women receiving antiretroviral drugs to Prevent Mother-To-Child Transmission (PMTCT) rose from 14 to 33 per cent. In this same period, the number of new infections among children fell from 410,000 to 370,000.

The Global Polio Eradication Initiative is the largest international public health effort in history. WHO, UNICEF and other organizations jointly collaborate on this initiative, which has led to a rapid decline in transmission of the wild polio virus. As a result, the number of countries where polio is still endemic has decreased to four as of 2007.

Progress has been made in Malaria control interventions, particularly through the use of insecticide-treated mosquito bed-nets, whose production worldwide jumped from 30 million in 2004 to 95 million in 2007. Large increases in funding and attention to Malaria have accelerated Malaria control activities in many countries, as a result of international funding from key philanthropic, bilateral and multilateral sources. India's DOTS programme for controlling TB is the fastest expanding programme, and the largest in the world in terms of patients initiated on treatment, placing more than 100,000 patients on treatment every month.

The Road Ahead: What Needs to be Done

Gender equality cannot be achieved unless action is taken on multiple fronts. For example, efforts to improve women's reproductive health require access to quality reproductive health-care and family planning services, as well as actions to address underlying issues of gender inequality in women's education, legal capacity, exposure to gender-based violence, stereotypes and gendered divisions of labour within the family, as well as broader issues of macroeconomic policy and global distribution of resources.

Several strategies have been suggested that include:

- Implementing a long-term multi-stakeholder, multi-sectoral and gender-sensitive approach, based on national AIDS plans.
- Creating closer linkages between HIV/AIDS interventions and sexual and reproductive health-care to reduce unsafe sexual risk-taking behaviours, and reduce sexually-transmitted infections, including HIV.
- Ensuring predictable and sustained funding to address the HIV/AIDS pandemic. The need to scale up programmes for HIV prevention and ensure universal access to treatment for HIV/AIDS for women and men.

- Developing sustainable national health systems, delivering quality services and retaining professional staff.
- Developing primary health-care systems to ensure universal coverage for essential health services, including for poor and under-served populations in rural areas and urban slums.
- Promoting mechanisms to substantially increase funding for research and development of essential drugs to treat tuberculosis, Malaria, HIV/AIDS and other infectious diseases.
- Adopting effective means to tackle HIV-related TB and mainstreaming DOTS–plus into DOTS to tackle multidrug-resistant TB.
- Ensuring adequate financing for key interventions under the Roll Back Malaria Partnership.
- Taking decisive action to control and treat neglected tropical diseases.
- Committing additional funding for the global partnership for affordable essential drugs.
- Promoting gender equality, equity and women's empowerment.
- Ensuring male involvement and responsibility in women's reproductive health.

No MDG can be realized in exclusion. Poverty control, education and gender equality are of paramount importance. For reducing HIV transmission from mother to child, highly-effective antiretroviral therapy as opposed to monodrug therapy (zidovudine), cesarian sections and avoidance of breastfeeding offer the best chances of survival although the feasibility of these measures is the limiting factor in resource poor settings. Same applies to expansion of DOTS and Malaria control measures. For rural women, under-reporting of TB and HIV along with poor compliance and inadequate treatment due to socio-economic constraints further compound the problem. So the issues of curbing the death jaws of highly-infectious conditions like HIV and TB cannot be propounded in isolation. The panacea does not lie with drugs alone but in combination therapy with education, upliftment and socio-economic empowerment of women.

Further Readings

Commission on the Status of Women Report on the 52nd Session, United Nations, 2008.

Committing to Action: Achieving the MDGs, Background note by the Secretary-General for the High-level Event on the Millennium Development Goals, United Nations, New York, September 2008.

The Millennium Development Goals Report, United Nations, 2008.

16

Millennium Development Goal 3

Towards Gender Equality and Women Empowerment

PRERNA PURI

> The MDGs encapsulate the development aspirations of the world as a whole. But they are not only development objectives; they encompass universally accepted human values and rights such as freedom from hunger, the right to basic education, the right to health and a responsibility to future generations.
>
> —Ban Ki-moon, Secretary-General, United Nations[1]

I

This paper examines MDGs and some issues of gender equality and women empowerment. Equality is a concept which has different meanings in different situations for people. Absolute equality is unattainable. In the context of women, most important is to recognize her first as a human being having a right to be born, to live and to grow into a normal human being. Even this basic right is not given to women and man claims to be a highly civilized being. The United Nations Population Fund declared gender equality as 'first and foremost, a human right'. The Beijing conference also declared that women's rights are human rights.

UNO has taken unprecedented, measures to improve the life of women, enacted several conventions, held world conferences on rights of women with binding resolutions to compel the states to implement them. Yet the facts tell a depressing story. It is not a reflection on the effectiveness of the UN but on the retarded psyche of man and male-dominated society which refuses to liberate its women members from the clutches of age-old traditionality and outdated modes of thinking and behaviour.

The Millennium Development Goals (MDGs) are the blueprint for a better world. MDGs are the international 'roadmap' for a concerted and concrete global action. They are the most broadly supported, comprehensive and specific development goals the world has ever agreed upon. They are the first set of quantitative and time-bound goals shared by developing and developed countries.

These were officially established at the Millennium Summit in 2000, where all world leaders present adopted the United Nations Millennium Declaration, from which the eight goals were promoted. These are eight international development goals that all 192 United Nations member states and at least 23 international organizations have agreed to achieve by the year 2015, using 1990 as a benchmark. The MDGs are both global and local, tailored by each country to suit specific development needs. They provide a framework for the entire international community to work together towards a common end – making sure that human development reaches everyone, everywhere. If these goals are achieved, world poverty will be cut by half, tens of millions of lives will be saved, and billions more will have the opportunity to benefit from the global economy.

The Millennium Development Goals (MDGs) were developed out of the eight chapters of the United Nations Millennium Declaration, signed in September 2000. There are eight goals with 21 targets, and a series of measurable indicators for each target. The following are the eight goals:

1. Eradicate extreme poverty and hunger: in 2003, an estimated 1.2 billion people were living on less than $1 a day. The first goal calls for halving this number. In many developing countries, the poor live on the margins of society, benefiting little from progress. They lack education, health-care, adequate shelter, personal safety, and regular income – all the things needed to improve their quality of life.
2. Achieve universal primary education: education is a powerful instrument for reducing poverty and inequality, improving health and social well-being, and laying the groundwork for sustained economic growth. It is essential for building democratic societies and dynamic, globally competitive economies. Providing universal primary education, however, remains a great challenge. There are currently 115 million children – 60 per cent of them girls – not in primary school, the majority living in South Asia and sub-Saharan Africa. The second goal aims that by 2015, all children, girls and boys, should be able to complete a full course of primary schooling.
3. Promote gender equality and empower women: in both rich and poor countries, gender discrimination persists, and its consequences are difficult to ignore. Nowhere is this more apparent than in some

developing countries, where traditional beliefs and practices put a high premium on boys' education, while girls are excluded. Even when girls start school, they are more likely to drop out for these reasons. Without at least a complete primary education, women face limited employment options, discrimination, lower pay, and less control over their health and well-being. The third MDG aims to achieve gender parity in the following areas:

- *Ratios of girls to boys in primary, secondary and tertiary education*
- *Share of women in wage employment in the non-agricultural sector*
- *Proportion of seats held by women in national parliament.*[2]

4. Reduce child mortality: keeping children alive and healthy, and enabling them to learn and thrive through adolescence, is imperative for the future of every country. According to the United Nations Development Programme (UNDP), on an average in developing countries, for every 1,000 children, 100 die before the age of 5. Around the world, thousands of children die every year from preventable causes: illnesses caused by contaminated water, inadequate immunization, injuries from war and civil conflict, high levels of poverty and malnutrition, HIV/AIDS and the high incidence of Malaria and tuberculosis. The fourth MDG aims to reduce the under-5 mortality rate by two-thirds, between 1990 and 2015.
5. Improve maternal health: in 2000, more than half a million women died in childbirth or from pregnancy-related complications. About 99 per cent of these deaths, many of them preventable, occur in developing countries. Infections, severe blood loss and unsafe abortions account for the majority of deaths. Goal 5 calls for reducing the rate of maternal mortality to 75 per cent by 2015 and to achieve, by 2015, universal access to reproductive health.
6. Combat HIV/AIDS, Malaria, and other diseases: the rampant spread of infectious diseases threatens to reverse development progress, reduce life expectancy and cut productivity. With an estimated 40 million people living with HIV/AIDS and 20 million deaths since the disease was first identified, AIDS poses an unprecedented health, economic, and social challenge on a global scale. The sixth goal calls to halt by 2015 and begun to reverse the spread of HIV/AIDS, the incidence of Malaria and other major diseases and to achieve, by 2010, universal access to treatment for HIV/AIDS for all those who need it.
7. Ensure environmental sustainability: our natural environment is the unequivocal basis of human survival. It is the foundation for all economic and, more importantly, human development. However, poorly-managed economic development that has resulted in

widespread pollution, land erosion and deforestation endangers the future of our natural resources – and our very survival. Because the environment provides the raw materials vital to sustaining human development, we must ensure that, in turn, international development policies work to preserve our natural environment. Goal seven aims at the following:

- *To integrate the principles of sustainable development into country policies and programmes; reverse loss of environmental resources*
- *To reduce biodiversity loss; achieving, by 2010, a significant reduction in the rate of loss*
- *To halve, by 2015, the proportion of people without sustainable access to safe drinking water and basic sanitation.*
- *By 2020, to have achieved a significant improvement in the lives of at least 100 million slum-dwellers.*[3]

8. Develop a global partnership for development: without key partnerships between rich and poor countries, the previous seven goals may not be achievable. Great opportunities for growth and development exist in today's fast-changing global economy, but many poor countries have been left behind, lacking access to new technologies as well as the resources to participate in the globalization process. The last goal aims to develop further an open, rule-based, predictable, non-discriminatory trading and financial system and to address the special needs of the least developed countries (LDCs), landlocked developing countries and small island developing states. It also aims to address the special needs of the debt problems of developing countries through national and international measures in order to make debt sustainable in the long term.

The MDGs are interrelated and strategic efforts must push for progress on all targets simultaneously. They remain the starting point and not the final steps for eradicating poverty, safeguarding human rights and human security and achieving sustainable development.

II
Gender Equality and Women Empowerment: A Cornerstone of Development

Kofi Annan, UN Secretary-General, Commission on the Status of Women, Beijing, 2005, said:

'Sixty years have passed since the founders of the United Nations inscribed, on the first page of our charter, the equal rights of men and women. Since then, study after study has taught us that there is no tool for development more effective than the empowerment of women. No other policy is as likely to raise economic productivity, or to reduce infant and maternal mortality. No other policy is as sure to improve nutrition and promote health – including the prevention of HIV/AIDS. No other policy is as powerful in increasing the chances of education for the next generation. And I also venture that no policy is more important in preventing conflict, or in achieving reconciliation after a conflict has ended. But whatever the very real benefit of investing in women, the most important fact remains: women themselves have the right to live in dignity, in freedom from want and from fear.'[4]

Gender equality and women's empowerment are two sides of the same coin: progress toward gender equality requires women's empowerment and women's empowerment requires increase in gender equality. The pairing of the two concepts of women's empowerment and gender equality into one MDG implicitly recognizes this. Both are an indispensable tool for advancing development and reducing poverty. Empowered women contribute to the health and productivity of whole families and communities and to improved prospects for the next generation.

Gender equality is also called gender equity, gender egalitarianism or sexual equality, i.e., equality of gender or sexes. In common parlance, the terms gender and sex are often used interchangeably; however, they are distinct concepts. Whereas sex of individuals is largely determined by biology, their gender is socially constructed and comprises the roles, rights, and obligations that attach to them on the basis of their sex.

Simon de Beauvoir explains in *The Second Sex*: 'One is not born a woman, but becomes one'. She explains: 'No biological, psychological, economic destiny defines the face that the human female assumes in the heart of society. It is civilization as a whole that elaborates this product, half way between the male and eunuch that one qualifies as feminine.' According to her, gender is socially constructed, a result of childhood socialization. Gender is a matter of becoming and this is subject to choice and change. Gender is a process open to social action and individual choice.[5]

Thus, gender equality is not only a women's issue. Millennium Project Task Force Report to the UN Secretary-General declares that 'gender equality and the empowerment of women – require fundamental transformation in the distribution of power, opportunities, and outcomes for both men and women. Genuine equality means more than parity in numbers. It means justice, greater opportunity, and better quality of life so that equality is achieved at high levels of wellbeing.'[6]

In spite of all this, discrimination against women and girls persists. It varies from country to country, region to region; no country or region is free of gender inequality. It is an irony that even UNO, which has enacted a number of conventions to improve the condition of women, has failed to improve the condition of women and has failed in implementing them in the UNO system.

Gender bias undercuts women's rights in many areas. Practices such as early marriage or poor health services result in high rates of maternal mortality. Violence against women and girls has reached extreme proportions in many parts of the world. Women's nutritional needs and health-care, particularly access to reproductive health services, are not given priority. The status of women and girls limits their ability to negotiate safe sex, fuelling the spread of HIV/AIDS. Women and girls bear enormous hardship during and after humanitarian emergencies, especially armed conflicts.

Over the past decade, gender equality and women's empowerment have been explicitly recognized as key not only to the health of nations, but also to social and economic development. The importance of gender equality and women's empowerment is underscored by its inclusion as one of the eight Millennium Development Goals. The Goal 3 of MDGs is 'to promote gender equality and empower women'. Gender equality is acknowledged as being a key to achieving the other seven goals. While only this goal explicitly addresses gender equality and the empowerment of women, it is now widely recognized that achieving gender equality and women's empowerment is central to fulfilling all the MDGs.

The United Nations Millennium Declaration, September 2000, emphasizes this point in these words: 'We also resolve to promote gender equality and the empowerment of women as effective ways to combat poverty, hunger and disease and to stimulate development that is truly sustainable.'

The United Nations Millennium Project to end world poverty by 2015 also claims: '*Every single goal is directly related to women's rights and societies where women are not afforded equal rights as men can never achieve development in a sustainable manner*.'[7] Thus, empowering women is an indispensable tool for advancing development.

Empowered women contribute to the health and productivity of whole families and communities and to improved prospects for the next generation. The target of Goal 3 is to eliminate gender disparity in primary and secondary education preferably by 2005, and at all levels by 2015. The indicators for the above target are:

1. Ratio of girls to boys in primary, secondary and tertiary education.
2. Ratio of literate women to men, 15–24 years old.
3. Share of women in wage employment in the non-agricultural sector.
4. Proportion of seats held by women in national parliament.

In 2005, the Millennium Project Gender Equality Task Force identified seven strategic priorities as critical to the achievement of Goal 3. Three specific groups of women were also identified, for whom action on these seven interdependent priorities is particularly critical, including poor women, adolescent women, and women and girls living in conflict and post-conflict settings.

The identified seven strategic priorities – which are considered the minimum necessary to achieve Millennium Development Goal 3 – are as follows:

1. Strengthen opportunities for post-primary education for girls while simultaneously meeting commitments to universal primary education.
2. Guarantee sexual and reproductive health and rights.
3. Invest in infrastructure to reduce women's and girls' time burdens.
4. Guarantee women's and girls' inheritance and property rights.
5. Eliminate gender inequality in employment by decreasing women's reliance on informal employment, closing gender gaps in earnings and reducing occupational segregation.
6. Increase women's share of seats in national parliaments and local governmental bodies.
7. Combat violence against girls and women.[8]

Ultimately success will depend on addressing not only these seven priorities, but also ensuring that all MDGs are addressed in a way that promotes gender equality and empowers women.

III
A Glance towards Targets

Position of Gender Parity in Education

First target of Goal 3 is elimination of gender disparity in elementary and secondary education. Schooling has innumerable benefits and yet a vast majority of girls are deprived of these. The significance of education in the empowerment of women was highlighted long ago by well-known feminist philosopher Mary Wollstonecraft in her book *The Vindication of the Rights of Woman,* published in 1792. She wrote: 'If boys and girls should have the same education and socialization pattern, women would show the right reasoning. Women do not miss reason by nature, but they miss cultural and social conventions (e.g., exclusion from education) to develop the gift.'[9] Thus the role of education as a catalyst of change is well established. Eliminating gender differences in access to education are key elements on the path to attaining gender equality and reducing the disempowerment of women. An analysis of indicators of education reveals that five years after the target date, gender parity in education has yet to be achieved.

Gender parity as defined by the UNESCO Institute for Statistics is the girls' to boys' gross enrolment ratio of between 97 and 103. In 1999, 39 countries out of total 171 achieved gender parity in both primary and secondary education. It increased to 53 in 2007. Still, the fact that over 100 countries have yet to reach the target is a source of concern. While developed countries have achieved gender parity in primary and secondary stages of school, developing countries still lag behind. The gender gap in school enrolment is more evident in secondary education, where many more countries are falling behind.

Table 1

Gender Parity in the Developing Region

Year	*No. of girls enrolled in primary school for every 100 boys*	*No. of girls enrolled in secondary school for every 100 boys*	*No. of girls enrolled in higher education for every 100 boys*
1998/1999	91	88	82
2008/2009	96	96	97

Source: MDG Report 2011.

In developing regions, 96 girls were enrolled in primary and in secondary school for every 100 boys in 2009. This is a significant improvement since 1999, when the ratios were 91 and 88, respectively. However, only three regions – the Caucasus and Central Asia, Latin America and the Caribbean, and South-Eastern Asia – have achieved gender parity in primary education (defined as a gender parity index between 97 and 103). Exceptionally, in Eastern Asia, girls slightly outnumber boys in primary school. Progress for girls has lagged in most other parts of the developing world, and equal access to education in the early years remains a distant target in Northern Africa, Oceania, Southern Asia, sub-Saharan Africa and Western Asia.[10]

Girls outnumber boys in higher education, except in the poorer regions: a very different situation emerges at higher levels of education. Worldwide, there are more young women than men enrolled in tertiary education. The ratio of girls' to boys' enrolment globally at the tertiary level rose from 96 in 1999 to 108 in 2007. But disparities among regions are dramatic. A large gap in favour of girls exists in the developed regions, CIS countries, Latin America and the Caribbean, and South-Eastern Asia. Far fewer female students than males have advanced to tertiary education in sub-Saharan Africa, Southern Asia and Oceania.

Available data shows that 60 per cent of countries have achieved gender parity in primary education, 30 per cent in secondary education and only 6 per cent in tertiary education.

Girls from poor and rural households face higher barriers to education: an analysis of primary school attendance in 108 developing countries by location of residence and household wealth reveals that gender parity has been reached in urban areas and among the richest 40 per cent of households. In contrast, girls are more likely to be excluded from primary education in rural localities and when they reside in the poorest households.

Gender disparities associated with poverty and rural residency are even more pronounced at the level of secondary education. Cultural attitudes and practices that promote early marriage encourage the seclusion of young girls or attach greater value to educating boys than girls and can create formidable barriers to gender parity.

The target of eliminating gender disparities in primary and secondary education by 2005 was missed. Ensuring that the opportunity is not lost again in 2015 will require renewed urgency and commitment, while gender parity is achieved.

Share of Women in Wage Employment in the Non-agricultural Sector

In addition to education, employment can also be an important source of empowerment for women. Employment, particularly for cash and in the formal sector, can empower women by providing financial independence, alternative sources of social identity, and exposure to power structures. Nonetheless, early-age marriage and child-bearing and limited access to education limit women's ability to participate in the labour market, particularly in the formal sectors. By contrast, male gender roles are compatible with employment and men are typically expected to be employed and be breadwinners for their families. Not surprisingly, men dominate most formal labour markets.

Paid employment for women continues to expand slowly and remains meagre in many regions: women have more income-earning opportunities than before. Overall, women occupy almost 40 per cent of all paid jobs outside agriculture, compared to 35 per cent in 1990. But almost two-third of women in the developing world work in vulnerable jobs as self-employed persons or as unpaid family workers. In Southern Asia, Northern Africa and Western Asia, employment opportunities for women remain extremely low. Women are also poorly represented in non-agricultural employment in sub-Saharan Africa. The situation of women in these regions, however, varies widely.

Women remain more vulnerable on the job front, assuming the largest share of unpaid work: although more women have been able to secure paid jobs outside agriculture, yet they have generally failed get access to decent work. Close to two-third of all employed women have vulnerable jobs, either as contributing family workers or as own-account workers.

The global financial crisis is creating new hurdles to women's employment: the 2008 financial crisis and high prices for primary commodities have eroded labour markets around the world.

Although men were hit hardest by the financial shock, women may be more profoundly affected over the long term: the gendered impacts on families and societies of remittances and labour mobility, including the risk of exploitation, particularly for female workers, are often overlooked.

Proportion of Seats held by Women in National Parliament

The universal declaration of human right states that everyone has the right to take part in the government of his/her country. The United Nations Economic and Social Council endorsed a target of 30 per cent women at all levels of decision-making by 1993. Equality and empowerment are essential components of human development. Equality in access to opportunities demands a fundamental restructuring of power in many societies. It includes equalization of political opportunities through voting rights and representation in legislative bodies and other actions aimed at limiting the excessive political power of feudal minority.

Political empowerment for women is regarded as a key driver for economic and social empowerment. The lack of representation of women in decision-making positions results in women's agenda not getting reflected and addressed in policies and programmes. Lack of critical numbers of elected women representatives impedes them from negotiating for important portfolios such as finance, home, defence, etc., which are generally termed as key portfolios and primarily controlled by men. It has been observed that women are allotted soft portfolios such as those related to women and children, information and culture, social welfare, etc., which are relatively less important and have correspondingly lesser resources, both financial and human. Women politicians point out that even within the political parties, women are rarely found in leadership positions. In fact, women candidates are usually fielded from 'losing' constituencies where the party does not want to 'waste' a male candidate.

Since 2000, the proportion of seats for women in parliaments increased from 13.5 to 17.9 per cent. Despite greater parliamentary participation, women are largely absent from the highest levels of governance. In January 2008, women accounted for 7 of the 150 elected heads of state and 8 of the 192 heads of government of United Nations member states.

Hence we find that even till now, women's voices are marginalized in national decision-making, country development priorities do not incorporate gender analysis and new delivery modalities fail to adequately consider gender dimensions This figure implies that politics is still predominantly a men's business, with men making up 82 per cent of parliamentarians.

The Beijing Platform for Action target of 30 per cent share of parliamentary seats for women has only been met by 20 countries to date, although none of these countries are in Asia. Today, Rwanda has the highest number of women parliamentarians in the world i.e., 48.8 per cent. The new Constitution of Rwanda adopted in 2003 guarantees a minimum of 30 per cent of parliamentary seats. Apart from Rwanda, women hold at least 40 per cent of the seats in four other parliaments: Sweden (47%), Cuba (43.2%), Finland (41.5%) and Argentina (40%).

IV
India and MDGs

> You can tell the condition of the nation by looking at the status of women.
>
> —Jawaharlal Nehru

India is the largest democracy in the world, with the second highest population in the world after China. Today India is one of the leading economies in the world and has the potential to play an increasingly important role in the evolving international economic and financial architecture. India was among the original members of the United Nations that signed the Declaration by United Nations and has been actively involved in the affairs of the United Nations since 1945. It has played an important role for constructive engagement in the world's affairs.

As an active member of UNO, the Indian government is firmly committed to achieving the MDGs. Targets have been set by policy-makers in India, and in some ways these are more ambitious than those stated in the MDGs. The realization of these targets in India is vital not only for attaining human development and economic growth within the country, but given its enormous size, they are critical for reaching the MDGs worldwide. As pointed out earlier, the MDG 3 'to promote gender equality and empower women' is a very important goal and is central to success of all other goals. Indian government is fully committed to the successful achievement of this goal. However, the condition of women in India today is far from happy and the government has much to do.

In India, normatively, women have been given an exalted position in society. During ancient times, they were treated at par with men even in political and philosophical spheres. However, down the centuries, the position of women in society deteriorated and politically they were pushed to the background. It was only in the 20th century, particularly during the freedom movement under the charismatic leadership of Mahatma Gandhi, that involvement of women was accepted as the natural course in India.[11]

After independence, our Constitution-makers enshrined the principle of gender equality in the Indian Constitution in its Preamble, Fundamental Rights, Fundamental Duties and Directive Principles. The Constitution not only grants equality to women, but also empowers the State to adopt measures of positive discrimination in favour of women. Consequent to this, various laws have been made to protect rights of women.[12]

However, even today, though India is developing economically and technologically by leaps and bounds, women continue to be discriminated against. We are still a male-dominated patriarchal society where the first preference is for sons. The 2001 census data for India revealed a sharp decline in the sex ratio for the population age 0–6, from 945 females in 1991 to 927 females per 1,000 males. The child gender ratio in the country has declined from 927 to 914 in Census 2011.[13] This is the most obvious indicator of position of girls and women in India. Social stereotyping and violence at the domestic and societal levels are some of the indicators. Discrimination against girl children, adolescent girls and women persists in parts of the country. The underlying causes of gender inequality are related to social and economic structure, which is based on informal and formal norms, and practices.

Considering the state of women in India, our commitment to achieve the MDG 3 'to promote gender equality and empower women' is still a distant one and stronger efforts need to be made to achieve the goal.

Progress in Achieving the MDGs to Promote Gender Equality and Empower Women in India

Education

Provision of educational opportunities for women and girls has been an important part of the national endeavour since Independence. Though it did yield significant results, gender disparities persist, more so in rural areas and among disadvantaged communities. There is gender equality in children's school attendance in urban areas; but, in rural areas, the female disadvantage in education is marked and increases with age. School dropout beyond primary school is a major problem, not just for girls, but also for boys. A consequence of high dropout beyond the primary school level is the low educational attainment of adults. Even among the population aged between 20–29 years, only 27 per cent of women and 39 per cent of men have 10 or more years of education.[14]

The target of MDG 3 is to eliminate gender disparity in primary and secondary education, preferably by 2005, and in all levels of education no later than 2015.

The indicator of this is the ratio of girls to boys in primary, secondary and tertiary education.

Education will lead to empowerment, securing the means of creating a social environment in which one can make decisions for social and individual transformation. It develops intrinsic capacity, inner transformation of one's consciousness to overcome barriers, access resources and change traditional ideologies. Empowerment, therefore, is possible only with access to education as a fundamental right.

Gender Parity Index (GPI) in enrolment at primary, secondary and tertiary levels is the ratio of the number of female students enrolled at primary, secondary and tertiary levels in public and private schools to the number of male students. To standardize the effects of the population structure of the appropriate age groups, the GPI of the GER for each level of education is used, i.e., GPI (GER) = GER (Female)/GER (Male). A GPI of 1 indicates parity between the sexes or no gender disparity. A GPI that varies between 0 and 1 typically means a disparity in favour of males whereas a GPI greater than 1 indicates a disparity in favour of females. Target 4 is intended to achieve GPI of 1 by 2005 for primary enrolment and by 2015 for all levels. In general, at the national level, the number of girls enrolled in all levels, i.e., primary, secondary and higher education is less than their counterparts. However, the female-male ratio in education has been steadily improving over the years. In primary education, the GPI ratio has gone up from 0.76 in 1990–91 to 0.98 in 2007–08, showing 29 per cent increase. In secondary education, the increase is from 0.60 in 1990–91 to 0.85 in 2007–08, thereby showing 42 per cent increase, and in higher education, it increased from 0.54 in 1990–91 to 0.7 in 2007–08, registering an increase of 30 per cent.

The target for eliminating gender disparity in primary and secondary enrolment by2005 has not been achieved in India as per the available data for *Gender Parity Index for Enrolment*, in the sense that though almost perfect parity was attained in the primary level of enrolment, it was not so in secondary level. However, by the cut-off line for achievement as internationally recognized, the target has been achieved for primary grade by 2007–08. The rates of increase in GPI signify India's on-the-track progress to achieving gender parity in enrolment by 2015, even for the secondary grade.

As per 2007–08 statistics, 15 states have already achieved gender parity at primary level and 16 more states are very close to the target. At secondary level, 13 states have already achieved the target and eight more states are nearing the target. The states/UTs in which GPI at secondary level is still very far from the target are Bihar (0.62), Madhya Pradesh (0.67), Rajasthan (0.58), and Dadra and Nagar Haveli (0.63). As of 2007–08, for the tertiary level, eight states have achieved MDG target. Kerala, Delhi and Andaman and Nicobar Islands have achieved GPI at I in all the three levels. While there is significant parity deficit in most of the states in favour of males, the states/UTs of Goa, Kerala, Punjab, Delhi, Andaman and Nicobar Islands, Himachal Pradesh, Chandigarh and Daman Diu have significant disparity in favour of females in the tertiary level of education.

A positive aspect is that the male-female gap in the literacy rate is declining age group of 15–24.

The literacy rate in India for (7+ years) in 2011 Census is 74.04 per cent. The corresponding figures for males and females are 82.14 and 65.46 per cent, respectively. The country has continued its march in improving literacy rates by recording a jump of 9.21 percentage points during 2001–11. The increase in literacy rates in males and females is of the order of 6.88 and 11.79 percentage points, respectively. An extremely positive development in the present decade is that the gap of 21.59 percentage points recorded between the male and female literacy rates in 2001 Census has reduced to 16.68 percentage points in 2011, mainly due to higher rate of increase in female literacy.

The female-male literacy rate for 15–24 years increased to 0.80 in 2001 from 0.67 in 1991. NSS (2007–08) results show that literates in the age group 15–24 years at all-India level constitute 86 per cent with 91 per cent being males and 80 per cent females. Thus, the ratio of literate women to men in the age group 15–24 years stands at 0.88 in 2007–08. The ratio of literate women to men in the age group 15–24 years could to exceed 1 by 2015, implying reaching a state of gender disparity against male youths in literacy by 2015. This attainment along with the attainment of gender parity in primary, secondary and tertiary levels of education can be a major gain for women in acquiring access to wider world of learning and development of skills, economic independence, authority of decision-making and self-determination.[15]

Various centre-sponsored schemes are being run by the government to strengthen school educations, which have benefited a large number of girls. In order to achieve the education standard of women, schooling is made completely free for girls in most states up to the higher secondary stage in government schools. Some of the female literacy programmes are:

The '*Sarva Shiksha Abhiyan*' or the '*Education for All*' Movement is a flagship programme of the Government of India for achievement of universalization of elementary education in a time-bound manner, as mandated by the 86th amendment to the Constitution of India, making free and compulsory education to children of ages 6–14 a fundamental right. SSA has a special focus on girls and children of weaker sections. Its main goals are:

1. All in school by 2005.
2. Complete 5 years of primary education by 2005 and 8 years of schooling by 2010.
3. Satisfactory quality with emphasis on education for life.
4. Bridge all gender and social gaps at primary level by 2007 and elementary level by 2010.
5. Universal retention by 2010

Early Childhood Care and Education (ECCE) is an important programme in freeing girls from sibling care responsibilities, leading to their regular attendance in school and in providing school-readiness skills to pre school children.

National Programme for Education of Girls at Elementary Level (NPEGEL) and the Kasturba Gandhi Balika Vidyalaya (KGBV): These are two focused intervention programmes for girls to reach out to girls from marginalized social groups in over 3,000 educationally backward blocks in the country where the female rural literacy is below the national average. NPEGEL provides for intensive community mobilization, monitoring of girls' enrolment in schools and thrust on ensuring that the content and process of education is sensitive to gender concerns. KGBV scheme is designed to encourage greater participation of girls in education at the upper primary level (VI to VII).

The *National Literacy Mission*, launched in 1988, aimed at attaining a literacy rate of 75 per cent by 2007. It imparts functional literacy to non-literates in the age group of 15–35 years. The *Total Literacy Campaign* is the principal strategy of the NLM for eradication of illiteracy. The *Continuing Education Scheme* provides a learning continuum to the efforts of the Total Literacy and Post-literacy programmes.

Mahila Samakhya Programme (programme for empowerment of women) started in 1989, and focuses on socially and economically disadvantaged women groups. It uses education as a tool for empowering women to achieve equality and emphasizes the process of learning, besides seeking to bring about a change in the perception of society in regard to women's roles.[16]

The Right of Children to Free and Compulsory Education Act (CFCEA) has come into force from April 1, 2010. Now Right to Education will be accorded the same legal status as the Right to Life as provided by Article 21A of the Indian Constitution. Every child in the age group of 6–14 years will be provided 8 years of elementary education in an appropriate classroom in the vicinity of his/her neighbourhood. Any cost that prevents a child from accessing school will be borne by the State, which shall have the responsibility of enrolling the child as well as ensuring attendance and completion of 8 years of schooling. No child shall be denied admission for want of documents; no child shall be turned away if the admission cycle in the school is over and no child shall be asked to take an admission test. Children with disabilities will also be educated in the mainstream schools. Prime Minister Manmohan Singh has emphasized that it is important for the country to nurture children and young people with the right education, so India's future as a strong and prosperous country is secure.

Non-agricultural Sector

In keeping with the predominantly rural nature of the Indian economy and the low average educational level of women, most women who work are employed in agriculture. For most women who work, employment is not intermittent but continuous and throughout the year. While the majority of employed women earn cash for the work they do, about 1 in 10 are paid only in kind and more than 2 in 10 receive no payment.

From the above data, it is clear that women lag significantly behind males in terms of work participation, employment, etc.

There are various laws implemented by the government to protect rights of working women and to prevent their exploitation. Some of these are: Beedi and Cigar Workers (Condition of Employment) Act, 1966; Bonded Labour System (Abolition) Act, 1976; Equal Remuneration Act, 1976; Legal Practitioners (Women) Act, 1923; Maternity Benefit Act, 1961. Despite various measures like these undertaken by the government and local bodies, inequality in gender still persists.

Table 2

Share of women in wage employment in the non-agriculture sector in India

Reference Year	*Area*	*Value*
1999–2000	Rural	15.09
	Urban	16.61
	India	16.00
2004–05	Rural	21.59
	Urban	19.00
	India	20.23
2009–10	Rural	19.6
	Urban	17.6
	India	18.6

Data: Millennium Development Goals India Country Report 2011.

Position of Indian Women in Representative Bodies

> As long as the women of India do not take part in public life, there can be no salvation for the country.'
>
> —Mahatma Gandhi[17]

Providing an enabling environment for women and men to participate equally in decision-making at all levels of government is essential in a democracy. India is the first country where since independence women have the right to vote to elect representatives to Parliament as well as the State Assemblies. Women have an equal right to contest any election subject to the fulfilment of other eligibility conditions. In independent India, women have held important political and administrative positions. India is second in Asia to have a woman Prime Minister. There are instances of women Cabinet Ministers, Chief Ministers and Governors. We also had a woman as the Head of the State of India. Despite the fact that Indian women have held important positions both at the national and international levels, women's participation in the political arena and in the decision-making bodies is not in proportion to their population, except in the local bodies. Their effective participation, even in these bodies, leaves much to be desired.[18]

Indian democracy is more than 60 years old now, yet the participation of women in politics has actually declined since the days of the freedom movement, both in quantity and quality. Statistical records show that there has been only a marginal increase in the last few decades in the number of women candidates fielded during the elections at the state and Central level. Moreover, their membership in the state legislatures is abysmally low, lower than their numbers in Parliament. Illiteracy, women's triple burden, patriarchal values, lack of access and control over income and other resources, restrictions to public spaces and insensitive legal systems continue to impair their effective political participation. This is compounded by the absence/inadequate availability of infrastructural facilities and support services to facilitate their participation.

The mechanisms to facilitate and protect women in political participation are not in place, such as a strong supportive constituency particularly for women, increased awareness of their rights and responsibilities as elected members, training and information dissemination on governance processes, gender sensitization of the male elected members, and so on.

Reservation for Women in Local Bodies: Encouraging Trends

Given the low representation of women in politics, there has been a consistent demand for more meaningful ways to increase their representation in decision-making bodies. In pursuance of this notion of empowerment of women, the Constitution (73rd Amendment) Act, 1993 and the Constitution (74th Amendment) Act, 1993 reserved seats for women at the local level bodies, namely, the panchayats and municipalities with the hope that these measures will set the trend to provide women their legitimate place in public life.

After these amendments, Articles 243D and 243T were added to the Constitution to provide that not less than one-third (including the number of seats reserved for women belonging to the Scheduled Castes and the Scheduled Tribes) of the total number of seats to be filled by the direct election in the local bodies (panchayats and municipalities) would be reserved for women and such seats may be allotted by rotation to different constituencies in the local bodies.

This, indeed, makes a historic beginning for the effective participation of women in the decision-making process at the grassroots level. In the elections to these local bodies, more than one million women have been elected every five years. It is but natural that a larger number of women have participated in these elections and this signifies a very encouraging trend for women's empowerment. Though it has taken time for women to translate their numerical strength into active participation in the rural and semi-urban areas, the results have been truly astounding.

Before reservation, the percentage of women in this area was merely 4.5 per cent, which after reservation has gone up to 40 per cent. More recently, with another amendment to Article 243D of the Constitution, reservation for women will increase in (i) the total number of seats to be filled by direct election, (ii) offices of chairpersons and (iii) in seats and offices of the chairpersons reserved for SCs and STs, to 50 per cent in all tiers of panchayats. The last 16 years of Panchayati Raj have thus succeeded in empowering marginalized groups, who have gained political representation and valuable experience. Many of them have successfully taken on the challenge of governance and brought about enduring social change through their close links with the community. Women have prioritized issues of health; education and access to basic services and in some cases have been able to ensure a significant change in living conditions for the entire community. The efforts and work of several women representatives in panchayats in Maharashtra, Gujarat and West Bengal have been widely acclaimed.

However, the battle to make the PRIs effective instruments of local rural governance is still an ongoing one. The women at the grassroots have to still battle against administrative apathy and listlessness, against ignorance and low awareness. For women, these odds are accompanied and intermeshed with deep-rooted patriarchal practices that determine and sanction norms of speech and behaviour both within and outside the home.

Reservation for Women in Parliament: Still a Long Way to go

So far, India has witnessed 15 General Elections to the Lok Sabha, or the Lower House of Parliament. As on November 2011, India, the world's largest democracy, had only 60 women representatives out of 544 members in Lok Sabha, while there were 26 female MPs in the 241–member Rajya Sabha.

The reservation for women in state assemblies and the national parliament has been a matter of public debate for quite some time now. Although increasingly women have stood for elections and have got elected as members of State Legislative Assemblies and Parliament, the number of women parliamentarians is not of expected level. Similarly, although the number of women in leadership positions at the local administration level has shown an encouraging trend, yet the proportion of women at senior levels of government remains low.

Attempts to have seats reserved for women in the Lok Sabha and the State Legislative Assemblies have had a chequered legislative history. After years of painstaking struggle by the women's groups, the Bill for women's reservation was introduced in Parliament as the Constitution (81st Amendment) Bill, 1996, on 12 September, 1996, and later in 1998 and 1999, respectively, without being passed.

Table 3

Proportion of Seats held by Women in National Parliament

	Number of Women members			*%*
	Lok Sabha	*Rajya Sabha*	*Total*	
1991			77 of 789	9.7
1999	52 of 544			9.6
2004	45 of 544	28 of 250	73 of 794	9.2
2007	47 of 544	25 of 250	72 of 794	9.1
2009	59 of 545	21 of 234	80 of 779	10.3
2011	60 of 544	26 of 241	86 of 785	10.96

According to data released by Inter Parliamentary Union (IPU), India ranks 98 in the world for proportion of National Parliament seats held by women.

More recently, under the Constitution (108th Amendment) Bill, 2008 India's politics took a decisive step towards change with its Upper House passing a historic Bill giving one-third representation to women in Parliament and state legislatures, crossing the biggest hurdle in the road towards political empowerment for women in the world's largest democracy.

V
What Needs to be Done?

> Looking ahead to 2015 and beyond, there is no question that we can achieve the overarching goal: we can put an end to poverty .... But it requires an unswerving, collective, long-term effort. Time has been lost. We have wasted opportunities and face additional challenges, making the task ahead more difficult. It is now our responsibility to make up lost ground – and to put all countries, together, firmly on track towards a more prosperous, sustainable and equitable world.
>
> —Ban Ki-moon Secretary-General, United Nations (1)

We are now nearing the last leg towards the target date – 2015 – by which the Millennium Development Goals are to be achieved. We have made important progress towards all eight goals, but we are not on track to fulfill our commitments. These tasks have now become more challenging because we face a global economic slowdown and a food security crisis, both of uncertain magnitude and duration.

Critics of the MDGs have also said that the target goals are oversimplistic and too quantitative. The indicators chosen for monitoring reflect only the data which already exists and do not take into account the myriad of differences among countries and cultures. 'Though the MDGs treat gender equality as an explicit goal, its indicators of progress nonetheless are reduced to mere numbers such as: the ratio of boys and girls at all levels of education; gender disparities in adult literacy; the percentage of women in waged employment in the non-agricultural sector; and the percentage of women holding seats in national parliament'. These indicators do not take into consideration other key areas for which there are no international comparable statistics such as the frequency of child-brides or violence against women, which have as much influence on how girls are educated and how much budget a government decides to set aside for them.

'Discrimination in girls' access to education persists in many areas, owing to customary attitudes, early marriages and pregnancies, inadequate and gender-biased teaching and educational materials, sexual harassment and lack of adequate and physically and otherwise accessible schooling facilities. Girls undertake heavy domestic work at a very early age. Girls and young women are expected to manage both educational and domestic responsibilities, often resulting in poor scholastic performance and early drop-out from the educational system. This has long-lasting consequences for all aspects of women's lives'.[19]

More than just increasing the figures and percentages, we need to aim for gender parity in accessing education by calling on governments and other relevant sectors too:

These are just a few of the many areas where work is urgently required:

1. Create an educational and social environment in which women and men, girls and boys are treated equally and encouraged to achieve their full potential, respecting their freedom of thought, conscience, religion and belief, and where educational resources promote non-stereotyped images of women and men.
2. Provide access for and retention of girls and women at all levels of education; targeted public policy and governance initiatives can help overcome gender inequalities. For example, removing school fees and providing incentives for girls to attend school can alleviate financial pressures on households. Building schools close to remote communities and recruiting local teachers can also narrow the gender gap in rural area.
3. Create a gender-sensitive educational system in order to ensure equal educational and training opportunities and full and equal participation of women in educational administration and policy-decision-making.
4. Develop training programmes and materials for teachers and educators that raise awareness about the status, role and contribution of women and men in the family, and society.

5. Provide funding for special programmes, such as in mathematics, science and computer technology, to advance opportunities for all girls and women.
6. Provide non-formal education, especially for rural women, in order to realize their potential with regard to health, micro-enterprise, agriculture and legal rights.
7. Scale up actions, increase financial resources and support – governments must accelerate the achievement of the MDG targets that equally benefit and empower women and girls, and ensure their access to education and health services, full and decent employment, and equal political participation and decision-making in all sectors.
8. Support women entrepreneurship, especially in rural areas – including through improved access to property and economic assets, microfinance, agricultural inputs such as seeds and fertilizers, training and markets.
9. Guarantee women's land and property rights through legal reforms.
10. Raise public awareness to reduce girls' domestic responsibilities and prevent early marriage and pregnancy.
11. Adopt comprehensive laws on all forms of violence against women and support awareness campaigns to prevent violence against women and girls.
12. Increase funding to provide adequate services and access to justice and redress to victims of violence against women.
13. Ensure a supportive environment to encourage the enrolment of girls in schools and reduce absenteeism and drop-out rates.
14. Hire more female teachers to act as role models and to promote girls' school attendance.
15. Promote gender-sensitive curricula and provide gender sensitization programmes for teachers and school officials.
16. Ensure that girls are provided with transportation to and from school.
17. Provide separate school sanitation facilities for girls and boys.
18. Enhance non-formal education for girls and women, such as vocational or skills training and literacy programmes.
19. Ratify and implement the Convention on the Elimination of All Forms of Discrimination against Women, and ILO Conventions on Equal Remuneration, Discrimination, Workers with Family Responsibilities, and Maternity Protection.
20. Step up efforts to implement decent work principles, such as social protection and freedom from harassment.
21. Enhance the participation of women at all levels of government and their role in other decision-making positions in the judiciary, the private sector, civil society and the media.[20]

Looking Ahead

Ten years ago, the nations of the world under the umbrella of UNO set goals to free humanity from the shackles of poverty, hunger, illiteracy, disease and discrimination. Gender equality and women empowerment was seen as an important goal which affects all other goals, women being the most vulnerable sections of all societies in the world even today. The nations of the world, including India, have made important progress in this effort and have achieved success in many areas. However, we are moving too slowly and the goals still seem very far. The difficulties have increased with the world facing the global recession. This has only added to the delay in achieving the goals set by the world community. These ongoing crises may also hold back progress towards gender equality, by creating new hurdles to women's employment. At worst, it could prevent us from keeping our promises. The need of the hour is to strengthen global cooperation and redouble our efforts to reach the MDGs and to make the world a better place to live in for all of us.

> Nothing arguably is as important today in the political economy of development as an adequate recognition of political, economic and social participation and leadership of women. This is indeed a crucial aspect of 'development as freedom'.[21]
>
> —Amartya Sen

Notes

1. *The Millennium Development Goals Report*, United Nations, New York, 2008.
2. Millennium Development Goals from Wikipedia, the free encyclopedia.
3. www.develomentgoals.com/environment/
4. *Breaking Barriers: Gender Perspectives and Empowerment of Women in Least Developed Countries*, UN-OHRLLS, United Nations, New York, 2006. www.Unohrlls.org/Userfiles/file/publications/Gender/perspectives.pdf.
5. Simone de Beauvoir, *The Second Sex*, Translated by H.M. Parshley, New York: Vintage Books, 1989.
6. UN Millennium Project, Investing in Development: A Practical Plan to Achieve the Millennium Development Goals, New York, 2005.
7. United Nations Millennium Campaign 2008, 'Goals # 3 Gender Equity'.
8. www.unmillenniumproject.org/documents/gender-Chapter1–3.pdf.
9. Mary Wollstonecraft, *Vindication of the Rights of Woman* (1792), London: Penguin Books, 1993.
10. *The Millennium Development Goals Report*, Department of Economic and Social Affairs, printed at the United Nations, New York, June 2011.

11. 'Reservation of Seats for Women in Legislative Bodies: Perspectives', Occasional Paper Series-1/2008, Rajya Sabha Secertariat, New Delhi, July 2008.
12. Constitution of India, Universal Law Publishing, Co. Pvt. Ltd., 2010.
13. Registrar General and Census Commissioner, Ministry of Home Affairs, GOI, New Delhi, India, 2011.
14. Sunita Kishor and Kamla Gupta, 'Gender Equality and Women's Empowerment' in India, National Family Health Survey (NFHS-3), India, 2005–06, Mumbai: International Institute for Population Sciences; Calverton, Maryland (USA): ICF Macro, 2009.
15. *Millennium Development Goals India Country Report 2011*, Central Statistical Organization, Ministry of Statistics and Programme Implementation, Government of India, New Delhi, www.mospi.nic.in.
16. *Millennium Development Goals India Country Report 2007*, Central Statistical Organization, Ministry of Statistics and Programme Implementation, Government of India, Sardar Patel Bhawan, Sansad Marg, New Delhi, http://www.mospi.gov.in.
17. Speech at Women's Conference, Sojitra, Gujarat in *Collected Works of Mahatma Gandhi*, Vol. 30, 27 December 1924–21 March 1925, p. 108.
18. Yogender Narain et al., 'Political Empowerment of Women', *Journal of Indian Institute of Public Administration*, Vol. LI, January–March 2005.
19. Eliminating Gender Disparity in all Levels of Education, www.ceeindia.org/mdgs/goals-3htm.
20. High-level Event on the Millennium Development Goals, United Nations Headquarters, New York, September 25, 2008. Fact-sheet issued by the UN Department of Public Information–DPI/2517.
21. Amartya Sen, *Development as Freedom*, Oxford: Oxford University Press, 1999.

17

MDGs, SAARC and Women

SHASHI UPADHYAY

The Millennium Development Goals (MDGs) are the most comprehensive, ambitious and broadly supported development goals ever embraced by the international community. It was in September 2000, that 189 countries met at the United Nations and reaffirmed their commitment to the Millennium Declaration, which broadly outlined the central concerns of the global community such as peace, security, development, environmental sustainability, human rights as well as democracy. They articulated a set of inter-connected and mutually reinforcing goals (MDGs), pursuing a global agenda for development in order to attain the vital targets of humanity and sustainable development. The eight MDGs are thus, the internationally agreed, time-bound and quantified targets for achieving, in most cases by 2015, the eradication of extreme poverty and hunger; achievement of universal primary education; promoting gender equality and empowering women; reducing child mortality; improvement in maternal health; combatting HIV/AIDS, Malaria and other diseases; ensuring environmental sustainability; and developing a global partnership for development.

In order to support the MDGs, at the global, national and regional level, the UNDP is both individually and collectively assisting and coordinating with a wide range of partners and countries across the world, development institutions, funding agencies, various commissions and regional organizations by way of strengthening their institutional capacity building and assisting then in formulating policies and programmes. Thus, unprecedented efforts are being made to set the course in order to meet out the comprehensive UN Development Agenda.

The South Asian Association for Regional Cooperation (SAARC) found in 1985 – comprising eight countries of India, Pakistan, Bangladesh, Sri Lanka, Nepal, Bhutan, Maldives and lately joined by Afghanistan – is a manifestation of the determination of the people of South Asia to work towards finding solutions to their common problems in a spirit of friendship, trust and understanding. The basic objective of the association is to accelerate economic growth, social progress and cultural development of the region and provide all individuals an opportunity to live in dignity and to realize their full potential.

With the advent of globalization, SAARC has moved beyond the region and sought to strengthen cooperation with developing countries, regional organizations and international development agencies with similar aims and purposes such as UNCTAD, ESCAP, UNICEF, ITU and UNDP. Presently it is making serious efforts to closely coincide with target-oriented Millennium Development Goals (MDGs) and their comprehensive agenda.

The beginning of 21st century has witnessed a revolution for gender equality. Recognition of the need to improve the status of women, comprehend the nature of gender inequalities in the region and introduce institutional mechanisms to enable movement towards equality has been the shared concern of all countries, as well. Ever since the launching of SAARC, issues related to women's empowerment and development have figured prominently on the SAARC agenda. In order to facilitate the MDGs' commitment at the global level and work closely in line with the global development agenda, a formal blueprint setting out SAARC Development Goals (SDGs) too was adopted at the 12th SAARC summit at Islamabad in 2004, in areas of poverty alleviation, education, health, and environment – all areas closely interlinked with the development of women for the period 2007–12. Thus, broadly consistent with the MDGs, the initiative of SDGs was expected to complement the regional endeavour for the attainment of MDGs in South Asia.

It is with the above context in mind that an attempt is made in this paper to explore and seek answers to questions such has how SAARC is closely coordinating with the development agenda of MDGs? What initiatives SAARC has undertaken with regard to women development? Is any progress visible in attaining the objectives of MDGs in South Asia? and finally, what are the hindrances in way of attaining gender equality in the region?

The paper is divided into five parts. Section I gives an introduction about gender and development followed by Section II discussing the position of women in South Asia. Section III highlights the initiatives undertaken by SAARC for upliftment of women in the region, Section IV deals with how SDGs and MDGs are partners of development and finally, Section V is a summation.

I
Gender and Development: Conceptual Framework

The contemporary era is witnessing how the 'women question' has interacted with the dominant national discourse of 'development'. In fact, gender equality and empowerment of women are not only being greatly debated but have become globally accepted norms in any discussion on development. The gender neutral approaches hitherto adopted have been questioned by the recognition of the asymmetrical impact of development on men and women. It is in this context that one needs to examine the co-relationship between the two. In simple words, development is defined as a process of change that meets the needs of the present without compromising the ability of the future generations to meet their own needs.[1] Amartya Sen, the Nobel laureate, views development as a process of expanding freedoms equally for all people.[2] It is within this framework of development that the international development community recognizes gender equality and empowerment of women being development objectives in their own right as embodied in the Millennium Development Goals 3 and 5. Ensuring gender equality and women's empowerment is essential, given the relevance of gender concerns to all the MDGs. This fact was recognized by governments at the September 2005 World Summit when it was collectively affirmed that progress for women is progress for all. It is quite clear, that the 21st century will be a century of much greater gender equality than the world has ever seen before.

The notion of 'gender' refers to the socially-constructed roles and socially-learned behaviour and expectations associated with males and females both.[3] 'Equality' means equal opportunities in terms of access to sources of livelihood, health and education as well as to social, economic and political participation without discrimination[4] and the term 'empowerment' is understood as the process of transforming the structures and institutions which directly or indirectly promote inequality, thereby ensuring equality.[5]

Though the recent trends interpret enhancement of women's position in the society as development and progress towards modernity but the fact is that all change is neither development, nor all modernity enhances women's status. Despite playing a multidimensional role, women have failed to get due recognition and equality status and are confronting multiple challenges, and lagging behind in the process of development and equality of status with men. Gender inequality is, in fact, a global phenomenon with variations in terms of degrees of discrimination and biases against women and it originates from relations of power and authority, class-religion-caste, ethnic hierarchies and socio-cultural traditions, customs and norms. Of late, not only has the importance of women's potential role in development increased manifold but gender equality is placed at the 'front and centre' of the global development agenda. The Millennium Declaration endorsed by the world's governments in September 2000 recognizes that gender equality and the empowerment of women and girls are among the most effective ways to 'combat poverty, hunger, disease and to stimulate development that is truly sustainable'.[6]

Since, elimination of poverty is placed at the centre of sustainable development and as women constitute on overwhelming majority of the world's poor, their advancement have to be regarded as the cornerstone of sustainable development and attaining gender equality. Apart from this, it is yet another most effective determinant and tool of development since all the basic norms that determine the position/status of women, such as her level of income, employment, education, health, political participation and the role she plays within the family, the community and the society combine not only to form important indicators of national development but human development as well. Therefore, women automatically become an important catalyst of change and a fundamental constituent of human development.

Gender equality is also visualized as smart economics simply because greater gender equality can improve economic efficiency; enhance productivity; improve development outcomes for next generations, create a sound base of human resources, ensure justice and human rights and finally, make the institutions more representative.[7] There is thus a close nexus between gender and human development (see Figure 1 for detailed overview).

The Figure 1 clearly exhibits a close relationship between gender and development. Empowerment of women and gender equality are, therefore, developmental objectives in their own right, and need to be essentially pursued with utmost sincerity for meeting the global aspirations of a just and equal society and achieving better development returns, inclusive growth, faster poverty reduction, sustainable development and accelerated progress toward the attainment of MDGs. In fact, increased investment in women is now considered as crucial for achieving the above objectives.

The recognition of gender equality and empowerment of women as developmental objectives is the culmination of years of determined advocacy and action by the international women's movements and conferences. The Stockholm Conference of 1972; declaration of the International Women's Year (1975); Convention on the Elimination of all Forms of Discrimination Against Women (CEDAW: 1979); Decade of Women (1975–1985); development approaches of 1990s; Agenda 21 of Rio Earth Summit (1992); World Conference on Women at Beijing (2005) and the Millennium Declaration (2000) have not only led to globalization of women's issues, but also manifested the awareness, need and importance

Figure 1

Gender and Human Development Nexus

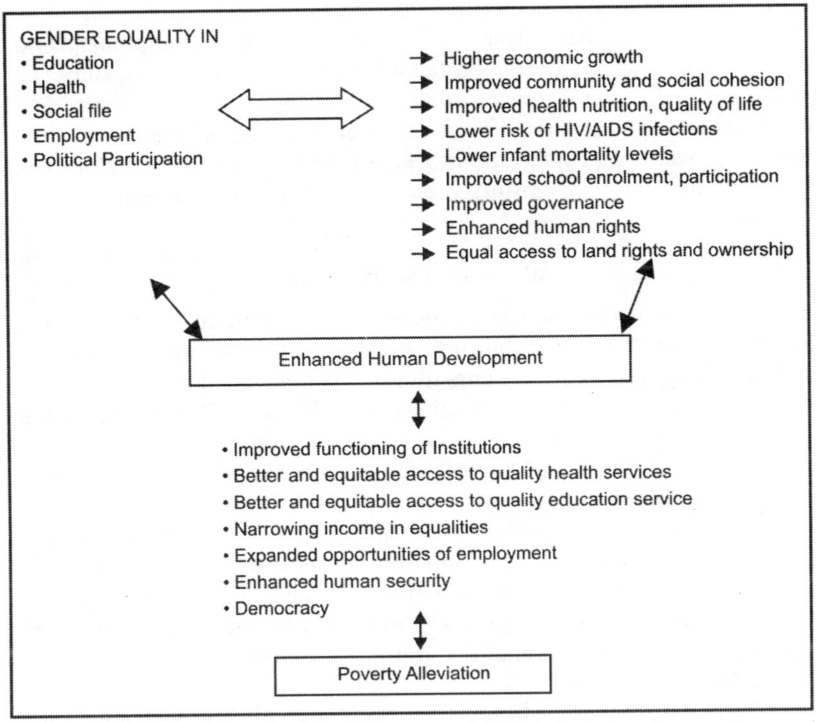

Source: Compiled on the basis of different facts available in Human Development Report of South Asia, 1999, 2000

of gender dimension and created a global consensus and positive momentum for gender mainstreaming and its incorporation in all aspects of development theory and practice. Consequently, women's empowerment and ensuring equality of status is enshrined as a universal goal in various international conventions and declarations.

The high priority accorded to Goal 3 (MDG) again reasserts global affirmation of gender equality as a core value of development. Though it is explicitly mentioned in two of the eight MDGs, but in reality it is an over-arching and cross-cutting concern that can enhance performance on every other indicator of human development and serve as critical channel of not only achieving the other MDGs but reducing the income and non-income poverty. Gender equality and empowerment of women will help to promote universal primary education (MDG 2) reduce under-5 mortality (MDG 4), improve material health (MDG 5) and reduce the likelihood of contracting HIV/AIDS (MDG 6).[8] Thus, it may be said that achieving MDG 3 will have definite advantage and influence over the other MDG and will automatically facilitate their attainment.

The above analysis clearly points out that since development is a process of expanding freedoms equally for all people, gender equality is a core objective in itself. There are close inter-linkages between 'women' and 'development'. In fact, the goals of development are essentially entwined with the progress, and upliftment of women and therefore any development without women is simply distorted, crippled and a partial paradigm.

II
Women in South Asia

The contemporary period has witnessed that women in South Asia have greatly expanded their capabilities over the last few decades and are in a position to assume more responsibilities, yet serious gaps continue in terms of gender equality and its different indicators. The women of the region still lag far behind in the process of development and stand isolated, unorganized and constrained by the socio-cultural and legal structures which not only restrict their access to resources but prevent them from coming to the forefront and joining the mainstream. The rights of women and their claim for equal status with men have remained as merely percepts partly enshrined in the legislations, but not effectively implemented. The region of South Asia is, therefore, defined as 'one of the least gender-sensitive and most gender-unequal regions in the world'.

Traditionally, women in South Asia enjoyed a high status but with the passage of time they have become victims of various socio-economic and political vices. South Asian women make up about 21 per cent of the world's female population and 44 per cent of the world's illiterate women. The region has one of the most distorted sex ratios in the world. There are 940 females for every 1,000 males.[9] The world's largest concentration of poor are here with more than 1 billion living on less than $2 a day. Women and children form a big chunk of this population.

Human development and gender share a close link. Though South Asia has emerged as one of the world's fastest growing regions with an average growth rate of 8 per cent sustained over the past five years, it still fares poorly in terms of the key indicators of development which contribute towards this marginalization and create gender disparity such as poverty, hunger and malnourishment, health, education and sanitation. Thus, despite a robust growth outlook, progress is hampered on account of poor development profile. A close look at the human development index will help to illustrate the argument further (see Table 1).

Table 1

Human Development Index

Region/South Asian countries	*Fiscal year*	*HDI value*	*HDI rank out of 187 total countries*
South Asia	2011	0.548	—
India	2011	0.547	134
Pakistan	2011	0.504	145
Bangladesh	2011	0.500	146
Afghanistan	2011	0.398	172
Sri Lanka	2011	0.691	97
Nepal	2011	0.458	157
Bhutan	2011	0.522	141
Maldives	2011	0.661	109

Source: Human Development Report 2011, UNDP, New York.

The index above shows that the South Asian countries are ranked by low, medium and high values of HDI. India, the biggest country, stands third behind Sri Lanka and Maldives. Sri Lanka had a high HDI value of 0.691, the highest in South Asia region. India is placed at the bottom of HDI compared to the developed countries of the world such as China and Russia. In order to attain a high HDI rank, the region has to work hard and make substantial progress in important sectors of health, education and gender, in particular. There is a close relationship between Human Development Index (HDI) and Gender Development Index (GDI). The region has suffered a substantial loss in HDI value mainly because of gender inequality and wide gender disparity. If the GDI is high, the HDI value is bound to be high and if GDI presents a grim scenario, its impact is bound to be visible on Human Development (see Table 2 for Gender Development Index of South Asia).

Table 2

Gender Development Index, 2011

Name of the country	*Gender Inequality Rank*
India	129
Pakistan	115
Bangladesh	112
Nepal	113
Bhutan	98
Maldives	101
Sri Lanka	74
Afghanistan	141

Source: HD Report, UNDP, 2011 and Global Gender Gap Report, 2011.

Table 3 shows that South Asian countries rank low in terms of gender inequality. India is placed at 129 rank out of 167 countries, which highlights that serious disparities exist in the country.

Table 3

Gender Disparities Profile of South Asia

Particulars	*India*	*Pakistan*	*Bangladesh*	*Nepal*	*Sri Lanka*	*Bhutan*	*Maldives*	*South Asia Weighted average*	*Developing countries*
Female Pop. Numbers (Millions) (2008)	571	86	79	14.5	10.2	0.32	0.15	761	2,715
Adult Female Literacy (as % of male) (2006–2007)	54	40	48	44	89	41	97	52	75
Female Life Expectancy (as % of male (2007)	105	101	103	102	111	106	103	104	106
Female Economic Activity rate (age 15+) (as % of male) (2007)	42	25	68	77	57	54	71	44	67
Female Professional and Technical workers (as % of total) (1999–2007)	—	25	22	20	46	—	49	25	—
Seats in Parliament held by Women (as % of total) (2009)	9	21	6	33	6	14	12	11	—
Gender-related Development Index (GDI) (2007)	0.594	0.532	0.536	0.545	0.756	0.605	0.767	0.582	—
Gender Empowerment Measure (GEM) (2007)	—	0.386	0.264	0.456	0.389	—	0.429	0.343	—
Female Earnings (as % of male (1999–2007)	32	18	51	61	56	39	54	33	—
Female Unemployment Rate (%) (2004–2007)	5.3	8.4	7.0	10.7	9.0	3.3	23.7	6.0	—

Source: Compiled from Human Development in South Asia 2009, Human Development Centre, Oxford 2009.

The status and rights of women in South Asia differ from country to country. Nevertheless, there are few commonalities shared by all countries of the region, such as:

(a) Patriarchy
(b) Deep-rooted poverty/malnutrition
(c) Ill-literacy/lack of higher education and technical facilities and knowledge
(d) Economic inequalities
(e) Socio-cultural discrimination
(f) Low political participation
(g) Domestic violence/human rights violation
(h) Health deficit

Gender discrimination in South Asia is deeply ingrained within the system of patriarchy,[10] which limits and confines women to subordinate role in all facets of life. It is a term used to refer to male domination; to the power relationship by which men dominate women; and especially, a system through which women are kept subordinate.[11] The subordination of women in the patriarchal-dominated societies of South Asia has been defined in terms of child marriage, dowry, polygamy, denial of ownership rights; and control of property, domestic violence, scarce share in economic resources; lack of access to education, and denial of information, along with lack of participation in decision-making. It is in these ways that patriarchal structures perpetuate the enduring gaps between the opportunities available to South Asian women and South Asian men. Attitudinal shift in the society as a whole along with education is a major pre-requisite to break out of this culture of patriarchy.

The gender inequalities in South Asia are most prominently observed in the economic sector. The economic discrimination they endure reinforces other discriminations and perpetuates low status for women. Globalization has no doubt benefited the urban educated women, but at the same time left vast majority of women in informal sectors to cope with the negative impacts of liberalization. Since most of the South Asian countries are agriculture-based, usually women in South Asia contribute significantly to the agriculture sector – basically labour (where work is confined to activities such as crop-processing, weeding, livestock rearing and post-harvest processing) in addition to regular household activities. The economic value is thus attributed to agricultural output and therefore, women receive either little or no compensation and recognition for their work (see Table 4).

Table 4 helps to draw a comparative picture of the female labour force in different countries of South Asia. The table highlights that over 50 per cent of the labour force comprises women in Bangladesh, Nepal and Bhutan as compared to India with 32.8 and Pakistan, the minimum with only 21.7 per cent. Women do not have control over the means of production, land ownership and income earned.

Apart from the agricultural sector, women are confined to other limited sectors, the vast majority being in traditional or service sector employment and others in poorly-paid manufacturing work. Of late, women have began to involve themselves not only in different kinds of work but in diversified sectors as well. Nevertheless, Women employees are subject to discrimination in pay and job security and are often targets of harassment at work place. The microfinance programmes for Women have not yet been mainstreamed.

Table 4

Female Percentage as Labour Force, 2009

Name of country	*Labour force participation rate (%)*
India	32.8
Pakistan	21.7
Bangladesh	58.7
Sri Lanka	34.2
Nepal	63.3
Bhutan	53.4
Maldives	NA
Afghanistan	33.1

Source: Human Development Report 2011, UNDP.

Education is a basic human right and educating women is considered a key to breaking the vicious circle of ignorance and exploitation and empowering them. It is also a key to overcoming oppressive customs and traditions that neglect the needs of girls and women. Though some progress has been achieved in the state of education, vast gaps remain in the educational achievements of men and women in the region. Except Sri Lanka and Maldives, there are large gender gaps in literacy and enrolment. The cultural beliefs and social practices too interface with each other to form multiple and overlapping disparities that exclude girls from their right to education. In fact, the Human Development Report presents a dismal profile of educational deprivation of women. It highlights that half of the South Asian adult illiterates are women. More than two-third of South Asians out of primary school children are girls. Nearly two-fifth of girls enrolled in primary schools drop out before grade 5 and finally one per cent female students are enrolled in the low vocational education.[12] This indicates the educational deprivation of women and girls in South Asia. Despite positive initiatives for widespread primary education and targeted programmes for secondary education in South Asian countries, there are wide gaps across countries in enrolment ratios between females and males.

Gender inequality increases all the more in higher education as well as in technical education (see Table 5).

Talking in terms of specific countries of South Asia, the educational achievements are found satisfactory in Sri Lanka and Maldives as compared to Pakistan, Bangladesh, Bhutan and Nepal.

Table 5

Adulit Literacy

Name of country	*Adult literacy rate % ages 15 and older*
Afghanistan	NA
Bangladesh	56
Bhutan	NA
India	63
Nepal	59
Pakistan	56
Sri Lanka	91
Maldives	NA
South Asia	61

Sources: Compiled from: World Development Report 2012, Gender Equality and Development, The World Bank, 2011.

Health and nutrition is yet another important area where gender inequality is highly visible. Women's health in South Asia is inextricably linked to social status. Health deficit and discrimination against women start even before birth and continue until death largely because of reasons like birth of a girl-child, early marriage, pregnancy, abortions, many children, etc. It is also found that malnutrition is one of the main reasons behind high morality rates in women. The rural women in the region also suffer from lack of access to health-care on account of relative inaccessibility of such facilities to them. The women in South Asia often face traditional taboos, based on cultural practices and religious beliefs against consulting doctors. The norms of early marriage continue to predominate, whereas the use of contraception is low. Strong preference for son, which is indeed an alteration of patriarchal society, has resulted in female foeticide. Women in South Asia are also vulnerable to many preventable and curable diseases such as tuberculosis, Malaria and hepatitis, when life becomes threatening as the diseases are exacerbated because of lack of information, poor health facilities, lack of sanitation facilities and safe drinking water. The female children are more prone to communicable diseases. There is generally discrimination against the girl child in terms of immunization as well as nutrition.

South Asian Women face legal discrimination as well. It is generally found that women have an unequal access to property, decision-making, fair justice and protection, mainly because the legal framework has largely been determined by religious-cultural practices and tradition of European jurisprudence.[13] These practices generally govern marriage, divorce, guardianship, adoption, inheritance and claim for property. Though all countries in the region are signatories of CEDAW and maintain constitutional guarantee of women's legal equality with men, nevertheless in many cases these guarantees are confounded or contradicted by other constitutional articles, amendments and laws, as well as by lack of political will to enforce these laws, combined with persistent customary practices which generally differ from country to country. For example, rules with regard to registration of marriage are not clear in most South Asian countries. Similarly, dowry or property exchange is known differently in each country so different kinds of rules persist. With special reference to Pakistan, it may be said that a woman who is marrying by choice can be charged with Zina (tax) and the existence of Muslim Personal Law in the country gives arbitrary and unconditional right to men regarding divorce and separation. Thus, it's clear that women are subject to gender-specific violence in all South Asian countries on account of ambiguity or lack of clarity in the articulation of rights and that creates space for misuse as well as discrimination.

Socio-cultural constraints across the region of South Asia play an important role in contributing towards the lower status of women. The cultural constraints in terms of class and ethnicity too work as impediments in attaining higher status. For example, Pathans and Baluchis of Pakistan observe a more rigid attitude and impose greater social restrictions on women. Ethnic differences in socio-cultural norms are equally visible in Nepal and in India. The Tibetan women in Nepal have a more equal status which is reflected in their greater control over the household assets and income in comparison with the Indo-Aryan groups where women's lower status is reflected in the system of inheritance and the work of lower status assigned to them. Similarly, the cultural divide between North and South India is reflected significantly when difference in women's status is considered to be higher in the southern states of India.[14]

Political participation of South Asian women is invisible in almost all governing institutions. Though women leaders dominate the political landscape in South Asia by representing major political parties, yet these powerful positions have not been translated into positive outcome for the majority of the women in the region. The Human Development Report of 1999 states:

- Women occupy only 7 per cent of the parliamentary seats.
- Only 9 per cent of the cabinet members are women.
- Only 6 per cent of positions in the judiciary are held by women.
- Only 9 per cent of civil servants are women.
- Only 20 per cent members of local government are women.[15]

The above facts highlight that there is not only political inconsistency but overall lack of commitment to women's empowerment and resistance to gender mainstreaming. Women continue to remain poorly represented in policy-making along with handling of administrative responsibilities. There is generally political and economic marginalization of women's departments and most women ministers are assigned or involved with 'soft' social sector posts. There is also found inadequate gender disaggregation of statistical databases and knowledge-bases (see Table 6).

Though political participation is increasing, women's effectiveness as local politicians is often hindered by lack of training; male backlash; along with corrupt, money-centred violent political culture. Thus, one can find that gender bias pervades at all levels of governance in South Asia and women have not been able to break through the glass-ceilings beyond certain limits, mainly because of the male-dominated social structures which often hinder the work of elected representatives.

Domestic violence is yet another inescapable reality of women's lives in South Asia as the social customs and attitudes that support violence against them are deeply entrenched and institutionalized at all levels - home, family, community and society. The pervasive culture of violence is a serious human rights issue and has affected women's fundamental right to life, food, shelter, security and political participation, which ultimately reduces their contribution to the society, economy and polity. Trafficking of women and girls within and across the countries of South Asia too has assumed alarming proportions and has drawn worldwide attention. The problem of missing girls at birth and excess female mortality post-birth in South Asia has assumed a serious dimension (see Table 7).

Women in South Asia are easy targets of environmental devastation. Bangladesh, India and Nepal face perennial natural disasters like droughts, floods, landslides and earthquakes. So the policy-makers in these countries face difficult choices with regard to current or future national development priorities in the counter of emergency recovery/ peace-building,

Table 6

Women Seats in National Parliament 2011

Name of Country	*% of female seats in National Parliament 2011*
India	10.7
Pakistan	21.0
Bangladesh	18.6
Sri Lanka	5.3
Nepal	33.2
Bhutan	13.9
Maldives	6.5
Afghanistan	27.6
South Asia region	12.5

Source: Human Development Report 2011 Sustainability and Equity: A Better Future for all UNDP, 2011.

Table 7

Missing girls at birth and excess female deaths in South Asia, excluding India (in thousands)

Ratio of girls at different ages	*1990*	*2008*
Girls at birth	0	1
Girls under 5	99	72
Girls 5–14	32	20
Girls 15–49	176	161
Women 50–59	37	51
Under 60	346	305
Total women	690	610

Source: The data is taken from World Development Report 2012: Gender Equality and Development, The World Bank, p. 121.

rehabilitation and reconstruction. In such a fragile environment, the situation of millions of marginalized and vulnerable women and children has been exacerbated, depriving them of their basic rights and entitlements.

In the above scenario, it is clear that women's position is dismal and it is obviously challenging for the countries of South Asia to achieve progress on MDG 3.

III
Women's Development in South Asia: SAARC Initiatives

Ever since launching of regional cooperation in South Asia in 1985, issues related to gender and equality for women have figured prominently on the SAARC agenda and cooperation has steadily grown in this area. The cooperation thus developed will enable the member states to achieve the ultimate goal of bringing women into the mainstream of development with independence and equality.

Initially, a technical committee on women-in-development was created under the erstwhile Integrated Programme of Action (IPA) and several meetings of the technical committees were held under IPA, which resulted in the formulation of a Regional Plan of Action (RPA) on women. This resulted in dissemination of technical information related to women-in-development generated by the member states and the preparation of several guide books and women's journals on specific themes to coincide with important events like SAARC summits.[16] It was on recommendation of the RPA that the year 1990 was designated as the SAARC Year of the Girl Child and subsequently the period from 1991–2000 was declared as the SAARC Decade of the Girl Child. During this period, several programmes and activities were initiated and a regional plan of action was drawn to observe the decade, to highlight the gender disparities in the region and to promote welfare of the girl child.

Apart from above mentioned, several short-term activities like seminars, workshops, training courses have taken place in areas such as women and law, women and environment; women education, women employment, women and agriculture and extension activities.[17] On a number of occasions, exhibitions on handicrafts and designs prepared by women have also been organized by the member states. A women's cell too has been established at the SAARC Secretariat to act as a data-bank and a storehouse of information on women-in-development in the region. The member states adopted 'Dhaka Resolution on Women' in 1995, which was later presented at the Fourth World Conference on Women in Beijing (1995). The Resolution provided additional inputs from SAARC countries to the Beijing Conference.

Women issues have been addressed at the highest political level in SAARC. It was on the occasion of the 11th SAARC Summit in Kathmandu that the leaders agreed to mobilize resources towards improving the social status of women and children, empowering them and ensuring their full participation in decision-making at all levels. SAARC also took a path-breaking initiative with the adoption of a Regional Convention on Combatting the Crime of Trafficking in Women and Children for Prostitution in 2002.[18] The civil society organizations and the media role in raising awareness about the inhuman treatment faced by the victims of trafficking was highlighted and appreciated at the 12th SAARC Summit in Islamabad. In 2004, the law enforcement agencies working in different countries were also included in SAARC.[19]

It was during the 14th SAARC Summit that the heads of government once again acknowledged that women's full participation in all spheres of society, including decision-making, is fundamental for the achievement of equality and development. The leaders reaffirmed women's empowerment as a major objective of regional cooperation and focused on the need to formulate regional projects addressing issues relating to women and children. The SAARC heads reinforced the need of women's economic empowerment and skill development while addressing key health issues and violence against women during the 15th SAARC summit at Colombo in 2008.[20] The leaders again reaffirmed their commitment to women equality on the occasion of 17th SAARC summit at Male and reiterated their commitment towards enhancing their status and ensuring equality. Yet another significant initiative was the signing of SAARC memorandum of understanding with the United Nations Development Fund (UNIFEM)[21] for Women to help the member states strive towards the goals of gender equality based upon the empowerment approach. In accordance with the MoU, SAARC and UNIFEM have developed a comprehensive SAARC Gender Database, which was launched by the SAARC Secretary General at the Sixth South Asian Regional Ministers' Conference by UNIFEM in New Delhi on January 17, 2010. The Gender Database contains record of violence against women and trafficking in South Asia and on women's health, including HIV/AIDS, and feminization of poverty. It will help in mapping the progress of women in the South Asia region.

Besides this, in an attempt to keep the Beijing spirit alive and to commemorate it, the South Asian governments in collaboration with UNIFEM regularly organized the regional conferences at the ministerial level in different countries such as at Delhi in 1996, Kathmandu 1998, Maldives 2000, Bhutan 2003, Islamabad 2005, and in Delhi in January 2008. These conferences deliberated on issues of violence, trafficking, female foeticide, political and economic empowerment, disaster preparedness, security, education and health.

The establishment of SAARC Chamber Women Entrepreneurs Council (SCWEC) on March 29, 2001 is yet another significant initiative with regard to women's development. SCWEC is a sector Council of the SAARC Commerce and Industries (SCCI), the apex business organization of the SAARC region. The council works with the objective of promoting, facilitating and networking among the women entrepreneurs of the SAARC region. Since the inception of SCWEC, a number of workshops, round-table conferences, seminars, training programmes and annual events have been organized and better opportunities for SAARC entrepreneurs created.[22]

Pursuant to a decision of the 11th summit (Kathmandu, 2002), the SAARC Autonomous Women's Advocacy Group (SAWAG) was formed to advocate mainstreaming gender and making recommendations on gender-related issues and programmes in the region. So far the group has addressed issues related to women's citizenship, political representation, trafficking and sexual exploitation, gender and HIV/AIDS, female education and literacy, legal rights, and economic empowerment.

Moreover, the SAARC Social Charter talks about promoting women and affirms the need to empower women through literacy and education and reaffirms its commitment to effectively implement the SAARC Convention on Combatting the Trafficking of Women and Children for Prostitution by involving the civil society. It finally affirmed that various regional-level mechanisms and institutions need to be developed in order to promote the advancement of women as an integral part of mainstream political, economic, social and cultural development of the region. A SAARC Network of Feminist Economists and an NGO, SAARC Women for Peace, was also set up.

All this shows there is an increased awareness on gender disparities and the need to address them at the regional level through mutual collaboration and understanding. It is in this context that SAARC has undertaken several initiatives at its level, such as organizing conferences and workshops, collaborating with the women's organizations, NGO, human rights organizations, the law enforcement agencies, and women's cells of all countries. Moreover, the appointment of women to the post of Secretary General of SAARC Secretariat is an important initiative towards promoting gender equality. Thus, one can say that despite several limitations, SAARC is taking measures to bring women to the front stage and generating positive goodwill.

IV

MDGs and SAARC Development Goals: Partners of Development

With less than five years left to achieve the MDGs, the South Asian countries are making serious attempts to reach them. A significant initiative in this regard was the setting up of SAARC Development Goals (SDGs). Four years after the inception of the Millennium Development

Goals, the regional heads of state from South Asia gathered at Islamabad for the 12th SAARC Summit (January 2004) to assess its progress and at the end released a report entitled 'An Engagement with Hope', wherein the Independent South Asian Commission on Poverty Alleviation (ISACPA) recommended and consolidated the MDGs to form the SAARC Development Goals (SDGs). These were formally endorsed during the 13th SAARC Summit at Dhaka (January 2006) for a period of five years from 2007–2012. The SDGs mandate covers several important development goals and is in a sense a roadmap for the implementation of SAARC Social Charter. Taking into consideration both the South Asian context and its specifities along with the relevant linkages with international goals such as that of MDGs; the SDGs include 22 priority goals divided into four clusters along with 75 indicators, eight of which pertain to livelihood, four to health, four to education and six to environment.

The basic inspiration that guided the formation of above SDGs, apart from the SAARC mandate, was to help the member states galvanize their developmental efforts and create a space in which all sections of society can be accommodated and jointly work towards fulfilling the national and regional priorities. The member states were also guided towards realizing the dream of complete alleviation of poverty from the region and finally to meet the international imperative for achieving the Millennium Development Goals (MDGs) by 2015. Thus SDGs reflect the collective vision of South Asian countries to address the developmental issues both regionally and internationally.

The SDGs clearly exhibit that goals and targets are interrelated with MDGs and most of the indicators of SDGs and MDGs are overlapping and complementary to each other. In fact, the MDGs have been localized and contextualized for South Asia through the SDGs. The MDGs and SDGs actually represent a partnership between the developed countries and the developing countries to create a conducive environment for sustainable development, and global interdependence. It is worth noting that all SDGs and their indicators are closely interlinked with the development of women and enhancement in her status. Thus, attainment of SDGs is directly linked to the progress made towards achieving MDGs. Each South Asian country was entrusted with individual responsibility to prioritize and formulate the specific targets and their indicators in their development plans.

It is difficult to locate the progress of SAARC Development Goals as the member states have taken a long time to chart a roadmap and to prioritize SDGs at the regional and national level. Nevertheless, the 15th SAARC Summit (Colombo, 2–3 August 2008) emphasized on undertaking sustained efforts, including developing and implementing regional and sub-regional projects towards the attainment of SDGs. The SAARC ministerial meeting on Poverty Alleviation (Male, 27 May 2008) reiterated its decision to have an inter-governmental mid-term review of the SDGs and to create an inter-governmental mechanism for the purpose. The 16th Summit (28–29 April, 2010 at Thimpu) also called for expeditious mainstreaming of SDGs in the national processes. Accordingly, the SAARC Secretariat organized the meeting of inter-governmental mechanism for the mid-term review of the SDGs and Plan of Action on Poverty Alleviation on 28–29 September, 2010. The preparation of SAARC Regional Poverty Profile (RPP), recommendations of Independent South Asian Commission on Poverty Alleviation (ISACPA) for observance of the 'SAARC Decade of Poverty Alleviation 2006–2015'[23] and working for SAARC Social Charter are some of the efforts in that direction. Before moving ahead to analyse SDGs' progress, it is necessary to have a look at the progress and status of MDGs in South Asia. An assessment of MDGs and SDGs will focus on the close partnership they share in moving on the path of development at global, national as well as regional level.

(a) Status of MDGs in South Asia

- While taking stock of the progress on eradication of extreme poverty which in context of MDGs in narrowly defined in terms of income, as the proportion of people living on less than $1.25 a day, the region as a whole is moving to be halfway to meet Goal 1. This is primarily due to the some decrease in poverty ratio's and sustained economic growth of the South Asian countries in the last decade. The smaller countries of Bangladesh, Bhutan, Sri Lanka and Maldives have grown over 5 per cent per year on average, while India and Pakistan have experienced 7–8 per cent growth. If this growth accelerates to 10 per cent a year, it is assumed that the region could attain single digit poverty rates by 2015.[24] Despite robust economic performance and rising optimism, doubts persist, because the region is still home to large numbers of extremely poor people. It is estimated that over three-fourth of South Asians live on less than US $2 per person per day. This indicates that South Asian poor are vulnerable to falling back to extreme poverty. In fact, there is greater inequity today as the benefits of economic growth have not equitably reached the poor and the marginalized, especially women. It may be argued that women in South Asia are highly vulnerable to poverty regardless of whether we define it in terms of income, basic needs or poverty of opportunity.[25] Poverty and gender inequality are closely interlinked in numerous ways, forming a vicious cycle that pushes millions of women and girls into a trap of constant denial of rights, deprivation and discrimination. Though poverty is feminized in most parts of the world, but in South Asia it truly has a women's face. Therefore, until the South

Asian countries break this vicious cycle of poverty, reaching MDG 1 continues to remain a challenge.

- This region may not be able to meet the nutritional targets of MDGs as South Asia suffers from the highest levels of hunger in the world, with just over one-fifth of the population not consuming the guidelines of 2,200 calories a day. This makes it the second-most hungry the region on earth. It has failed to decrease the proportion of hungry and un-fed in the last 20 years. Almost every second child is underweight. The situation is even worse for those under-5 with almost 50 per cent of children in this age bracket underweight. Gender disparities also exist with only 46 per cent of boys being underweight as compared to 49 per cent of girls. It is generally found that boys are favoured over girls in times of food scarcity. The severity of malnutrition is found to be high in India, Pakistan, Nepal and Afghanistan. Bangladesh may achieve the nutritional goal partly due to the scale-up of community-based nutrition programme.[26] Thus, South Asia is off-track in terms of achieving this goal and may not be in a position to achieve its targets before 2050.
- South Asian countries have made good progress on the educational front over the last 25 years and are likely to reach MDG 2 if the consistency is maintained in the educational standards of the region. The region has witnessed marked improvement in the enrolment ratios in primary education. This ratio has increased from 75.3 per cent in 1991 to 89.7 per cent in 2008.[27] India, Bangladesh and Nepal have made noteworthy achievements in this regard. Pakistan lags behind other countries in achieving the goal of universal primary education. The most impressing part is the reducing of gender gap – girls now enjoy educational parity with males in terms of primary school enrolment. The enrolment ratio of girls in primary education was 87.5 per cent in 2008 compared to 66.7 per cent in 1991.[28] Maldives has 95 per cent per cent female enrolment in primary education. These developments are noteworthy considering that only two decades back, the female primary school completion rate in the region was almost 20 per cent points below that of males. Thus, gender equality in terms of education has shown perceptible improvement.
- Gender equality and women empowerment are the main determinants to attain other MDGs. Reaching MDG 3 continues to remain a difficult task. As mentioned above, girls are at parity with boys in terms of the primary enrolment rate. However, the gender gap is more pronounced for the secondary and tertiary levels. There is also gender inequality in adult literacy rate in all the South Asia countries. A recent UN report observes that 74 girls were enrolled in tertiary education as compared to 100 boys in South Asia. Though it is

decreasing fast, the region of South Asia still performs unsatisfactory vis-à-vis the rest of the world and other developing regions. Yet another indicator of female equality is the proportion of females in wage employment in the non-agriculture sector. Although there is some progress, it is still not prepared to reach the MDG targets by 2015 and still has the lowest share in the world (tied with sub-Sahara Africa). Yet another indicator of equality, the MDGs include the proportion of national parliament seats taken by women. South Asia has made huge progress in the last 5 years with massive increase in political participation. In fact the number of women in parliamentary seats can now be compared to the developed countries. If the current trends persist, South Asia may have the highest number of women taking parliamentary seats in the world by 2015.

- The region suffers from the second highest child mortality rates in the world with over 7 per cent of children dying before completing 5 years of age. Reducing child mortality and reaching MDG 4 is again a challenge for South Asia. Though some progress is visible and both under-5 mortality and infant mortality rates have declined significantly. The under-5 mortality reduced from 125 in 1990 to 76 in 2005, whereas infant mortality declined from 83 in 1990 to 58 per 1,000 live births in 2005[29], and the proportion of children being immunized too has increased rapidly in the last 10 years. Despite this reduction, the progress in this regard continues to remain insufficient to achieve the target of reducing by two-third the child mortality rate by 2015.
- Maternal mortality is yet another serious challenge for the region. Despite substantial investment in health sector by governments, donors and NGOs, women in countries across the region continue to suffer from maternal mortality. In fact, South Asia is categorized with second highest maternal mortality rates in the world.[30] Though a recent UN study observes that 'between 1990 and 2008, maternal mortality in South Asia declined by 53 per cent', the region lags far behind in several indicators closely interlinked with maternal mortality such as nutrition, sanitation, discrimination, violence and gender equality, affecting the health-seeking behaviour of most of the girls and women. The health-care system in South Asia is weak in addressing the needs of pregnant women. Therefore, it may by submitted that the region is off-track and is unlikely to reach MDG 5 of improving maternal health by 2015.
- Progress on MDG 6 is slow and mixed. South Asia seems to be on the track in terms of achieving the goals of combatting contentious diseases such as TB and Malaria, though Pakistan and Afghanistan are two countries where the disease has posed major risks. In case of

HIV/AIDS infections, it is on the rise and gender norms and gender inequality play a critical role in spread of HIV infections, making South Asia a fertile ground for the rapid spread of infection. According to the estimates of the National AIDS Control Organization of India, currently 20 to 25 per cent of HIV infections in India are among girls and women[31]. Violence undermines the ability of women to access HIV/AIDS prevention, care, support and treatment programmes and the disease in turn contributes to an increased risk of violence because of the stigma and discrimination experienced by those who are infected or affected by the disease. There is thus a dynamic interplay between spread of HIV/AIDS and gender-based violence in South Asia. Bangladesh, Nepal and Sri Lanka are rapidly developing local epidemics among those groups most vulnerable to HIV. Thus, it may be said that reaching MDG 6 is a challenge for South Asia.

- Progress on MDG 7 is very uneven. In order to attain MDG 7, South Asia needs massive investment for drinking water supply and sanitation coverage. To fulfill MDG 7, in rural areas alone over 105 million people need to gain access to drinking water and at least 400 million must have sanitation. Though India has made considerable progress in providing access to drinking water, it is found that nearly 2/3 Indians have no access to sanitation. Inadequate sanitation is a problem for all, but more so for women and girls. Similarly, the other South Asian countries too are not in a position to fulfill the targets laid down in MDG 7 and therefore, reaching the goal seem to be a distinct dream.

The overall scenario in South Asia on most MDG targets has been dismal and significantly below the target levels, as compared with other countries of the world. There is need of a well-coordinated regional response to the vexing problems of the region in a time-bound implementation process, possibly through the SAARC framework.

The above analysis highlights the mixed performance of the region in the attainment of the MDGs. However, efforts have been made to localize MDGs through SDGs by mainstreaming them in the planning process of the countries with a sense of priority and urgency; by revisiting the targets suitable for the country; by adopting revised targets in their national plans and further breaking down and adjusting these targets at the state and local-level planning.

(b) National Trends of SDGs

The formation of SDGs is a testament of the determination of the South Asian countries in advancing the MDGs amidst several constraints and challenges. A close look at the list of SDGs may help us to have a better understanding of the interlinkages it has with MDGs and how they are partners of development.

SAARC Development Goals (SDGs) 2007–2012

Livelihood SDGs

Goal 1 : Eradication of hunger poverty
Goal 2 : Halve proportion of people in poverty by 2010
Goal 3 : Ensure adequate nutrition and dietary improvement for the poor.
Goal 4 : Ensure a pro-poor growth process
Goal 5 : Strengthen connectivity of poor regions and of poor as social groups.
Goal 6 : Reduce social and institutional vulnerabilities of poor, women and children.
Goal 7 : Ensure access to affordable justice.
Goal 8 : Ensure effective participation of poor and of women in anti-poverty policies and programmes.

Health SDGs

Goal 9 : Maternal health
Goal 10 : Child health
Goal 11 : Affordable health-care
Goal 12 : Improved hygiene and public health

Education SDGs

Goal 13 : Access to primary school for all children, boys and girls.
Goal 14 : Completion of primary education cycle
Goal 15 : Universal functional literacy
Goal 16 : Quality education at primary, secondary and vocational levels.

Environmental SDGs

Goal 17 : Acceptable levels of forest cover
Goal 18 : Acceptable levels of water and soil quality
Goal 19 : Acceptable levels of air quality
Goal 20 : Conservation of bio-diversity
Goal 21 : Wetland conservation
Goal 22 : Ban on dumping hazardous waste, including radio-active waste.

The SDGs' schedule reflects that they have been prepared within the broad framework of MDGs. The SDGs have been incorporated by the South Asian countries in their national development plans and sincere attempts are being made to attain them.

In Afghanistan, the eighth member of SAARC, it is found that though the country has made some positive advances in area of economic development, health-care and education, the overall progress is uneven, far too slow and confronts several challenges. Gender inequality constitutes a major impediment to human development. It is estimated that about 6.6 million Afghans do not meet their minimum food requirements. Women and children constitute the majority. The country has the lowest life expectancy rates (44 years).[32] With regard to universalization of elementary education in Afghanistan, the girls' access to education has increased over the years in urban areas but the situation is poor in rural areas and additional resources are needed to improve and increase this access. In terms of the adult literacy rates, Afghanistan ranks lowest in the world. Only 23.5 per cent of the population above 15 years of age can read and write. More surprisingly, only an estimated 12.6 per cent of women are literate, compared to 43.5 per cent for men.[33] The maternal mortality rates are highest among the SAARC countries.[34] Though a significant increase in the number of female health workers has increased female access to health-care, still the health indicators of both women and children continue to remain exceptionally low basically on account of malnutrition. Despite the dismal health scenario, the trend to empower women politically is found encouraging in Afghanistan. Of late, 25 per cent of the seats have been allotted to women in Wolesi Jirga (Lower House) of the national Assembly.[35]

The landlocked state of Bhutan has made notable progress in all 22 SDG goals. Since the State is guided by the philosophy of Gross National Happiness (GNH), it attaches equal importance to all sectors and has mainstreamed all SDGs in its sectoral developmental plans of health, education, poverty alleviation, rural development, women development and environment. So far as the SDG status in gender equality is concerned, over the years Bhutan has developed a strong institutional mechanism at both governmental and non-governmental level which is not only working for the cause of women but has also taken several initiatives enhance the status of women. The SDG trends indicate that gender parity significantly improved at both primary and secondary levels. The ratio of girls to boys at primary level increased from 82 per cent in 2000 to 99.4 per cent in 2010. It has fared even better at secondary level, where initially in 2000 the ratio of girls to boys was only 78 per cent but in 2010 it surpassed the targets to 103.50 per cent.[36] There is also a steady increase in the number of females joining the civil services from 21.23 per cent in 2000 to 31.62 per cent in 2011. However, the number of females at decision level is still very low. The health SDGs focus on significant improvement in maternal mortality ratios; the percentage of births attended by skilled personnel increased from 24 per cent in 2000 to 64.5 per cent in 2010.[37] Though the incidence of Malaria and tuberculosis have decreased, women in rural areas are vulnerable to HIV/AIDS infections. With regard to share of women in employment, women have dominance in agriculture and forestry economic activities with 65.3 per cent of females and 54 per cent of males.[38]

Bangladesh too is committed to achieve the SAARC Development Goals within the given time-frame and it has integrated the Millennium Development Goals and SDGs within the broader agenda of its national economic targets. The SDG trends in Bangladesh indicate that the country, has made remarkable progress in the areas of primary schooling, girls' education, female economic participation and birth control. Although the development goals have moved towards their targets, the performances have been uneven. Bangladesh has achieved successive in attaining gender parity by attaining more than 100 per cent enrolment in primary as well as secondary school education. Since 1990, the primary school enrolment has increased 1.4 times from 11.9 million in 1990 with 6.6 million boys and 5.4 million girls to 16.7 million in 2008, half of whom are girls.[39] However, the trend in territary education is virtually stagnant with around 57 per cent. The adult female literacy rate is 54.74 per cent. Under the health cluster of SDGs, the maternal mortality rates declined from 322 in 2001 to 194 per 100,000 live births in the country, which is about 40 per cent drop from previous survey. The proportion of births attended by skilled health personnel too has increased as compared to previous decades. Reversing the past trend from 2001 when the female life expectancy was lower than male, it is found that women now live longer than men.[40] Political empowerment of women seems promising, as the share of women in national parliament is gradually found increasing from 12.7 per cent in 1991–95 to 13 per cent in 1996–2000, and then 12.4 per cent in 2001–06 and finally, 19 per cent in 2008.[41] However, in the other areas of decision-making such as the bureaucracy and high-level jobs, women's presence is negligible. Similarly, the share of women in employment (wage/self/organized/ unorganized) is found to be 31.5 per cent, according to Bangladesh employment survey. The budgetary allocation for women's development was 25.96 per cent of the total budgetary amount in 2010–11.

Nepal is one of the poor and least-developed countries in the world with almost one-third of its population living below poverty line. Due to prolonged period of relative political instability in the country, the delivery of social services remained poor and as a corollary the progress indicators reflect the MDGs and SDGs' position as far from satisfactory. Nevertheless, Nepal is committed to reach them. With regard to progress on gender equality and women's empowerment, it is found that politically women in Nepal are aware and active. The proportion of women representatives in national assemblies has increased by 8 per cent in the decade from 1998–2008. The educational SDGs with regard to gender parity are not very encouraging. There is significant gender gap in primary schooling and adult literacy, which needs to be done away. The most worrying aspect of SDGs indicators of Nepal is the high maternal mortality rates.[42]

India, the biggest member of SAARC, registered an unprecedented GDP growth rate but has been disappointing in delivery of social services and depicts a depressing state of human development and therefore, lags behind in attaining satisfactory performance in reaching MDGs and SDGs. With regard to gender equality and women's empowerment, there are serious disparities found in women's access and control over resources, which is reflected in social development indicators of health, education, nutrition, as well as the occupational status. India has incorporated the SDGs in its national development plans. The 11th Five Year Plan (2007–12) reaffirms this commitment and provides a comprehensive strategy for inclusive development and identifies 26 measurable indices of performance relating to poverty, education, health and environment, all sectors broadly identified in SDGs and closely linked to women's development. Apart from this, the government has taken up several policy initiatives to bridge gender disparities in the area of education such as the Sarva Shiksha Abhiyan launched in 2000, which targets the most educationally-backward areas with low female literacy rates and the other is the National Programme for Education of Girls at Elementary Level.[43] It may be said that the aforesaid initiatives and programmes are gradually helping to reduce the gender gaps in the educational sector. The ratio of girls attending school has shown improvement from 55 per cent in 1999–2002 to 93 per cent in 2007–2009.

The inadequacy of health sector, scarcity of financial commitments and poor infrastructure have resulted in poor health of women. In fact, reproductive health is the largest contributor to the Gender Inequality Index in India. The maternal mortality figure stands stagnant at a high level of 450 per 10,00,000 live births and the adolescent fertility rate is 68 births per 1,000 live births. It may thus be submitted that apart from raising the enrolment ratios at primary level with due gender balance, India is lagging far behind the targets set under development goals.

Pakistan too has a long way to go in order to reach MDG 3 and SDGs promoting women's equality. The country has charted out a well-planned Medium Term Development Framework (MTDF) where the human development targets have been fixed in line with the Millennium Development Goals and SDGs. There are wide gender gaps in Pakistan which inhibit efforts to ensure gender parity. Though the ratio of girls in primary enrolment increased over the years, the adult female literacy is just over one-third compared to nearly two-third of adult females. The MTDF has set targets for the overall adult literacy, along with promoting quality education. With regard to health SDGs, the maternal mortality rates remain high and the country has started several health programmes, and established new health units and rural health centres.[44] Women in the country are politically active. Reaching MDGs and SDGs remains distant in Pakistan unless the socio-economic scenario improves.

Sri Lanka, the island nation, outperforms all other SAARC countries in case of its socio-economic and human development indicators. The nation has made considerable achievement in gender equality and women's empowerment. The goal of universal primary education for both boys and girls is almost achieved; the indicators show 100 per cent enrolment for girl students. Apart from this, significant decline in maternal mortality rates has occurred as more women have gained access to family planning and skilled birth attendance – almost 98.5 per cent in 2007. Thus, Sri Lanka has outperformed the SAARC countries so far as SDG indicators are concerned.[45]

To sum it up, South Asian countries have given high priority in national policy implementation to achieve MDG/SDG goals. The governments have implemented several schemes, programmes and projects. The civil society and NGOs of respective countries are also playing a crucial role in reaching the development goals, but the task at hand is very challenging and unfulfilled.

(c) SDGs at the Regional Level

SAARC has grown over the years. It has vastly expanded and developed the necessary mechanisms as well as the infrastructure to pursue, monitor and coordinate the various programmes, projects and schemes to reach the eight MDGs and SDGs formulated under the different clusters. It is generally felt that the economic and social development cannot be ensured without optimum utilization of human resources and therefore, the significance of human resource development has been emphasized as well as recognized by SAARC. In this context, SAARC has also established various regional centres. A few among them are as follows:

Table 8

SAARC Regional Centres

Regional Centres	*Country*	*Year of establishment*
SAARC Agriculture Information Centre	Dhaka	1988
SAARC Tuberculosis Centre (STC)	Kathmandu	1992
SAARC Meteorological Research Centre (SMRC)	Dhaka	1995
SAARC Human Resource Development Centre (SHRDC)	Islamabad	1999
SAARC Forestry Centre (SFC)	Bhutan	2008
SAARC Disaster Management Centre (SDMC)	New Delhi	2006

Source: www.saarc.sec.org

Since illiteracy is identified as one of the major factors contributing to region's economic backwardness and social imbalance, education was included as an area of cooperation under the purview of the technical committee on human resource development. In this context, SAARC Chair, Fellowship and scholarship schemes are in operation in the region. A SAARC Consortium of Open and Distance Learning (SACODIL) has been created with a view to standardize curricular and mutual recognition of various educational and vocational courses. Similarly, a South Asian University too has been set up at Delhi. The multi-campus university will help to develop excellence in higher education in the entire region and strengthen cooperation on educational matters through exchange of academics, experts and policy-makers. Training programmes on capacity-building of women too have been organized.[46] Thus, the education SDG can be pursued and coordinated at the regional level through SAARC.

SAARC has also initiated various policies and programmes at the regional level to combat the resurgence of communicable diseases like Malaria, TB and other water-borne diseases. Member countries have identified centres to act as local points on selected diseases in the region. The SAARC Tuberculosis Centre (STC) establish in Kathmandu in 1992 may be mentioned here. It plays a important role in the prevention and control of TB by way of coordinating efforts of the national TB control programmes of the member states. The year 2004 was designated as the SAARC Awareness Year for TB and HIV/AIDS. Apart from preparing audio-visual documentaries on prevention and control of these diseases, various awareness programmes have been organized from time to time at various levels. Special publications regarding communicable diseases have been distributed in SAARC countries in all seven regional languages. SAARC has also recognized the importance of the rich heritage of traditional systems of medicines in the region for meeting the basic health needs of the people and tried to develop it. A pilot tele-medicine project connecting one/two hospitals in each of the SAARC countries with super-speciality hospitals in India too has been started. A special focus is laid on maternal and child health, including immunization, establishing of blood banks and developing sick child care units along with vaccine storage units.[47] Thus, it may be said that health SDGs can be pursued through SAARC at the regional level.

The SAARC Human Resource Development Centre was established in Islamabad in 2002 with an objective of undertaking research, training and dissemination of information on human resource development issues such as health, education, gender, poverty and environment. Thus, SDGs can be pursued at this level as well.

Several committees have been set up and programmes undertaken for alleviation of poverty and environmental sustainability at regional level. Regional cooperation initiatives also include efforts at capacity-building by South Asian countries on bilateral basis. Here special mention may be made of SEWA (Self-Employed Women's Association) set up by India as part of post-war reconstruction programme in Afghanistan to train women in embroidery, weaving, food processing, packaging, environment regeneration, marketing and management skills. This kind of initiative will contribute to creating self-employment opportunities for women.[48] Thus, social infrastructure on solid foundations of education and health can be build through regional cooperation in South Asia and help in achieving gender equality while pursuing MDGs and SDGs.

V

Summing up

The Millennium Development Goals (MDGs) adopted by the United Nations in 2000 are most exhaustive and universal in nature. They have not only succeeded in raising global awareness but also shaped a broad vision that remains an overarching framework for the developmental activities of the world. With the 2015 deadline in mind, all the South Asian countries are advancing their efforts towards attaining the MDGs, both at the national level and regional level. In order to work intensely for MDGs, the SAARC Developmental Goals were adopted under the four broad clusters of livelihood, education, health and environment. All South Asian countries have mainstreamed the SDGs in their national planning process with a sense of high priority. The MDGs and SDGs are thus identified as partners of development.

The importance of gender equality and women's empowerment is widely realized in order to bridge gender discrimination in access to resources. Gender equality will create a fair society, raise economic productivity and help to advance other developmental goals. Therefore, mainstreaming women's empowerment and equality in policy formulation is vital for building sound social infrastructure. Ever since the launching of SAARC, issues related to women and their development have figured prominently on the SAARC agenda and several initiatives have been taken in this area from time to time.

While mapping the progress of South Asian countries in reaching the goals set under MDGs/SDGs, they are found far from impressive. There is serious disjuncture across South Asia between the stunning growth rates and desolate performance on all indicators of human development as represented by MDGs/SDGs. While some progress is visible on issues related to literacy and primary school enrolment ratios, the region lags far behind the targets in field of maternal health and prevention of fatal diseases, access to improved sources of sanitation and gender equality.

This may be attributed to a number of reasons. At the outset it may be mentioned that poverty is the most intimidating challenge, consequently each country is facing unique challenges while pursuing the MDGs/SDGs with subsequently variable results. The regional association of SAARC has its own limitations, and therefore cannot pursue the developmental agenda beyond political will of the national governments of SAARC countries. Though all South Asian countries have democratic forms of government, they are weak and corrupt and not accountable. The stability of the region is often at stake. India and Pakistan, the two major states of the region, are often at loggerheads and that imposes serious limitations on the smooth functioning of SAARC to pursue SDGs/MDGs. With regard to specific MDG 3 and SDGs pursuing women's development, it may be highlighted that apart from sorry state of gender equality in each South Asian country, monitoring the development goals from a gender perspective is often hindered by the restricted number of indicators and a shortage of quality data. Therefore, no South Asian country has made substantive progress on this goal. Funding of projects related to women's upliftment is another serious issue.

Finally, it may be concluded that building an improved social infrastructure base is a gradual process. Given the socio-economic similarities of South Asian countries, a systematic, comprehensive and coordinated regional mechanism of SAARC can help the region move towards attaining the MDGs/SDGs. Increased investment in schemes that benefit women may help to produce a healthier, better educated and literate workforce which may finally create a sound base of human resources and work towards reaching MDG 3. However, national-level determination, political will and sincere efforts and faith in SAARC are required to achieve the development goals and maximize benefits from regional cooperation.

Notes

1. Krishna Ahooja-Patel, *Women and Sustainable Development: An International Dimension*, New Delhi: Ashish Publishing House, 1995, p. 2. Also see, Dhanlaxmi Dash, *Women Environment and Health*, Delhi: Mangal Deep Publications, 2005, pp. 196–211.
2. See for details, Amartya Sen, *Development as Freedom*, Oxford: Oxford University Press, 1999.
3. *Human Development in South Asia 2000: The Gender Question*, Mahbub-ul-Haq, Human Development Centre, Karachi: Oxford University Press, 2000, p. 24.
4. Imtiaz Alam (ed.), *SAPNA: South Asian Studies*, Vol. XIII, SAARC, Free Media Foundation, 2006 p. 310.
5. Sudha Nayar, *Women's Empowerment in South Asia*, New Delhi: Navyug Publishers & Distributors, 2008, pp. 1–8.

6. United Nations Millennium Declaration, p. 20; UN Documents, UN General Assembly 2000, September 18, 2000.
7. *World Development Report 2012: Gender Equality and Development*, The International Bank for Reconstruction and Development, 2011, p. XX and p. 4.
8. Ibid., p. 4.
9. *Human Development in South Asia, 2000*, op. cit., p. 2.
10. Ibid., p. 3.
11. Ibid., p. 25.
12. Ibid., p. 104.
13. Prem R. Bhardwaj (ed.), *Gender Discrimination: Politics of Women Empowerment*, New Delhi: Anamika Publishers & Distributors, 2005, p. 71.
14. V. Kanesalingan (ed.), *Women in Development in South Asia*, New Delhi: Macmillan India Ltd., 1989, p. 46.
15. *Human Development in South Asia 2000*, op. cit., p. 136.
16. Sudhir Kumar Singh (ed.), *Handbook of SAARC: Sixteenth Summit and Beyond*, New Delhi: Pentagon Press, 2012, p. 26.
17. Ibid., p. 26.
18. Kathmandu Declaration, 2002, SAARC Secretariat.
19. Islamabad Declaration, January 6, 2004.
20. Colombo Declaration, August 2–3, 2008.
21. *UNIFEM*, http://www.unifem.org.in/2/17/2010, pp. 1–5.
22. See http://www.scwec.com/
23. *South Asia Development and Cooperation Report 2008*, RIS, Research and Information System for Development Countries, Oxford University Press, 2008, p. 139.
24. Shantayanan Devarajan and Ijaz Nabi, *Economic Growth in South Asia: Promising, Un-Equalizing ... Sustainable*? South Asia Region, World Bank, Washington DC, June 2006.
25. *Human Development in South Asia 2006*, op. cit., pp. 39–63.
26. See http://go.worldbank.org/ Global Monitoring Report, 2006.
27. Andrew Jackson and Anil Singh, *Measuring South Asia's Progress Towards the Millennium Development Goals*, South Asian Network for Agriculture & Social Development (SANSAD), 2009, p. 7.
28. Ibid.
29. *Human Development in South Asia 2007: A Ten-Year Review*, Mahbub-ul-Haq, Human Development Centre, Karachi: Oxford University Press, 2008, p. 36.

30. *Human Development in South Asia 2004: The Health Challenge*, Mahbub-ul-Haq, Human Development Centre, Karachi: Oxford University Press, 2005, p. 47.
31. Ibid.
32. For details, see *Human Development Report, Afghanistan*, Centre for Policy and Human Development, Kabul University, 2011 and also see, Anil K. Singh and Ram Gati Singh, *SAARC Development Goals: Commitments and Achievements*, South Asian Network for Social & Agricultural Development, New Delhi, 2009, p. 33.
33. Adult Literacy Rate, Gender Info, UN Data, United Nations Statistics Division, March 2008.
34. See note 32, p. 42.
35. Ibid., pp. 39–41.
36. *SAARC Development Goals, Mid-Term Review Report 2011, Bhutan*, Gross National Happiness Commission, November 2011, p. 45.
37. Ibid., p. 36.
38. Ibid., p. 30.
39. *SAARC Development Goals, Bangladesh Country Report 2011*, Planning Commission, Government of People's Republic of Bangladesh, p. 45.
40. Ibid., pp. 35–40.
41. Ibid., p. 29.
42. See for details, Anil K. Singh and Ram Gati Singh, op. cit., pp. 103–15.
43. *South Asia Development and Cooperation Report, 2008*, RIS, Oxford University Press, 2008, p. 144.
44. See for details, Anil K. Singh and Ram Gati Singh, op. cit., pp. 119–32.
45. Ibid., pp. 137–49.
46. *South Asia Development and Cooperation Report, RIS*, Research and Information System for Developing Countries, Oxford University Press, 2008, p. 147.
47. Ibid., p. 148.
48. Ibid., p. 149.

18

Millennium Development Goals and Women's Health in Rajasthan

MEETA SINGH

The turn of the century marked unparalleled progress for humankind the world over as also for India, where the quantum jumps ranged from space to medicine to economy to information networks and to an endless list of super achievements.

But the turn of the century also rang a warning bell that the fruits of this progress were unevenly distributed and this inequity was responsible for misery and indignity for millions across the world. In September 2000, representatives from 189 countries came together to adopt the Millennium Declaration of which India too was a signatory. This declaration is a commitment by the international community to address the world's development challenges of poverty and hunger, illiteracy, gender inequity and inequality, ill-health and disease, environmental degradation and global inequities in development. Through the Millennium Development Goals (MDGs), targets and indicators were set so that a blueprint was available to chart out the path of action to reach the desired results till 2015. The MDGs have thus become the universal framework for development and the means for developing countries and their partners to work together, towards a common end – making sure that human development reaches everyone, everywhere. If these goals are achieved, world poverty will be cut by half, tens of millions of lives will be saved, and billions more will have the opportunity to benefit from the global economy.[1]

The MDGs in a nutshell encompass various development issues which though separate are deeply intertwined. These goals are:

Goal 1. Eradicate extreme poverty and hunger
Goal 2. Achieve universal primary education
Goal 3. Promote gender equality and empower women
Goal 4. Reduce child mortality
Goal 5. Improve maternal health
Goal 6. Combat HIV/AIDS, Malaria, and other diseases
Goal 7. Ensure environmental sustainability
Goal 8. Develop a global partnership for development

However, considering that the deadline of 2015 is approaching fast, the progress on the MDGs has been far from satisfactory. To bolster the efforts and speed up action, the international community met again. In September 2010, at the global summit on the Millennium Development Goals (MDGs), United Nations Secretary-General Ban Ki-moon and heads of states and governments, along with the private sector, foundations, international organizations, civil society and research organizations, kicked off a concerted world-wide effort to save the lives of more than 16 million women and children. Since the initiation of the MDGs in 2000, several new targets were added and indicators designed to provide added impetus to achieve the goals.

In case of MDG 5, the scope of the targets has been expanded since 2007. Target 5A, thus, aims to reduce by three quarters the maternal mortality ratio, while the additional target 5B is set to achieve universal access to reproductive health by 2015. The original indicators are the maternal mortality ratio and proportion of births attended by skilled health personnel, while the added indicators include contraceptive prevalence rate, adolescent birth rate, antenatal care coverage (at least one visit and at least four visits during the entire pregnancy) and unmet need for family planning. This scope is also narrow because maternal health needs to be more comprehensive and cannot be limited to the targets 5A and 5B. Maternal health must encompass the life-cycle approach, extending from womb to tomb and must include physical, mental and social well-being and not merely absence of disease. It has to be looked at as a continuum, ranging from nutritional and reproductive and sexual literacy needs of adolescents and women and men to post-partum care. Safe and effective contraception, access to safe abortions and freedom from violence are as much a part of maternal health as safe deliveries, whether in institutions or within homes.[2]

India being a signatory to the Millennium Declaration is committed to achieving the MDGs. The expectations and hope held out at the beginning of the century is dampened by the slow and somewhat tardy movement that belies the MDG promise. Towards the realization of MDG 5, the Government of India has launched several programmes intended at improving maternal and child health, namely, National Rural Health Mission (NRHM), National Urban Health Mission (NUHM), Reproductive and Child Health (RCH) Programme and the Integrated Child Development Scheme (ICDS). The National Population Policy (2000) and the National Health Policy (2002) also attempt to capture the essence of the MDGs.[3]

Though MDG 5 is linked in one way or another to all the MDGs (especially MDG 1, 3 and 4), it is also the most off track. Attainment of the MDGs portends to be a humongous task for governments and health systems. Globally, over half a million women die every year during pregnancy or childbirth, and over 90 per cent of these largely preventable deaths occur in developing countries. India's maternal mortality ratio (maternal mortality ratio is defined as the number of maternal deaths per 100,000 live births) stands at 450 per 100,000 live births, against 540 in 1998–1999. The figures are way behind India's Millennium Development Goals, which call for a reduction to 109 by 2015, according to UNICEF. The link between the MDGs and accountability is nowhere clearer than here: governments that answer to women would invest in preventing these deaths.[4]

For an emerging global economic power with unprecedented medical progress, India continues to have unacceptably high maternal mortality levels. Of every 70 Indian girls who reach reproductive age, one will eventually die because of pregnancy, childbirth, or unsafe abortion, compared to one in 7,300 in the developed world. More will suffer preventable injuries, infections and disabilities, often serious and lasting a lifetime, due to failures in maternal care.

'Destiny' or 'fate' brought this upon them, say many of the families that experience maternal deaths, unaware that as many as three in four might be prevented if all women and girls had access to appropriate health care. In fact, after more than a decade of programming for reproductive and child health with few results, the Indian government acknowledged the problem and in 2005 took steps under its flagship National Rural Health Mission (NRHM) to improve public health systems and reduce maternal mortality in particular. Recent data suggests it is having some success: all-India figures show a decline in maternal deaths.

This decline, however, is small in relation to the scope of the problem, and camouflages inter and intra-state disparities. Some states like Haryana and Punjab actually showed an increase in maternal mortality. Significant disparities based on income, caste, place of residence and other arbitrary factors persist even within every state, including those that appear to be improving access to care for pregnant women and mothers.

Poor maternal health is far too prevalent in many communities, particularly marginalized Dalits (so-called 'untouchables'), other lower castes, and tribal populations. These inequalities, particularly gender inequality, have hampered India's march towards the MDGs.[5]

Though there have been small gains by way of improvement in adult sex ratio and increase in female life expectancy of women in India, there is little cause for joy. One out of every 140 women in the country runs the risk of dying during childbirth. An average Indian woman's life expectancy is only 66 years, which is among the lowest in the world. Less than half (49%) of women in the country use some form of modern contraceptives. Further, gender disparity is reflected in the Census of India 2011 data of the country's child sex ratio, which shows a decline from 927 girls to 1,000 boys in the 0–6 year age group in 2001 to just 914 girls in the year 2011.[6]

Rajasthan: An Overview

Rajasthan is one of the largest states of India, occupying 10.41 per cent of the country's area. It is home to 5.5 per cent of India's population. It comprises 33 districts, 237 blocks and nearly 43,000 villages. Population of Rajasthan as per 2011 Census is 6.86 crore/68.6 million which is much higher than 2001 Census, which recorded 5,65,07,188 (5.65 crore/56.5 million). Child sex ratio at 883 in the state is below the national average of 914. Rajasthan ranks 5th among those states with lowest child sex ratio (Haryana 830, Punjab 846, Delhi 866, Chandigarh 867, Rajasthan and Maharashtra 883). Even, the adult sex ratio in Rajasthan at 926 is below the national average of 940, a rise by seven points since 2001 to record the highest figures in the country since 1971. The rising population in the state is also reflected in the population density, which now stands at 201 persons per sq km against figures of 165 and 129 in 2001 and 1991, respectively. On the significant side, Rajasthan has also shown an improvement in the female literacy rate that in 2011 stands at 52.66 against that of 43.9 in 2001. But even this figure stands way below the national average of 65.46. In fact, this is the lowest female literacy rate in the country and is closely followed by Bihar at 53.33.[7] Approximately 66 per cent of its population is engaged in agriculture and 77 per cent population resides in rural areas. And, 26 per cent of the state's rural population lives below the poverty line.[8]

Social Dimensions of Maternal Health

Maternal health is a complex issue and even though it may seem, on the surface, an area of health dealing with women in the child-bearing age group of 15 to 49 years of age, but a deeper analysis reveals that a woman's health throughout her life-cycle has a direct bearing on the 'maternal' phase of her life. Gender discrimination in India, and especially so in the feudal state of Rajasthan, puts the female in a position of disadvantage even before she is born.

For millennia, among Indian parents, there has existed a deeply internalized preference for sons, and it cuts across religious/caste divisions, economic segments, rural/urban divides and education levels.

In contrast, a daughter is seen as an economic liability due to the expense of her dowry and wedding. Though the practice of dowry is officially prohibited by a 1961 law, it continues nevertheless. A daughter is also seen as a social liability since she needs to be protected and married off into a family of equal or higher social status, in whose house she will live. According to one idiom, raising a girl child is like 'watering another man's garden'. The birth of a girl child is more an occasion of lamentation than joy.[9]

As the girl child grows older, she faces discrimination in terms of nutrition, health care, mobility, opportunities for education and employment. As she attains puberty, she faces further stumbling blocks in the form of myths associated with menstruation, in attaining her full potential. Low self-esteem, poor nutritional status, anaemia, low levels of literacy and awareness, absence of skills to enable her to find gainful employment coupled with early marriage, early and frequent child-bearing, and inability to negotiate contraception choices with her partner combine together to result in compromised maternal health status. Pressure to bear sons often results in sex selection followed by repeated sex-selective abortions if the foetus is female. This aggravates already existing anaemia and lowers immunity, thus increasing the susceptibility to infections, which may lead to lifelong morbidity in the form of low backache, vaginal discharge and lower abdominal discomfort and pain.

Economic theory of supply and demand leads us to believe that if women are fewer in number than men, this scarcity will enhance their status, as they will be much sought after by men who want to marry and have children. However, this is far from the truth. A study from Haryana, a state with the second lowest sex ratio, illustrates that the scarcity of women, instead of increasing their value, has led to a manifold increase in violence against them.

Haryana's extremely low sex ratio (830 in 2011 Census of India) has made it very difficult for men to find brides locally. But this has in no way produced any decrease in dowry demands or enhancement of the status of local women. Rather, it has led to the buying, selling and reselling of women; the trafficking, abduction and sexual exploitation of women; marriage at much younger ages; and implementation of harsh measures to keep women under male control. Despite their scarcity, Haryana's women are subjected to more atrocities, rapes, forced marriages, prostitution, polyandry and social turmoil than in past decades.[10]

Socio-cultural Beliefs and Health Implications

Certain traditions and cultural beliefs also contribute to negative outcomes of pregnancy, like aggravating already existing anaemia by refusing to take Iron Folic Acid (IFA) tablets. The iron tablets are held responsible for imparting dark complexion to the child. It is so assumed because the tablets are black in colour and the stools dark following ingestion of iron tablets – kaali goli se chhora kala paida hoga (black pill will give a dark complexion to newborn). The Indian society places great premium on fair skin and the innocuous iron tablet is blamed for dusky, dark skin colour that the unborn foetus may acquire. According to National Family Health Survey 2005–06, one in every two girls and women between the ages of 15–49 years are anaemic in Rajasthan.[11] Thus, iron supplementation for pregnant mothers is a key element of ante natal care. Iron deficiency anaemia is the most common micro-nutrient deficiency in the world and a major threat to safe motherhood and to the health and survival of the foetus. It contributes to low birth weight of the newborn, decreased resistance to infection and increased fatigability in the pregnant woman. The provision of Iron Folic Acid tablets to pregnant women to prevent nutritional anaemia forms an integral part of the safe motherhood services offered as part of the Reproductive Child Health Programme. The medical recommendation dictates the consumption of 100 IFA tablets during pregnancy. This simple step to ensure a healthy mother and baby is not followed because of a local, cultural myth. This fact underscores the need for awareness campaigns to counter the misconceptions.

In some rural areas, women are encouraged to consume smaller meals so that the foetus is small and the delivery is relatively easier. In reality, nutritional deficiencies in women are often exacerbated during pregnancy because of the additional nutritional requirements of foetal growth. Instead of balanced, wholesome and nutritious diet in appropriate quantity, when the dietary needs are not met the outcome of the pregnancy is bound to be unfavourable in the form of low birth weight babies who are more likely to die in infancy.

In some families, dairy products like butter, milk, curds, etc., which are white in colour are forbidden to the pregnant woman as it is believed that these foods get deposited on the body surface of the foetus. These deposits are thought of as a 'dirty' substance that must be scrubbed off and removed from the skin of the newborn soon after birth.

In medical parlance, this white cheesy material is called Vernix and serves several purposes, including moisturizing the infant's skin and facilitating passage through the birth canal. It also serves to conserve heat and protect the delicate newborn skin from environmental stress. Vernix is composed of sebum (the oil of the skin) and cells that have sloughed off the foetus' skin and is a perfectly normal phenomenon. It peels off on its own in a few days' time and must not be scrubbed off the baby's skin. On the contrary, the newborn must be kept warm after delivery and not bathed immediately after birth as has been the common practice in the past.[12]

It is important also that the newborn not be administered honey or *ghutti* (a proprietary concoction of jaggery and some herbs traditionally given to newborn babies). The baby must be put to the mother's breast as soon as possible to suckle on the colostrum and establish successful breastfeeding. Colostrum is the first milk the breasts produce in the early days of breastfeeding. This special milk is low in fat, and high in carbohydrates, protein, and antibodies to help keep the newborn baby healthy. It is extremely easy to digest, and is therefore the perfect first food. It is low in volume but high in concentrated nutrition for the newborn. Colostrum has a laxative effect on the baby, and helps in passing early stools, which aids in the excretion of excess bilirubin and helps prevent jaundice.

The advantage of putting the newborn to breast helps the initiation of the breast-feeding cycle. While it provides high-quality nutrition to the newborn, it also prevents engorgement of milk in the mother's breasts, a painful condition that may develop into a breast abscess and need surgical intervention. Customarily, this colostrum is often expressed and removed as 'dirty milk' and the newborn deprived of its first natural vaccine. Modern science advocates exclusive breastfeeding till six months of age. This practice of exclusive breastfeeding helps release hormones that relax the mother and make her feel more nurturing toward her baby.[13]

Breastfeeding soon after giving birth increases the mother's oxytocin levels, making her uterus contract more quickly and reducing post partum bleeding.[14] For breastfeeding women, long-term health benefits include less risk of breast and ovarian cancer and 23 per cent lower risk of coronary heart disease.[15]

Thus, local cultural practices can have a direct bearing on the pre and post partum health of the mother. Changing age-old customs and behaviour need to be instituted in a manner that is culturally acceptable, based on scientific evidence and sensitively delivered. Challenging mindsets and attitudes translates into huge efforts in terms of strategies and time to translate into actual behavioural and attitudinal change among communities.

The Need for Action

The Indian Constitution grants its citizens a life of dignity, complete well-being, all-round development, prosperity and freedom. Under this promise, it is the responsibility of the state that maternal health is protected and ensured as a human right. Maternal death is a gross violation of human rights. The government would do well to invest in women to produce far-reaching economic and social benefits. Serious political and administrative will is required to achieve the MDG 5.

In September 2010, the United Nations launched the 'Global Strategy for Women's and Children's Health'. The special event during the MDG Summit was called 'Every Woman, Every Child' and carried in its name an important message: that every woman, whether she lives in a wealthy urban centre or remote village, should have access to the basic health services she needs; and that every child has the right to a healthy future. This is a matter of fundamental equity.

'The Global Strategy marks a distinct departure from business as usual. Previous efforts have generated progress but tended at times towards the piecemeal. The Global Strategy is truly comprehensive: it addresses the full range of issues that affect the health of women and children; brings all the key actors together under one umbrella; and it integrates what they are doing – their objectives and programmes – into one coherent approach.'[16]

At the UN MGD summit, India's Health Minister also made lofty claims and promises. 'India launched a community-based strategy for revitalizing primary health-care to provide universal access to basic health services. This process is being implemented under the National Rural Health Mission and is essentially focused on providing quality care under the Reproductive and Child Health Programme. Almost US $3.5 billion are being spent on these efforts annually. Based on evidence, 235 out of 600 districts have now been identified for a more focused approach to achieve Millennium Development Goals 4, 5 and 6. Though these districts account for 35 per cent of the population, they also account for nearly 70 per cent of maternal and infant mortality, high levels of fertility and high levels of morbidity and mortality on account of infectious diseases. Under this approach, facilities are being strengthened for providing excellent quality of care alongside strategies for demand generation through a well-structured conditional cash transfer scheme.

It is our belief that the interventions mentioned above would enable us to achieve our goals within the given time-frame. India remains committed to ensuring the effective use of domestic and donor aid in this regard and, as a responsible stakeholder of the global community, continuing to assist in extending technical advice to countries in greater need. India pledges its commitment to achieve the MDG health goals within the time frame of 2015.

Though this commitment is well made, the ground realities tell a different story. The promise of quality of care is far from being kept. Indeed more funds have been invested into health-care by the Indian nation than ever before, but sufficient human resource is lacking and optimum utilization of available health care personnel and facilities is riddled with unequal distribution of doctors and paramedics, posts lying vacant, emergency obstetric services not in place and paucity of skills in considerable proportion of the workforce available in rural areas. This concern is raising uncomfortable questions regarding the training imparted to the medical, nursing and paramedical workforce. There is also a massive shortage of hospital beds (with a world average of 2.6 hospital beds per 1,000 people, India stands at 1.1 hospital beds per 1,000). As a result, our hospitals are overcrowded beyond capacity and long waiting periods in the Outpatient centres and Casualty Departments are the norm.[17]

Cost of health care is a leading cause of rural impoverishment.[18] India's conditional cash transfer scheme, the Janani Suraksha Yojana (JSY), is supposed to address this issue by providing cash to support costs related to institutional deliveries. Of the 20,032 deliveries recorded in 2008 in the survey, roughly one in four families (5,042 deliveries) reported that they needed to borrow money or sell property or jewellery to pay for the associated costs. For women who had an institutional delivery, this proportion rises to almost a third (3,071 of 10,073). Even worse, of the 2,438 women who received JSY and had their last institutional delivery in 2008, 912 (37%) said they had to sell their property or jewellery. More than half of these women (53%) belonged to the two lower wealth quintiles (40%), which roughly correspond to the poverty level in the country. Since JSY promotes more institutional deliveries without really covering the full costs, the programme might in fact be exacerbating the indebtedness of women in poverty, rather than helping.[19]

Maternal health is a function of both poverty eradication and focused food and nutrition security of all women in the reproductive age, including in particular the pregnant and nursing women.

The India Country Report 2009 states that the estimate of maternal mortality ratio (MMR) quoted is drawn from Sample Registration System (SRS)-based studies. The estimates quoted state that the national MMR level has come down from 398 in 1997–98 to 254 in 2004–06, a 36 per cent decline over 6 years, compared to a 25 per cent decline in the preceding 8 years from 1990–1997. Therefore, India would reach an MMR of 135 in 2015, falling short of the target of 109 by 26 points. According to the UNICEF's 'State of the World Children 2009', the MMR for the year 2005 for India was 450. A clear comparative study between those two figures of the SRS and UNICEF is needed to see where the similarities and differences lie and what really is the correct MMR for India.[20]

The India Country Report 2009 also does not refer to the failure of distribution of Vitamin A and IFA tablets to pregnant mothers in the context of safe motherhood. Distribution and intake of Vitamin A and IFA tablets have serious implications for safe pregnancy and constitute a care that far precedes the presence of trained or skilled personnel at delivery. The ICDS programme in India is specifically designed for this but studies show serious gaps leading to unacceptably high levels of anaemia threatening mortality for the mother. Distribution of Vitamin A and IFA tablets to pregnant mothers and ensuring their intake would be an important measure in reduction of MMR and needs to be monitored as an indicator.[21]

The Scenario in Rajasthan

Maternal Mortality Ratio

The women in Rajasthan are much more vulnerable to maternal mortality in comparison to the women of other states. According to experts, maternal mortality ratio (MMR) in Rajasthan is eight times higher than other states due to complications during pregnancy period. The risk of mortality caused by complications during delivery is twice as high in Rajasthan as compared to other states. With a maternal mortality rate of 388 per 1,00,000 live births, Rajasthan has the third highest MMR in the country. Severe nutritional deficiency anaemia and pre and post-natal health complications are cited as the main challenges to check MMR. Owing to lack of proper and timely medical facilities, one woman dies every five minutes due to pregnancy-related causes.[22] Nearly 60 per cent of these mothers die during the post partum period. Haemorrhage causes 37 per cent of all maternal deaths followed by sepsis (11%), abortion (10%) and obstructed labour and hypertensive disorder (9%).[23]

Proportion of Births Attended by Skilled Health Personnel

Delivery by a skilled birth attendant is another important indicator, which has a direct impact on maternal mortality. The fourth common review mission of NRHM Rajasthan in February 2011 states that under the JSY, institutional deliveries have increased from 28 per cent to 70 per cent.[24]

Since 1992–93, the country has shown progress in improving the availability of skilled health personnel (doctors, nurses or midwives) to assist in deliveries. Just over half (53%) of the women in India are assisted by trained health workers while giving birth to a child.[25] In Rajasthan, till 2005–06, more than 70 per cent births were taking place at home.[26]

Ante-natal Care

As per the fourth common review mission of NRHM Rajasthan, 73 per cent women who gave birth in the five years preceding the survey, received ante-natal care from a health professional (34% from a doctor, and 39% from an Auxiliary Nurse Midwife/Lady Health Visitor/nurse/midwife or other health personnel) for their last birth. One-quarter of the women did not receive any ante-natal care.

In urban areas, 90 per cent of women received ante-natal care from a health professional, compared to 69 per cent of rural women. Despite substantial improvement in the coverage of ante-natal care for mothers, only 4 in 10 women in Rajasthan received at least three ante-natal care visits for their last birth in the past five years.[27]

Adolescent Birth Rate

In Rajasthan, the average age of marriage is 17.2 years.[28] Although child marriages are officially discouraged through compulsory education for girls and despite massive awareness campaigns and laws that make the minimum age of marriage 18 for girls and 21 for boys, girls are married at an earlier age, thus jeopardizing their opportunities for education and participation in the workforce. In addition, early marriages contribute to earlier sexual experiences, earlier childbirth and higher possibilities of maternal mortality. Adolescent birth rate (per 1,000 women aged 15–19 years) in Rajasthan was calculated at 98 births. Approximately 16 per cent of women aged 15–19 years began childbearing in Rajasthan.[29]

Contraceptive Prevalence Rate and Unmet Need of Family Planning

Despite the 15 per cent increase in the current contraceptive use since NFHS 1 in Rajasthan, only 47 per cent women in Rajasthan reported contraceptive usage during NFHS 3. The contraceptive prevalence rate (any method) was calculated at 66 per cent in urban areas and only 41 per cent in rural areas. With an increase in contraceptive use, the unmet need has declined but still remains high at 15 per cent.[30]

What Needs to be Done?

Covered below are some of the gaps that need to be bridged to bring about substantial improvement to women's health in Rajasthan. However, this is in no way exhaustive as health issues cover a much larger plethora of areas that need to be addressed.

Training Needs

The fourth common review mission of NRHM Rajasthan 2010 report acknowledges that quality training of all categories of personnel, and institutions is urgently needed at the districts and is an important area of health sector reform that requires immediate action. This training must include capacity-building in skills as well as sensitization and attitudinal change towards the social determinants of health like gender, equity and equality.

Human Resource

Although within the NRHM process, Rajasthan has initiated increase of human resources for health, specifically in recruitment of accredited social and health activists (ASHAs); the state continues to report a significant gap between required and posted health functionaries at all levels. This is more so in the case of rural medical officers, junior and senior specialists, nurses, Auxiliary Nurse Midwives and laboratory technicians. There are 851 vacancies for junior and senior specialists, 225 for senior medical officers, 763 for medical officers and 424 for rural medical officers.

Additionally, across the state, 15 posts for the deputy chief medical officer remain unfilled. This situation reflects that the state is yet unable to fulfil its role in providing quality health services to majority of people as it is expected to under the NRHM. Similarly, there is a shortage of more than 2,000 nurses, 1,700 Auxiliary Nurse Midwives, 4,57 laboratory technicians and 2,880 other staff. The state is trying to address this key challenge through ad hoc and contractual appointments.[31] The gap in numbers of health-care providers appropriately positioned is imperative to improve the lagging indicators.

Proper Implementation of Innovative Schemes

Supplementary initiatives have also been undertaken by the Government of Rajasthan and include schemes[32] that provide dietary support, facilitate transport and provide additional personnel like the Yashoda (community worker trained in basic neo and post-natal care) to improve the quality of period of stay in the health-care facility for mother and baby after the delivery. Yashoda helps initiate post partum care (breastfeeding; weight of the baby; oral polio vaccine; BCG vaccine against tuberculosis and home-based care). The Yashoda scheme thus provides an additional female support worker to assist the newly-delivered baby and mother. Some of the other schemes include the BPL First Delivery Desi Ghee Scheme, where clarified butter is provided to women living below poverty line. This is given with the view to nurse the women back to health in keeping with the local tradition of serving clarified butter to women after delivery during the post partum period. The Kalewa Scheme is yet another scheme that serves hot nutritious meal to all women in the post partum period to encourage them to stay at the health-care facility for at least 48 hours after delivery. These schemes are innovative and if implemented properly and sensitively, can go a long way to repose confidence regarding quality care linked to institutional delivery.

Additional Efforts

The state has also made specific interventions[33] that include Maternal Death Audit in all districts, Mobile Medical Units at the block level, referral transport provision at block level, drugs and supplies for maternal health, recruiting and training of additional Auxiliary Nurse Midwives, hiring of specialists at First Referral Unit (FRU) @ ₹ 60,000 (1,400 USD approx) per month, establishment of a midwifery resource centre and operationalizing of Emergency Ambulance Services (ambulances bearing the number 108 available for transport of patients from residence to the health-care facility offered at no cost).

In addition, community mobilization through Village Health and Sanitation Committees and involvement of the Panchayati Raj (locally elected governance) needs to be strengthened. Periodic and constant capacity-building through adult pedagogy would lead to ownership and sustainability of health issues by the community.

Despite these measures, the implementation of the schemes and programmes leaves a lot to be desired. Paucity of trained human resource, corruption, that prevents the benefits from reaching to the designated beneficiaries, insensitive and rude behaviour by health-care personnel, especially in the labour rooms, systemic flaws in management, unhygienic conditions, lack of privacy and confidentiality, and overcrowding in hospitals are stark reminders of the huge gaps that prevent expected improvement in the maternal health scenario of the state.

A case in point is the death of 17 women due to pregnancy-related causes in a tertiary government hospital in Jodhpur in the short span of a little more than two months[34] (outlookindia.com May 28, 2011). Though contaminated intravenous fluid is blamed as the culprit, the cause of the maternal deaths has not been conclusively established so far. Such instances of medical negligence lead to loss of faith in health systems and could prove a serious blow to the ambitious institutional delivery drive in the state under the JSY. Safety concerns must be addressed in the case of all institutional deliveries if the scheme is to attain the desired outcome. Institutional deliveries should essentially mean safe deliveries for JSY to be a successful scheme.

Considering that a great majority of maternal and newborn deaths can be prevented through simple cost-effective methods, better health services, community involvement and male participation, improving the status of maternal health is possible through a well-planned, inclusive and systemic strategy. Maternal health-care must be available, accessible, sensitive and of high quality to actually translate into achieving MDG 5. If not, it is a violation of a woman's right to life, health, equality and non-discrimination and will result in MDG 5 being wide off the mark.

Action Plan

While some of the strategies suggested are already in place, cautious monitoring of the quality of services and internal and external appraisal systems are needed to ensure transparency, accountability and efficiency.[35] Future strategies[36] must include focus on the following key areas:

1. Increase investments in maternal and newborn health – people can access health services without fear of out of pocket expenditure. Central to the corrections is a need to abolish user fees, as well as decrease and phase out all out of pocket expenditure in the public health care facilities.
2. Strengthen health systems – NRHM can improve on its designs to achieve the objectives of providing free, non-discriminatory, universal access to comprehensive and quality health services to all.
3. Expand the purview of maternity health – there is need to recognize women not only as mothers but as individuals with rights and entitlements and with differing needs as per age and their social environment. Therefore, there is need for programmes to address women's health beyond the narrow focus of maternal health, which should include issues of violence, gender discrimination, adolescents, single women, aged women along with mental health and nutrition.
4. Improve inter-sectoral co-ordination – there is a need to reinforce the importance of social determinants that have implications for health status and equity. This needs greater inter-sectoral coordination between the health department and related sectors. Housing, urban health, food security, safe water, health planning for disability and mental health are public health issues that need urgent attention.
5. Strengthen maternal, newborn and reproductive health through motivated, skilled human resource and well-equipped health-care facilities. Government has to develop adequate qualified health-care personnel at different levels by creating enough publicly financed professional and technical educational institutions to produce such human resources in health as are needed.
6. There is need for recognition and role-clarity of non-doctor health professionals. There should be better representation of the nursing cadre in the directorate and role in decision-making process and senior management. Nursing councils need to be strengthened. Similarly, all other non-doctor health professionals should have more roles in the decision-making process and senior management. There should be better avenues of skill upgradation of non-doctor health professionals as well as scope for lateral entry and promotion to senior posts.
7. Ensure that information and services are available, accessible, sensitive and respectful to women.
8. A system of community monitoring also needs to be in place to encourage community involvement and service uptake towards a client-centred, demand-driven approach to ensure quality care.

9. Community involvement to educate and sensitize boys and men on gender and discrimination issues, explain the role of the father in determining sex of the child so that women are not held responsible and blamed for giving birth to daughters, get over son preference and appreciate and understand the value of the girl child, get rid of harmful cultural taboos, support single women and promote life-skill education among adolescents. NGO participation can go a long way in strengthening the ability of civil society and community groups to advocate for improved implementation of the Protection of Women Against Domestic Violence Act (PWDVA) 2005, the Preconception and Prenatal Diagnostic Techniques (Prevention of Sex Selection) Act (PCPNDT) 1994, and the Prohibition of Child Marriage Act (PCM) 2006. This would help in combatting sex-selection, child marriage and violence against women – social evils that directly impact women's health. The benefits of these efforts will mean healthier, better educated women who are more productive economically, and able to take better care of their children. Targeted investments in maternal, newborn, and reproductive health make women and newborns healthier, and can have a dramatic, lasting impact on the economic and social fabric.

When a woman dies or becomes ill, her children are much more likely to leave school, to suffer from poor health, and even to die themselves. Her production and income are lost both to her family and to her community.

While safe childbirth and post-natal care saves lives and reduces maternal mortality, planned childbirth offers greater choices to couples so that they can enjoy fulfilling sexual relationships without fear of pregnancy and are able to exercise their reproductive right to choose if, when, how many and at what interval they want to have children.

To speed up the march to attain the MDGs, three core strategies need to be followed. These are essential for improving vital health services for mothers and their newborns and include:

1. Access to family planning – counselling, services, supplies.
2. Access to quality care for pregnancy and childbirth – ante-natal care, skilled attendance at birth, including emergency obstetric and neo-natal care, immediate post-natal care for mothers and newborns.
3. Access to safe abortion services – so that all women can access the right to safe abortion services under the Medical Termination of Pregnancy Act, 1994.

Ensuring that these three strategies are in place will translate into sound investment as promoting maternal and newborn health is cost-effective. Better maternal health services mean other services also improve (e.g., accident and emergency and blood transfusion facilities).

Providing efficient family planning services reduces the rate of unintended pregnancies, which leads to fewer unsafe abortions.

If we achieve MDG 5, it will directly support other MDGs by empowering women, reducing child mortality, enabling the fight against HIV and helping to reduce poverty and promoting universal primary education. Happy and healthy mothers augur well for their children, families, societies, nations and indeed, the world.

Notes

1. *The Millennium Development Goals Report 2007*, United Nations, www.un.org/millenniumgoals/pdf/mdg2007.pdf
2. D. Goel and S.D. Gupta, *Millennium Development Goals in Rajasthan: A Review*, March 2010.
3. *Millennium Development Goals in India 2010: A Civil Society Report*, Wada Na Todo Abhiyan, September 2010.
4. www.unifem.org/progress/2008/mdgsGender5.html
5. No Tally of the Anguish-Accountability in Maternal Health Care in India, Human Rights Watch, October 2009.
6. *Census of India* 2011 – provisional report.
7. *Census of India* 2011 – provisional report.
8. *Planning Commission of India Report 2011.*
9. M. Singh and V. Mohan, 'Rise of Sex Selection in India', *Democracy at Large*, Vol. 2, No. 1, 2005.
10. M. Rathi, 'Female Foeticide: Haryana's Experience', *People's Democracy*, Vol. 29, No. 29, July 20, 2005.
11. *The Hindu*, April 20, 2010.
12. MedicineNet.com – www.medterms.com/script/main/art.asp? articlekey = 9402.
13. P. Stuart-Macadam and K. Dettwyler, *Breastfeeding: Biocultural Perspectives*, New York: Aldine de Gruyter, 1995, p. 131.
14. S. Chua, S. Arulkumaran, I. Lim, N. Selamat and S. Ratnam, 'Influence of Breastfeeding and Nipple Stimulation on Postpartum Uterine Activity', *Br J Obstet Gynaecol*, Vol. 101, No. 9, 1994: 804–5.
15. S. Ip, M. Chung, G. Raman et al., 'Breastfeeding and Maternal and Infant Health Outcomes in Developed Countries', *Evid Rep Technol Assess* (Full Rep), Vol. 153, 2007: 1–186.
16. United Nations MDG Summit 2010 – press release.
17. *Indian Express*, May 27, 2011.

18. S. Bonu, I. Bhushan, M. Rani and I. Anderson, 'Incidence and Correlates of 'Catastrophic' Maternal Health Care Expenditure in India', *Health Policy Plan*, Vol. 24, No. 6, 2009: 445–56.
19. A. Das, Deepa Rao and A. Hagopian, 'India's Janani Suraksha Yojana: Further Review Needed', *The Lancet*, Vol. 377, Issue 9762, January 22, 2011, pp. 295–96.
20. *Millennium Development Goals in India 2010*, op. cit.
21. Ibid.
22. N. Bhowmick, 'India Takes Step Forward in Tackling Maternal Health', www.guardian.co.uk/global February 3, 2011.
23. Sample Registration System, Ministry of Health and Family Welfare, Government of India, 2009.
24. Coverage Evaluation Survey (CES) 2010.
25. Save the Children's 'State of the World's Mothers 2011' report.
26. International Institute for Population Studies, National Family Health Survey (NFHS-3), 2005–2006, Mumbai.
27. Ministry of Health and Family Welfare, Fourth Common Review Mission, Rajasthan: MOHFW, 2010.
28. International Institute for Population Studies, National Family Health Survey (NFHS-3), 2005–2006, Mumbai.
29. Ibid.
30. Ibid.
31. Ministry of Health and Family Welfare, Fourth Common Review Mission, Rajasthan: MOHFW, 2010.
32. Ibid.
33. Ibid.
34. Outlookindia.com May 28, 2011.
35. Focus on 5. Women's Health and the MDGs. Author: Women Deliver. No. of pages: 22. Publication date: 2009.
36. Deliberations during the first Public Health Resource Network, National Convention, 30 April–1 May, 2001.

19

Globalization, MDGs and Women

Political Dimensions and Implications

NAVNEET KUMAR VERMA

Today's world is governed by the spirit of 'globalization', 'privatization', 'liberalization' and the concept of 'global village'. The term 'globalization' refers to a set of processes that increasingly create an environment for free flow of international finance and information leading to an integrated world economy. It emerged post-1980s and was hailed as a new ideological movement capable of tackling social, economic, political, administrative, environmental and technological problems of humanity at the global level. As the movement was backed by US and international aid agencies, so it was thrust on small and large governments with a great force, leaving them with no option but to follow. It centred on '... application of the ideas and institutions of the market economy to the world as a whole'.[1] Consequently, the impact of globalization was sure on every aspect of human life at the global level. Various social, political, economic, environmental and cultural institutions were found to be at receiving end of this globalization trend. The concept of free flow of international finance and world-wide access to information has led to the weakening importance of national territorial boundaries. Consequently, the institution of nation-state came under attack. Furthermore, the concept of globalization is also projected as the only way of development. Making a prophetic statement about globalization as the only way of development precludes any other possibility of alternative, which further makes it a contested concept. Here, a distinction is necessary between a natural outcome of evolution of human social, political and economic institutions as a result of development in technology and a global political project to nurture the interests of large governments and international corporate finance.[2]

Earlier the development of people and nation was closely linked with more and more industrialization through national economic management, but the globalization project seeks development through global economic management by powerful governments, transnational corporations and international multilateral institutions like the International Monetary Fund (IMF), the World Bank (WB) and the World Trade Organization (WTO). Now, the primary vehicle for development was linked to free circulation of goods, services and capital. However, the term 'globalization' lacks a precise definition but the term being essentially economic in character is an agreed fact. According to McMichael[3], certain strands of globalization include:

1. An emerging consensus among the policy-makers favouring market-based rather than state-managed development strategies
2. Centralized management of global market by G-7 states,
3. Implementation of (global management) rules by multilateral agencies: The World Bank, International Monetary Fund (IMF), World Trade Organization (WTO),
4. Concentration of market power in the hands of transnational banks; and
5. Subordination of the former second and third world states to (G-7) global forces.

Political Aspects

Thus, the increasing importance of 'market' over 'politics' is suggestive of reordering of priorities by different countries. In this sense, the globalization concept is not only a description of today's world but a political and ideological movement powerful enough to affect all the nations. It was projected that '... the globalization market relationships would be the guarantee of peace in the world'.[4] This 'Brownean movement' is replete with good and bad ideas. Undoubtedly, it's opening up possibilities and increasing interdependencies between the nations. The process of increasing interdependencies and transnational linkages '... implies a diminishing importance of national borders and the strengthening of identities that stretch beyond those rooted in a particular country or region'.[5] It is aimed towards removing every barrier put up by the nation-state. And national identity is to give way to global identity. The global agenda of transnational corporations (TNCs) is to make the world an open play-field for them. The supporters of globalization aim to create a global village with one economy. They wish to replace an earlier world system of Cold War period which was divided on the cultural, political and economic lines with a new world system of one culture, one polity and one economy. The powerful agents to execute the desires of transnational corporations are available in the name of Bretton Woods institutions IMF, World Bank and regional development banks. These institutions succeeded in imposing a whole new regime of 'General Agreements on Trade and Tariffs (GATT), which was expanded and institutionalized into the World Trade Organization (WTO) in 1995'[6], the Agreement on Trade-related Aspects of Intellectual Property Rights (TRIPS), and the Agreement on Trade-related Investment Measures (TRIMS) with an intention to bind present and future governments of rich and poor countries alike '... to certain predetermined institutional forms and policies. They confer privileged rights of citizenship on corporate capital, while constraining the power of the nation-state and the democratic rights of its citizens'.[7] This agenda has enforced the poor nations competing with the rich nations on unequal terms. It has led to shrinkage of development space for developing countries as they are forced to follow the policies written into multilateral agreements. In a detailed analysis of TRIPS agreement, it was pointed out that patent holders (developed) countries, especially US and EU, use TRIPS agreement as a starting point for any discussion with patent using (developing) countries. The agreement '... covers protection of trademarks, copyrights, industrial designs, data secrets, and patents'.[8] The developed countries ask for tighter implementation of intellectual property rules, forcing the developing countries to fetch out more money for use of patents. In the context of poor economy, a country is pressured to cut back expenditure on development sectors and public provisions for citizens. Non-compliance is again met with threat of withdrawing aid as well as supporting the rival country of geopolitical importance. Similarly, the Agreement on Trade-related Investment Measures (TRIMS) purports to 'avoid trade and investment distortions' and any attempt by developing country to impose 'performance requirements' on foreign firms in relation to local content, export requirements and mandatory purchase of goods by public agencies from local suppliers are categorized as distortions. The agreement seeks to put a ban on all these kinds of regulations. Undoubtedly, the agreement is in favour of easy operation of TNCs at the global level. The developing countries are merely to follow the dictates of powerful governments and TNCs. Under the agreement, the complainant has to provide evidence to show that 'specific requirement is distorting' and can bring the errant country to 'Dispute Settlement Mechanism', but mere assertion by dominant actors is enough to put pressure on developing countries. Thus, TRIMS also narrows the scope of interventionist capacity of the nation-state. In the same manner, the General Agreement on Trade in Services (GATS), another product of Uruguay Round (1986–1994), seeks to remove barriers to trade in services. The range of services includes almost everything from education, health, garbage collection to water supply, etc. Its main intrusion is felt in the realm of public services being provided by the developing states as their full and original commitments to their citizens. The provisions of

GATS bring the governments of developing countries in competition with well-established firms of developed nations. Obviously, these agreements go against the interests of developing countries and are skewed in favour of developed countries.[9] Rather, the developing countries are required to take up non-market measures to deal with problems of poverty, illiteracy, malnutrition and unemployment.

Furthermore, the actions and decisions taken in one country can affect the other countries. Here, the question arises whether the country has the 'capacity to choose and decide' on the question of integration of domestic economy with global economy. Since this very capacity has been challenged and weakened through these agreements, it indicates loss of 'political' at the expense of 'economic'. The direct consequence of globalization process is reduction in the area of intervention of an elected government. The strategy of weakening the interventionist capacity of government has been quite successfully attained through increasing control over market. 'It's the movement of finance capital that signals the helplessness of many regimes. It is once again the rootlessness of finance capital that raises question of responsibility.'[10] Anytime a government chooses to act otherwise, the global actors threaten it of withdrawing the international finance, thereby forcing the government to follow the dictates of international financial institutions. In other words, global actors like WTO, IMF and WB combinedly exercise global governing powers to override various regulations of elected governments of developing countries. Unelected bureaucrats and staff of global actors define rules and regulations of multilateral treaties, which are binding on other member states. Thus, 'the potential global regime is only formally multilateral, as states lose capacity as sovereign rule-makers'.[11]

The concept of nation-state is primarily based on the existence of territorial boundaries. In a defined territory the political community is allowed to have an independent and sovereign authority. In this context, the nation-states have been controlling the economic fate of the respective country. Boundaries are a 'necessary condition for autonomous national policies'.[12] Recent developments in the area of technology and communications have rendered the territorial boundaries as 'ineffective and redundant'. Of late, we find no reference being made to 'people and government'; rather every effort is made to control the whole economy of the world without any reference to national political community and government. The breaking down of political boundaries of State is conducive to promote the professed agenda of multinational corporations, (hereafter, MNCs), the standard-bearer of globalization. Consequently, the State as an institution comes under attack and its commitment to people is weakened through institutional mechanism of globalization forces. Specifically, the nation-state is forced to withdraw from the core commitment of social security sector and is further asked to cut back its size and lose control over market. Ironically, all these decisions are taken by multilateral agencies and the national government merely acts as an implementer of the decision. Therefore, the chief attribute of 'sovereignty' comes under attack at the hands of international financial institutions.

The withdrawal of nation-state from social security sector is particularly dangerous with respect to interests of poor strata of political national community. Nonetheless, the nation-state is compelled to withdraw from social welfare sector under the pressure '... from global capital for reduced taxes and labour costs ...'.[13] Therefore, an important political implication is noticeable in delinking politics from economy as the political commitment to welfare of poor sections is withdrawn on pure economic ground of cutting of expenditure. The 'retreat of the state' is mainly in the realm of social welfare sectors, thereby affecting poor strata of domestic population. Furthermore, the national governments are also forced to abdicate their social commitments under the pressures of MNCs for privatization of 'public amenities such as electricity, gas, water, transportation, telecommunication and health, which provide a highly profitable regular income which is free of risk and where prior investment made by governments is good for decades to come'.[14] Resultantly, the ownership and control over these public assets change hands from public to private. The rationale for privatization is, all the time, coined in the name of 'better services' so as to initiate changes in the economic system. A serious implication of privatization can be easily seen on deteriorating conditions of poor population or people with no requisite purchasing power. 'The mushrooming of super-specialty hospitals in India while the public health-care system verges on collapse tellingly brings this out.'[15]

The changes introduced in the economic structure of a particular country are presented in the name of efficiency and competition. Thus, 'efficiency', 'competition', 'technology' and 'digital governance' are given primacy over social goals. The upsetting of domestic priorities is considerably important from the perspective of developing nations. Moreover, the project of globalization becomes further alienated when it's perceived to have been imposed from outside.[16] In order to integrate fully with the global economy, the nation-state has been found working as a facilitator to implement the global agenda of MNCs. Here the nation-states are forced to support the lines of GATT and WTO. A major political implication of this process is evident in shifting of power from nation-state to TNCs (transnational corporations).

Emergence of supranational identities like EU and NAFTA has further lessened the relevance of nation-state in the changing world. Sovereignty is found to be divided and it's further elaborated that '... any conception of sovereignty which assumes that it is an indivisible, illimitable, exclusive and perpetual form of public power is defunct'.[17] But so long as the state has the right to go to war and the capacity to create an organization to control the operation of MNCs within national territory, the concept of sovereignty has relevance to us. Therefore, the importance of national government lies in its capacity to decide whether it is there to protect the interests of citizens or go by the dictates of international financial institutions. The point is to emphasize the objective circumstances in which a nation-state has to perform in today's world. 'Global economic integration is an empirical fact, but it is hardly the only reality. About 80 per cent of the more than five billion people in the world live outside global consumer networks'.[18]

The advocates of globalization specifically sought to enlarge the scope of global market by 'making the fruits of modern technology available to all countries of the world with almost all sections of the people benefiting (as the spread of cellphones, for instance, in developing countries testify). Apparently, globalization is providing a big help in achieving the Millennium Development Goals and poverty elimination everywhere. It cannot be denied that there is force in these contentions. However, the influence may not have been all that benign.'[19] The concept of globalization was promoted with 'alluring ideas like individual freedom and efficiency' but in reality it favours 'particular elite economic interests' and discriminates against poor segments of developing states.[20]

Another major political fallout of the globalization process is reflected in a kind of competition amongst units of federation, especially in India. A visible impact of globalization is observed in direct contact of sub-national governments with international agencies. Earlier, the federal government used to control trade activities of sub-national governments. In response to balance of payment crisis in 1991, the Government of India implemented structural adjustment programmes and the economy got stabilized for a short period of time. But 'attention turned to the states as the fiscal situation deteriorated after showing some improvement and the consolidated fiscal deficit crept up to nearly the same level as at the onset of the crisis, and deficits in state budgets turned out to be a major contributory factor'.[21] Populist measures like free power to farmers, implementation of Fifth Pay Commission recommendations and upward movement of interest rates resulted in a greater than before fiscal deficit of state governments in India 'as the fiscal deficit of many states rose to over 5 per cent of GDP and in quite a few, over 7 per cent'.[22] Consequently, state governments were asked to tide over the fiscal crisis by adopting certain reform measures like rationalization of stamp duty, reform of property tax, urban planning reforms, etc. In order to avail loan from federal government to deal with fiscal crises, the state governments subjected themselves to these conditionalities and thus the autonomy of sub-national governments came at stake. An essential feature of federalism was curbed as a consequence of globalization. Furthermore, state governments started competing with each other to attract foreign investments in their respective states. It has led to incite a kind of competition amongst them, disregarding the aspirations and ambition of people inhabiting the state. Rather it has made them vulnerable to impact of trade as reduced barrier to trade easily affects their economy. Price fluctuations in international market show its impact on lives of farmers and agricultural workers as coconut growers in Kerala and tea growers in Tamil Nadu 'were exposed to acute price fluctuations as a result of changing rules of international trade. A sharp fall in prices of groundnuts driven by competing imports from South-east Asia hit groundnut producers. Increased exposure to trade and the resulting volatility in prices have not been conducive to domestic sovereignty of their respective governments either'.[23] Secondly, the attitude and tendency of developed states are also found to be changing vis-à-vis the less developed states. Recently, an adverse remark made by the Chief Minister of Andhra Pradesh blaming the less-developed states for arrested growth of the country shows the tendency of leaving the poor brothers of the society to fight for themselves. With the shrinking of space to control developmental policies by respective governments, it's the poor and lower strata of the society who are going to be hit the most. The problem of victimization of poor sections of society is conspicuously evident in developing countries. The point is well described as '... (h)aving only an old car in a world where everyone else owns a top-of-the-line Mercedes may be psychologically as painful as starving to death while everyone else enjoys a lavish dinner. However, in the latter example someone dies whereas in the former the choice to survive physically is always there.'[24] Logically, the protest against the globalization process has to come from the poor and disadvantaged sections of the society.

Responses from Below

The arena of protest by poor sections in developing countries is demarcated by the functioning of democracy. So the question of democracy is also linked with the globalization process. The political protests are an expression of their discontentment with globalization process. It is important because democracy and politics cannot kick the weak and poor but the market can kick the weak and poor. The hegemonic ideology of globalization and its overemphasis on governance finds political protests as antagonistic to development. The state comes in direct conflict with political protests of people. The political parties and pressure groups make use of their politics to grab state power and, in turn, become vehicles of globalization forces, promoting interests of international financial institutions and MNCs. Therefore, people-based protests take place outside of political space of formal institutional protests of political parties and pressure groups. The globalization-affected people strive to create space for political struggles with a view to counter negative effects of globalization. It may be called politicization of poor and deprived sections as a consequence of globalization. Such mass-based protests are visible with newer ways of political protests such as 'Jan Sunwai' (public hearing), 'Saamajik Ankekshan' (social audit), 'Dharna' (sit-in), 'Nukkad Natak' (street play), 'Padyatras' (big walkathons) and 'Film-Manchan' (film show). These strategies are resorted to bring awareness about the issue in hand as well as '... to form transnational alliances aimed at democratizing the global power structure'.[25] With an emphasis on globalization, the enemies of people are multiple. The poor citizens have to fight with the state, local power structure, law and order machinery, bureaucracy, political parties, trade unions and MNCs, as well. People-based struggles are aimed to establish people's control over resources like land, water, forests, etc., as well as forcing the authorities to make laws in accordance with people's wishes like Right to Information Act in India. The formal political institutions and authorities are blamed squarely for their incompetence and incapacity to protect the deprived sections of society.

The political formations are also gradually changing with an '... emerging trend towards decentralization of power all over the world primarily as a part of the process of liberalization. ... The emergence of the new states of Jharkhand, Chhattisgarh and Uttarakhand and similar demands for the creation of separate Vidarbha, Telengana, Bodoland, Gorkhaland and now Harit Pradesh can be explained in terms of changing economic and political formations ...'.[26] Non-centralization is an organizing principle. In the name of creating small political formations, the aspirations of regional movement are being fulfilled, giving an impetus to regional and local movements. Here, the globalizing forces meet with localism. Ironically, small states are not in a position to meet the global challenges. And the domestic national government can easily shift the responsibility on to unacceptable global actors, over whom they have no control. 'President Cardoso claimed that he did not rule Brazil because globalization was swallowing up less powerful states.'[27]

Millennium Development Goals (MDGs)

Looking at ineffectiveness of most nation-states in tackling the problems of inequality and poverty, the United Nations called a meeting of world leaders at the turn of millennium. In this Millennium Summit,[28] the leaders committed themselves to adopt an ambitious programme to end poverty by 2015. It was realized that the benefits of globalization were not evenly distributed amongst nations and people. Although '(t)he benefits of globalization are obvious: faster growth, higher living standards, new opportunities. Yet a backlash has begun, because these benefits are so unequally distributed, and because the global market is not yet underpinned by rules based on shared social objectives.'[29] The need for shared social objectives highlighted the problems of negative effects of globalization on world population. Undoubtedly, the process of globalization opened up the possibilities of integration of nation-states to deal with issues of humanity at global level. There is no sign of disappearance of nation-state but issue of governance poses a serious challenge. With an objective to make human life better throughout the world,[30] the Millennium Declaration specifically mentioned to make globalization 'a positive force for all the world's people'.[31] Consequently, Millennium Development Goals were developed with an objective to achieve them in a target time of 15 years. These goals were identified as follows:

Goal 1. Eradicate extreme poverty and hunger
Goal 2. Achieve universal primary education
Goal 3. Promote gender equality and empower women
Goal 4. Reduce child mortality rate
Goal 5. Improve maternal health
Goal 6. Combat HIV/AIDS, Malaria, and other diseases
Goal 7. Ensure environmental sustainability
Goal 8. Develop a global partnership for development

These eight international development goals had 21 targets to achieve by 2015.

Location of Women

The Goal 3 to promote gender equality and empower women mentions three primary targets to be achieved by 2015. It sought to eliminate gender disparity in primary and secondary education preferably by 2005, and at all levels by 2015. The indicators to measure gender equality were developed as ratios of girls to boys in primary, secondary and tertiary education, share of women in wage employment in the non-agricultural sector and proportion of seats held by women in national parliament. According to a UN report on MDGs,[32] progress in development and girls' education are positively related as disparity in favour of girls increases significantly with level of development and higher level of schooling. As per the report, there is a significant increase in enrolment at primary level but the disparity continues at secondary level and tertiary level. 'Available data show that 60 per cent of countries have achieved gender parity in primary education, 30 per cent in secondary education and only 6 per cent in tertiary education.'[33] It was also reported that girls belonging to poor families suffer the most because generally, in matters of education these families give preferential treatment to boys. Therefore, innovative steps like removal of school fee for girls and incentives to attend school will be beneficial for an increase in their enrolment at primary level as it will lessen financial burden on poor families. The developing states need to commit with renewed energy to attain gender equality. Moreover, the issue of gender parity gets more complicated when viewed against their ratio in employment. 'The employment situation of women is particularly dismal in Oceania and Southern Asia, where the largest share of women's employment is as contributing family workers – 64 per cent and 46 per cent, respectively. These labourers, also known as unpaid family workers, are family members who freely give their time to family-owned businesses.'[34] When the financial crisis hits the market and prices of daily commodities go up, its effect can be easily seen on women's employment. Their pace of unemployment is fast and their prospect for reemployment is slow. Looking at such vulnerability of the women, non-market interventionist measures are deemed necessary to enable them to survive in these volatile circumstances. Furthermore, their level of political participation is low but is on the rise, slowly. 'The proportion of seats held by women in parliament continues to rise slowly, averaging 18 per cent across all chambers of parliament as of January 2009. Women hold 30 per cent or more of single or lower chamber seats in 24 countries and 30 per cent or more of upper chamber seats in 15 countries .... Proportional representation electoral systems enable a greater number of women to be elected than majority electoral systems .... Worldwide, women are entering a greater variety of political leadership positions. As of January 2009, women reached the highest parliamentary position – presiding officer – in 31 parliamentary chambers. This figure has remained more or less constant for the past decade. During 2008, a woman took up the post of Speaker for the first time in Pakistan, Romania, Rwanda, Serbia and Uzbekistan. There were 15 women serving as heads of state or government in March 2009, compared to nine in 2000 and 12 in 1995.'[35] These indicators throw a light on significance and role of nation-state in achievement of goal of gender equality and empowerment of women. It is of paramount importance how a state agency provides rights, responsibilities, resources and opportunities to the women and their level of participation in policy-making institutions reflects their engagement with the state. The concept of gender equality refers to a stage of human social development in which an individual secures rights, responsibilities and opportunities on the basis of his or her abilities and not on the basis of being born male or female.[36]

In this context and changing scenario, the women in developing countries have been the most neglected lot. They are not part of the political process at both the levels – domestic as well as global. Everybody agrees that the women should have right to education, employment and vote. But they have been deliberately kept away from their right to education, employment and high public offices. In the changed scenario, the women are posed as commodities. They, on the whole, are victims of globalization. Moreover, a poor woman is a victim twice-over. Being poor, she cannot get the benefits of development and as a woman, she is deliberately kept away from the benefits of development by blocking her access to education, employment and high public offices. The question remains unanswered whether globalization has succeeded in changing the status of poor women and, increased the opportunities or been able to make it a women's world. For a traditional society like India, the answer is an emphatic 'No'. Instead, it has worsened their situation, marginalized their position and put them at war with various other groups, including the local government.

The women in traditional societies are facing an inherent cultural conflict. The democratic aspirations of the women are linked with their demand for increasing control over the processes of decision-making, especially the decisions affecting them.

Interests of women are different and dependent on socio-cultural realities. If women participate and protest against any policy, it does not mean that it's a feminist protest. Therefore, the social conditions become important. In Latin America, women demonstrated and organized, not because there was a feminist movement but because they could not feed their families.[37] The understanding of social conditions makes us aware of marginalization of women in the globalization project. Therefore, social conditions dictate the right approach to development. Any approach which is blind to prevailing social conditions is short of changing the scenario. The gender approach to development does not see women as a special category to give a ladder to climb up. Rather it tries to enable them to become economic and political agents to direct development. If their means of income are augmented then it will generate demand for goods and services, thus directing the economy. Similarly, if they are given an opportunity to participate in public decision-making bodies then it will create space for them to claim rights and have a voice to make women-oriented policies, thus directing politics.

The inherent cultural conflict is evident in the day-to-day lives of women in developing countries. Since democracy is often conceived as a western concept, therefore any attempt by women to take advantage of democracy is met with 'criticism' and 'violence'. With the rise of participation by marginalized groups like women in the political process, the scope of violence against women is also rising. Social conflict is also on the rise. Women activists are attacked for their dress, speech, lifestyle and progressive ideas. The case of Bhanwari Devi in India is handy to narrate the plight of women activists in the so-called 'globalized' world. Women in Third World nations are left to fight the structures of patriarchy, domestic government, bureaucracy, powerful groups and agents of global forces. In this context the emergence of various new social groups is a logical development. The supporters of 'globalization' and 'localization' are from the same population and country. The real emancipation of women lies in devising strategies to fight them at multiple levels. In India, if right to vote and reservation in Panchayati Raj Institutions are available to fight the domestic government, then the world-wide access to various other similar movements through internet gives an opportunity to create linkages at international level. The location of women in development perspectives and their inclusion in Millennium Development Goals create space for women to claim rights. 'In the current global context of increasing disparities, dreadful pandemics such as AIDS and the widespread recognition of the scourges of persistent hunger and unemployment all seem to converge in women's location in poverty. It seems crucial to make a quantum leap in ideation to fulfill women's aspirations and struggles for justice.'[38] The concern for gender cuts across MDGs and shows a way to engage the 'excluded' and 'discriminated' in development paradigm.

Society is violence-ridden. Men-in-uniform are visible quite often. Various other protest movements are taking place. Multiple groups are facing multiple groups. So the women's movements have to locate their work in broader political struggle while understanding the specific impact of globalization on women. There is lack of research to know the specific impact of globalization on women. The UN has to develop a synergetic relationship with women's movements to heal the wounds inflicted by globalization.

'The multiple struggles of women in relation to national development, in relation to politics and in relation to their own families and lives shaped the Indian women's movement after independence.'[39] The struggle of women has been further multiplied by the globalization process.

The political implication of the rise of pro-globalization forces in domestic politics means further marginalization of women and strengthening of patriarchal character of the society. The hope lies on the fighting spirit of women's movements. 'The existence of women's movements also affects men ... because the goal is ... to create a humane, free and just society ...'.[40]

Pointers for Hope

In the changed scenario, the organizing of various women's movements is to take place outside the government. More and more 'politics' and active participation for greater control over decision-making processes form the political activities of women. 'The hope lies now with the NGOs like ...

Manushi, Sewa and also the new social movements like anti-arrack movement, Chipko movement, anti-sati and anti-dowry movement focusing on the issues relating to the women workers and dowry victims'.[41] The hope is not unfounded in the sense that the economy and society can be made more humane and just only by changing the gender principle in it. The women activists try to locate gender principle in every other formal organization so that they could secure a more humane and just organization. Resultantly, the focus of women activists in times of globalization in India is centred on devising strategies '... to bring about gender justice in the realm of personal laws, including strengthening the hands of democratic sections within religious communities attempting to reform personal laws to bring about gender justice'.[42] The slogan 'mobilization against globalization' holds the hope for a more equitable economic and social order and changing of 'gender' principle in it to make it more humane.

Notes

1. Ministry of Foreign Affairs, 'Copenhagen Seminar for Social Progress 1997', 1998, Denmark as quoted in Ninan Koshy, 'Political Dimensions of Globalisation', *Economic and Political Weekly (EPW)*, May 5, 2001, p. 1513.
2. Ninan Koshy, ibid.
3. A.P. Barnabas, 'Globalization and Transformation of Indian Rural Social Structure', *The Indian Journal of Public Administration*, Vol. XLV, No. 4, October–December, New Delhi, 1999.
4. Wolfgang Sachs (ed.), *The Development Dictionary: A Guide to Knowledge as Power*, London: Zed Books, 1992, p. 105.
5. Peter Newell, 'Global Challenges to the Future State', *Seminar*, Vol. 503, July 2001.
6. Helen V. Milner, 'Globalization, Development and International Institutions: Normative and Positive Perspectives', Review Essay, *Perspectives on Politics*, Vol. 3, No. 4, December 2005, p. 833.
7. Ninan Koshy, op. cit., p. 1514.
8. Robert Hunter Wade, 'What Strategies are Viable for Developing Countries Today? The World Trade Organization and the Shrinking of Development Space' (2003), in J. Timmons Roberts and Amy Bellone Hite (eds.), *The Globalization and Development Reader: Perspectives on Development and Global Change*, Malden, MA (USA): Blackwell Publishing, 2007, p. 278.

9. For a detailed analysis of these agreements in respect to perspective of developing states, see Robert Hunter Wade, op. cit., pp. 277–94.
10. Shiv Vishwanathan, 'The Problem', *Seminar*, Vol. 503, July 2001.
11. Philip McMichael, 'Globalization: Myths and Realities (1996)', in J. Timmons Roberts and Amy Bellone Hite (eds.), op. cit., p. 225.
12. David Held, *Political Theory and the Modern State: Essays on State, Power and Democracy*, New Delhi: Maya Polity, 1998, p. 230.
13. Ninan Koshy, op. cit., p. 1515.
14. Ibid., p. 1517.
15. Amaresh Bagchi, 'Globalisation and Federalism: Uneasy Partners?', *EPW*, September 20, 2008, p. 43.
16. Peter Newell, op. cit.
17. David Held, op. cit., p. 234.
18. Philip McMichael, op. cit., p. 217.
19. Amaresh Bagchi, op. cit., pp. 43–44.
20. Rahul Varman, 'A Skewed Global Order', *EPW*, September 20, 2008, p. 31.
21. Amaresh Bagchi, op. cit., p. 47.
22. Ibid., p. 47.
23. Ibid., p. 46.
24. Rajat Acharyya and Sugata Marjit, 'Globalization and Inequality: An Analytical Perspective', *EPW*, Vol. 35, No. 39, September 23, 2000.
25. D.L. Sheth, 'Globalisation and New Politics of Micro-Movements', *EPW*, Vol. 39, No. 1, January 3, 2004, p. 50.
26. Ashutosh Kumar, 'Globalization and After', *EPW*, Vol. 37, No. 4, January 26, 2002.
27. Peter Newell, op. cit.
28. The Millennium Summit was called by the United Nations and was attended by many world leaders. It was held for three days from 6 September to 8 September, 2000 at the United Nations headquarters in New York city. Its purpose was delineated as to reformulate the role of the United Nations at the turn of the 21st century.
29. Millennium Report of the Secretary-General of the United Nations, *We the Peoples:* Executive Summary, II. Globalization and Governance, http://www.un.org/millennium/sg/report/summ.htm.
30. In spite of unprecedented economic gains, 1.2 billion people have to live on less than $1 a day. Millennium Report of the Secretary-General of the United Nations, *We the Peoples:* Executive Summary, III. Freedom from Want.
31. Resolution of United Nations General Assembly, 55th Session, A/RES/55/2 http://www.un.org/millennium/declaration/ares552e.pdf

32. United Nations, *The Millennium Development Goals Report 2009*, New York, 2009.
33. Ibid., p. 20.
34. Ibid., p. 21.
35. Ibid., p. 23.
36. Augusto Lopez–Claros and Saadia Zahidi, *Women's Empowerment: Measuring the Global Gender Gap*, World Economic Forum, Geneva, Switzerland, 2005, p. 1.
37. Vinay Bahl, 'Cultural Imperialism and Women's Movements' in Sheila Rowbotham: 'Builder of Bridges', *EPW*, Vol. 30, No. 43, October 28, 1995.
38. Devaki Jain, *Women, Development, and the UN: A Sixty-Year Quest for Equality and Justice*, Hyderabad: Orient Longman, 2005, p. 164.
39. Brinda Karat, 'The Multiple Struggles of Women', *Frontline*, October 3, 1997, p. 90.
40. Vinay Bahl, op. cit.
41. Ashutosh Kumar, op. cit.
42. Nivedita Menon, 'Refusing Globalisation and the Authentic Nation: Feminist Politics in Current Conjuncture', *EPW*, Vol. 39, No. 1, January 3, 2004, p. 103.

References

Acharyya, Rajat and Sugata Marjit (2000) 'Globalization and Inequality: An Analytical Perspective', *Economic and Political Weekly*, 35(39), September 23.

Appelbaum, Richard P. and William I. Robinson (eds.) (2005) *Critical Globalization Studies*, New York: Routledge.

Bagchi, Amaresh (2008) 'Globalisation and Federalism: Uneasy Partners?', *Economic and Political Weekly*, September 20.

Bahl, Vinay (1995) 'Cultural Imperialism and Women's Movements in Sheila Rowbotham: Builder of Bridges', *Economic and Political Weekly*, 30(43), October 28.

Barnabas, A.P. (1999) 'Globalization and Transformation of Indian Rural Social Structure', *The Indian Journal of Public Administration*, XLV(4), October–December.

Basu, Kaushik (2007) *The Retreat of Democracy and Other Itinerant Essays on Globalization, Economics, and India*, Ranikhet: Permanent Black.

Dubhashi, P.R. (2002) 'People's Movement against Global Capitalism', *Economic and Political Weekly*, 37(6), February 9.

Held, David (1998) *Political Theory and the Modern State: Essays on State, Power and Democracy*, New Delhi: Maya Polity.

Jain, Devaki (2005) *Women, Development, and the UN: A Sixty-Year Quest for Equality and Justice*, Hyderabad: Orient Longman.

Karat, Brinda (1997) 'The Multiple Struggles of Women', *Frontline*, October 3.

Koshy, Ninan (2001) 'Political Dimensions of Globalisation', *Economic and Political Weekly*, 36(18), May 5.

Kumar, Ashutosh (2002) 'Globalization and After', *Economic and Political Weekly*, 37(4), January 26.

Menon, Nivedita (2004) 'Refusing Globalisation and the Authentic Nation: Feminist Politics in Current Conjuncture', *Economic and Political Weekly*, 39(1), January 3.

Mukherji, Rahul (2004) 'Privatisation, Federalism and Governance', *Economic and Political Weekly*, 39(1), January 3.

Newell, Peter (2001) 'Global Challenges to the Future State', *Seminar*, 503, July.

Rajan, Sudhir Chella (2007) 'Global Politics and Institutions: A 'Utopistic' View', *Economic and Political Weekly*, 42(41), October 13.

Roberts, J. Timmons and Amy Bellone Hite (2007) *The Globalization and Development Reader: Perspectives on Development and Global Change*, Malden, MA: Blackwell Publishing.

Sachs, Wolfgang (ed.) (1992) *The Development Dictionary: A Guide to Knowledge as Power*, London: Zed Books.

Satapathy, C. (2000) 'Role of the State in the E-World', *Economic and Political Weekly*, 35(39), September 23.

Sheth, D.L. (2004) 'Globalisation and New Politics of Micro-Movements', *Economic and Political Weekly*, 39(1), January 3.

United Nations (2008) *The Millennium Development Goals Report 2008*, New York.

United Nations (2009) *The Millennium Development Goals Report 2009*, New York.

Varman, Rahul (2008) 'A Skewed Global Order', *Economic and Political Weekly*, September 20.

Vishwanathan, Shiv (2001) 'The Problem', *Seminar*, 503, July.

20

Millennium Development Goals, Armed Conflicts and Women's Rights in North-East India

MANJU SINGH

Gender equality and women's empowerment are essential for achieving the Millennium Development Goals (MDGs). Gender equality helps to accelerate achievement of each goal. If there is progress in striking gender equality, it will lead to attainment of other development goals. If women are not being benefited from the progress in achieving the MDGs, as much as men, then it presents an accountability issue for national governments and international institutions alike. India's North-East region has experienced four decades of political unrest, frequently escalating to insurgency and armed conflict. This violence has been devastating for the communities involved but within communities, women suffer the most. This paper attempts at examining women's vulnerabilities in those conflict-ridden societies and how women have to deal with violence.

The MDGs aim at achieving gender equality and women empowerment but we find a dismal and gloomy picture of MDGs in North-East India. The region has a complex history of under-development resulting in what we see as the region of silent wars and revolts. With slow development in the North-East, both during British rule and thereafter, education lagged and the economy got stagnant. Many of the available bureaucratic jobs were taken by aspiring candidates from other parts of India, especially from Bengal because Assam, the largest state of North-East, had been under the Bengal Presidency for more than 50 years.

After independence in 1947, the Indian government was frugal with development initiatives, leaving the North-East region economically handicapped. At the same time, exploitation of Assam's rich natural resources, fertile land and forests attracted migrant labour from poorer regions of India.[1]

It is difficult to pinpoint one reason for the endemic conflict in the region but lack of economic development to benefit native people, the impression that outsiders exploit the region's resources, the growth of ethnic/linguistic nationalism, and the lack of serious efforts at nation-building through education and other institutions are important factors. Though the intensity and the experience of conflict varies from different groups and communities (as the region is far from homogeneous), the violence affects all those who live there. Some conflicts begin with a demand, made by an ethnically-defined group, for some form of self-determination, ranging from greater autonomy to complete secession from the Indian Union. Other conflicts have their genesis in competition for scarce resources, between different ethnic groups.

In response to insurgency, the Central Government has sent para-military troops into the North-East. At the same time, the government keeps a significant military presence in the region because there are international borders on all sides. The insurgency and the presence of the military and para-military forces affect the work people do and how they do it. Militarization affects every aspect of life – from work roles to children's play where children too play war, making their own toy guns. Thirty years of conflict means that most of the children have grown into adulthood without any experience of peace. Everyone lives in an atmosphere of fear, an atmosphere conducive to further conflict and instability.

Though all suffer, women are the most affected because of their economic roles and vulnerability to physical, mental and sexual violence. Their daily lives are a constant struggle, whether in situations of open conflict or protracted low-intensity war.

Before discussing the effect of the conflict on women in greater detail, there is need to discuss women's status in the North-East. There is a general impression that because women are more mobile and visible, women's status is higher than elsewhere in India. Often people assume that women's autonomous movement and economic participation mean a degree of equity between men and women. This assumption behind the belief is that violence against women is not a major issue as it is in other parts of India. Unfortunately, that is not the case. Although tribal societies throughout the world are celebrated for their egalitarian treatment of women, it would be more productive to focus on changes in their roles. If we examine customary laws regarding women's rights and day-to-day practice, it is clear that women are far from equal.

Women at Workplace

Feeding the family has always been women's responsibility. The North-Eastern women have traditionally worked in the fields but their work has been affected by political unrest. In a village of Kohima district of Nagaland, for example, women worked alone in the fields until late afternoons. In the last decade, fear of rape and molestation by armed security forces has forced the change. Women must either stop working early and lose income, which they can ill-afford, or ask men to accompany them to protect them. By asking men for protection, women lose both power and autonomy in family as well as society.

A related problem is the migration of men away from rural areas and the loss of their agricultural labour, and of their presence as protectors. Men initially made up a significant percentage of the agricultural workforce, particularly in Nagaland and the hill districts of Manipur, but their numbers are declining as they flee the conflict, join the insurgency, or take up non-agricultural work outside their villages. As a consequence, their contribution to the family decreases, leaving women more responsible.

Conflict Situation

Militant political organizations, driven by the desire for self-determination, recruit young men for rural areas. This leads to political unrest and the intrusion of the security forces, who then pressure villagers to reveal the names and whereabouts of the insurgents. Clearly, militarization has meant relentless violence in these communities, especially against women. When house-to-house searches are carried out, women become the victims of physical and sexual violence by the armed forces. They are accused of protecting the 'boys'. In these situations, men may be working elsewhere or are themselves under suspicion of supporting insurgency. In either case, they are unable to protect the women, and most of the women experience a sense of helplessness.

In conflict situations, women are the worst suffers. They are abducted and raped by both militants (non-state actors) and security forces. Women become victims of conflict when their male partners succumb to bullets and they are burdened with the task of running the family single-handedly and to bring up children on their own. Conflicts in North-East have given rise to several women-headed households. In all conflict zones, women have invariably been held as cultural symbols. This implies the imposition of a dress code and other rules of good conduct which non-state actors impose on them. Women have to comply to these diktats for fear of their lives. Take the case of Manipur, where a plethora of underground groups have dictated that women should wear the traditional 'phanek' ostensibly to support the weaving industry, which has long been a popular cottage industry of that state. Women who tried to oppose it faced dire consequences.

In areas of intense conflict of the North-Eastern region of India and Kashmir, human rights activists and organizations, all actors in the conflict are males. There has been very little attempt to see how conflict impinges on women. For instance, women are often abducted and raped by both militants (non-state actors) and security forces. This happens because, as stated earlier, women are seen as cultural symbols and raping a woman is equivalent to inflicting injury on the entire group or society. Woman do not exist as individuals, they are part of a family and the larger society. When men are killed in conflict, their wives often have to become the bread winners and sustain the hearth and home, which is a huge responsibility. Conflicts, particularly in the North-East, have given rise to several women-headed households.[2]

Women of North-East and Politics

Women in North-East have been discriminated in the field of politics. In all the eight states, not more than 5 per cent women are represented in the state legislature. In the 15th Lok Sabha, there are only three women representative from all eight states of the North-East and in Rajya Sabha there is only one, Syeda Anwara Taimur from Assam.

To add to that, there is a strong resistance in the tribal states of North-East to the implementation of the 73rd Constitutional Amendment allowing for the creating of the Panchayati Raj system, which is aimed at empowering women politically by providing reservation of 33 per cent seats for women. The pretext is that traditional institutions are already in existence and they are best able to serve the needs of people at the grassroots. But the question is whether these democratic institutions are democratized or another male bastion. This is the point of conflict that needs to be discussed and debated.[3] This might be due to the fact that traditionally women have been debarred from participating in traditional grassroots institutions like the Dorbar or the Village Councils. Politics is still seen as a male bastion where women have no right to meddle in. A woman's social space is so well-defined that she would consider it unbecoming to intrude into the political space, which she has believed for centuries to be the legitimate space of a man.

Denied Equality Status

Tracing back India's pre-independence period, socio-economic and legal status of women was totally denied under the Mitakshara and Dayabhaga system of Hindu Law. In the post-independence period, Constitution of India was drafted in a proper democratic manner and amended from time to time. Articles 14, 15(3), 16, 19, 38, (2), 39(a), 51(a)(e) are important for giving equality to women. Still women could not achieve their legitimate share and rights due to the subordinate status in the society, submissive role and lack of education, mainly due to the patriarchal system. Even in matrilineal society as in Meghalaya, women are discriminated against in many areas and thereby, Indian Constitution has been minusculated.[4]

Human development is impossible without gender equality. Men and women must be equally empowered in the design and implementation of key decisions that shape their life. As long as women are excluded from the development process, human development as a whole will remain weak and lopsided.

As per the provisional report of Census 2001, North-East states are, of course, far ahead in women literacy rate in comparison to many other states of India except Kerala, Puducherry and Punjab. But women are not represented proportionately in all spheres of life. According to the provisional report of 2011, Women Literacy rate in Mizoram is 86.13 per cent, Tripura 65.41 per cent, Nagaland 61.92 per cent, Assam 56.03 per cent, Meghalaya 60.41 per cent, Sikkim 61.46 per cent, whereas in Kerala it is 87.85 per cent, Chandigarh 76.65 per cent, Puducherry 78.13 per cent.[5]

Political power is the central theme through which participation in all spheres of life can be channelized. Till date since women are not fairly represented in state and national politics, automatically predominantly male set-up sits in judgement. Women organizations are persistently urging for introducing women in decision-making agencies but without entry into legislatures, it is not possible.

Situation is the same in the North-Eastern region. Legislators have never seriously discussed the issue relating to women equality and infirmities. It is unfortunate to mention here that being a state of matrilineal society, Meghalaya does not have women's courts, State Women Commission and proportionate representation in Dorbar, politics and higher administration and even in higher judiciary. Due to lack of sufficient and competent women in politics, higher administration, higher judiciary and other institutions, important issues concerning women are neither implemented nor pursued.

Women Molestation in North-East India

Rape cases, of late, have become a regular phenomenon in North-East region. Laws relating to women are mostly defective. Positive laws are hardly followed by the society in favour of women. In some places, of course, laws are amended and made stringent, e.g., rape laws. But due to non-changing of police investigation system and procedural laws and the system of conducting cases, benefit could not be availed and in the name of trial, rape victims are humiliated in the court of justice. Supreme Court in the case of 'Domestic Women's Forum V/S Union of India (1994)' has elaborately discussed the pitiable condition of victims. The situation becomes worse than the rape itself and significant observation has been made and stress laid on the urgent need for radical change in the attitude of defence councils and judges. A suggestion has been made to form a Criminal Injuries Compensation Board to compensate the victims, whether or not a conviction has taken place.

Because of non-existence of proper laws to remove the grievances of working women, the Supreme Court, in its landmark judgement in 1997 on 'Sexual Harassment of Women at Work Place', issued stringent guidelines both to governmental and non-government institutions to book the offenders by forming complaint committees headed by women, to protect the dignity of women at work place. North-eastern states are yet to follow the said guidelines. As a result, not a single committee has been set up as per the direction of the Supreme Court. Due to ignorance, women bodies equally have not put pressure for the implementation.

Domestic Violence

Domestic violence is one of the biggest problems due to alcoholicism in most of the North-Eastern states. The protection of women from Domestic Violence Act was brought into force by the Indian government on October 26, 2006. The Act is supposed to provide quick protection and relief to women facing domestic violence. This Act has not helped in solving the problem of domestic violence as many of the women living in tribal belts are ignorant about it.

Though it is said the women in the North-Eastern region are in a much comfortable position compared to the women in other parts of India, the inner current is more or less same if the condition is closely observed.

Women Trafficking and Arms Trafficking in India's North-East Region

India's North-East, especially Meghalaya, has become a supply zone for trafficking and the flesh trade. There are a number of reasons for this. One is the international boundary the region shares with Bhutan, China, Myanmar and Bangladesh. Conflict situations result in major displacement. This adds to the already prevalent phenomena of economic impoverishment that forces people to migrate. It also increases the vulnerability of women and children. A number of highways turn into a dubious network for trafficking. Thus, viewing North-Eastern India from this perspective, it is clear that young girls of this region are vulnerable. As the region has been for quite a while now witnessing ethnic and armed conflict, a major result has been displacement of the people.

There are various factors which have a cumulative effect and manifest in problems like trafficking of children and young women. The Supreme Court of India's order of banning the felling of timber in Meghalaya no doubt was a commendable step in attempting to protect the larger environment, but it took shape as a serious problem as there was no alternative given by the Government to the rural population whose means of livelihood was dependent on timber. Thus, it led to pushing rural populations to migrate to urban areas looking for employment and better standards of living. Prostitution as another problem arises due to such larger issues of socio-economic conditions. Proximity to the infamous Golden Triangle facilitated the free flow of narcotics, arms and so on through the region. Also, the extremely porous international boundary adds to the problem. Illegal arms trade was done along with flesh trade across the borders. In 2008, some Myanamarese girls were caught with arms during trafficking in Mizoram.

There are many examples which show how some recruiting agencies in the name of offering 'jobs like air hostess, free education in US/UK, free food and lodging facilities' have trapped many children and young women from North-Eastern region.

There is need to involve the media as a partner in disseminating information and spreading awareness among the community at large. Impulse NGO Network, partnering with other organizations such as INGON, a child rights organization, held a series of meetings and called press conferences for sensitizing on the issue. Some of the issues addressed included the legal procedures involved, various conventions and laws and the role of the citizens. Human trafficking is a crime and cannot be solved by an NGO alone, but by collective efforts.

Due to decades of armed violence in North-East region, many children have been left orphaned and thousands internally displaced. Due to the ongoing conflict, many young people from the region have migrated to metropolitan cities in India such as Delhi, Mumbai, Chennai, Bangalore and others in search of education and jobs. The armed conflict situation in India's North-East has and can continue to be used to traffic children and young women from the region and civil society and governments need to stay vigilant over this. Many of the routes where women are trafficked in North-East region are also the routes where small arms and narcotic drugs are also trafficked. It's time we do something about it.

As a step in spreading awareness about the region and to curb the stereotypical notions about the North-Eastern people, school and college curriculum can play an important role.

There is need for a vigilant civil society and concerned citizens to work in solidarity with one another to bring the problem to an end. In doing so, keeping a strict vigilance on the recruitment agencies is needed. There is a need to start a sensitizing movement to bring about a culture of respect for livelihood, human rights, semblance of peace and justice. The Government of India should act with greater commitment to bring the problem of human and illegal arms trafficking to an end.

Women Groups

Women's groups and collectives have existed since the beginning of the 20th century in North-East India, long before the Government of India promoted the formation of Mahila Mandals (women's organizations), as part of the Community Development Programme inaugurated in 1952. Women's collective strength, a unique feature of the North-East, has been responsible for bringing about many a change in society. For example, Manipur has a history of women's activism against unjust colonial economic policies from the early 20th century. In the 1970s, Manipur witnessed the formation of Meira Paibi, literally meaning the Torch Bearers, where women would go around their localities with lit torches and detain young men who were caught drinking and misbehaving in public. By the 1980s, the Meira Paibi began to alert the community about the presence of Army patrols and sometimes negotiate with the Army when men of their community were detained. Meira Paibis are acknowledged for their influence within the community and outside.

The Meitei inhabit the riverine valleys and wetlands of the lower Eastern Himalayas in India's North-East. Like those of many other indigenous peoples of the region, the Meitei lands were divided by the British and turned over to the emerging state of India, Myanmar and Bangladesh in the decolonization process in the mid-20th century, giving rise to ongoing, low-intensity armed conflict. Still today, peaceful and armed opposition groups are demanding independence or greater autonomy from the Indian government. India's North-East is under a near-constant state of emergency, with tensions frequently erupting between locals and the Indian security forces.

The women of Manipur are highly politicized, Meira Paibi is a women's association and one of the largest grassroots human rights movements in the region, comprising virtually the entire adult Meitei female population in every Meitei town and village. It is the watchdog of civil rights at the community level, initiating and engaging in campaigns against rights violations, such as arbitrary detention, cordon and search operations, and torture committed by the security personnel of the federal government of India.

However, the Meitei women of Meira Paibi are less concerned with women's rights, and believe that they must 'get general civil rights implemented first.' This is perhaps the inevitable attitude of people in a situation of violent strife that has lasted for generations and where civil rights are routinely flouted. The tendency to dismiss women's rights is also due to the Meitei culture, which prides itself on the traditionally high status and prominent role of its women. Consequently, many women are reluctant to see themselves as objects of human rights violations particular to their gender.

But the Meitei women do suffer from rights abuses because of their gender, and they are not accorded adequate protection. Increasingly, Indian security personnel assault women for their support of opposition groups as a means of demoralizing and insulting the Meitei community at large.[6] Research by the Imphal-based Centre for Organization, Research and Education (CORE), in 2000 suggests that incidences of violence against women, including rape, are increasing at an alarming rate.

The Meitei women are ultimately more concerned with human rights abuses committed by the Indian government than they are with their rights as women. Consider these two contrasting incidents. In 1997, during a routine cordon and search operation, security forces raped a woman, holding her husband at knife-point outside the room while her seven-year-old son, bedridden with polio, witnessed the crime. For months, hundreds of thousands of Meira Paibi members, supported by human rights activists and organizations, protested on the streets of Imphal. Yet, in 1999, a young woman was physically threatened with violent reprisal by community activists when she chose to be sexually involved with a trooper of the security forces. In this case, the public was widely sympathetic to the activists.

In Imphal it is found that unless women's rights contribute to the common understanding of the community's greater political cause, they do not resonate among the local women, nor are they likely to be implemented.

The Mahila Samitis of Assam played an important role in the freedom struggle. They came out in large numbers to fight for the country's independence during the Non-Cooperation Movement. We must remember that at that time women were not considered chaste if they were involved in the public domain such as acting in theatre, films, in political meetings or demonstrations. During Civil Disobedience Movement, 18 women were arrested.[7] Guneswari Debi of Nagaon was the first woman to be jailed, along with another in connection with the movement. During 1930–31, a women's force or Bahini was formed in the town of Golaghat under the leadership of three women – Swaranlata Barua, Rajkumari Mohini Gohain and Basantlata Hazarika.

Research on Mahila Samitis tells us that the first Mahila Samiti was established at Dibrugarh in 1915, followed by another at Nagaon in 1917 and the next at Tezpur in 1919. Apparently, all three were formally registered in 1928. It is therefore worth highlighting the process through which these Mahila Samitis came into being in Assam, especially between the years 1915–1926. The samitis which were formed between 1915 and 1920 had similar ideological content and a strong Gandhian influence. At this juncture, it is necessary to extol the dedication and ingenuity of women like Chandraprabha Saikia, who motivated other young women through their speeches and their fight against the evils of opium addiction, child marriage and subservience of women. Illustrative of Saikia's vision and courage is an incident that occurred at the 1925 All Assam Sahitya Sabha's Annual Convention. Custom decreed that the women's section, in this gathering, be segregated by a partition of bamboo reed matting, ensuring both invisibility and silence. Chandraprabha Saikia (better known as Saikiani), perhaps the first woman ever in Assam to speak from a public platform, protested sharply against the segregation, likening the partition to a 'cage imprisoning a lioness' in her own home. This head-on attack inspired some of the women present to tear down the matting and stamp on it in a symbolic gesture of liberation.

Several activists like Chandraprabha Saikia, Guneswari Devi, Dwariki Kachari and Rajkumari Mohini Gohain undertook extensive tours of the villages to mobilize rural women. This is perhaps a major factor which eventually resulted in the formal establishment of Mahila Samitis. In 1926, the state-level apex body of Mahila Samitis was formed under the name of Assam Pradeshi Mahila Samiti. Saikiani, secretary of this apex body, shouldered the responsibility of coordinating and facilitating the various Mahila Samitis into a strong force. Her efforts resulted in the formation of district Mahila Samitis under which came the primary or village Mahila Samitis. A majority of existing Mahila Samitis are affiliated to the apex Assam Pradeshik Mahila Samiti. Their objectives include maternity and child-welfare, mass education, social reforms and weaving projects. A logical fallout of this initiative was the consolidation of many Mahila Samitis through the Community Development Programme of 1952, which tried to ensure intelligent participation of women in community development activity. For years the activities of Mahila Samitis revolved around nutrition programmes, weaving projects under bank loan and so on. That is the fate of women's organizations in a scenario where conflict is all-pervasive. Despite the fairly visible role of women in the ongoing situation of conflict, human rights violations were committed by the state machinery in the early days of conflict. Now there are as many violations committed by non-state actors too. Fear is the underlying factor, which cuts across many of the women's organizations. Equally critical is the very nature of patriarchy and today's conflict situation, which perpetuates silence among women and disproportionate power relations between them and men. The Assam Movement, led by students and the newly-formed Assam Gana Parished (AGP) of 1980s, was characterized by mass representation of women. But none of these women made it to the ranks of decision-making bodies, be it the AGP office or any students' union bodies. One also did not see any individual woman or a member of a Mahila Samiti address the mis-doings of those people (who they supported during the Movement), who subsequently became political leaders and ministers. Drawing-room discussions, particularly among middle class women, hint at the way women worked for the Movement and got nothing out of it. Very few, however, ask whether they were used – a question that irks many of us.

This is the crux of the problem. Mahila Samitis have not been able to question the bastion of power structure, which is predominantly male, be it in the Congress, AGP or in any political party of the past or present. In addition, women have not questioned the factors that have led to corruption, scams and economic instability in the state. The Right to Information Act (RTI) should be taken up as a direct tool by Mahila Samitis, social organizations and the concerned public. This despite the fact that the rural populace, in most parts of Rajasthan, have worked on RTI and have succeeded in making the state and district agencies accountable.

Another problem that is seen in the internal functioning of Mahila Samitis is the utter lack of documentation of their past efforts. Yes, we find excellent record-keeping in their 'proceeding books' but no documented narrative, which would bring out an analytical viewpoint and the worth of their remarkable efforts. It is only thanks to the ingenuity and imaginative writings of writers and novelists within Assam, who wrote about these women, that we still have some information on the past.

However, women of Mahila Samitis are not usually a part of their internal management system. This relates directly to democratic decision-making. Under normal circumstances we find that women have less institutional power than men to meet needs and realize interests. We find that their vulnerability lies not only in differences of roles and responsibilities but also in hierarchies of power and privileges. In a narrower sense, it is startling to find that something similar happens within the internal functioning of Mahila Samitis of Assam. Finally, heads of samitis like presidents and secretaries hold the reins of power for too long. This discourages democratic functioning as well as a host of potentialities, such as younger women joining the fold.

Speaking of external factors, Mahila Samitis have to be analysed in relation to State delivery systems – to see what works and does not work for civil society, and women in particular. This encompasses issues like health-care services, free flow of rations under PDS and so on. It should also be seen in the context of how women are positioned in local governance. And finally it should be seen in the context of rights that women ought to know and wield in their favour. That women are not well informed of certain rights and have no access to opportunities is a serious matter – a matter that needs intense discussion among women and men all over the North-East.

Domestic violence and violence against women (VAW) in conflict situation are two categories that overlap, making analysis obscure rather than focused. For instance, a woman in Kokrajhar, who was assaulted by two Armymen, was rejected by her husband on grounds that she complied to 'their wishes'. She was beaten up by him before being sent out of the house. Did women of Mahila Samitis address these problems or were they sent away by the family on the pretext that this was a personal matter? The All Bodo Women's Welfare Federation addressed the issue but added that popular support from the public and the government was lacking. There are examples of young women leaving their villages because of factional fighting between militant groups or because of the Army, which conducts frequent house searches. To avoid any kind of violence in such situations, these young girls often migrate to cities like Guwahati and find employment as maids. Research by several NGOs has found that maids often run away from their employers and finally land up as sex workers in the process of looking for alternative employment.[8] Women's organizations have to recognize, in real terms, this duality of domestic violence and VAW in conflict situations and find strategies to deal with it locally and collectively. This is where the issue of legal literacy and the awareness of one's legal rights becomes an important agenda for people working on women's rights and development.

Though influential in some aspects, most women's organizations and groups have no decision-making powers in local governance. This is one of the main problems of women's organizations all over the North-East. Acute problems of communication have prevented some of the dedicated members in reaching out to village-level Mahila Samitis. The distancing of the middle class from the realities of rural life – its culture and socio-economic situation – has widened the social disparities. More stress has to be laid on the part of the apex and district-level Mahila Samiti members to involve rural women in direct economic action programmes and discussions on gender inequality, non-recognition of women's work capacity. Almost all of the 5,000-odd rural Mahila Samitis in Assam are not getting access to information about struggles and successes that other organizations have experienced in the rest of the country, let alone what state agencies have to offer them. There is a lack of institutional support and district-level women's organizations are not able to do anything about it because they themselves are in a disadvantaged position.

A radical change in a pragmatic and realistic sense can rejuvenate scores of women both at the urban and rural level, if they are able to invest some thinking and debate on their basic rights enshrined in the Constitution as well as in the UN's Universal Declaration of Human Rights.

New women's groups have been formed in recent years which have rightly made attempts at mobilizing women, both at the urban as well as rural level. Several of these organizations have emerged, perhaps, as a reaction to the inertia of existing Mahila Samitis, which they criticize as lacking in ideological consciousness. Some have emerged in response to the increase in alcoholism and drug abuse amongst the youth. Needless to say, the rate of crime against women has gone up. It is of vital importance, therefore, to revamp the district and primary Mahila Samitis, whose weak functioning is not just a result of women's immobility or the inherently repressive social system but of poor documentation, poor financial or infrastructural functioning, total lack of exposure to the rights issues and lack of self-esteem amongst a majority of the women.

Notwithstanding their influence in public debate and social factors in society, women's collectives and organizations in Assam are not a part of decision-making in policy matters or in local governance. Thus, professional networking with women's groups all over the country and new links and exchange of ideas can well put our Mahila Samitis in a significant position of achievement.

In Nagaland, every village, town, and district has a women's society, a mother's welfare association bearing either the name of their area or of their tribe. Moreover, every church has a women's wing. Women's organization, such as Lotha Eloe Hoho, Chakhesang Women's Welfare Society, Angami Women's Organization, and the Naga Mothers' Association (NMA), were formed during the 1970s and the 1980s. The NMA is credited for mediating in the Naga peace process and for carrying out intensive campaigns against killings and bloodshed.

In 1955, a Naga women delegation went to Governor Jairamdas Medhi with an appeal to stop all kinds of atrocities and violence. Thus, the peace initiative from the women is neither new nor alien to the Naga culture. What is important is that Naga insurgency and the political turmoil in North-East has compelled the women to be organized among themselves, which in turn consolidated their efforts directly or otherwise.[9]

The politics of North-East in general and of Nagaland in particular took a radical turn during 1975–76, when the Government of India signed Shillong Accord on 11th November, 1975 with a few Naga leaders, who, ignoring the general sentiments of the Naga movement, agreed to accept the Indian Constitution instead of their own. The importance of Shillong Accord was that it led to intra-group rivalry and dissension within NNC. The point to note here is that the women as such played no significant role in signing the Shillong Accord, but the political turbulence of that period affected the Indo-Naga peace process and provoked Indian security forces negatively, which had a direct bearing on the women. One example can be cited, where on 18th May, 1979, a BSF Jawan raped a 60-year-old woman. In protest, the Angami Women's Welfare Association organized a strong resistance movement and demanded the removal of BSF from the village. The movement created enormous pressure on the government.[10]

The atrocities following the unrest in North-East helped the women unite among themselves around their own tribal affiliations. Rita

Manchanda has rightly opined that 'several of the most active women's organizations in Nagaland and Manipur emerged as a direct response to such atrocities'.[11] Another cause that facilitated women's mobilization on such a large scale was the emerging social problems, particularly alcoholism and drug abuse among the Naga men, during late 1970s and early 1980s. The politically excluded section, the Naga women, became socially vulnerable as well, as a consequence.[12]

It is interesting to note that though the initiatives of women organizations in this part of the country were not apparently visible at the state level, these grassroots level groups were gaining strength both organizationally and ideologically. We should emphasize on the ideological orientation and consolidation of different organizations towards trust-building and peace-making because this phase of attitudinal change had a far-reaching consequence in Naga women's intervention in the general settlement of this issue.

In 1984, Naga Mothers' Association (NMA) was established in Kohima as a state-level voluntary organization with the objective of eradicating all social evils. Neidomo Angami, one of the founding members of NMA, popularly known as the mother of peace, served as its General Secretary from 1984 to 1994. In an article 'Naga Women's Intervention', Shimray has clearly pointed out the holistic attitude of NMA to facilitate peace, eradicating violence and malpractices. A few lines from that are mentioned here.[13]

'The main objectives are to serve as a channel of communication for Naga women's mutual interest and welfare, to eradicate social evil and exploitation; to promote active participation in socio-political life ... and to maintain peaceful living ...'

NMA, the apex body of Naga women's organizations, came up at a time when the entire North-East became what may be called 'the theatre of the longest state versus community conflict in South Asia'. The whole situation got more complicated as the Nagas became involved in intra-group conflict leading to large-scale deaths and displacements. Therefore, NMA prioritized its 'Stop All Bloodshed Campaign' and started extending support to all grassroot-level women organizations. And the result was evident. Kofi Annan, in his speech to the UN Security Council on 26 July, 2000, opined that besides representing the Naga women's concerns, the NMA is also working against what he calls 'homicidal militarization' of Naga children.[14]

What has made the entire North-East a 'virtual killing field' is the Naga-Kuki clash that is going on since 1992 and to divert the attention of the Naga insurgents, the Government of India, for strategic reasons, encouraged the Kukis against the Nagas. Anuradha Chenoy[15] has pointed out that the women are 'either victims' or 'part of the infrastructure support' in these struggles and conflicts. NMA has used all possible ways to convince both the warring Nagas and the Government of India that the Naga problem will not be solved through violence. All through it has paved the way for reconciliation by 'keeping open the channels of communication between warring groups'.[16]

In fact the contribution of NMA as a whole can be analysed at three levels, each in turn reinforcing the other. Though the Naga tribes are patriarchal, the position of women in their society is not much degraded. As has been observed by Shimray, 'many of the Naga parents prefer their first-born child to be female.'[17] NMA has fully utilized this cultural tradition to project itself as the symbol of peace and human integrity. The role played by NMA at all the levels is based on this agenda. As a civil society organization, it has two faces – social and the political. The social face of this organization has, undoubtedly, helped mobilize the common people, which in turn legitimizes NMA to speak politically.

At the village level, NMA is more social than political. Here the primary objective of this organization is to combat alcoholism, drug addiction and other malpractices and social evils. They try to make aware the women of the danger of these social evils and motivate them to establish a good Naga society. Needless to say that NMA gets large-scale support from Naga civil society in return. While acting as a social welfare organization, NMA organizes workshops and training programmes for women so that they can become conscious citizens and can play a role, at least indirectly, in the ongoing peace process. It is, however, its political side in the sense that through campaigning NMA tries to make women aware of the current political situation and the need for peace in this region also. It should be made clear that women in Nagaland in general and NMA in particular have little and very insignificant role in the formal political process.[18]

At the district level, NMA acts as an apex body of women's organizations and tries to extend its cooperation to respective women's organizations at the village level to mobilize women. Here NMA is more concerned with protecting the dignity of Naga women in general. Whenever there is a violation of human rights, they protest. Similarly, at this level, NMA speaks of the developmental issues without which, they believe, 'there cannot be peace in Nagaland'. But these mothers have no access to policy-making, which, as Brara points out, is highly unfortunate. At this level, also, NMA is more social in its vision.[19]

The political project of NMA aiming at peace-making and general solution to Naga problem is clearly evident at the state level. While this organization, as a first step towards trust building, has started a dialogue with opposing factions NSCN-IN and NSCN-K, it is only with their initiatives that a conducive situation is expected to come up for the dialogue between these two antagonistic groups. In doing so, the members of NMA had to take the risk to their life. As a result of the meetings with the underground leaders of both factions, at least it has been established that a permanent solution to the Naga problem could be achieved through the joint efforts of these groups. At the same time NMA always supports the ceasefire and demands the withdrawal of the 'Armed Forces Special Powers Act' as a part of its peace initiatives.

In 1994, NMA launched its famous 'Shed No More Blood' campaign and constituted NMA Peace Team. NMA believes that the problem of Nagaland is political and therefore it requires political solution. It always tries to create a space for dialogue and negotiation. Neidonuo Angami, the most active member of NMA Peace Team, says that 'people-to-people dialogue is essential for the solution of Naga problem'.[20] So in 2002, 70 delegates under the leadership of NMA went to New Delhi to meet different civil society groups and convinced them of the critical political situation of the North-East. It was a journey of conscience that put the negotiations outside the conference room.

Thus NMA attempts to reconstruct Naga politics on a new basis, though from outside the formal political process, where, till now, they have little role to play. The women are not allowed in Naga village councils or in Naga Ho Ho, their apex body. However, the activities of NMA at these three levels – village, district and state – are well-coordinated and reflect their sincerity in establishing peace and developing confidence among different warring groups and the officials of Government of India. They have started the process of reconciliation and have been successful, at least partially, to create a space for people-to-people dialogue. Now it is the duty of others to accommodate these initiatives in their own political agenda.

Watsu Mongdung is among a few women organizations, that have not joined NMA. They are also working for the Naga women. It is mainly Ao women's association, but having extraordinary organizational skills, this association has been able to extend its influence over other tribal communities. Watsu Mongdung always fights to protect the rights of the Naga women and organizes protests whenever it is violated. During the time of natural disasters also, this association plays an active part in rescue activities.

What is done by NMA in Nagaland is done by Naga Women's Union of Manipur (NWUM) in Manipur. Since 1994, when it was established as an apex body of all Naga tribal communities in Manipur, NWUM is working as a sister organization of NMA. Like NMA, its peace initiatives also include trust-building and human integrity. But the only difference is that this organization does not follow 'the motherhood politics' like NMA that has enabled this organization (NMA) to enjoy more credibility.[21]

As mentioned above, the effectiveness of women's organizations in working against violence is limited by their identification with ethnic agendas. This has special consequences when Meira Paibis are fighting the cause of Meiteis and the Naga Women's Union of Manipur for Nagas of Manipur's hill districts. Women then become implicated in inter-community hostility. However, there are sincere efforts to build networks of women across ethnic groups, especially in support of women's rights and conflict resolution. To date, women's groups involved in conflict management have done so in reaction to immediate incidents without any long-range commitment to this issue. At present, there are a number of new initiatives to engage groups in conflict resolution by training groups, developing mechanisms to share local and international experiences of conflict management, theorizing information for meaningful application to specific situations, and systematizing peace-building efforts.

North-East Network

North-East Network (NEN) is a women's organization set up in 1994 with a focus on woman's human rights in response to the preparatory process of the World Women's Conference in 1995. Ever since its inception, NEN's goal has been to empower women of North-East around issues of peace, livelihood, and reproductive health conflict and governance through capacity building, awareness raising networking, research and advocacy. The goal is to ensure a fundamental change in the region's development perspective from needs to rights.

NEN's growing concern with the region's conflicts is one of the main reasons why the organization took up research in conflict areas, followed by training women and facilitating a process for policy advocacy. NEN realized that it had to create an awareness and understanding of concepts such as Violence Against Women (VAW), and human rights.[22]

NEN has been using a combination of national and international mechanisms in its advocacy efforts and disseminating information about them in English and local languages to different groups about human rights, peace and conflict resolution. At the international level, NEN has been consistently using alternative reporting strategy to raise critical concerns of the region at CEDAW and ESCR committees. It has also been engaged with process of UN special rapportours and UN Resolution 1325 through international partnership.

NEN has been working in Assam, Meghalaya, Nagaland and New Delhi, adopting diverse strategies corresponding to the local situations. Perspective building leading to conceptual clarity and advocating for effective implementation of laws related to women, particularly at the grassroots level, has been an important part of NEN's work in Assam and Meghalaya. NEN Nagaland focuses on creating a conducive environment using innovative ways of engaging youth in all its activities, ranging from livelihood options to arts and cultural forms, to environmental issues.

Conclusion

It is the prime duty of the government and NGOs to promote women to take up responsibility to represent the women community, by providing them necessary facilities. Women are not less talented to work hand in hand with men for the development of the country; what is needed is a change of perception of the government, society, politicians and the NGOs. A package of training techniques is needed which includes confidence-building, leadership development, etc. Without a Central statute like reservation, women cannot come out to participate on a large-scale to take part in politics, mostly against the money and muscle power. Nor would men voluntarily relinquish their seats of power for women. Without entering into the political arena, striving for gender equality, human rights, involvement in decision-making, etc., is nothing but like 'crying in the jungle'.

Conflict, whether between ethnic groups demanding autonomy against the military or between rival ethnic groups, not only brings new dangers and burdens to women's lives, it threatens gains in other areas, and undercuts the possibilities of women working together. In attaining MDGs in North-East, our greatest concern is bringing women together to fight inequality and to fight against armed conflict. Our challenge is to try to bring women together across ethnic lines to work for peace, since it is only in peacetime that they will be able to improve their situation. Although awareness of gender discrimination and women's rights has increased, yet there is still a long way to go.

Notes

1. See Akhil Ranjan Dutta, *Human Security in North East India*, Guwahati: Anwesha, 2009, p. 249.
2. For details, see S. Subramanian, 'Thinking through Justice', *Economic and Political Weekly*, May 2010, p. 37.
3. Patricia Mukhum, *Gender Perspective of Human Rights*, New Delhi: Reliance Publishing House, 2007, p. 104.
4. Minati Sharma, *Human Rights of the Women in India and North East in Particular*, New Delhi: Reliance Publishing House, 2007, p. 125.
5. Ibid., p. 126.
6. The Local Meitei women feel proud in calling themselves the mothers of the militants because they are fighting to restore their lost ethnic supremacy.
7. Amlendu Guha, *Planter Raj to Swaraj*, New Delhi: ICHR, 1977, p. 174.

8. Findings made in the community-based research on 'Gender and HIV/AIDS in Assam' done by NEN, January 2000.
9. Sowmajit Patra, 'Contribution of Undervalued Women in North-East Politics', *The Indian Journal of Political Science*, September 2009, p. 927.
10. Ibid., p. 928.
11. Rita Manchanda, *We Do More Because We Can: Naga Women in the Peace Process*, Nepal: South Asia Forum for Human Rights, 2004, p. 92.
12. S. Patras and S. Mannas, 'Integrative Reconciliation: Mothers in Naga Movement', *Economic and Political Weekly*, Vol. XLIII, No. 10, 2008.
13. U.A. Shimray, Naga Women's Intervention, December 2004, www.manipuronline.com
14. See for Kofi Annan's statement, www.e_pao.net
15. Anuradha Chenoy, 'Still a Man's World', *Business Line*, www.theindusbusinessline.com of 11.02.2005.
16. R. Manchanda, op. cit., p. 94.
17. U.A. Shimray, op. cit.
18. Sowmajit Patra, op. cit., p. 930.
19. V.N. Brara, 'Women's Role in Human Rights and Peace in the North-East', *PUCL Bulletin*, February 2002.
20. Also refer, Fareed Kazmi, *Human Rights: Myth and Reality*, New Delhi: Intellectual Publishing House, 1987.
21. See J.A. Joyce, *The New Politics of Human Rights*, London: Macmillan, 1978.
22. R. Manchanda, op. cit., p. 95.

Index

adult literacy
  in South Asia, 255
adverse child sex ratio, 150
  in Haryana, 150, factors
    responsible for, 150–51
Agarwal, B., 43, 55
Anker, Richard, 45

Baylis, J. and Steve Smith, 96, 97
Beauvoir, Simon de, 226
Beneria, L. and S. Bisnath, 188
Beneria, L., 43
Berry, Thomas, 11
Bhatt, E.R., 192
Boserup, E., 41, 98
Braidotti, R., E. Charkiwicz, S. Häusler and S. Wieringa, 46, 47
Brara, V.N., 323
Bubeck, D., 48
Buvinic, M., 41

casino capitalism, 13
caste/kinship-based organizations
  in Haryana, 153–54
  in rural India, 147
Castells, Manuel, 184
Chadha, G.K. and P.P. Sahu, 75, 77
Chenoy, Anuradha, 322
Chipko movement, 6
Chowdhry, Prem, 147, 150
civil society, 6
Constitution of India, 112, 198, 235, 282
cultural mix, 8
culture industry, 38

Daly, M., 43
DAWN, 45
Deshmukh-Ranadive, Joy, 55
development, 3, 5, 95, 247
  agents, 6, 22
  concept/meaning/definition, 3, 34, 95–96, alternative model of, 96–97
  from a gender perspective, 40–47
  Gandhi-Nehru debate over, 23
  impact of, on women, 97–98; on tribal societies, 101
  theories, 34–37
Dickinson, T., 188

Eaton, Heather, 9, 12
economic globalization, 139
Economic Survey, 81, 82, 83, 85
Emmanuel, A., 42
empowerment, 55, 114, 247
  definitions of, 55–56, 100
equality
  concept of, 222

female literacy programmes
  in India, 235–36
female workforce
  in India, 56–57, structure of, 57–58; working conditions for, 58–60
Frank, A.G., 42
Fraser, N. and L. Nicholson, 45
free market, 11
Friedman, T.L., 185

GAD, 44
gender equality, 222, 248, 309
  and women empowerment, 225–28
gender gap/bias
  in India, 111, challenges before, 117–20; strategies to overcome, 120–22
gender
  inequality/disparity/discrimination, 24
  in India, 280
  in South Asia, 252–58
gender parity, 228
gender
  and development, 247–50
  notion of, 247
gender-human development nexus, 249
Giddens, Anthony and Will Hutton, 9, 10, 12, 17
Giddens, Anthony, 183
global village, 293
globalization of mothering, 17
globalization, 8, 66, 132, 166, 182, 293
  as a historical process, 10–11
  aspects of, political, 294–99
  definitions/meaning of, 9–10, 37–39, 60, 183–84
  environmental consequences of, 132–38
  impact of, on women, 15–20, 186–88
  negative effects of, 185–86
  strands of, 294
  the current scenario, 11–15
globalization-driven development paradigm, 39, 47, 66
globalization-Islamization interface
  in the Indian subcontinent, 166–79
Gorringe, Timothy, 13
Government of India, 67
Gray, Mary, 184
Greene, Graham, 186
growth with greener face, 97

Harrison, D., 42
Haryana, 148
  caste/kinship in, impact of, 148–50
  sex ratio in, 280
HDR, 55
hill women, 105
  profile of, 105–8
Hirst, P. and G. Thompson, 185
Hirway, Indira, 76
HIV/AIDS
  in India, 216, and women, 216–17
honour-related crimes, 161–62
human development, 36, 47, 111
  in South Asia, 251

Indian women
  impact of globalization on, 66–93
  political participation by, 112–17
Islamic Fundamentamentalism
  in Bangladesh, and women's rights, 176–79

Islaization
in Pakistan, and women's rights, 171–75
process of, 166

Jhabvala, Renana and Shalini Sinha, 78, 91

Kabeer, N., 41, 42, 43, 44, 45, 55, 95
Kaushik, Asha, 38
Khap Panchayats
in Haryana, 154–58, patrilineal inheritance of, 158–59; limitations/support structure of, 159–63
khap
concept of, 154
Khor, Martin, 66
knowledge economy, 9
Korten, David, 14
Kothari, S., 191
Kumaon (a region in Uttarakhand), 99
political economy of, features of, 99
women in, 105–7, status of, 99–100

Lerner, Gerda, 98
Lewis, Robert Arthur, 15
literacy
in India, 235

malaria
in India, 214, and women, 217–18
mammon worship, 38
Manchanda, R., 322
Marchand, M.H. and J. Parpart, 49
market-friendly state, 63
maternal health, 279, 284
social dimensions of, 279–80
MDG 3, 227, 249
MDG 5, 2m77, 278
MDG 6, 212, 250
and women, 215: the global scenario, 212–3; the Indian situation, 213–18
MDGs, 37, 211, 223–25, 245, 272, 276–77, 300–1, 309
in India, 232–40
in South Asia, 262–65
locating women in, 301–4
Mehta, Nira, 80
Mies, M. and V. Shiva, 46
Mill, James, 111
Millennium Summit/Declaration, 276, 277, 300
Millett, Kate, 98
Mitra, Arup, 79
modern state
Gandhi-Nehru debate over, 23
Moghadam, V.M., 188
Mookherjee, M., 49
Moser, C.O.N., 41, 42, 44
Mukerji, A.B., 148
Muslim women
in India, 166, and their rights, 169–71

National Literacy Mission, 236
National Rural Health Mission (NRHM), 278
Nehru, J.L., 113
Nehruvian state, 27
New York market crash, 13
NGOs, 188
in India, growth of, 190
North-East India, 309
domestic violence in, 314
women in, 310, impact of armed conflicts on, 311–12; molestation of, 313–14
Nussbaum, Martha, 19

Okin, S.M., 48
Olsen, R.N. and A. Coppin, 45

paper money, 12
Parekh, B., 49
Parpart, J., 43, 46
Pateman, C., 48
patriarchy, 98
  and women's subordination, 98
petroleum century, 12
Phillips, A., 48
Pilger, John, 13
Planning Commission, 67
political status of women, 112
  in India, 112–17, 237–40
postmodernism
  of Gandhi, 22–27
Pradhan, M.C., 154

Quit India movement, 24

Rajasthan, 199
  demography of, 279
  women's status in, 199–200
Ram Raj
  of Gandhi, 24
Rees, T., 48
Rhode, D., 48
Robeyns, I., 48
Rogers, B., 41
Roy, Ram Mohan, 113

SAARC development goals, 266
SAARC, 246
  and MDGs, 260–72
Sarva Shiksha Abhiyan, 235
Scheper-Hughes, Nancy, 18
second-class citizens, 114
Sen, A., 243, 247
Sen, G. and C. Grown, 44
Sen, G. and S. Correa, 188
73rd constitutional amendment, 107, 115
74th constitutional amendment, 115
Shimray, U.A., 323
Sklair, L., 39
socio-cultural beliefs
  in India, and health implications, 281–82
South Asia, 250
  gender development in, 251
  human development in, 251
  MDGs in, 262–65
  women in, 250–58
  women's development in, 258, role of SAARC in, 258–60
Squires, Judith, 49
sustainable development, 36, 97

Tiger economies, 11
Tocqueville, A., 189
tuberculosis
  in India, 213–14, and women, 218

UN Decade for Women, 16
UN, 99
UNDP, 36, 56
unorganized activity, 5
unorganized development, 5

Vepa, Swarna S., 79
village/gram swaraj, 24
  of Gandhi, 24
voluntary associations, 6
  in India, 6

WAD, 43
Waylen, G., 41, 43, 46
WED, 46
weightless economy, 9
well-being
  parameters of, 19
WID, 41

Wollstonecraft, Mary, 228
women
  and development, 6, 97–98, approaches to, 40–47
  and globalization, 15–20
  and MDGs, 215
  in agriculture, 102–3
  in India, political status of, 112–17; media projection of, 198, 201–3
  in media, 203–4
  media portrayal of, 200–3
women's development
  in South Asia, 258, role played by SAARC in, 258–60
women's empowerment, 100, 309
  political dimension of, 126–31
  strategies for, 101
women's groups
  in North-East India, 316–25
women's health
  in India, 279, impact of socio-cultural beliefs on, 281–82
  in Rajasthan, 285–86, strategies to improve, 289–90
women's NGOs, 189
  in the context of globalization, 190–93
women's subordination, 98
women's trafficking
  in North-East India, 314–15
World Bank, 47

Young, I., 48